Ralph Le Fevre

ESTHER M. OLIVER

Wife of the author, to whom this book is dedicated in recognition
of the active aid and encouragement, without which
the work would not have been undertaken
or carried through.

HISTORY OF NEW PALTZ

NEW YORK

AND

ITS OLD FAMILIES

(FROM 1678 TO 1820)

INCLUDING THE HUGUENOT PIONEERS AND OTHERS WHO SETTLED
IN NEW PALTZ PREVIOUS TO THE REVOLUTION

BY RALPH LEFEVRE

President New Paltz Huguenot, Patriotic, Historical and Monumental Society ;
Corresponding Member Huguenot Society of America ;
Thirty-four years Editor of New Paltz Independent

ILLUSTRATED

FORT ORANGE PRESS
BRANDOW PRINTING COMPANY, ALBANY, N. Y.
1903

Facsimile Reprint

Published 1992 by:

HERITAGE BOOKS, INC.
1540-E Pointer Ridge Place, Bowie, MD 21706
(301) 390-7709

ISBN 1-55613-629-3

A complete catalog listing hundreds of titles
on history, genealogy, and Americana available
free on request

PREFACE

IT is natural for the people of any country or community to feel an interest in the history of their ancestors. Even the most savage nations have carefully cherished traditions of the deeds and prowess of their forefathers.

To every man the honorable fame of his progenitors is an incentive to emulate their noble deeds.

In the early settlement of New Paltz and its history for nearly a century afterwards there is such a touch of romance, such a blending of the stern realities of frontier life with the harmony of the poet's golden age, such noble examples of devotion to the cause of religious liberty, such brotherly kindness toward each other as exiles for a common cause, that the example should not be lost to posterity.

Our old men are falling around us. The traditions which they cherished are perishing with them. What is to be saved from oblivion must be saved now—in this generation.

With these feelings we have undertaken the task of gathering up the scattered links of history and joining them in a chain that should stretch down from the days of the Patentees.

In writing the history of New Paltz it is not to be expected that the record of its early settlers can be carried back of the time when our ancestors fled from France. Louis XIV was not satisfied with driving his Protestant subjects out of the country and confiscating their lands and goods.—Their very names were obliterated from baptismal and genealogical records. The record of the marriage of

Louis DuBois, at Manheim, in 1655, shows that he was the son of Chretian DuBois, of Wicres. The old register at the little village of Wicres has been examined and found to contain the registry of the baptism of three sons of Chretian DuBois, but in each case the Christian name of the son is torn out, in accordance with the orders of the French king. The same is no doubt the case with the other church registers in France in which the names of the Huguenot settlers of New Paltz might otherwise still be found.

TABLE OF CONTENTS

CONTENTS

ILLUSTRATIONS

History of New Paltz

CHAPTER I

WITH modesty, yet with confidence, we make the claim that the early history of no other portion of our land can excel in interest that of New Paltz. With the exception of Kingston no other place in this part of the country was settled at so early a date. The New Paltz church was organized exactly forty years before the first church was erected in Poughkeepsie. Col. Jonathan Hasbrouck, grandson of one of the early settlers of New Paltz, built Washington's Headquarters at Newburgh. Col. Lewis DuBois, a great-grandson of one of the early settlers at New Paltz, built what was doubtless the first house at Marlborough, on the river front. Two other New Paltz men, John and Abram Bevier, were the first settlers in the town of Wawarsing.

Peter Guimar, of Moir, in Sanaigne, who was one of the pioneers of Orange county and one of the seven men who made a settlement in 1690 at what is now Cuddebackville, at the stone fort, which was for half a century an outpost of civilization, married Esther, daughter of Jean Hasbrouck, one of the New Paltz patentees.

But it is not only because New Paltz was the cradle of surrounding settlements, nor only on account of its antiquity, that we claim for New Paltz the most interesting place in the history of the early settlements. It is not because the New Paltz patentees purchased the lands of the

Indians before William Penn had performed a like gracious deed, with like peaceful results, in Pennsylvania; it is not because New Paltz was one of the few Huguenot settlements in this country, and perhaps the only one in which the stock of original settlers was not speedily overwhelmed in a flood of new-comers from other European nationalities; nor yet is it because the little community existed for half a century to some extent as a miniature republic—must we say aristocracy?—in which the Dusine exercised judicial and legislative powers, and the church owned no higher authority than its own membership. No; it is for none of these facts, though rendering the history of New Paltz so unique and peculiar, that we claim for it the most interesting place in the narrative of early settlements. But it is for one other circumstance, coming down to our own day; it is because at New Paltz, as in no other place in our country, the homesteads have been handed down in the family ever since the first settlement. In the house in which I was born my father lived before me, my grandfather spent his days there, my great-grandfather dwelt there. A few rods off my great-great-grandfather's house was built. In the old street in our village the Deyo house, the DuBois house and the houses of the two Hasbrouck brothers came down in the same family for nearly two hundred years.

While New Paltz was, to a great extent, the cradle of surrounding towns, the Huguenots kept their grip on their own old homesteads, and their conservatism we consider a more remarkable point, by far, than the early date of the settlement. In church matters this point in their character is still more noticeable, and whether the settlement at New Paltz is acknowledged to be the most interesting of any in the country or not, there can scarcely be a doubt that this claim will be conceded in regard to the Reformed Church in our village. Over 200 years ago our church organized. By the grace of God it has grown and flourished from that time until the present day. For fifty years of its history the records, still in existence, were kept to a great extent in French; for seventy years longer in the Holland tongue, and afterwards in English. But, now that we have stated what there is peculiar in the early history of New Paltz, we must go back to show the causes that led up to that settlement.

Two hundred and twenty years have passed since the first settlers reared their humble homes in New Paltz. Of the history previous to that time we know but little. We only know that they left their native land, on account of religious persecution, and after a residence of a short period in that portion of Germany, known as the Paltz, or Palatinate, came to the New World, from 1660 to 1675. The history of the French Huguenots, in their own country for a century preceding, had been a history of blood. The Reformation had not been slow to take deep root, and among the names of French reformers is that of sturdy John Calvin, whose fame has spread wherever Protestantism has obtained a foothold; but while, partly from political causes, the reformation succeeded in England and in the north of Germany, in France it had to fight, almost from the first, against the power of the court, the priesthood and the prevailing popular sentiment. Nevertheless the Huguenots numbered in their ranks many of the nobility and a great portion of the most intelligent people. Three civil wars had raged between the Catholics and the Protestants.

The massacre of St. Bartholomew in 1572, which was planned by Catharine De Medici, the wicked mother of Charles IX, the king, and was intended to destroy the

Protestants at one blow, had but strengthened their hands. Although outnumbered, ten to one, by the Catholics, they had gallantly sustained themselves in arms, upheld, in part, by moral support from Germany, as well as more tangible aid from Queen Elizabeth, of England. The death of Henry III left the Protestant Henry, of Navarre, as the legal heir to the crown, but the Catholics were determined that no heretic should sit on the throne of France. For years Henry waged an unequal war for his inheritance, with a courage and a gallantry that made his name famous, but the odds were too great; he found himself forced to give up his religion or continue a hopeless contest. He chose the former alternative, declaring that "the crown was worth a mass." Shortly afterward, in 1598, he granted the celebrated Edict of Nantes, which secured to Protestants freedom of conscience and all political and religious rights.

In 1610 Henry met his death at the hands of an assassin, and the Protestants being left without a protector their troubles again commenced. In 1628 Rochelle, which had been their stronghold and had been in their possession for seventy years, was taken, after a siege of fourteen months, during which so desperate a resistance was made that the population of the city was reduced, by war and famine, from 30,000 to 5,000 souls. Notwithstanding that Rochelle was wrested from their grasp, while Richelieu managed the realm, yet this was done rather as a political measure, because Protestantism threatened to become a state within a state, than for the purpose of religious persecution. Richelieu was no bigot; in the thirty-years' war he aided the Protestants and the Huguenots could not complain much of persecution during his administration or that of his successor, Mazarin. But from the time of Mazarin's death, in 1661, when Louis XIV himself assumed the reins of authority, until the formal revocation of the Edict of Nantes, in 1685, which was the last act in a series of persecutions, the Protestants of France suffered greatly. Before the formal revocation. of the Edict whole troops of dissolute soldiers were let loose upon them, and frightful barbarities followed.

Half a million of subjects of the French king left their native country and fled to foreign lands. Borne on this wave of immigration and prizing liberty of conscience above everything else, the brave-hearted men, who afterward settled New Paltz, fled across the frontier, and found an asylum in that part of Germany known as the Palatinate or Paltz—the name being borne now only by a castle on the Rhine. Here they could not long remain in peace, for the armies of their cruel monarch, in the wars which he almost constantly carried on with other European powers, repeatedly invaded and ravaged the Palatinate. In 1664 an army under Turenne, one of his generals, desolated that province without mercy, and it may be at this time some of our forefathers resolved to cross the Atlantic and escape from their merciless foes.

At this time the Huguenots were flying to different portions of the New World, as well as Europe, for protection. As early as 1625 several families settled in New York, then in possession of the Dutch, and were the first permanent settlers. Others were to be found in Virginia, Rhode Island, Massachusetts, and especially in South Carolina, where a large portion of the most honored names are of Huguenot origin. Scattered like leaves by the autumn blast, they were tossed hither and thither, and it is probable that by 1663 a score or more had found their way to Kingston—

called Esopus by the Dutch—then a flourishing village. We know that Louis DuBois, who was one of the first New Paltz immigrants, had been there two or three years at least before that time. In 1663 Kingston was burned by the Indians, and the wife and three children of Louis Du-Bois, the Walloon, as he was called, were among those carried away captive.

This Louis DuBois, who became the leader of the settle-ment at New Paltz, was usually called Louis, the Walloon, the Walloons being the residents of that part of Flanders lying between the Scheldt and Lys. He was born in the hamlet of Wicres, near Lille, in the province of Artois, in French Flanders, October 27, 1626, and was the son of Chre-tien DuBois, whose farm is still pointed out. Louis moved to Manheim, on the Rhine, the capital of the Palatinate, or Paltz, a little principality, now incorporated in Baden, and there he married Catharine Blancon, the daughter of a burgher residing there, named Matthew Blançon, who was also a native of Artois. Manheim was, at that time, a refuge for the Protestants from the neighboring parts of France, and Baird, in his Huguenot Emigration, says: "The Le-Fevers, Hasbroucks, Crispells, etc., were associated with Louis DuBois at Manheim."

Anthony Crispell was the first of the New Paltz patentees to come to America. He came in company with his father-in-law, Matthew Blanchan,* on the Gilded Otter, arriving at New York in June, 1660. Governor Stuyvesant gave Blan-chan a letter to Sergeant Romp, in Esopus, whither they at once proceeded.

Louis DuBois, who was also a son-in-law of Blanchan, probably came over on the ship St. Jan Baptist, which

---

* There is no uniformity in the early records in the spelling of French surnames and therefore none is attempted in this book.

landed August 6, 1661. Blanchan had sojourned in England before crossing the ocean, and probably his two sons-in-law, likewise. Blanchan, DuBois and Crispell all got land at Hurley. In 1661 Louis DuBois' third son, Jacob, was presented for baptism at the church at Kingston, as still shown by the church register, that being one of the earliest entries.

In 1663, June 10, Hurley and part of Kingston were burned by the Indians, and the wife of Louis DuBois and three children were among those carried away captive. Likewise the two children of Matthew Blanchan, Jr., and the wife and child of Anthony Crispell.

Three months afterward an expedition under Captain Kregier, sent from New York, recovered the captives; surprising the Indians at their fort near the Hogabergh, in Shawangunk. The story, which is dear to the Huguenot heart of New Paltz, is that when Captain Kregier and his company, directed by an Indian, attacked the savages at their place of refuge near the Shawangunk Kill, they were about to burn one or more captives at the stake, and the women commenced singing the 137th Psalm, which so pleased the red men that they deferred the proposed death by torture, and in the meantime Captain Kregier's band, with Louis DuBois and others, arrived and rescued the captives from a horrible death, Louis DuBois himself killing with his sword an Indian who was in advance of the rest before the alarm could be raised. Captain Kregier's report says nothing about this. However, we shall not give up the tradition as it contains nothing irreconcilable with the report of Captain Kregier, which deals mainly with the fighting done by his soldiers, while tradition would dwell more upon the condition of the captives.

The tradition concerning the impending fate of the wife of Louis DuBois at the time of rescue is not credited by Mr. E. M. Ruttenber, the Orange county historian, who states his objections as follows:

"The story was repudiated as a statement of fact, first, on the authority of Indian customs. We do not recall a single instance where a woman was burned at the stake by the Indians. They killed female prisoners on the march sometimes, when they were too feeble to keep up, but very rarely indeed after reaching camp.—Mrs. DuBois and her companions had been prisoners from June 19th to September 5th, or nearly three months before they were rescued from captivity. During all that time they had been guarded carefully at the castle of the Indians, and held for ransom or exchange, to which end negotiations had been opened, the Indians asking especially the return of some of their chiefs who had been sent to Curaçoa and sold as slaves by Governor Stuyvesant.

Second: documentary evidence concerning the events of that period is entirely against the tradition. The written record is, that when the Dutch forces surprised the Indians, the latter were busy in constructing a third angle to their fort for the purpose of strengthening it, instead of being engaged in preparations for burning prisoners. (See Kregier's Journal.) The prisoners were found alive and well, and no complaint is recorded of any ill treatment, not even that their heads had been shaved and painted, as had been customary. Every night, says the record, they were removed from the castle to the woods, lest the Dutch should recover them before negotiations for their release were consummated. The entire drift of the record narrative is against even the probability of an intention to burn, much more so of preparation to do so."

In answer to Mr. Ruttenber's objections we will say, that it is probable that the Indians had heard of the presence of the Dutch soldiers at Kingston, but supposed they would tarry there longer before marching on their stronghold, and that being enraged at the failure of their negotiations for the exchange of their captives for their chiefs who were prisoners at Curaçoa, they determined to burn them at the stake.

Tradition states that during the advance for the rescue of the captives, an Indian, who was no doubt a scout and had fallen asleep, was killed by Louis DuBois with his sword near Libertyville, before the savage had opportunity to let fly his arrow. His death prevented the news of the approach of the white men being given to their savage foes. The Indians at the fort were taken by surprise; a squaw, named Basha, who had gone to the spring a short distance north of the fort for water, raised an alarm and Louis Du-Bois shot her with his gun and she fell in the spring, which still bears her name. The settler's dogs, which had accompanied the party, rushed on and the cry "White men's dogs" was raised. The Indians in the ensuing fight lost their chief and twenty-one men killed and thirteen prisoners. Captain Kregier lost five men killed and six wounded. He recovered twenty-three women and children who had been captured by the Indians at Kingston and Hurley. The Indian fort was surrounded with palisades as thick as a man's body and fifteen feet high, but it was not yet completed. The surprise of the Indians was so complete that tradition states that Louis DuBois's wife started to run with the others at first, but was recalled by the voice of her husband, exclaiming in his excitement, "Stop, 'Trene, or I'll shoot you."

In 1665 the LeFevre brothers, Simon and Andre, came to Kingston, and in April united with the church at that place. They had been at Manheim in the Palatinate, but their native spot in France is not known. It is possible that they were of the kindred of James LeFevre, the great French preacher and reformer, who was from Etaples, on the English channel, in the ancient province of Picardy. They were unmarried men, probably quite young, when they came to Kingston.

The English conquest of the New Netherlands took place at about this date, and the unsettled condition of the provinces prevented the coming of other Huguenots to Kingston for a time.

In the spring of 1673 came Jean Hasbrouck and his wife, Anna, daughter of Christian Deyo, and their two unmarried daughters, Mary and Hester. Jean and his brother, Abraham, who came later, were natives of Calais. Jean brought with him his certificate of church membership.

In 1673, likewise came Louis Bevier, who was a cousin of the Hasbrouck brothers, and his wife, Maria LeBlan.

About three years later came Hugo Freer and his wife, Mary Hays, and their three children, Hugo, Abraham and Isaac.

Abraham Hasbrouck sailed from Amsterdam in 1675 and landed at Boston. Shortly after he joined his brother in Kingston.

Probably the last of the Patentees to cross the ocean were Christian Deyo and his son, Pierre. Pierre's wife, Agatha Nickol, and their child came with them; likewise his three unmarried sisters, Maria, Elizabeth and Margaret, who afterwards became the wives respectively of Abraham Hasbrouck, Simon LeFever and Abraham DuBois.

There was now quite a number of Huguenots at Kingston and Hurley. No doubt they longed for a settlement of their own where they might speak their own language and form a community by themselves. Kingston was dropping its character as a trading post. The traffic with the Indians, in furs, was becoming less profitable. The cultivation of the soil was becoming more and more a necessary occupation. The fertile lowlands of the Wallkill had doubtless recurred again and again to the recollection of Louis DuBois. In the meantime the colony of New York had finally passed from the control of the Dutch to the English. Edmund Andross was the Colonial Governor. Among the Huguenot settlers at Kingston, at this time, was Abraham Hasbrouck. He had served with Edmund Andross in the English army. He was a native of Calais; had emigrated to Manheim, and in 1673 to America, settling finally in Esopus.

The Huguenots, being desirous of forming a settlement of their own, were indebted, to some extent, to the acquaintanceship of Abraham Hasbrouck with Governor Andross for the grant of so fine a tract as they obtained. It is related that Governor Andross wanted them to take more land along the river to the southward, as far as Murderer's Creek, but upon examining the land they found it so rough they declared they did not want it.

Four months previous to the grant from Governor Andross the land was purchased of the Indians, and the article signed bestowing upon Louis DuBois and his associates the territory comprising the Paltz patent, occupying all the present town of Lloyd, about two-thirds of New Paltz, one-third of Esopus and one-fourth of Rosendale. In the records

of the patentees—as these twelve men were called—long
preserved in an ancient trunk in the Huguenot Bank at New
Paltz, is the copy of the document signed by the Indians
on their part, and by Louis DuBois and his associates; likewise by Jan Eltinge and others, as witnesses. This is dated
May 26, 1677. Here is likewise the confirmation or grant
from Governor Andross, covering the same territory, dated
September 29, 1677. The four corners of the patent were
Moggonck—now Mohonk; Juffrou's Hook, the point in the
Hudson where the town line between' Lloyd and Marl-
borough strikes the river; Rapoos—Pell's Island, and Tower
a Toque, a point of white rocks in the Shawangunks near
Rosendale Plains.

The papers relating to the matter in the Patentees' trunk
are in Dutch and are translated by Rev. Ame Vennema as
follows:

By approbation of his Excellency Governor Edmond An-
dras, dated April 28, 1677, an agreement is made on this
date, the 26th of May, of the year 1677, for the purchase of
certain lands, between the parties herein named and the undersigned Esopus Indians.

Matsayay, Nekahakaway, Magakahas, Assinnerakan, Wa-
wawanis acknowledge to have sold to Lowies du Booys
and his partners the land described as follows: Beginning
from the high hills at a place named Moggonck, from thence
south-east toward the river to a point named Juffrous
Hoock, lying in the Long Reach, named by the Indians
Magaatramis, then north up along the river to the island
called by the Indians Raphoes, then west toward the high
hills to a place called Waratahaes and Tawaentaqui, along
the high hills south-west to Moggonck, being described by

the four corners with everything included within these boundaries, hills, dales, waters, etc., and a right of way to the Ronduyt kill as directly as it can be found, and also that the Indians shall have the same right to hunt and to fish as the Christians, for which land the Indians have agreed to accept the articles here specified:

40 kettles, 10 large, 30 small; 40 axes; 40 adzes; 40 shirts; 400 fathoms of white net-work; 300 fathoms of black network; 60 pairs of stockings, half small sizes; 100 bars of lead; 1 keg of powder; 100 knives; 4 kegs of wine; 40 oars; 40 pieces of "duffel" (heavy woolen cloth); 60 blankets; 100 needles; 100 awls; 1 measure of tobacco; 2 horses— 1 stallion, 1 mare:

Parties on both sides acknowledge to be fully satisfied herewith and have affixed their own signatures *ad ut supra.*

Matsaya x his mark; Waehtonck x his mark; Seneraken x his mark; Magakahoos x his mark; Wawateanis x his mark; Lowies Du Booys; Christian de Yoo x his mark; Abraham Haesbroecq; Andrie Lefeber; Jan Broecq; Piere Doyo; Anthony Crespel; Abraham Du Booys; Hugo Freer; Isaack D. Boojs; Symon Lefeber.

Witnesses: Jan Eltinge; Jacomeyntje Sleght; Jan Mattyse. Agrees with the original. W. La: Montague, Secry.

I do allow of the within Bargaine and shall Grant patents for y Same when payments made accordingly before mee or Magistrates of Esopus.

Andross.

We the undersigned persons, former owners of the land sold to Lowies du Booys and his partners acknowledge to have been fully satisfied by them according to agreement,

we therefore transfer the designated land with a free right
of way for them and their heirs, and relinquishing ferever
our right and title, will protect them against further claims,
in token whereof we have affixed our signatures in the presence of the Justice, Sheriff, Magistrates and Bystanders,
on the 15 September, 1677, at Hurley, Esopus Sackmakers,

Witnesses: Sewakuny x his mark; Hamerwack x his
mark; Manvest x her mark; Mahente; Papoehkies x his
mark; Pochquqet x his mark; Haroman x his mark; Pago-
tamin x his mark; Haromini x his mark; Wingatiek x his
mark; Wissinahkan x his mark; Mattawessick x his mark;
Matsayay x his mark; Asserwvaka x his mark; Umtronok
x his mark; Wawanies x sister in his absence called Wara-
wenhtow; Magakhoos x her mark; Wawejask x his mark;
Nawas x his mark; Tomaehkapray x his mark; Sagaro-
wanto x his mark; Sawanawams x his mark; Machkamoeke
x his mark.

Witnesses: Jan Eltinge; Roelof Henderyckx; John Ward;
Gars x Harris; Albert Jansen.

Testis: Thomas Chambers; Hall Sherrife; Wessel Ten
Broeck; Dirck Schepmoes; Hendrik Jochensen, Joost de Yadus;
Garit x Cornelise; Lambert x Huybertse.

Mattay has publicly proclaimed and acknowledged in the
presence of all the Indian bystanders that the land had been
fully paid for in which all concurred.

Testis: W: Montague, Secr.

•The grant by Gov. Edmund Andross, confirming this purchase from the Indians, is in English as follows:

                          Edmund Andros, Esqr.

Seigneur of Sansmarez, Lieut. t Governor Generall under

his Royall Highness: *James* Duke of Yorke & Albany &c.
of all his Territoryes in America. *Whereas* there is a certain piece of Land att Esopus, the which by my approba-
con and Consent, hath been purchased of the Indian Proprietors, by Lewis DuBois and Partners; The said Land
lyeing on the South side of the Redoute Creek or Kill, beginning from the High Hills called Moggonck, from thence
stretching South East neare the Great River, to a certain
Point or Hooke, called the Jeuffrous Hoocke, lyeing in the
long Reach named by the Indyans Magaatramis, then North
up alengst the River to an Island in a Crooked Elbow in
the Beginning of the Long Reach called by the Indyans
Raphoos, then West, on to the High Hills, to a place called
Waratahaes and Tawaratague, and so alongst the said High
Hills South West to Moggonck aforesaid; All which hath
by the Magistrates of Esopus been certifyed unto mee, to
have been publiquely bought and paid for in their presence;
As by the returne from theme doth and may appeare:
Know yee that by vertue of his Ma, *ties* Letters Patents,
and the Commission and authority unto mee given by his
Royall Highness, I have given, Ratifyed, confirmed and
granted, and by these presents doe hereby give, ratify, con-
firme & grant unto the said Lewis DuBois and Partners,
Thatt is to say, Christian Doyo, Abraham Haesbroecq,
Andries Lefevre, Jean Broecq, Pierre Doyo, Laurens Biverie,
Anthony Crespell, Abraham DuBois, Hugo Frere, Isaack
DuBois, and Symeon LeFevre, their heyres and Assignes,
the afore recited piece of Land and premises; Together
with all the Lands, Soyles, Woods, Hills, Dales, meadowes,
pastures, Marshes, Lakes, waters, Rivers, fishing, Hawking,
Hunting and fowling, and all other Profitts, Commoditys,
and Emoluments whatsoever to the said piece of land and

I do allow of the within bargain; and shall grant Patents for ý same; when payments made accordingly before mee or Magistrates of ...

ANDROSS

ORIGINAL DEED WITH SIGNATURES OF GOV. ANDROSS AND INDIANS IN TOWN CLERK'S OFFICE, NEW PALTZ

SIGNATURES OF WITNESSES TO ORIGINAL DEED

premises belonging, with their & every of their appurtenances, & of every part and parcell thereof; *To have and
to hold* the said piece of Land and Premises, with all and
Singular the appurtenances unto the said Lewis DuBois
and partners their heyres and Assignes, to the proper use
and behoofe of him the said Lewis DuBois and partners
their heyres and Assignes for ever. *And* that the planta-
cons which shall bee settled upon the said piece of land bee
a Township, and that the Inhabitants to have liberty to
make a High Way between them and the Redout Creeke or
Kill for their Convenience. Hee, the said Lewis DuBois
and partners their heyres and Assigns, Returning due Surveys & makeing improvem't thereon according to Law;
And Yielding and paying therefore yearely and every yeare
unto his Royall Highnesse use as an acknowledgment or
Quitt Rent att the Redout in Esopus five bushells of good
Winter Wheat unto such Officer or Officers as shall be
empowered to receive the same:

Given under my hand and Sealed with y Seale of the
Province in New Yorke this 29th day of September in the
29th yeare of his Ma'ties Reigne, Anno Domini 1677.

Andross.

Examined by mee,
Matthias: Nicolls, Secr.

The final action taken by Governor Andros in regard to
granting the patent appears in the Documentary History
of New York as follows:

Upon request of Louis DuBois and partners at Esopus,
that they may have Liberty to goe and settle upon the land
by them purchased on the South side of the Redout Creek,
at their first convenience, these are to certify that they have

Liberty so to do, Provided they build a Redoute there first for a place of Retreat and Safeguard upon Occasion:

Action in New York, November, 1677.   E. Andros.

ALL PROBABLY LIVED AT HURLEY—THE NEW VILLAGE (THREE MILES FROM KINGSTON)

From the Kingston records it appears that Andre LeFevre one of the New Paltz Patentees owned a house and lot at Hurley which he sold, June 29, 1680, to Hyman Allertson Roosa. This house he had bought of the executors of Cornelius Wynkoop. It also appears from the same records that about 1678 Simon LeFevre the Patentee transferred for his father-in-law Christian Deyo a lot and house at Hurley to Cornelius Wolverson.

Thus is afforded additional evidence that the New Paltz Patentees were residents of Hurley before coming to New Paltz. We know of no evidence that a single one of the number lived in Kingston. It has been shown that Anthony Crispell lived at Hurley and never moved to New Paltz, the treaty with the Indians was made at Hurley, Louis DuBois was a magistrate at Hurley, Abraham Hasbrouck the Patentee married the daughter of Christian Deyo at Hurley. Abraham Deyo, son of Pierre the Patentee was born at the same place. Quite possibly we may yet find houses once owned by New Paltz Patentees still standing in the ancient village of Hurley. It would no doubt be laborious but perhaps not impossible to trace the ownership down to the present day.

CHAPTER II

All the Frenchmen at Kingston did not move to New
Paltz.   On the church records at the former place are
found the names of Perrine, Depuy, Gasherie, Delemater
and others, not to be found on the church book at New
Paltz.   Anthony Crispell, although having a share in the
New Paltz patent, never moved there, but remained at
Hurley.   The eleven who came to New Paltz were, to a
considerable extent, related to each other.   Abram and
Isaac DuBois, the latter but eighteen years of age, were the
sons of Louis; the two Deyos were father and son.   The
two Hasbroucks were brothers, and so were the two Le-
Fevers.   Four of the patentees, Abram DuBois, the two
Hasbrouck brothers and Simon LeFever, married the four
daughters of Christian Deyo, who was usually called Grandpere or Grandfather.   Andries LeFever did not marry.

From Kingston the little party came to New Paltz in
three carts, and the spot of their encampment, about a
mile south of the village, on the west side of the Walkill,
is still known as "Tri-Cor," in English three carts.   Tradition relates that when they alighted one of the party read
for them the 37th Psalm.

In 1686, Louis DuBois, who had been the leader of the
settlement, returned from New Paltz to Kingston, where
he purchased a house, and lived ten years, until his death
in 1696.   His son, Isaac, had died six years before at the
early age of thirty-one.

More Land Wanted

At the outset the Patentees had quite as much land as they wanted, but it was only a few years before they were ready to acquire more land, as shown by the following paper in the Patentees' trunk in the Dutch language, dated 168⅔, applying for permission to purchase lands of the Indians, which translated literally reads as follows:

To the Hon. Justice of the Court now in session at Kingston,

We citizens of New Paltz inform your Honor that we must keep a great fence between us and the Indians, and that the Indians are disposed to sell us their land to their New Indian Fort. We therefore humbly petition your Honor to give us a further hearing upon the approval of His Excellency the Governor, and we will then give satisfaction to the Indians. We remain your servants, In the name of the citizens of New Paltz.

Abraham Hasbrouck,
Jean Hasbrouck,
Louis Baijvier.

Permission is granted to the citizens of New Paltz to purchase of the Indians, on approval of His Excellency the Governor, the unpurchased lands, to wit: Sewakanamie and Sewankonck, to the New Indian Fort.

By order of the Special Session Court held in Kingston, February 13, 168⅔.

Rv.nd d La Monragerh.

This purchase of land was never made.

Deed of Gift to Jean Cottin, the Schoolmaster

To the general reader there is no paper in the Freer collection of greater interest than the copy of the deed of gift to Jean Cottin, the schoolmaster, of a house and lot in the little settlement in 1689, just eleven years after the first settlers arrived on the ground. The copy was made in 1707. The paper is in good French, the writing legible, but the lines and the words in the lines crowded so close together that it is difficult to read it on that account. A rough translation is as follows:

We the undersigned gentlemen, resident proprietors of the twelve parts of the village of New Paltz, a dependency of Kingston, county of Ulster, province of New York, certify that of our good will and to give pleasure to Jean Cottin, schoolmaster at said Paltz, we to him have given gratuitously a little cottage to afford him a home, situate at said Paltz, at the end of the street on the left hand near the large clearing (creupelbose) extending one "lizier" to the place reserved for building the church and continuing in a straight line to the edge of the clearing, thence one "lizier" to the extremity of the clearing to the north, thence running along the street and continuing to the west (couchant soliel) as far as the extremity of the clearing, and we guarantee the said Cottin that he shall be placed in possession without any trouble and we allow said Cottin to cut wood convenient to his purpose for building and he is given the pasturage for two cows and their calves and a mare and colt. We the proprietors at the same time agree among ourselves, for the interest of our own homes to request said Cottin that he will not sell the above mentioned property to any one not of good life and manners, and we are not to keep said Cottin as schoolmaster longer than we think fit and proper.

Done at New Paltz, August 1, 1689.

Thus signed: Abraham hasbroucq, pierre doio, Jean hasbroucq has made his mark HB, hugue frere has made his mark X, Abraham dubois, Isaac dubois, Louis dubois, Anthoine Crespel, Louis Beviere, Lisbette doyau has made her mark E. D.

We Anthoine Crespel and Estienne Gacherie certify that this copy is true, just and conformable. In evidence we have signed.

Anthoine Crespel.
Estienne Gasherie.

Kingston, October 9, 1707.

In presence of me,
      D. Wynkoop,
        Justice of Peace.

This deed of gift throws a strong light on the character of the Huguenot settlers at New Paltz. It shows that they highly prized education, that they already had a schoolmaster, only eleven years after the date of the first settlement, and that they treated him with great kindness; it shows, moreover, that they had a lot reserved for a church, that they objected to a sale of property to any person "not of good life and manners," and their business ideas were sufficiently practical that they did not care to bind themselves to employ Jean Cottin as schoolmaster longer than they saw fit and proper.

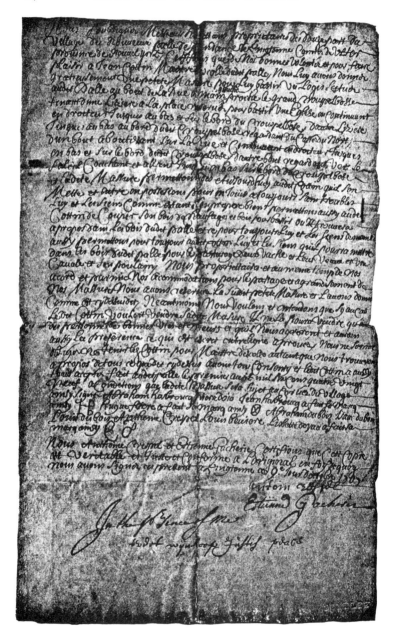

DEED OF GIFT TO JEAN COTTIN

The French Schoolmasters at New Paltz

In the early history of New Paltz two men stand out as pastors and two as schoolmasters in the little community. The two French pastors, Rev. Pierre Daillie and Rev. David Bonrepos have had their names and memories preserved in the church records, but it is only within the past few years that documents have been brought to light showing who it was that taught the school in those early days. In the same building in which the Huguenot pastors preached the gospel and baptised the children on their occasional visits to New Paltz, in the years preceding 1700, two other Huguenots of learning and ability gathered their little flock to instruct them in secular learning on week days and probably in religious matters on the Sabbath, in the absence of the pastor.

It is greatly to the credit of the New Paltz people that they organized a school as well as a church at so early a date. In their kind and liberal treatment of their instructors they set an example to people of the present day.

Neither of these French schoolmasters left descendants. One bequeathed his little property to the church at New Paltz; the other his considerable estate to the church at Kingston.

From 1696 to 1700 the children in the little community were taught by Jean Tebenin, as is shown by the certificate, in French, among the papers that have come down in the family of Isaac DuBois the Patentee, which is as follows:

Nous Ministers & Anciens de L'Eglise françoise aux palls de la province del la Nole York dans L'Amerique, certifions que le Sr. Jean Tebenin ayant demeure avec nous pendant l'espace de quatre ans pour maistre d'escole & pour L'Instruction de nos enfans, a toujours fait le devoir d' un bon &

veritable christien, frequenté nos saintes assembles, & participé a sacrement de la cene du Siegneur—c'est pourquoi Nous le recommendons. [There is here a small portion of the document illegible, but the signatures are plain.]

Aux palls ce May 1700.

> D. Bonrepos, pasteur.
> Jean hasbrouck anciens.
> * * Bayvier.

On the back of the paper is written:

Atestation pour Jean Tebenin faite Au pals Lan 1700.

That is:

Attestation for Jean Tebenin, made at the Paltz in the year 1700.

Translation.

We, minister and elders, of the French church at the Paltz of the province of New York in America, certify that Mr. Jean Tebenin having lived with us during the space of four years for schoolmaster and for the instruction of our children, has always done the duty of a good and true Christian, frequented our holy assemblies and partaken of the sacrament of the Lord's supper—therefore we recommend him.

At Paltz, the — May, 1700.　　D. Bonrepos, Pastor.
> Jean hasbrouck,
> —— Bayvier, Elders.

Jean Tebenin may have again taught the school at a later date. We have no evidence on this point. He certainly lived at New Paltz at a much later date. In his will, dated in 1730, and preserved in the Patentees' trunk, he gives his property to the church at New Paltz, with the special request that if the French language should cease to be used his copy of the Bible be sold and the proceeds given to the poor.

As the Huguenots at that time had no religious schools or seminaries, either in France or America, the poor old schoolmaster's apprehension was sure to be realized. When the old French ministers were dead there was none educated in the French tongue to stand in their stead.

We have no further information concerning Jean Tebenin except that he was godfather at one or two baptisms of children at New Paltz.

The other French schoolmaster at New Paltz was Jean Cottin. He was a prominent man in the community, and lived many years at New Paltz. Afterwards he moved to Kingston, married the widow of Louis DuBois the Patentee and for many years carried on the mercantile business.

Jean Cottin's name appears on the church records at New Paltz in 1690 as godfather at the baptism of Hendricus, son of Pierre Deyo. He was the schoolmaster as early as 1689. For about ten years after this date he resided at New Paltz.

In 1701, Jean Cottin sold a house and lot in this village to Hugo Freer, the deed, in French, being still among the Freer papers. This was certainly the house and lot which the New Paltz people had given him, the deed of gift being turned over to the purchaser and still preserved among his papers.

We have no record showing the date of the marriage of Jean Cottin and Catharine, widow of Louis DuBois the Patentee. The first record we have bearing on this point is in 1703, when at the baptism of a negro slave girl in the church at Kingston she promises to serve her mistress, Catharine, and her master, Jean Cottin, faithfully as long as they live and she shall then be free.

The widow of Louis DuBois the Patentee was a rich
woman for those days. In his will Louis had performed
the very unusual act of bestowing on her the full half of the
property, in case she should marry again. Louis had moved
from New Paltz to Kingston in 1686, and died there ten
years later. Mrs. DuBois' father, Matthew Blanshan, was
a very rich man. Probably much of the property in the
family had come from him.

Be that as it may, Jean Cottin sold his house and lot at
New Paltz, moved to Kingston, married the widow of Louis
DuBois and engaged in the mercantile business, which he
carried on for about twenty years. Among the Freer papers
are a number with his signature. One is written in English, with a delightful French brogue. In a letter still preserved among these old papers Mr. Cottin duns the recip-
ient in a very polite manner, saying: "You pay others; me
you neglect."

When Jean Cottin died, about 1723, he left his property,
including his account books, which were in the French language, to the church at Kingston. These account books
are still in the chest containing the papers of the Kingston
church.

HOUSES BUILT BY THE PATENTEES

The first settlers all undoubtedly lived on what is now
called Huguenot street in this village. About thirty years
after the first settlement, the log houses of the pioneers
began to be superseded by the stone houses which have
come down to the present day.

Commencing on the south end of the street, on the west,
Jean Hasbrouck lived on the site, now the Memorial House.
This house bears the date of 1712, and there is not the

shadow of a doubt that it came straight down from Jean to his son, Jacob, then to his son, Jacob, Jr., then to his son, Colonel Josiah, then to his son, Levi, from whom it passed to his son, Josiah, after whose death it was sold with his other real estate and became the property of Jesse Eltinge.

The house across the street now owned and occupied by Abm. D. Brodhead and previously by his grandfather, Sheriff Abm. A. Deyo, Jr., has come straight down from one Abm. Deyo to another from the time of the first Abm., grandson of Christian, the patentee.

In this house Senator Jacob Hardenburgh was born, his father, Richard Hardenburgh, renting the farm at this time, while its owner, Judge Abm. A. Deyo, resided at Modena.

The house now owned and occupied by Mrs. Mary Du-Bois Berry's heirs has come as straight down in the family as either the Hasbrouck or Deyo houses mentioned. This house still bears, in large iron figures, the date of its erection, 1705, and on the eastern wall, fronting on the street, may be seen the port holes—now closed with brick—which, in the ancient times, had been provided as precautions, un-needed, however, against the attacks of the savages.

Across the street, with its gable-end to the road, stands the original Bevier house, which, however, passed into the possession of the Eltings considerably over 100 years ago. This was the Elting store for a considerable time before the Revolutionary war, and between this establishment and the Hasbrouck store, in the house first described, the sharpest kind of rivalry existed. In the chimney of this house, until recently, the date, 1735, was to be seen. But the house was evidently built at two different times, and the portion with the chimney and date quite certainly was built last.

Passing on still further to the north, the next house, now

owned by Isaiah Hasbrouck, has come straight down from Abm. Hasbrouck, the patentee. We have traced its ownership to the widow of Daniel, son of Abm., the patentee.

The house of Simon LeFever, the patentee, stood on the north end of the present church yard. It passed from the possession of Simon to his son, Andries, then to his son, Simon, then to his son, Andries, usually called Flagus, who died about 1811, and left no son. This house was torn down when the present brick church was built, and the stone went into the foundation of the church edifice.

We have now come to the last stone house on this street. This was the Freer house, but the Freers moved out of the village 160 years ago, and about 100 years ago this house was occupied for a long time by the Lows.

We have now stated where each of the patentees lived except Abram and Isaac DuBois, who, being young, doubtless lived with their father, while Andre LeFevre, having no wife, did not need a house. Anthony Crispell, as we have stated, never lived at New Paltz, but his daughter, who married Elias Ean, located, about 1712, some four miles north of this village, on the homestead where their descendants still reside.

Simon LeFevre died young and his widow married Moses Cantain, who occupied the homestead at New Paltz until the LeFevre boys were grown, and then removed to Ponckhockie. The last survivor of the patentees was Abm. DuBois, and his grave in the old church-yard in our village is the only one of those of pioneers that is marked by a stone. It is a large flat stone, picked up in the field, and marked "1731, Oct. 7, A. D. Bois, S V R viver of 12 Patentees."

Pierre Deyo, son of Pierre, the patentee, met a sad and

tragic fate; going alone to search a direct route eastward to the Hudson river, he never returned. Long afterward the buckle of a truss that he had worn was found at the foot of a tree. He may have died from sudden illness, or from the arrow of an Indian.

DRESSMAKING IN THE OLD DAYS

Among the papers in the Freer collection is one in good French, showing that at so early a date as 1699 the New Paltz people were sufficiently advanced in the refinements of life to have regularly taught dressmakers. A translation is as follows:

This day, the twenty-seventh of October, 1699, Sara Frere, daughter of the late Hugues Frere, an inhabitant of the Paltz, has by the advice of Hugues Frere, her brother, as her guardian, promised to bind herself to serve in the capacity of dress maker's apprentice, during the space of three years, to commence the first of December next, to Mr. David de Bonrepos or to Blanche du Bois, his daughter-in-law, dress maker, and to obey them in all things that are reasonable and proper; and that the said David de Bon-repos and Blanche du Bois promise also and bind themselves to feed her, board her, and educate her in the fear of the Lord, and to furnish her with whatever shall be necessary, having regard to her habits and manner of bringing up, during the space of three years, and above all, to teach her the trade of dress making, and at the end of the said three years, to give to her the same number of clothes, both dresses and underclothes, as she will bring with her on entering the house of the said David de Bonrepos or Blanche du Bois, and to teach her to read and write, in so

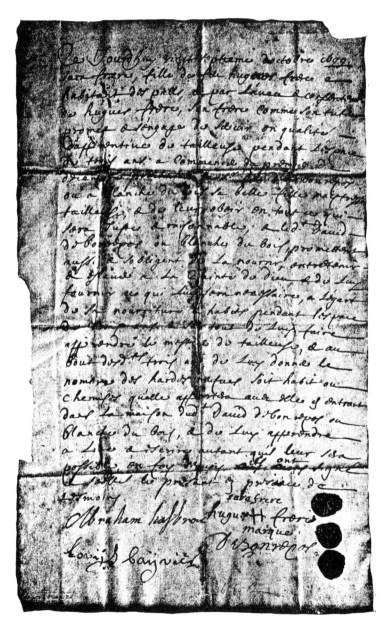

CONTRACT OF SARAH FREER TO LEARN DRESSMAKING TRADE.

far as it shall be possible for them (to do so) ; in token of
which they have signed and sealed these presents in the
presence of witnesses.

Sara frere (Seal)

hugues H frere (Seal)

mark

de Bonrepos (Seal)

Abraham hasbrouc

louys bayvier.

The First Sales of Land

One of the first sales of land of which we have any record
was by Anthony Crispell to Louis Bevier of a lot in New
Paltz, in 1699.

Crispell, it must be remembered, never moved to New
Paltz, but continued to reside in Hurley. The following is
the record in French in the county clerk's office at Kingston :

Fut present en sa personne Anthoine Crespel Laboureur
demeurant a Horly Countes de Ulster Cognois et Confesse
avoir vendue Cedes et Quettes Transportes et par Ces
presentes vendet de Laisse et Transport a Louis Beviere
Laboreur dem. au nouveau palle une certaine terre dans un
Crouspelbose Joignant Le village du dit palle faisant une
part de douze part suiuant quil a estes partages par Les
proprietaire du dit palle La dite part Joignant d'une Leziere a la Pasture Abraham du Bois et dautre Leziere
a Louis Beviere dun bout du Costes du mydy sure La
Wasmater Land Et loutre bout du Costes du Nort
Joignant Les heritier de Simon Leffebre. Et moy Le dit
Crespel promes faire Jouir et garantir at dujours et a per-
petuites Sans trouble et aupechaneus Le dit Beviers luy et

3

ses heritier et La dite Vente faite moyennaunt La somme de Cens quarante squipe de bles que moy Le dit Crespel ay Receu Content et tunt quitte Le dit Beviers et tous Autres en ffoy de quoy.

Jaye signes fait a quinstoune ce dixi ane Jour de Avril six Cent nonante neuff.   Antoin Crespel.

Jean Cottin.

Jaque Du boois.

     Tes moins.

The following is a translation:

Personally appeared Anthony Crespel a laborer living at Hurly County of Ulster who declares and confesses to have sold, ceded, released, conveyed, and by these presents sells, releases and conveys to Louis Bevier, laborer living at New Palle, a certain piece of land in a thicket adjoining the said village of Palle making one of the twelve parts according to the partition by the proprietors of said Palle. This said part is bounded by the pasture of Abraham DuBois and by Louis BeVier on one side at the south it bounds on the Washmaker's land and on the other side at the north on the heirs of Simon Leffebre. And I, the said Crespel, promise to have the said Bevier enjoy and hold thereof without trouble and hindrance; and said sale has been made upon payment of the sum of 140 schepels of wheat which I the said Crespel have received to my satisfaction and absolve thereof the said Bevier and all others.

In testimony whereof I have signed this.

Done at Quinstoun this 10 day of April, 1699.

                          Antoine Crespel.

Jean Cottin.

Jaque DuBoois.

     Witnesses.

DEED FROM ANTHONY CRISPELL TO HUGO FREER

Another sale of land at a still earlier date was from Anthony Crispel, the Patentee, to Hugo Freer, son of the Patentee, of a pasture at New Paltz. The original deed in French is among the papers of the Freer Collection.

A translation is as follows:

I, the undersigned, Anthoine Crispel, laborer, dwelling at Harley (Hurley), acknowledge that I have sold, conveyed, transferred and delivered to Hugue Frere Junior, dwelling at the Paltz, a pasture, with all my pretentions thereto, as it lies and extends, situated in the tract of the Paltz, adjoining the pastures of the late Simon le Febvre, and in consideration of fifty bushels of wheat * * (Ms. effaced) as follows: Twenty-five bushels of wheat and twenty-five bushels of flax, at the current price, to be paid in four consecutive years, as follows: twelve and a half bushels each year; and I promise to assure and guaranteee the said Hugue Frere, Junior, him and his, forever and in perpetuity (in his possession). Done at the Paltz, the eleventh of September, one thousand six hundred and ninety three.

anthoine crespel.

(mark H de Hugue Frere   )

louys bayver,   Jean Cottin,
witness.   witness.

CHAPTER III

THE FRENCH RECORDS OF THE NEW PALTZ CHURCH

The French records of the church are in a small book containing seventeen pages, about 6 x 8 inches, which has always been in the care of the pastor of the church. The paper is of coarse quality and somewhat yellow with age, but the writing is perfectly legible. The following translation of these records was made by the late Wm. E. DuBois, of Philadelphia, in 1846:

January 22, 1683. Mr. Pierre Daillie, minister of the Word of God, arrived at Paltz, and preached twice the Sunday following, and proposed to the heads of the families to choose by a majority of the votes of the fathers of the families an Elder and a Deacon, which they did, and chose Louis DuBois for Elder and Hugh Frere for Deacon to aid the minister in the management of the members of the church, meeting at Paltz, who were then confirmed to the said charge of Elder and Deacon. The present minute has been made to put in order the things which appertain to said church.

October 14, 1683. Baptised two children of Pierre Doyau ———— and [one] named Peter, the other Mary. Abraham Rutan, Godfather, and Mary Petilon, Godmother, to the first, of the other Abraham DuBois, Godfather, and Margaret Doioie (Doyau), Godmother.

October 21, 1683. Baptised a child of Simon LeFevre and Elizabeth Doioie, named Isaac. Isaac DuBois Godfather, and Marie Hasbrouck, Godmother.

April 28, 1684. Baptised a child of Isaac DuBois and Marie Hasbrouck, named Daniel. Godfather, Louis Du-Bois, and Catharine Blancon, Godmother.

September 23, 1684. Baptised a child of Abraham Ruton [Rutemps] and Marie Petilon, named Daniel. Godfather, Louys DuBois, Catherine Blancon [Blanjean], Godmother.

October 23, 1684. Baptised a child of Abram Hasbrouck and Marie Doioie, named Joseph. Godfather, Jacob Du-Bois, Marie Doioie, Godmother.

April 4, 1685. Baptised a child of John Hasbrouck and Anne Doioie, named Elizabeth. Godfather, Pierre Doioie, and Elizabeth Doioie, Godmother.

April 6, 1685. Baptised a child of Louis Bevier and Mary Leblanc, named Louis. Abm. Hasbrouck, Godfather, and Mary Doioie, Godmother.

April 17, 1685. Baptised a child of Abraham DuBois and Margaret Doioie, named Abraham. Louis DuBois, Godfather, and Catharine Blancon, Godmother.

October 28, 1685. Baptised a child of Simon LeFevre and Elizabeth Doioie, named John. Pierre Doioie, Godfather, and Mary Doioie, Godmother.

March 20, 1685-6. Baptised a child of Abm. Ruton [Rutemps], named Paul. Hugh Frere, Godfather, Hagar Meckel, Godmother.

The year one thousand, 1686, the 17th of October, was baptised a child of Abm. Hasbrouck and Mary Doyo, a son. His name is Solomon. The Godfather, Louis Bayvier, the Godmother, La-Toynelle.

April 15, 1688. John Hasbrouck and Anne Doyo have baptised a child named Jacob. Godfather, Louis Bayvier, Godmother, Mary Leblanc.

April 19, 1688. Abram Ruton and Mary Petilon had

baptised a child named David. Godfather, Peter Doyo. Godmother, Jane Vilar.

April 16, 1689. Peter Doyo and Agatha had a daughter baptised named Madaline. Godfather, John Hasbrouck, Godmother, Margaret Doyo.

April 16, 1689. Louis Bevier and Mary Leblanc had a daughter baptised named Esther. Godfather, John Hasbrouck, Godmother, Esther Latoinelle.

April 16, 1689. Isaac DuBois and Mary Hasbrouck had a son baptised named Benjamin. Abram DuBois, Godfather, and Anne Doyo, Godmother.

October 13, 1689. Louis Bevier had a son baptised named Solomon. Godfather, Isaac DuBois, Godmother, Anne Doyo.

October 13, 1689. Abraham DuBois and Margaret Doyo had a daughter baptised named Rachel. Godfather, Abm. Hasbrouck, Godmother, Mary Doyo.

October 13, 1689. Elizabeth Doyo had a daughter baptised named Mary. Godfather, Hugh Frere, Godmother, Anne Hasbrouck.

October 16, 1689. Abraham DuBois and Margaret Doyo had a daughter baptised named Leah. Godfather, Solomon DuBois, Godmother, Mary Leblanc.

May 14, 1690. Isaac DuBois and Mary Hasbrouck, his wife had a son baptised, who was named Philip. John Hasbrouck, Godfather, and Esther Hasbrouck, Godmother.

May 14, 1690. Abram Rutemps and Mary Petilon had a daughter baptised named Esther. Abm. Hasbrouck, Godfather, and Esther Hasbrouck, Godmother.

June 7, 1690. Hugh Frere, son of Hugh Frere, his father, and Mary Haye, his mother, was married by Mr. Daillie to Mary Leroy.

June 9, 1690. The gentlemen of the consistory of Paltz

have placed in my hands two sealed bags, saying that in
one there is a hundred and forty francs in zewannes [wam-
pum] and in good silver, in the other they say there is four
hundred francs, zewannes, in good silver.

> Abraham Hasbrouck, Witness.
> mark of (x) Hugh Frere, Elder.
> Louis Bevier, Witness.

June 28, 1690. Isaac DuBois died at his home in Paltz.

August 3, 1690. A daughter of Abram Rutemp died,
aged about 6 months.

August 9, 1690. Isaac Frere, son of Hugh Frere, died,
aged about 18 years.

October 12, 1690. Mr. Dallie baptised a male child of
Pierre Doyeau. John Cottin, Godfather, Esther Hasbroucq, Godmother. His name is Henry.

October 14, 1691. Abraham Hasbrouck and Mary Doyeau, his wife, had a boy baptised, called Jonas. Abram
Hasbrouck (son of John Hasbrouck), Godfather, Anne Hasbrouck, Godmother.

October 17, 1691. Hugh Frere, Jr., and Mary Leroy,
his wife, had a boy baptised named Hugh. Abram Frere,
Godfather, Mary Frere, Godmother.

October 24, 1691. Abram Rutemp and Mary Petilon, his
wife, had a boy baptised called Peter. Godfather, Peter
Guimar, Godmother, Esther Hasbrouck.

April 18, 1692. Mr. Dallie married Peter Guimar, a
native of Moir, in Saintonge, son of Peter Guimar, and Anne
Damour (his father and mother), and Esther Hasbrouck,
native of the Palatinate, in Germany, daughter of John
Hasbrouck and Anne Doyeau (her father and mother).

May 21, 1693. Abram DuBois and Mary Deyo, his wife,

had a daughter baptised named Catharine. Louis DuBois, Jr., Godfather, Trinque (Tryntje), wife of Solomon DuBois, Godmother.

May 21, 1693. Hugh Frere and Mary Ann Leroy, his wife, had a son baptised named Isaac. Dennis Reille, Godfather, and Hagnette, Godmother.

May 21, 1693. Moses Quantin and Elizabeth Deyo, his wife, had a son baptised named ———. Peter Guimar, Godfather, Rachel Hasbrouck, Godmother.

April 28, 1694. Abram Frere married to Haignies Titesorte.

May 5, 1694. Anne Doyo died in the Lord, aged 50 years.

December 8, 1695. The wife of Hugh Frere died in the Lord.

May 31, 1696. Mr. Bonrepos baptised a daughter of Hugh Frere and Mary Leroy (her father and mother), having come into the world the 5th of May, 1696. Her name is Mary. Abram Hasbrouck, Jr., Godfather, Rachel Hasbrouck, Godmother.

May 31, 1696. Mr. Bonrepos baptised a daughter of Abram Frere and Haiquiez Titesorte (her father and mother), [she] came into the world the 15th day of May, 1696, her name is Nelleties. Louis DuBois, Godfather, and Elizabeth Titesort, Godmother.

May 31, 1696. Mr. Bonrepos baptised a son of Abram Hasbrouck and Mary Doyo (his father and mother), his name is Benjamin. Abraham Doyo, Godfather, Mary Frere, Godmother.

October 23, 1698. Richard Viltfil and Madelin Chut have caused to be baptised a child, his name is (?). Louye Bayvier, Godfather, Marian [Bayvier?], Godmother.

October 23, 1698. Abraham Frere [and] Achsah, his

wife had a child baptised, his name is Solomon. Moses Quantin, Godfather, Rachel Hasbrouck, Godmother.

July 2, 1699. Jacob Clarwater and Mary, his wife, had a child baptised, his name is Abraham. Godfathers, Abram Hasbrouck, Solomon DuBois; Godmother, Mary Doyo.

July 3, 1699. John Bevier, Abm. Bevier, Isaac Hasbrouck, Christian Doyo, Jacob Frere, Rachel Hasbrouck, Sarah DuBois were received at the table of the Lord in the congregation of the Paltz by Mr. Bonrepos, minister of the Word of God.

October 22, 1699. Louis DuBois [Jr.], was received at the table of the Lord in the congregation of Paltz by Mr. Bonrepos, minister of the Word of God.

October 15, 1699. Mr. Bonrepos baptised a daughter of Hugh Frere and Mary Anne Leroy, her name is Esther. Godfather, John Tebenin, Godmother, Achsah (?) Titesorte.

May 19, 1700. Richard Viltfil and Madaline Chut, his wife, had baptised a son, his name is Daniel. Hugh Frere is Godfather and Marianne Leroy, Godmother, by Mons. Bonrepos, minister of the Word of God.

Isaac DuBois, son of Louys DuBois and Catharine Blancon [Blanjean on Kingston record], was married by the minister, after three announcements on three Sundays previous, to Marie Hasbrouck, daughter to John Hasbrouck and Anne Doyoie.

June 19, 1700. Andrew LeFevre and Samuel Bevier were received at the table of the Lord in the congregation of the Paltz, by Mr. Bonrepos, minister of the Word of God.

June 19, 1701. Louis Bevier (Jr.) married to Rachel Hasbrouck.

February 20, 1702. Christian Doyo and Mary Leconte were married in this town of Paltz.

Daniel DuBois has paid 5 francs and 10 —— too much.
John LeFevre owes 3 francs. Henry Doyo has paid 22
francs and 15 —— too much. Louis DuBois has paid 88
francs and 5 —— too much. Hugh Frere 3 francs, 5 ——
too much. Joseph has paid 3 francs, 5 —— too much.
Abram Doyo has paid 5 francs, 15 —— too much.

Recapitulation by translator of names of French Families,
or Surnames of the record in their order:

DuBois, Rutamps (or Ruton), Frere, Daillie (Rev.), Viltfil, Chut (?), Bevier, Quantin, Hasbroucq, Clarwater, Doyau,
Leroy, Bonrepos (Rev.), Meckel, Petilon, LeFevre, Blancon
(Blanjean), Leblance, Lationelle, Vilar, Guimar, Haye, Cottin, Reille, Titesorte, Leconte, Tebenin.

The record extends from 1683 to 1702. There is a single
entry in Dutch, dated 1718.

There appears at least eight different handwritings in the
record. Also the autographs of Abram Hasbrouck and
Louis Bevier. The latest entry in the handwriting of Louis
DuBois is dated March, 1686. The last notice of Rev. Mr.
Daillie is April, 1692. The first of Rev. Mr. Bonrepos,
May, 1696.

CHAPTER IV

The Blending of French and Dutch at New Paltz

The question is occasionally raised as to when the first marriages took place between the French settlers at New Paltz and the Dutch.

There has been a wide-spread but very erroneous impression that matrimonial alliances between the Huguenots, who came to New Paltz, and the Dutch took place at a very early date and even before crossing the Atlantic.

A careful examination of the records shows that none of the Patentees and not many of their children intermarried with the Dutch. A considerable proportion of the children and grandchildren of the Patentees married people of French descent, not residing at New Paltz. Among these appear the names, Gumaer, LeConte, Blanshan, Vernooy, Montanye, Le Roy, Cantine and Ferree.

Solomon DuBois, of Poughwoughtononk, son of Louis the Patentee, was the first New Paltz man to make the experiment of selecting a wife outside the Huguenot fold. In 1691 Solomon and his wife Tryntje Gerritsen, whose name bespeaks her Dutch origin, had a son, Isaac, presented for baptism.

The first young man of Dutch origin to marry a New Paltz woman and locate within the bounds of the Patent was Jacob Clearwater, whose residence was at Bontecoe. In 1699 he and his wife, Mary Deyo, had a son, Abraham, presented for baptism. But Jacob Clearwater did not leave descendants permanently residing at New Paltz.

There were a few and only a few other marriages between the Dutch and those of the children of the Patentees who. located at New Paltz, as follows: Abraham Deyo married Elsie Clearwater in 1702; Roelif Eltinge married Sarah DuBois in 1703; Jacob Freer married Altje Van Weyen in 1705; Joseph Hasbrouck married Ellsje Schoonmaker in 1706; Hendricus Deyo married Margaret Van Bummell in 1715; Solomon Hasbrouck married Sarah Van Wagenen in 1721. Other children of the Patentees, who settled outside of New Paltz, intermarried with the Dutch to a greater extent.

In the third generation there were quite a number of intermarriages with the Dutch, in certain families, but fewer, we think, than are generally supposed. In the LeFevre family, out of twenty-one grandchildren of Simon LeFevre, the Patentee, who grew to maturity and married, not one selected a partner of the Holland race. One married Col. Johannes Hardenbergh, Jr., who was of German origin, and one married Jacob Hoffman, who was of Swedish ancestry. All the rest united with people bearing French names.

Elias Ean, whose nationality is not known, was the first man, not the son of a Patentee, to settle at New Paltz and remain there permanently. He married Elizabeth, daughter of Anthony Crispell, the Patentee, and located about four miles north of the village on a farm, that has come down in the family until the present day. Elias Ean's name appears on the tax list of 1712, and when the first stone church was erected in 1718, just forty years after the settlement, Elias Un (in Dutch Ean) was the only person, beside the Patentees and their children, who assisted in the work.

The first man who was certainly of Dutch origin to locate here permanently was Roeliff Eltinge, who married Sarah, daughter of Abraham DuBois the Patentee in 1703. It was not, however, until about a score of years later that he moved from Kingston, where he held the office of justice of the peace, and located at New Paltz. His family was the first that was certainly of Dutch origin to take root at New Paltz and flourish here.

The Low family, which was of Dutch descent, had a number of representatives at New Paltz for a long period, both before and after the Revolutionary war, but finally all died out or moved away.

Next to the Eltings, the Van Wagenens were the most prominent among the Dutch to settle and remain permanently at New Paltz. But the Van Wagenens did not come until a much later date than the Eltings, the name of Petrus Van Wagenen, the progenitor of the family at New Paltz, not appearing on the church book here until 1766.

Although the French and Dutch at New Paltz no doubt harmonized, yet the line of demarcation is plainly seen in the strife between the Cœtus and Conferentia parties, which for a time split the Dutch church in America into two hostile factions. The Conferentie party, which claimed that each dominie must be ordained by the home church in Holland, seceded from the New Paltz church and in 1766 erected a church building near Mr. W. H. D. Blake's present residence, about two miles from our village. This church was called by the old people "the owl church," probably because the woods near by was a favorite haunt for owls. In the list of persons who built the Conferentie church appear the names of four Eltings, three Lows, Petrus Van Wagenen and Abraham Ean. The names of a small portion of the DuBois family, but no other names of French origin, appear in the list of those who built the Conferentie church.

When the second stone church was built in our village in 1772, the Dutch element, which had seceded and built the Conferentie church, rendered no aid. About ten years afterwards peace came, and in 1783 the Conferentie church organization was, as stated in the church book, "in the fear of God, in love and mutual friendship united with the old congregation of the New Paltz."

Thenceforward there was peace and harmony in the church, and the New Paltz people who bore names of Holland origin have been certainly quite as faithful in support of the church as those bearing Huguenot names.

In the blending of races, which took place at New Paltz as well as elsewhere in New York, there were other elements beside the French and the Dutch. The Brodheads were English; the Auchmoodys, Scotch; the Hardenberghs, German; the Ronks and Terpenings from Flanders; the Bruyns, Norwegian. The ancestors of the Wurts and Goetcheous families were Swiss. By the mixture of these various nationalities the people of New Paltz had become a composite race at the beginning of the last century.

In this mixture of races there was little infusion of English blood until the Quaker settlement at Butterville, about 1810. The New Englanders swarmed into what is now Orange county, a portion coming by way of Long Island; but on the lower Wallkill they found the ground occupied and did not enter.

The Dutch language was not abandoned at New Paltz because of an influx of English-speaking people. Neither, may we say, had the French tongue been previously abandoned because the Dutch element had come into the town in large numbers. No doubt the influence of church and school and of surrounding communities brought about a change in the language. The father of the writer has told him that he did not learn to speak English till he went to school. This was not an exceptional case. No doubt there were many in this community who knew no tongue but the Dutch until they went to that famous Irish schoolmaster, Gilbert Cuthbert Rice, who from about 1815 to about 1825 taught the young ideas how to shoot in different communities in the vicinity of New Paltz. Quite probably the grandparents of some of the children who thus learned to talk English had themselves known no tongue but the French until they went to school, and there from a Dutch-speaking schoolmaster and Dutch-speaking children learned to use that language.

A story that has come down to us from the old people relates that when the three brothers, sons of Isaac LeFevre, were living in the three stone houses on the banks of the Wallkill at Bontecoe, a child sent from one of the houses to another to borrow some article asked for it in Dutch and was indignantly told to go back home and learn to ask for it in French. This was about 1760, and the story shows that even where the children were of pure French blood, as was the case at that time with the Bontecoe LeFevres, they had somehow learned to speak in Dutch, but received a stern rebuke for using that tongue.

CHAPTER V

COLLECTIONS OF OLD PAPERS

From time to time, since the matter of the local history of New Paltz has attracted attention, various collections of old papers and documents have been brought to light. Valuable collections of ancient documents are owned in the families of the late Messrs. Edmund Eltinge and Samuel B. Stilwell.

The largest and most valuable assortment of old papers was that in the possession of Mrs. Theodore Deyo. This contained not only papers relating to the Deyo family, but many others. It is stated that when the British burned Kingston, in the time of the Revolution, is was supposed that they would march up the Wallkill and burn New Paltz, likewise. It must be remembered that in colonial days the practice of having valuable papers recorded in the county clerk's office was not as general as it now is. In order to have their papers in a safe place, the New Paltz people brought them to the residence of Captain Abram Deyo, whose house is now owned and occupied by his great-great-grandson, Abm. Deyo Brodhead. Here they were placed in a large chest and buried in the cellar. After the fright was over, and the British had returned to New York, some of the papers were not reclaimed by their owners. The chest containing the papers was taken from the residence of Capt. Abm. Deyo to that of his brother, Philip Deyo, on the Paltz Plains, and remained there during his life time and that of his son, Andries, and also while Theodore Deyo, who was

4

the son of Andries, kept the old homestead. When he moved it was taken to the new residence of the family, where it remained.

One of the most valuable collections of ancient documents is that which has come down in the family of Isaac DuBois, the Patentee. Among the papers are the following:

A quit claim from Mary, widow of Isaac DuBois, the Patentee, to her son, Daniel, for her interest in the real estate of her husband. This is dated 1718.

A release from Andre, Isaac and Jean, sons of Simon LeFevre the Patentee, to their sister Mary, wife of Daniel DuBois, for their share in certain lots of land lying in and near the village. This is dated 1713.

A will in French of Daniel DuBois, dated 1729. The handwriting is plain, and each letter distinct from beginning to end of the document. The first page is nearly taken up with a complete and extended declaration of faith in the Christian religion, which is in striking contrast with the plain businesslike form of the wills of the present day.

A paper which is in Dutch is dated 1741 and contains the signatures of Daniel DuBois, Isaac LeFevre, Simon Le-Fevre and Matthew LeFevre.

Another valuable paper is dated 1742 and is a bond given by Jean LeFevre to Garret Kateltas, when the former purchased of the latter the land in Kettleborough on which Jean's sons, Abraham and Andries, settled.

A large collection of ancient documents has come down in the Freer family, many of them dating back to the time of Hugo Freer, senior, son of Hugo the Patentee.

Some of the most ancient of these papers have been framed in glass and placed in the Memorial House; others have been placed in a small trunk, in which a portion of them had been previously kept. This little trunk is about six inches long and four inches wide. It bears the initials H. F. and has a blacksmith-made handle. There are among these ancient papers about thirty in the French language and a few in Dutch and English. A considerable portion are fully 200 years old. They include letters, wills, receipts, deeds and warrants.

One of the most valuable papers is a copy of a deed of gift in 1689 from the New Paltz people to their schoolmaster, Jean Cottin, of a house and lot. Among the other papers in the little trunk are the following:

A deed from Jean Cottin to Hugo Freer of a house and lot in this village, probably the property above mentioned, dated 1701.

Three receipts in the handwriting and containing the signature of Louis DuBois the Patentee, each dated in 1695, the year before his death.

Two receipts in the handwriting and containing the signature of Abraham DuBois the Patentee.

Two receipts in the handwriting and containing the signature of Moses Cantain, the ancestor of the Cantine family.

A paper containing the signature of Peter du booys, who was a nephew of Louis DuBois the Patentee, and ancestor of the Dutchess county DuBoises.

A warrant, in English, in the handwriting and with the signature of Roelif Eltinge, ancestor of the New Paltz Eltings, who was at the time of writing, 1710, still residing in Kingston and was already a justice of the peace.

A paper in the handwriting and containing the signature of Solomon DuBois, son of Louis the Patentee.

The will of Hugo Freer the Patentee.

The will, in Dutch, of his son, Hugo, senior.

A deed dated 1693 from Anthony Crispell the Patentee to Hugo Freer for a lot of land in this village, probably the first sale of real estate at New Paltz, the pay to be made partly in wheat and partly in flax seed.

Papers with the signatures of Rev. Pierre Daillie and Rev. David Bonrepos, the two French pastors at New Paltz.

Letters of friendship and business addressed to Hugo Freer from New York and Quebec.

Bills from merchants in New York, showing the high prices for goods in ordinary use and the very low price paid for country produce in those old days.

An order for grain to be delivered at the mill of Johannes DuBois at Greenkill, in the present town of Rosendale, dated in 1701, and showing that there was a mill there at that early date.

Deeds to Hugo Freer, senior, son of Hugo the Patentee, from his two sisters, who married and located at Schenectady, and from his brother Jean, who located at Kingston, for their share of their father's estate.

A deed, in English, from Abraham Freer to his brother, Hugo, senior, for his two sittings in the first stone church.

Papers with the signatures of Louis Bevier the Patentee and Abraham Hasbrouck the Patentee.

A tax list of 1712, showing that at that time the Patentees and their children constituted almost the entire taxpaying population of the precinct. Four of the Patentees were still alive.

The oldest paper is dated 1677—the year of the Patent. It does not seem to be a paper of much importance.

Many of these documents are specially useful in determining the original orthography of the names of the early settlers at New Paltz. This can not be determined from the church records, because the minister performing the ceremony evidently recorded each name as he thought it ought to be spelled, without asking the parent of the child baptised how he was accustomed to spell it.

Among the more modern papers in this collection are a mass of documents, including a will of Jonas Freer, a letter from Aaron Burr, a letter from Col. Abraham Hasbrouck, of Kingston, and other papers of interest to members of the Freer family.

Most of the papers have not been fully translated, but have been examined to a sufficient extent to give a clear idea of their contents.

THE PATENTEES' TRUNK

For about 100 years, commencing with 1728, the administration of affairs, in this town, regarding land titles, etc., was in the hands of a board of twelve men, elected annually, who represented the original twelve patentees. The trunk, containing records that remain, was for a great number of years at the Huguenot Bank, in this village. About 1850, at a public meeting, a committee was appointed to examine the old trunk and report what documents it contained. Some of the papers are in French and others in Dutch, but the majority are in English. These papers have since been placed in the safe in the town clerk's office. The most important papers in the Patentees' trunk were as follows:

1st. A copy of the purchase of the patent, signed by the Indians on their part, and by Louis DuBois and the other patentees.

2d. The confirmation of the title to the patentees by Edmond Andross, Colonial Governor of New York, given September 29, 1677.

3d. A document dated February 13, 1682, with reference to negotiation concerning the purchase of land to the southward as far as the "New Indian Fort." This was situated at Shawangunk.

4th. An agreement entered into April 21, 1728, by which the institution of the "Twelve Men" was established to fix the title to lands, previously divided, and to distribute the remainder by lot.

5th. Two contracts, one dated 1744 and the other 1774, entered into by the owners of the patent, binding themselves to pay all assessments by the "Twelve Men" for legal expenses in defending the claims of title of any of the owners.

6th. An Act of the Legislature confirming unto the owners, the partitions of land made by the "Twelve Men." This is dated in 1785 and is signed by Gen. George Clinton as Governor.

CHAPTER VI

The Spelling of Various Family Names

The question is sometimes asked as to what is the original orthography of various family names of people in New Paltz and elsewhere in Ulster county. The question can not be answered from the church records, but in some cases can be decided from the original signatures of the Patentees. The earliest records in the Dutch church at Kingston and the Huguenot church at New Paltz show different ways of spelling the same name.

Turning to the translation of the French records of the New Paltz church in the very first entry, October 14, 1683, we find the baptism of two children of Pierre "Doyau." Their godmother was their father's sister, Margaret "Doioie," wife of Abraham DuBois. Their baptism was not performed by a back woodsman, who did not know how to spell, but by Rev. Pierre Daillie, a learned man, who before he left France was a professor in the university of Saumur. Yet here in the same entry he spells the name of the brother Doyau and of the sister Doioie. In 1686, three years after this first record, we find the name of Anna, another sister of the same family and wife of John Hasbrouck, spelled Doyo. Here are three different methods of spelling the family name now written almost uniformly Deyo.

If there had been any established form of spelling the name the ministers would undoubtedly have spelled it that way.

In the treaty with the Indians, made in 1677, Pierre, the

Patentee, wrote the name Doyo, his father, Christian, did not write his name, but makes his mark and the name is written deYoo.

Another yet more striking instance of different ways of spelling the same family name is that of the two Hasbrouck brothers. In the treaty made with the Indians for the purchase of the patent, Abraham Hasbrouck writes his name Hasbrocq, and his brother, Jean, writes the name Brocq, without the prefix Has. In the same paper we find that the name of the leader of the band of Huguenots is spelled Lowies DuBooys, and that of his son, Abraham, is spelled in the same way; the name of the LeFevre brothers is spelled Lefebre, and Freer is spelled as at the present day. In the agreement among the owners of the patent in 1728 we find the three sons of Simon LeFevre, the Patentee, each spelling the name LeFevre; two of the Hasbroucks wrote the name Hasbrocq, while another had the present spelling; the DuBoises and Beviers spelled the name as at present; Freer is written Freer, while the three signatures of Deyos are all spelled differently—one writing Doio, another Doiau and another Doyo.

Rev. Randall R. Hoes in the preface to the translation of the records of the Dutch church at Kingston speaks thus of the orthography of the various family names:

"The orthography of the proper names in these Registers is quite in keeping with a practice of the early times in which they were written.—It never seems to have occurred to these university-bred Dutch Domines of the Kingston church to inquire how various persons presenting themselves for marriage, or their children for baptism, spelled their own names, but these names having been pronounced in their hearing, they recorded them phonetically, according to the prompting of their ears, or arbitrarily, according to the dictates of their fancy. This practice, however, involved no unusual inconsistency, for the orthography of the Dutch language, even in Holland, as respects both common and proper names, was not wholly settled until late in the eighteenth century. Some of our most familiar family names of to-day are recorded on these pages in half a dozen or more different ways, and in many instances variations in spelling occur even in the same baptismal or marriage entry. It is therefore impossible in any case whatever to state, at least by the aid of these Registers, the exact original orthography, even if any existed, of particular family names among our Dutch settlers.—This remark applies, moreover, to all of the early civil and ecclesiastical records of the Dutch, whether in this country or in Holland, and to a large extent also to those written in English, as it was not before the commencement of the present century that any marked degree of uniformity was observed in the orthography of a very large number of proper names.

"The variations in spelling in the Kingston Church Registers are even more involved and confusing than usual, owing to the fact that Domines Mancius, Meyer, and Doll, and also Domine Cock, of East Camp, an advisory friend of the Kingston church, who during the "Coetus" and "Conferentie" difficulties, repeatedly officiated there at baptismal and marriage ceremonies, were not Dutchmen, but Germans, and naturally displayed German tendencies in their orthography."

CHAPTER VII

Moving Out and Moving In

Isaac LeFevre, son of Simon LeFevre, the Patentee, Hendrick Deyo, son of Pierre, the Patentee, and Jacob Freer, son of Hugo Freer, the Patentee, located about 1720 in what is still known as Bontecoe, about four miles north of this village, the last named nearly on the north bounds of the patent, and their descendants have continued to the present day to occupy, in great part, the land settled on at this time by their ancestors. The name Bontecoe was, perhaps, bestowed in remembrance of the Dutch vessel Bontecoe, called in contemporaneous English history "Spotted Cow," which made several voyages from Holland to America, bringing over a number of Huguenot emigrants, though we have no certain information as yet that any of the people who located at New Paltz crossed the ocean on the Bontecoe.

There is equally good reason for supposing that the proper orthography is Bon-ter-cou, meaning "neck of good land" and applied to the fertile necks of land on the banks of the Wallkill.

About the year 1720, Roelif Eltinge, son of Jan Eltinge, a native of Drenthe, in Holland, came from Kingston to New Paltz. He married the daughter of Abm. DuBois, the patentee, and from that day to this the Eltinges have been men of influence and greatly respected in New Paltz.

Although the Paltz patent included about 36,000 acres of land, yet the sons and grandsons of the original settlers were, from time to time, obtaining fresh grants of land to the south of the original grant, while others emigrated to Duchess,

Orange and Greene counties, likewise to other parts of the State, and to New Jersey and Pennsylvania. Wherever they settled the Huguenot stock usually took root.

But the emigration was only the swarming out. The old colony of New Paltz continued to thrive, although its growth was slow.

In 1720 the church of logs in which they had worshiped God gave way to a stone structure.

Previous to this time, and after the departure of Rev. Pierre Daille for Boston, Rev. David Bonrepos preached at New Paltz, not as a stated pastor but as a supply.

The Dutch Language Superseding the French

During this time the French language was giving way and the Dutch taking its place. It is as difficult to determine how long the French language was used at New Paltz as it is to say how long the Holland tongue was spoken. Very old people still talk in Dutch occasionally. When the writer was a child it was the custom for the old people to talk in Dutch when they did not want the children to understand what they were saying. Father informed us that he never learned to speak English until he went to school. The first and second generations of the New Paltz people probably talked French altogether.

The French language was evidently never much used in important legal documents at New Paltz, though it was doubtless the common speech of the people for at least half a century after the first settlement. The country being under English rule, and Kingston being a Dutch settlement, it was natural that official documents in the state or county archives, although relating to a French-speaking community, should be written in the English or Dutch tongue. In receipts and papers of that nature given by one person to another in the little community the French language was used and many of these papers are still in existence. In the old graveyard the oldest tombstones have English inscriptions. On the church book the first entry in Dutch was in 1718. One of the few papers in French that have been preserved in the "Patentees' trunk" is a little slip, dated 1729, commencing thus: *"Daniel Hasbrouck a paise a jacobus brun pour le vilage un demy pistole,"* etc. In family collections many papers in French have come to light.

Perhaps the most noteworthy papers in the French language in the Patentees' trunk are the two wills of Jean Tebenin, one of the two French schoolmasters of the little settlement. One of these wills is dated February 20, 1719, and the other November 14, 1730. The testator, who had no wife or children, left his property to the church, and mentions particularly his French Bible, which, if the French language should be superseded by the Dutch, must be sold and the proceeds given to the poor in the church.

TERRITORY FORMERLY PART OF THIS TOWN, BUT NOT WITHIN
THE PALTZ PATENT

It must be noted that the town of New Paltz, at its greatest extent and before it had been dismembered, included much territory not within the original bounds of the Patent, which extended only about a mile south of this village. This additional territory, included in the town, comprised a number of smaller patents, which had become, either by purchase or by grant from the colonial governors, the property of descendants of the Paltz patentees.

In 1685, only eight years after the Huguenots settled at New Paltz, a tract of 5,000 acres, at Guildford, was granted

to James Graham and John Delavall.   On this tract lived
a number of years afterwards, Ellsje, the widow of Joseph,
son of Abraham Hasbrouck, one of the Paltz patentees.
She outlived her husband about forty-one years, raised a
large family and here some of her descendants still till the
ancestral acres.   The original grant is in possession of
Joseph Hasbrouck, Jr.

The next grant, in point of time, was doubtless that from
Gov. Dongan, to the original Louis DuBois, lying prin-
cipally on the west side of the Wallkill and extending from
the Paltz patent to the Guilford patent.   Louis, in his will,
makes mention of the fact that this tract had been granted to
him by patent dated June, 1688.

Edmund Eltinge had in his possession a release, dated in
1729, from the then proprietors of the Paltz patent, for
the sum of six pence, to Solomon and Louis, Jr., of any
claim they might possibly have against this tract, granted
their father.   On this tract, on the west side of the Wallkill,
Solomon and Louis, Jr., had located, the former taking the
northern part of the tract and Louis the southern part.

The next grant of land, in point of time, was probably
that to Captain John Evans by Governor Fletcher, in 1694,
which comprised an immense territory extending from New
Paltz patent southward into Orange county.   This grant
was annulled by the Legislature five years afterwards, and
we find reference to this fact in one or two subsequent
grants.

The next grant, adjoining the Paltz patent on the south,
was of 1,200 acres, June 30, 1715, to Hugo Frere, Sen., the
son of Hugo the Paltz patentee, and to his sons, Hugo, Jr.,
Thomas and Isaac.   On this tract his descendants are still
cultivating the soil granted to their ancestors in 1715.

In 1721, January 21, was granted the Garland patent of 2,000 acres, taking in the Kettleborough and Ireland Corner neighborhoods. On this tract Garret Ketaltas was a freeholder, in 1728, and on this tract Andries and Abram Le-Fevre and Daniel Deyo resided about thirty years later and here a number of their descendants still live.

In 1748 there was granted to Noah Eltinge and Nathaniel LeFevre 3,000 acres, lying on the Paltz Plains and extending eastward and also including some land on the west side of the Wallkill. On a portion of this grant some of their descendants are still living.

Lastly, in point of time, was the grant, in 1753, in the name of George II, King of England, to Abraham Hasbrouck, of Kingston, Louis Bevier, of Marbletown, and Jacob Hasbrouck, Jr., of New Paltz, of several parcels of land, petitioned for, which, as stated in the grant, did not exceed 2,000 acres, and was part of the tract formerly granted to Capt. John Evans and afterwards vacated and lay on both sides of the Paltz River, some parts lying to the southward of the Paltz patent and some parcels southward of the grant to Noach Eltinge and Nathaniel LeFevre. The parchment, containing this patent and the great seal of the colony, attached, was in possession of Mr. Samuel B. Stilwell, who resided on part of the tract and was a descendant of the Abm. Hasbrouck, of Kingston, to whom one-third of this patent was granted.

The First Public Highway

The first highway, probably, in this town, was laid in 1738, when a highway was laid out, as stated in the record, for the purpose of enabling the people to get to church at New Paltz and Kingston. The route stretched from one to another of the old stone houses along the Wallkill, north from our village to the northern bounds of the patent, crossing the Wallkill by a scow, just this side of the Bontecoe school-house. The marks are yet to be seen where this old road had been worked down below the level of the surrounding soil. About forty years later this road was abandoned and a new one was constructed about one-eighth of a mile farther east, above the reach of high water. As a consequence of this removal of the high-way, nearly all the old settlers had to construct lanes from their houses. About a mile north of the village the new high-way drew so near to the old that an angle was made, and the old highway was used for the rest of the route to the village.

DISPUTES IN REGARD TO THE BOUNDARIES OF THE PATENT

The first grant, from Governor Andross, did not define the boundaries of the patent very clearly. In 1722 an attempt was made to fix exactly the corner of the patent at Paltz Point (or as it is now called Mohonk) as is shown by the following document:

"These are to certify that the inhabitants of the town of New Paltz, being desirous that the first station of their patent, named Maggonck, might be kept in remembrance, did desire us, Joseph Horsbrook, John Hardenburgh, Roeleft Eltinge, Esq., Justices of the county of Ulster, to accompany them and there bring Ancrop, the Indian, then brought us to the High Mountain which is named Maggrnapogh at or near the foot of which hill is a small run of water and a swamp which he called Maggonck and the said Indian, Ancrop affirms it to be the right

Indian names of the said places as witness our hands this
nineteenth day of December, 1722.

> "JOSEPH HASBROUCK,
> "HARDENBERGH,
> "ROELOFF ELTINGE.

"ULSTER COUNTY, ⎱ ss:—
"April 16th, 1723. ⎰

> "Recorded for said county, Records in lib. CC. fol. 205.
> "J. GIL. LIVINGSTON,
> "Clerk."

In regard to the boundary line between the Paltz patent and
the patent of Louis Dubois, on the south, there was also
trouble, and in 1729 the line was surveyed by Caldwallad_r
Colden, Jr. A letter from Josiah DuBois written in 1850 says
in regard to a certain stone on the west bank of the Wallkill:

"I have a deposition on parchment of Abm. DuBois, the
patentee, who makes oath that he saw an Indian named Bontecoe stand, at the place where this stone is with one foot on
one side of the brook and the other on the other, and heard
him say the lands on his right belong to the DuBoises and those
on his left to the Frenchmen." The boundary line between
New Paltz and Marbletown, and also between New Paltz and
the Hardenbergh patent on the north were also matters of dispute. It was claimed that the Hardenbergh patent included
Dashville Falls, and it was alleged on the part of the New Paltz
people that the surveyor had been bribed by the present of a
cow to run the line so as to deprive New Paltz of the valuable
water privilege. The bounds of the patent as finally determined, left the Falls in the Hardenbergh patent.

The boundary line between New Paltz and Marbletown was

not settled until after the revolutionary war. The top of the mountain was the line, but it was impossible to determine exactly where the top of the mountain was. We have in our possession an ancient document containing the proceedings of a meeting at which Dr. George Wurts, the first Wurts in this place, was Chairman, and Isaac LeFever, clerk, at which the representatives of the different Paltz families bound themselves to stand together in contesting the claims of Marbletown. In the suit which followed the Paltz people employed Aaron Burr as their attorney and won the case.

CHAPTER VIII

A Pure Democracy

The government of New Paltz in the earliest period was evidently a pure Democracy, the heads of families gathering in a body to frame regulations for the general welfare. This fact is plainly set forth in the following:

New Paltz Orders

RECORDED

We inhabitants of ye Niew Pals in generall are mett together ye 23th day of Feb. 1711-12 to conclued concerning all our fences of the Land as also of the pastures, to the plurality of Votes according to the order of the Warrant to the Constable directed;

First of all we shall begin to ye kill or kreek next of Solomon Dubois to ye Aest of sd Solomon and then the fence shall run to ye bounds of Abraham Dubois, from thence along a run of watter and then to the pasture of Louis Bevier, and the sd fence is to be made of three Rails and of three and fifty inches high, and then ye sd Louis Bevier is obliged to make and repare a good and sufficient fence a Long his pasture to ye East until he Comes to Abraham Dubois, and then Jacob Hasbroucq shall make or have a good Sufficient fence of the same high as here above mentioned until he comes to the pasture of Daniel Dubois neer of the tourelle or neest and then the gate Shall be Set according as it is ordered or concluded, then the N. Pals town Shall together make the fence from Jacob Hasbroucq, to the sd. gate and so we shall begin the vasmakerslant fences to the kill or kreek at the Landing place, to the erf of John Hasbroucq and every one of us must make his part or share at six Raeles as now is and them that have theirs erf opposite the P. Vasmakersland they shall make and maintaine a good and sufficient fence to the house of Hugue Frere, as also at both sides of the street and between the Erfs a good and close fence to be made, it is also said that ye fences of the Creupelbos shall begin to the house of Hugue frere and so a Long the above sd Creupelbos so fare as hath been measured, and them that have a part or lots in sd Creupelbos they shall make and hold a good and sufficient six Railes fence of fifty three inches high there he now is at present. And to the end of sd fence shall begin the bosh fence of three Railes of the same high as here above mentioned and so along to the kill or kreek neer of Abraham Frere so as it is now deeld and devided Now to the other sides of the kill or kreek to the West we shall begin to the long macos or long bondecoe and shall be made and kept as now is at present and of the same high to the time that wee think fit to join him together. ——

As also the fences of ye petit macos or litle bondecoe shall be made and kept as now is at present and of the same high as above sd. for ye time of two year and then shall be sett a long de mountaing in ye best convenient place that we think sutable, and then will be joined to the high bridge fences & from sd bridge to the kill or kreke near Solomon Dubois to the West; Every one shall make and kepe his fences good and sufficient at three Reals and of ye same high as aforesd.——

More concerning the old pastures every one is oblidged and bound to doe as his Nebourgh that is to say the just half of ye fences of five Raels or other wise & that good and sufficient.——

And as for ye kettel doing Damage and so taken they shall

be put in pound by him that shall there unto be chosen or impoured by the inhabitants of sd place.

And each and every horse or Cow beast so taken in damage shall pay a piece nine pence for a fine, the one half for him thereunto chosen, and the other half for the toune.   And as for the hogs they shall have no Liberties for to Runne free; but as for the Sheeps they may runne free until that time that they goe in Dammage in ye Corne or in the pastures, provided ye fences be good and sufficient as for the first time Warning shall be given Charitably to ye owner to kepe them out Dammage, but if they are once more taken in Dammage they shall pay for a fine 3 pences a peace.   And as for the horses which Rune upon the Land in the fale they shall be taken away the 30th of September otherwise they shall pay the fine hereabove sd.   Concerning all the fences here before mentioned, Each and Every one is oblidged and bound to make and kepe his owne fence at the time Limitted or ordered by him thereunto chosen to take notice of sd. fences, but in case any one neglict or will not doe or make his fence he shall pay for a fyne six shellings, and the Viewers of fences shall make or have made the sd fence or fences at his owne charge as ye Law Dirrect in such case.

Here is farther Concluded for them that leaves any gates open, it be with a malicious intend, or neglict they shall pay for a fine three shellings.—And the money so Received of the finnes shall be imployd to pay the cost and charges of the touwne, and such person or persons thereunto chosen to Receive the sd fines shall be accoumptable or give an accounts yearly to ye touwne.

Recorded p.

W. Nottingham Clerk.

LAND WORKED IN COMMON

There is good evidence that in the early settlement the land was worked in common. In the bends of the Wallkill four spots of fertile land were known as Grote Bontecoe, Kline Bontecoe, Bontecoe in Haning and Bontecoe. Grote Bontecoe was certainly worked by the settlers in common, and there is good reason to believe that other lands were also so worked.

THE GOVERNMENT OF THE DUSINE

In 1728 there were twenty-four proprietors at New Paltz, and at that time was instituted the government of the Twelve Men or Dusine. They were chosen annually, and had power to act and set in good order and unity all common affairs. These twelve men exercised the power of dividing lands by lot, in the Paltz patent, and giving title by parole, without deed.

They made rules in regard to fence building, and imposed fines for violation of these rules, in fact they exercised, to some extent, judicial as well as legislative powers, until in 1785, when the town was incorporated in the State government, and by special Act of the Legislature the grants and partitions of the Dusine were confirmed. It does not appear that any appeal was ever taken to the Colonial Government from the acts of the Dusine. There were divisions of land into lots among the proprietors at two different times, the land being set off in regular tiers, numbering from one to twelve.

There were, besides the Dusine, regularly chosen town officers whose duties were distinct from those of the twelve men. The latter were chosen annually at town meeting and were descendants either in the male or female line from the patentee whom they represented.

The Dusine were elected by *viva voce* vote annually just before the poll opened. In the latter period of their existence about the only power exercised was to settle disputes concerning land titles.

This government of the Dusine has no parallel in the colonial history of America. It was transplanted from the banks of the Rhine to the banks of the Wallkill. We are told that the only other European colony in which it had existed was a Huguenot settlement founded at about the same time in South Africa.

The document establishing the government of the Dusine or Twelve Men is one of the papers that have come down in tne Patentees' trunk. It is in English, as follows:

To all Christian People to whom These presents shall come or in any ways may concern *Greeting*. Whereas Edmond Andross Esq'r Seigneur of Sansmarez, late Governor General under his Royal Highness James Duke of York and Albany &c., of all his Territorys In America By his Letters Pattent bearing Date the 29th Day of September in the Year of our Lord 1677 Did Give, Ratifye, Confirme and Grant unto Lewis DuBois and partners, that is to say, Christian Doyo, Abraham Hausbroecq, Andries Lefevre, Jean Broecq, Pierre Doyo, Laurens Bivier, Anthony Crespell, Abraham DuBois, Hugo Frere, Isaac DuBois and Simon Lefever their heirs and Assignes All That certain piece of Land lyeing at the South side of Rondout Creek or Kill begining from the High Hills Called Moggonck from them Stretching South East near the great River, to a certaine point or hook called the Juffrous Hoocke, lyeing in the long Beach named by the Indians Magaatranics, then North

up along the River, to an Island in a Crooked Elbow, In the
beginning of the long Beach Called by the Indians Raphoos
then west on the High Hills to a place called Waratahoes and
Tawarataque and soo along the said High Hills South West
to Moggoncck aforesaid *To hold* unto the said Lewis DuBois
and partners their heirs and Assignes, to the proper use and
behoof of him the said Lewis DuBois and partners their heirs
and Assignes forever.

And Whereas the aforesaid Patentes in their life time and
since their Decease their Severall heirs or Assignes have Severally according to their Just Rights and Interests therein held
Enjoyed and Improved some part of the aforesaid Land and
premises Commonly known by the name of New Paltz, accordingly to the Severall Divisions and partitions that have
been made between them by Parale without Deed, and the
other parts thereof yet Remaining In common and Undivided
Now Know Yee That we whose names are under written and
who have Signed and Sealed These presents being owners and
Interested In the aforesaid Pattent, for the Good Order Regulation benefitts and profitts of the freeholders and Inhabitants
in the said Pattent as likewise for the Maintaining, Preserving,
Defending and Keeping Whole and Entire the full Right Title
benefitts propertys and advantages belonging or in any wise
appertaining unto the aforesaid freeholders and Inhabitants by
Vertue and Authority of the above mentioned Pattent and of
the Several Conveyances and Last Wills and Testaments of
the aforesaid Pattentees and of their heirs and Assignes and
for makeing good and firme the aforesaid Divisions and partitions made by the aforesaid Patentees in their lifetime and
since their Decease by their Severall heirs and Assignes and
for makeing a further and more perfect Division and Partition
of the undivided Lands and premises now lyeing in Common

and Undivided and unimproved within the bounds of the aforesaid Pattent *have* Thought fitt and Convenient and we Doe by
these presents Covenant and Grant to and with each other,
that there shall and may be Yearly and every Year forever
hereafter Chosen and Elected for the purposes above mentioned
by the pleurality of Votes of the freeholders and Inhabitants
within the aforesaid Pattent Twelve good able and sufficient
men freeholders and Inhabitants who have an interest within
the said pattent Representing the aforesaid Twelve Pattentees,
That is to say out of every of us who are owners and occu-
piers, or hath a Right In each of the aforesaid Pattents Shares
Respectively One, which Election shall and may be held Yearly
and every Year at the New Paltz aforesaid on the first Tuesday
in April and in Case any of the freeholders being so Chosen
and Elected as aforesaid Refuse Denye and will not Serve tnat
Then he shall provide one who is likewise an owner and hath
a Right in the same Pattentees Share in its Stead and place,
who not being produced or Doth not appear within a fortnight
after the Election to be held as aforesaid, Then the other
Elected men shall Nominate and take one who is an owner
and hath a Right within the said pattentees share to Act in
his Stead *And we* Doe by These presents every of us severally
in behalf of ourselves our heirs Executors Administrators and
every of them and not Joyntly Give Grant and Bequeath unto
the aforesaid Twelve men or the Major part of them to be
elected and Nominated in manner as aforesaid full power and
Authority to Act and Sett in Good order and unity all Common
Affairs, Businesses or things comeing before them belonging to
or concerning the Right Title Interest or property of the
Township of the New Paltz aforesaid and Commonalty within
the said Pattent According to Law or Equity and to the best
of their knowledge and understanding And That if it should

soe happen that the aforesaid Twelve men to be elected as aforesaid Should Disburse any money for Charges or other Expenses for Defending and preserving the Right Title Interest and property of the Township of the New Paltz afores'd, and the Commonalty within the said Pattent, That then we and every of us Respectively according to our Respective Rights and Interests in the aforesaid Pattent shall bear and pay an equall proportion of the afores'd Charges and expenses soe beene at by the aforesaid Twelve men or any of them, and that they, the said Twelve men Shall and may Give Deeds of Partition or other proper Conveyances in Law for the Confirmation and Assertaining Each man's Just Share and Dividend of the aforesaid Divided land and premises according to the aforesaid Severall Devisions and partitions thereof made by the aforesaid Twelve pattentees in their lifetime and by the Severall heirs and Assigness since their Decease *And we* Doe by these presents further give and Grant unto the aforesaid Twelve men to be Elected and Nominated as aforesaid or the Major part of them full power and authority to make a further and more perfect Division and partition of the aforesaid undivided Land and premisses or soe much thereof as they shall from time to time see cause fer or think convenient which Devision is to ɒe made in manner and forme following That is to say That the said Undivided Lande and premises or such part thereof as they shall from time to time see cause fer or think convenient shall be laid out in Twelve Equal Shares and Devisions soe that the one is not of more Vallue than the other and Then the aforesaid Twelve Shares or Devisions shall be numbered and then the aforesaid Twelve men shall Draw Lotts for the same and such Share or Division as falls to the Lotts of the aforesaid Twelve men Respectively Shall be and remaine to the proper use benefitt and behoof of us who are properly Interested in the Respective pattentees Share they are soe elected and chosen for according to our Just Shares and Interests therein for which the aforesaid Twelve men are to Give Deeds of conveyance for the same, *And* that the same shall stand and Remaine as a full and perfect partition and Severance for the same, *And* that after such partition and Alottment made in manner as aforesaid *We* whose names are under subscribed and who have signed and sealed these presents Respectively and our heirs and Assignes shall stand to and agree to the said partition and Alottment soe to be made in manner as aforesaid according to the true Intent and meaning of these presents And shall permit and suffer the same to stand Remaine and Abide in its full Strength and force forever as if we ourselves had been present and consented thereto and Gave Deeds of partition for the same And That the said Twelve men or such thereof as there shall be others Chosen in their stead at the End of the Year shall be accountable to the New Elected And Soe Yearly and every Year forever hereafter And soe having faithfully Served they shall be Duely and lawfully Dismissed and Discharged for their proceeding in behalf of the Township and Commonalty as aforesaid. — And Now fer the True performance of all and singular the Articles Covenants and Agreements as aforesaid soe far as the same are to be performed by us Severally and Respectively, Each and every of us whose name are hereunder Subscribed, Doe and Doth Severally bind himself his heirs, Executors and Administrators In the sum of fifty pounds currant money of the province of New York, to be paid unto each and every the other of us his heirs Executors and Administrators, upon the non performance of any of the Articles Covenants or Agreements aforesaid which on our severall and Respective parts are to be Done and performed According to the True Intent

and Meaning of These presents In Witness whereof we have
hereunto of one Assent and Consent Sett our hands and affixed
our Seales This Twenty-first Day of April In the first Year
of his Majestys Reigne Anno Dom One Thousand Seven
hundred and Twenty-Eight.

Abraham du bois	(seal)	Samuel Bevier	(seal)
his		Daniel DuBois	(seal)
Hugo x frere	(seal)	Jacob hasbrouck	(seal)
mark		hanrey doyo	(seal)
Andre le fevre	(seal)	daniel has broucq	(seal)
isaac le Fevre	(seal)	Yan een	(seal)
yean le fevre	(seal)	his	
Solomons has broucq	(seal)	Hugo-hu-Frere Junr.	(seal)
Abraham Bevier	(seal)	her	
Louis bevier	(seal)	Elizabet Een	(seal)
his		Sara een	(seal)
John x Teerpenningh	(seal)	mark	
mark		MariaMagdalena-M-Een	(seal)
Abraham doiau	(seal)	mark	
Crestian doio	(seal)	matys slecht juneyer	(seal)
Jacob Frere	(seal)	Anthony Yelverton	(seal)

Sealed and Delivered by the within Subscribers Abraham
DuBois, Hugo Frere, Andri LeFever, Samuel Bevier, Daniel
DuBois, Jacob Hasbrouck, Isaac LeFevre, Jean LeFevre, Solo-
mon Hasbroucq, Henrey Doyo, Daniel Hasbroucq, Jan Een,
Hugo Frere Junr., Abraham Bevier, Louis Bevier, John Teer-
penningh, Elizabet Een, Sara Een, Maria Magdelena Een,

Mattys Slecht Junr. and Abraham Doiou, Jacob Frere, In the presence of us,

AHasbrouck.

J. Bruyn, Junr.

Sealed and Delivered by the within subscriber Cristiaen doyo in the presence of us: My 15: 174—.

Isaak Doyo.

Johannis Lefever.

Sealed and Delivered by the Within Subscribed Anthony Yearenton in the presence of us April 8 Annoy: Dom: 1752.

abraham van der marken.

Jacobus Has brouck.

Ulster ⎫
County ⎭ —Ss.

Be it remembered that on the Eight Day of May in the year of our Lord one thousand seven Hundred and Seventy one, Personally, Came before me Dirck Wynkoop Junr. Esqr. one of the Judges of the Court of Common pleas for said County Coll. Abraham Hasbrouck whome being Duly sworn on the Holy Evangelist of Almighty God Deposeth and saith that he wass present and saw, Abraham Dubois, Hugo Frere, Andri LeFever, Jacob Frere, Samuel Bevier, Daniel Dubois, Jacob Hasbrouck, Isaac Le Fever, Jan Le Fevere, Salomons Hasbroucq, Hanrey Deyo, Daniel Hasbroucq, Jan Een, Hugo Frere Jun. Abraham Bevier, Louis Bevier, John Teerpenningh, Elizabet Een, Sara Een, Maria Magdalena Een, Mattys Slecht Jun. and Abraham Deiou, Syn, Seal and Deliver the within Deed, as their Voluntary act and Deed for the use, therein mentioned, and that at, Same Time, Jacobus Bruyn Junr, and

himself Subscribed their names thereto, as, Witnesses, and
also, Abraham Deyo, acknowledged, at same time, before me
that he had Executed the same deed as his Voluntary act and
deed for the use therein mentioned, and that at the same time
of Executing this deed, he was underage, but that now acknowl-
edges, that the same is his Voluntary act and deed and at
same time also appeared, Isaac Doyo, whom being duly sworn
on the holy Evengelist of Almight god deposeth and saith, that
he was present and saw Christian Doye Syn Seal and deliver
the within deed, as his Voluntary act and deed for the use
therein mentioned, and that, at same time Johannis Lefever
and himself Subscribed their names thereto as Witnesses and
also, that on the Tenth day of said month Jacobus Hasbrouck,
being duly sworn, as aforesaid saith that he wass present and
saw Anthony Yelverton, syn seal and De Liver the within
deed as his Volutary act and deed for the use therein mentioned, and Also, that at same time Abraham Van dermercken
and himself had Subscribed their names thereto as Witnesses,
and I have perused the same and find no Material Erezures,
nor Interlinations therein. Wherefore I do Alow the same to
be recorded——   D : Wynkoop Jun.

CHAPTER IX

The Indians and Hunting Stories

The Indians make but a small figure in the early history of New Paltz.   There is no account of their having ever troubled the inhabitants a particle.   This was because the Paltz people had honestly paid for the land and treated the Indians kindly.   The last remains of the red men in this locality are said to have lived in a little village on the south bank of the Plattekill, where it empties into the Wallkill.   Many arrow heads, both of the kind used in hunting and in war, have been picked up in that locality.   The Normal School grounds were an Indian burying ground.   An Indian skeleton, with large beads, obtained no doubt from some Dutch trader, was dug up near Mr. Low's brick yard when the railroad was in process of construction.

In the sale of the patent the red men reserved a tract called Ah Qua, southeast of Perrine's Bridge, on account of supposed mineral wealth.

Old stories relate that at butchering time they would visit the farmers' yards to select bits of the entrails of the slaughtered animals.

The few remaining at that time went off with Sir William Johnson, the Tory leader in the Revolutionary war.   Now and then one would come around with baskets to sell.   Once a member of such a company was drowned in the Wallkill, at Libertyville.   Then they came no more, saying that the drowned man "spooked" them.   One of the last of the Indians was called Tottoi.   He would make maple sugar and trade it off for bread. When he died he was wrapped in a coffin of bark and buried by Daniel and Levi Van Wagenen. Probably the last visit of the Indians to this place was about 1820, when two of them came to the reservation at Ah Qua. It is related that at one time Indians came near Dashville and cut some timber for baskets. Some of the people started to drive them away, but Ezekiel Eltinge said "let them alone; they have the right." His remark was no doubt on account of the reservation at Ah Qua.

The Indians kept up the custom of holding kint-a-koys at Ah Qua after the whites had settled around. They would sing and feast as well as dance, and borrow vessels in which to prepare the food for these occasions. No matter how clean these vessels were when borrowed the Indians would wash them. The exact spot on which these kint-a-koys were held was about a half a mile southeast of the Bontecoe school-house, where the house and garden of the late Abm. Freer were located. The Indian title to the reservation at Ah Qua was probably never extinguished, but finally the tract was sold for taxes and in that way became the property of the whites.

There was a family of Indians that would come and live in a hut in the woods of Cornelius DuBois (now the W. H. D. Blake place), and with his permission cut down any timber they desired, which they would manufacture into scoops and baskets. Stephen G. DuBois tells us that when he was a small child he visited this Indian family many times. There was a little Indian, called Jake, the grandson of the old Indian, who was the head of the family, and who used to shoot squirrels from the trees with his bow and arrows. Stephen tells us that one day, when he was on a visit to the hut, little Jake showed a skill with the bow and arrow nearly equal to that of his grandfather, by shooting a spider on the opposite side of the shanty. After a while the old Indian, who was the head of the family, was accidentally drowned in crossing the Wallkill, which he frequently did to visit a white man, named "Mocky" Wackman, who lived on the other side of the Wallkill, with whom he was very friendly. After his death the family offered a portion of his clothing to "Mocky," who, thinking it a pity to take any of the poor Indian's clothes, declined the gift, when the garment was instantly tossed in the fire.

The following story Aunt Judy Jackson relates as having happened in her childhood days, about 1812, when she was a slave in the family of Jeremiah Merritt on the county house plains:

Her master in the fall had taken her behind him on horseback and started for the mountain to bring up the cattle which had been running at large in the woods. It was growing late in the fall and it was time to bring up the stock for the winter.

Suddenly as they were riding along they came upon an Indian wigwam. Merritt jumped off the horse which he left in her charge and entered the hut. He remained there a long, long time. At last she grew tired and moving up to the wigwam pushed open the door. There were about a dozen Indians sitting on the floor engaged in making baskets. One man, who seemed to be the chief, had a ring hanging from his nose. Merritt was talking with the Indians and did not go to the mountains to get the cattle that day. Aunt Judy is positive that those Indians were spies who had come probably from Canada to get what information they could in the interest of the English Government. She says, moreover, that Merritt was a tory and this accounted for the long talk he was having with the Indians in the wigwam. The visit of the Indians attracted great attention and the people from all the country around went to see them.

Mrs. Edward McEntee's recollections of her early childhood days, as related to us, contain more accounts of the Indians than the recollections of any of the other old people with whom we have talked. They probably remained longer in the locality about Rosendale Plains than elsewhere in this vicinity. On the east side of the road was an Indian burying ground. One of the neighbors attempted to plow it up, but the red men made him stop. The Indians had bark wigwams scattered through the woods. The spot where one of these had stood would be marked long after it had disappeared by a patch of tansy, that being a favorite herb with the red men. She says she saw the Indians many times when a child. They were kind people if treated well. In their wigwams they would lie on the floor with their feet to the fire. Sometimes they would pass the house, the pappooses strapped to their fathers' backs. The little ones would laugh and call to her. When she was a young woman she lived at Benjamin Van Wagenen's in this village. The Indians would come and shoot with bow and arrow at copper coins at a distance of about fifty yards. If they hit the penny they would keep it. (This was a travelling company.) When she was a small child an Indian woman would call at the house and delight to play with her, sometimes lifting her up by one arm, but this her mother forbade for fear of injury. At one time there was a wigwam right by her grandfather's door. When the first Freer located at Bontecoe an Indian set up his wigwam in the clearing. Sometimes he would lie drunk on the door-step. He was not disturbed and after a time went away.

A story related by Aunt Judy Jackson is as follows:

When she was a slave in the family of Andries P. LeFevre at Kettleborough, about 1820, six Indians came dressed in women's clothing. They lurked about the neighborhood for some time. At Mrs. Andries J. LeFevre's they tapped on the window. At Matthew LeFevre's they entered the house and talked but little, but asked for buttermilk. The buttermilk was brought from the cellar and then it was discovered that they had on male attire under their female apparel. After a while Daniel Deyo, of Ireland Corners (grandfather of Dr. Abm. Deyo), had the Indians arrested and found that they were armed. They said that they wanted to find John ——. Now John —— resided in the neighborhood and had confessed to perpetrating an inhuman act of cruelty upon an Indian family. He had entered an Indian wigwam (just where Aunt Judy did not know), and finding a squaw and her pappoose had asked the squaw to go and get him a drink of water. While she was gone he picked up the papoose and threw it into a pot of boiling water on the fire. He then hid and escaped the fury of the Indians, who, however, hunted him for years. The Kettleborough people told the Indians that they did not know who John —— was. He was living, however, in the neighborhood, and his house at Jenkintown is still standing.

STOLEN BY THE INDIANS

Stephen G. DuBois and his sister, Mrs. Hand, tell us the following story as having been related to them by the old folks, but which must be simply another version of the capture of the wife and children of the original Louis DuBois, at Kingston. The event, as related to them, when they were children, took place at Libertyville and is as follows:

A woman named Katrina DuBois (they do not know her husband's name) was carried away captive by the Indians, with an infant in her arms and a child at her side. The husband followed in pursuit. He saw a savage in the act of drawing his bow. In his haste and nervousness he could ¡.ot get the arrow to fit the string. Before he could shoot, DuBois sprang upon him and ran his sword through him with such force that it struck into a tree behind him. This happened near Lewis Hasbrouck's present residence, in Libertyville, by the brook now called the Stenykill. DuBois' wife, not recognizing the pursuers, started to run with the Indians. DuBois then shouted to his wife, *"Trene, stop, or I'll shoot you."* Then she recognized his voice and returned.

Both Mr. DuBois and his sister, Mrs. Hand, repeat this story, positively and emphatically, as being told to them by the old people.

Elihu Schoonmaker likewise remembers hearing this story in his young days and says that a black oak tree, at the locality described above, was pointed out to him as marking the spot where DuBois slew the Indian with his sword.

Some Hunting Stories

One of the most interesting chapters of the history of New Paltz might be given to the hunting stories of the olden times. One of the most undoubted truthfulness is that of Hons Decker, of Shawangunk, who pursued a deer from rock to rock at Paltz Point, until it had descended to its last place of refuge on table rock, called by old people Ephriam's Point. Having no gun, he seized the animal by the horns, and a contest of strength ensued. A companion, who was with Decker, cried out that the infuriated creature would fling him over the cliff, but the intrepid man replied that if he did he would pull him back. Finally, with the aid of his pocket knife, the prize was secured.

Another hunting story is that of Peter LeFevre, grandfather of the writer, and Louis Hardenburgh, grandfather of the late Senator Jacob Hardenburgh, formerly of Kingston. Louis was a sturdy blacksmith, his shop being located on the public highway about four miles north of this village. Peter LeFevre lived in the old stone house still standing near by. These two followed a bear to her den in the Gerhow region, and Hardenburgh entering the den, slew the brute—an exploit requiring as much courage, perhaps, as the famous adventures of General Putnam and the wolf. But another version of this story is that one of the hunters shot into the den and killed the bear before Hardenburgh entered it.

Major Isaac LeFevre, of Swartekill, a famous surveyor in his day, was once employed to make surveys in the neighborhood of Paltz Point (Sky Top), about 1820, and on drawing toward the rockiest portion of the mountain his employer (Mr. Mullenix) told him to stop, that the rest of the mountain might be left for the foxes. Major Isaac asked him if he would give it to him for his day's work. The reply being in the affirmative, he received twenty acres for his day's work. This he afterwards transferred to Mr. Pell, of Esopus, and it is well settled that this identical tract was the highest part of the mountains, which was never owned by John F. Stokes and was not secured by Mr. A. K. Smiley until some years after his purchase of Mohonk.

One day when Major Isaac Lefevre was going out on a surveying expedition he shot an elk. He dressed the animal and hung it up in a small tree. On his return in the evening he found a deer had been smelling in the carcass of the elk and become fastened by his horns. He dispatched the deer and thought he had done quite as good a day's work at hunting as at surveying.

Wild turkeys were found in the woods in this vicinity in the old times. Levi Schryver informs us that the locality in Esopus, which still bears the name of *Calicoon* (turkey) hook, was noted in old times for the wild turkeys found there.

Aunt Judy Jackson's stories concerning the wild animals that roamed the forest in her young days are very thrilling. There were more wild beasts in the Libertyville neighborhood, when she was there, than in the Kettelborough neighborhood, where she afterwards lived. Once, in her childhood, when she was a slave in Jeremiah Merritt's family, she was bringing home the cows when she saw a panther crouched on a limb of a tree overhead. He paid no attention to her but sprang for the cows. He missed his prey and the cattle scattered widely, bellowing as they ran. Shortly afterwards the panther attacked a cow belonging to Cornelius DuBois. He was tearing her hind quarters when seen. The cow was not dead, but died of her injuries. The panther escaped to the woods.

When Aunt Judy was a slave at Andries P. LeFevre's a panther was shot in the woods of his father, Philip. The ball hit the ferocious beast in the head. He made one tremendous spring for the man who shot him. The man dodged and the panther fell dead on the ground. Aunt Judy says that she has "seen a sight of wild animals in her day, but the panther is the savagest of all."

Wolves and bears were quite numerous, especially on the west side of the Wallkill. Cornelius DuBois, the youngest of the name, brother of Josiah DuBois of Poughwaughtenonk, had a narrow escape from being killed by wolves. He was skating on the Wallkill, alone, when two wolves came out of a pine woods, on the east side of the Wallkill, near Libertyville, and chased him. By skating he kept ahead of them, but growing tired he bethought himself of the dogs at a neighboring house, near the stream. He whistled to the dogs. They came and fought with the wolves. The dogs were killed, but Mr. DuBois escaped with his life.

It must be remembered that these stories which Aunt Judy tells are not what she has heard from older people, but what occurred in the neighborhood while she lived there.

Cornelius DuBois (father of the one just spoken of) owned land on the east side of the Wallkill and had a barrack there where he kept sheep. Farmers stored much of their hay in barracks in those days. Aunt Judy had herself seen wolves in pursuit of these sheep.

Bears would also come around. At one time Aunt Judy noticed that some animal had been injuring the corn in the field. She thought the damage had been done by a cow, but it proved to be the work of a bear.

One man started alone in pursuit of the animal and followed him to the mountain. Others followed and found the man dead, having, it is thought, run himself to death.

WILD PIGEONS AND LARGER GAME

In those days, about 1820, game was still quite abundant. Nearly every year great flocks of wild pigeons would come and almost every family was provided with nets for catching them and likewise with stool pigeons. Catching pigeons was a favorite sport. Stephen G. DuBois relates that one day as he was riding, on horseback, in company with about a dozen others, to attend town meeting at the Paltz, the pigeons passed over their heads in immense numbers.

Peter W. DuBois' father, Wilhelmus, was quite a hunter, and he and John Fuller, grandfather of Wm. Fuller, killed many bears and wolves, before the digging of the Delaware &

Hudson Canal, but after the construction of the big ditch these wild animals did not venture to cross it.

One of the last wolves trapped by Fuller was on the Mullenix place on the mountains. In this case Fuller had intended to bring the captive alive to Libertyville, but the farmer seeing the destroyer of his sheep in the trap exclaimed "You are the one that has been killing my sheep," and slew him on the spot.

Another story about one of the last wolves caught in this vicinity is concerning one caught on the Mathusalem Eltinge farm, which extended from Springtown up to Bontecoe Point. In this case, too, the wolf was brought, alive, in the trap.

Mr. Edward DuBois, of Marlborough, favors us with an account of the capture of the very last wolf in this portion of the country which was trapped by Fuller in the winter of 1826 or '27. Mr. DuBois says:

"It was a field day for Libertyville. I was quite young at the time, yet I recollect his bringing the beast alive with the trap on its leg into my father's kitchen, where Mr. Blake now lives. * * The bronzed hunter and the captive wolf, the old cellar kitchen, and an old oaken table, upon which two terror stricken urchins—a younger brother and myself, sought refuge, are among the clearly defined impressions of my childhood."

Desperate Fight with a Bear

Mr. J. Nelson Terwilligar gives us an account of a famous bear hunt that happened about 1820, when he was a lad of sixteen. Henry Williams, a famous hunter, and another hunter named Watkins had followed a bear all the way from Tucker's Corner, through New Paltz, crossing the Wallkill at what is now Luther Hasbrouck's place, and running him into a hole in the rocks near Bontecoe Point. The hunters went home and returned the next morning. They found the bear, who was a very large fellow, and Watkins shot and wounded him. The bear instantly turned and gave chase. Watkins climbed a tree but the bear was too quick for him; seized and pulled him down and got on top of him. Then Williams took a hand in the fray and proceeded to hammer the bear with his gun and took him by the ears to pull him off his comrade. Finally the bear was killed and Mr. Terwilligar tells us he had a piece of the meat which was very fat. Watkins long bore the marks of the fight, the bear's teeth having left wounds in his head as large as a man's fingers.

CHAPTER X

PROPERTY HOLDERS AT NEW PALTZ IN EARLY DAYS

TAXPAYERS IN 1712

The first tax list which we have found is among the Freer papers and is as follows showing the amount of property in 1712:

The freeholders, inhabitants, residents & sojourners of the New Paltz in the county of Ulster, their real and personal estate rated & assessed on the 16th day of January 171⅔ by the assessors chosen for the same on their oaths to pay at the rate of three pence half farthing per pound, to pay said county quota, layd by an act of General Assembly, entitled an act for the levying of ten thousand ounces of plate or fourteen thousand five hundred forty-five Lyon dollars:

Abraham Doyo.........£ 45	Abraham freer.......... 25
Christian Doyo........ 50	Jacob freer............ 25
Pieter Doyo........... 45	Elias Uin............. 35
Henry Doyo........... 45	Solomon Dubois........ 100
Abraham Hasbrouck.... 200	Louis Dubois.......... 75
Louys Bevier.......... 300	Joseph Hasbrouck....... 25
Jean Hasbrouck........ 150	Tunis Jacobse.......... 10
Mary Dubois.......... 150	Hendrick Van Weye..... 15
Abraham Dubois....... 270	Jacob Clearwater....... 5
Andrew Lefever & Com-	Gerrit Lambertse....... 5
pany............... 240	Jan Terpening......... 5
Hugo ffrer........... 75	Total..............£1895

Total tax £24, 13 shillings.

A True Copy.

Wm. Notingham,

Clerk.

The freeholders Inhabitants Residents & Sojorners of the New paltz in the County of Ulster theire Reall and personall Estate are Rated & assessed on the 18th day of January 71⅔ by theassessors Chosen for the same on theire oaths and are to pay after the Rate of three pence halfe farthing p pound to pay said County Quota Layd by an act of Generall assembly but tuled an act for the Levying of ten thousand ounces of plate or fourteen thousand five hundred forty five Lyon Dollars—

		£	s	d	fur
Abraham Dojo	45£	0	11	0	2½
Christian Doyo	50£	0	13	0	L
Pieter Doyo	45£	0	11	0	2½
Henry Doyo	45£	0	11	0	2½
Abraham Haasbroeck	200£	2	12	L	0
Louys Bevere	300£	3	10	L	2
Jean Hasbroeck	150£	L	19	0	3
Mary Du bois	150£	1	19	0	3
Abraham Du bois	270£	3	10	3	3
André Lefever & Copany	240£	3	2	6	0
Hugo frere	75£	0	19	6	1½
Abraham frere	25£	0	6	6	0½
Jacob frere	25£	0	6	6	0½
Elias Uin	9£	0	9	L	1½
Salomon Dubois	100£		6	0	2
Louis Du bois	75£	0	19	6	1½
Joseph Haasbroeck	25£	0	6	6	0½
Teunis Jacobse	10£	0	2	7	1
Hendrek van wye	15£	0	3	10	3¾
Jacob Clerwater	5£	0	L	3	2½
Gerret Lambertse	5£	0	L	3	2½
Jan Teerpenengh	5£	0	L	3	2½
Totall Sume	1095£	24	13	5	½

A True Coppy Jb Wottingham Clarke

TAX LIST OF 1712

The above list shows that in 1712 four of the original Patentees were still alive, namely Abraham and Jean Hasbrouck, Louis Bevier and Abraham DuBois, also Mary widow of Isaac DuBois. The other tax payers are sons of Patentees, namely: the four sons of Pierre Deyo, the three sons of Simon LeFever, three of the four sons of Hugo Freer, two sons of Louis Du-Bois, Joseph, son of Abraham Hasbrouck. The only other persons on the tax list are Elias Uin the ancestor of the Ean family, who married Elizabeth, daughter of Anthony Crispell the Patentee, Jacob Clearwater, who was a brother-in-law of Abm. Deyo and resided at Bontecoe, Jan Terpening who also resided at Bontecoe, and was from Flanders; also Tunis Jacobse (Clearwater), Hendrick Van Weye and Garritt Lambertse.

THE BUILDING OF THE FIRST STONE CHURCH

The next list of this nature that we have at New Paltz is the names of those who built the first stone church in 1720 which is found in the French records of the church as follows: Samuel Bevier, Louis Bevier, Jr., Abraham Doyo, Christian Doyo, Henry Doyo, Abraham DuBois, Solomon DuBois, Louis Du-Bois, Jr., Daniel DuBois, Philip DuBois, Andre LeFevre, Isaac LeFevre, Jean LeFevre, Mary Hasbrouck (widow of Abraham the Patentee), Jacob Hasbrouck, Joseph Hasbrouck, Hugh Freer, Abraham Freer, Jacob Freer, Elias Un.

The last named, who is the ancestor of the Ean family, is the only person not of the Patentee families who assisted in building the church. Abraham DuBois was the only one of the Patentees living in 1720. Abm. DuBois long survived his associates and lived until 1731.

FREEHOLDERS IN 1728

The next list in point of time is found in the Documentary History of New York, page 971, and contains the names of all the freeholders in the precinct in 1728, as follows: Samuel Bevier, Christian Deyou, Hendrick Deyou, Peter Deyou, Solomon Hasbrouck, Jacob Hasbrouck, Daniel Hasbrouck, Hugo Freer, Hugo Freer, Jr., Isaac Freer, Jacob Freer, Lewis DuBois, Jr., Solomon DuBois, Abraham DuBois, Daniel Dubois, John LeFevre, Andries LeFevre, Isaac LeFevre, John Terpening, Dirck Terpening, Augustus Vandemark, Nicholas Roosa, Peter Low, Garrit Keetaltas, Rœloff Eltinge, Esq.

NEW PALTZ TAX PAYERS IN 1728

The following list of New Paltz taxpayers in 1728 is in the county clerk's office at Kingston:

Elsie Djou [widow of Abraham]	£ 23	Peter Low	5
Christian Djou	30	Solomon DuBois	69
Hendricus Djou	30	Louis DuBois	67
Peter Djou	19	Abraham DuBois	193
Jacob Deyo [Jacobus?]	1	Daniel DuBois	99
Moses Deyo	1	Abraham Clearwater	1
Solomon Hasbrouck	42	Jan Terpenning	10
Daniel Hasbrouck	62	Samuel Bevier	95
Jacob Hasbrouck	92	Louis Bevier	26
Andries LeFevre	40	August Vandemárk	2
Jan LeFevre	52	Anthony Westbrook	4
Isaac LeFevre	31	Roelif Elting, Esq.	10
Hugo Freer	69	Nicholas Roosa	13
Jacob Freer	6	Mattys Slecht	10
Hugo Freer, Jr.	12	Col. Jacob Rutson (non-resident)	5
Jonas Frere	1	Garret Keeteltas	5
Widow of Elias Ean	20		

LIST OF SLAVEHOLDERS IN 1755.

The next list of property holders of any kind that we find is a list of slaveholders in 1755 in the Documentary History of New York. Samuel Bevier, Philip Bevier, Jacobus Bevier, Abm. Bevier, Christian Doyo, Abm. Doyo, Peter Doyo, Jr., Sarah Hasbrouck (widow of Solomon), Benjamin Hasbrouck (Wallkill), Daniel Hasbrouck, Jacob Hasbrouck, Lewis Du-Bois, Solomon DuBois, Benj. DuBois, Hendricus DuBois, Simon DuBois, Hugo Freer, Isaac Freer, Mary LeFevre (widow of Isaac), Petronella LeFevre (widow of Simon), Nathaniel LeFevre, Abm. LeFevre, Andries LeFevre, Abm. Hardenburgh, Geesje Ean (widow of Jan), Anetje Vandemark, Noah Eltinge, Capt. Josiah Eltinge.

Abm. Hardenburgh and Solomon DuBois each owned 7 slaves, Simon DuBois 6 and others a less number. The list shows that in 1755 all the sons of the Patentees were dead except Solomon and Louis DuBois, Jr., Samuel Bevier, Daniel and Jacob Hasbrouck.

VALUE OF THE PRECINCT OF NEW PALTZ IN 1765

We copy from a collection warrant dated at Kingston, August 27, 1765, the list given below of the estimated value of the real and personal estates of the precinct of New Paltz. The warrant was signed by "Dirck Wynkoop, Jr., John Dumond, Charles Dewit, Elias Depuy, Abraham Hardenburgh, Johannis H. Jansen and John Wandle—Supervisors elected and chosen for the several towns, manor and precincts of Ulster county." It was issued to raise money, pursuant to an Act to raise £52,000 for paying 1,715 men to be employed in an expedition against the French fort at Crown Point and against the Indians : and to raise £100,000 for paying the ex-

penses of 2,600 for the invasion of Canada; and also to raise
£100,000 and £60,000 for like purposes under other Acts. One
hundred and thirteen pounds, three shillings eight pence and
one-fifth of a farthing was the amount to be collected from the
precinct of New Paltz. This precinct then included the present town of New Paltz, the whole of Lloyd and parts of the
towns of Rosendale, Esopus and Gardiner.

The warrant directed that after the tax was collected it
should be lodged in the hands of Col. Abraham Hasbrouck,
county treasurer, retaining the fees.

In 1765 there were only six Townships in the entire county,
viz: Kingston, Marbletown, Hurley, Rochester, Shawangunk
and New Paltz.

Dirck Wynkoop, Jr., represented Kingston; Abraham Hardenburgh, New Paltz; Johannes H. Jansen, Shawangunk;
Elias Depuy, Rochester. The remaining three Supervisors,
viz: John Dumond, Ch. Dewitt and John Wandle must have
represented the towns of Hurley and Marbletown and a precinct or manor not yet organized into a Township.

An estimate or list of all the estates real and personal of all
the freeholders and inhabitants of the precinct of New Paltz
in 1765:

NAMES.	VALUE.		NAMES.	VALUE	
Peter Dujou	£31	s 1	Johannis Dujou	£ 9	s 0
John Terwilliger	14	2	Petrus Low	7	0
Abraham Harden-			Abraham Bevier	50	2
burgh	65	16	Gerret Frere	7	5
Abraham Hasbrouck			Jacobus Bevier	10	0
(for his farm)	71	3	Benjamin DuBois	29	10
Hendricus Dubois	55	10	Johannis Dujou, Jr.	4	10
Philip Dubois	8	0	Solomon Low	3	10
Cornelius Dubois	65	12	Jonas Frere	25	0

NAMES.	VALUE.		NAMES.	VALUE.	
Christopher Dujou	..£15	s1?	Abraham Vandemark.	£ 9	s 1
Christiaen Dujou, Jr..	1	5	Benjamin I. Frere....	10	10
Moses Dujou........	7	0	Petrus Hasbrouck....	12	16
Jacobus Hasbrouck...	13	2	John Hasbrouck.....	12	10
Johannis Frere......	15	8	Lewis Bevier........	19	2
Benjamin Frere......	8	4	Nathaniel Lefever	23	0
Hugo Frere........	1	5	Catholinetie Lefever..	3	0
Jacob Frere........	12	0	Noah Eltinge........	49	5
Hugo Frere, Jr......	16	16	Dominie Monriches		
Benjamin Dujou.....	16	0	Geotschius	1	8
David Akker........		12	Lewis Dubois........	17	15
The estate of Marynus			Abraham LeFever...	21	10
Van Aken........	2	10	Andries Lefever.....	27	12
Daniel Lefever.......	17	0	Samuel Schoonmaker.	1	0
Petrus Lefever......	21	12	Petrus Schoonmaker..	1	0
Johannis Lefever.....	24	12	Catholinitie Bevier		
Abraham Een.......	18	17	(widow)	1	10
Nathaniel Dubois	23	0	George Stover.......	1	16
Jacob Hasbrouck, Jr..	65	0	Frederick Hyms.....	4	0
Abraham Dujou.....	50	0	Joseph Griffen.......		3
Matthew Lefever.....	1	18	Joseph Terwilliger ...	6	10
Simon DuBois.......	42	0	Jonathan Terwilliger.	16	2
Marritie Dubois (wi-			Isaac Frere..........	14	10
dow)	4	·0	Joseph Frere........	3	10
Josiah Eltinge........	66	15	Petrus Van Wagenen.	8	10
Roloff J. Eltinge......	1	3	Abraham Van Wage-		
Abraham Eltinge....	3	12	nen	1	13
Petronella Lefever ...	5	0	Abraham Donaldson..	17	14
Andries Lefever, Jr...	14	0	Michael De Vou.....	3	0
Winetie Hasbrouck...	48	5	Robert Hurs........		5
Johannis M. Low....	6	12	David Auchmoody ...		5

NAMES.	VALUE.		NAMES.	VALUE.	
Thomas Woolsey....	£ 5	s 5	Oliver Gray........	£	s10
Israel Koole.........	2	1	Phelick Ransom......	2	17
Alexander Mackey...	1	2	Nathaniel Wyard....	1	0
James Turtle........	1	17	Abraham Hass.......		15
John Woolsey.......		5	Lewis Pontinear.....	1	0
Peter Koleman......		6	Robert Sergeant.....	1	12
James Wheeler......	2	7	Joseph Coddington...	4	0
James Hurta........		14	Daniel Dujou........	2	7
Murry Lester........		16	Abm. Dujou, for the		
Valuntine Parkus....	2	16	estate where his son		
Ebenezer Gilbert.....	5	0	Daniel lives on.....	5	0
Ebenezer Parkus.....	1	4	Jacob DuBois........	15	0
Livelet Hubble.......	3	8	James Hue..........	1	0
Christiaen Dujou.....	1	12	Martinus Bakeman...		6
Richard Monion.....			Moses Nap.........	1	0
Michael Palmiter....		13	Hendrick Wasemiller.		4
Anthony Yarnton....	1	18	Petrus Vandemerk...		10
Abraham Brister.....	3	6	Daniel Frere........	1	12
Johannis Presslar....	1	15	Christiaen Achtmoemy	1	0
Jadediah Dean.......	1	8	William Frere.......	1	6
Simon Crandle.......	1	0			
William Ellsworth...		12	Total value.....£1,354 s18		

This assessment roll is valuable, not only as showing who were taxpayers and the amount of each assessment in 1765, but it is still more useful because with the aid of some corroborating evidence, we are able to determine where nearly all of the larger taxpayers lived.

It is evident that the assessor in making out the roll commenced at the south bonds of the precinct as it then was at what is now Tuthill and continued on the west side of the Wallkill until reaching the north bounds of the Patent at Mud

Hook; then crossing the Wallkill returned to the village on the east side of the stream and then passed on south to the Plains and Kettelboro; thence east to Jenkintown and the Freer patent, and finally picked up the small taxpayers along the Hudson River and elsewhere.

As far as the Huguenot names on the roll are concerned it must be remembered that in this list we are dealing with the grandsons of the Patentees.

Commencing with the first name on the list, Peter Deyo is the son of Hendricus and lived at Tuthill where he had descendants living until modern times. Peter and his son had a patent for land in Shawangunk.

Abraham Hardenbergh, who was Supervisor and one of the heaviest taxpayers lived in a stone house, recently tumbled into ruins, just below Tuthill. Here the family had a large tract of land. Abraham Hardenbergh's grandsons Abraham and Jacob, were the last of the name to occupy the land of their ancestors, Abraham living in the fine, old brick house near the Guilford church and Jacob on the old homestead, where Crines Jenkins who married Jacob's daughter Rachel afterward lived.

Abraham Hasbrouck who comes next and is assessed for the heaviest amount is Col. Abraham Hasbrouck of Kingston. This farm at Guilford is still owned in the family. Col. Abraham Hasbrouck was probably the most prominent man in the county in his day.

Hendricus and Cornelius DuBois are brothers, sons of Solomon. Philip is Hendricus' son. Hendricus lived on the Capt. Jacob M. DuBois place of our day, Cornelius a short distance south of where Capt. W. H. D. Blake now lives, Philip kept a public house at Libertyville. Cornelius and Hendricus were men of large means and influential in the community as their descendants are at the present day.

Abraham and Jacobus Bevier are brothers, sons of Samuel and grandsons of Louis the Patentee. Abraham lived just south of Butterville. His wife was Margaret, daughter of Roelif Eltinge, the first of the name at New Paltz. Their son Abraham moved to Chenango county.

Benjamin DuBois was the first of the name at Springtown and his descendants still reside there and until recently a little further north. Benjamin is the son of Daniel and grandson of Isaac the Patentee.

Jonas Freer is the son of Hugo, senior, and grandson of the Patentee. Jonas lived at Kline Bontecoe on what is now the R. V. N. Beaver place. His descendants reside in various places in this vicinity. Garret Freer is the nephew of Jonas and son of Hugo, jun. of Bontecoe.

Christopher Deyo lived at Springtown. He is the brother of Peter and Johanes, whose names have appeared on the list and of Benjamin, whose name comes later. Christopher is the ancestor of Rev. Paul T. Deyo.

Moses Deyo is the son of Christian and grandson of Pierre the Patentee. He and his son Christian, Jr. reside where their descendants have since lived and near where James E. and Matthew Deyo now reside.

Jacobus Hasbrouck is the son of Solomon. He probably owned the Simon L. DuBois farm. At any rate his son Benjamin owned it and gave a life estate in it to his son.

We have now come to the Freer settlement at Mud Hook and Bontecoe. Hugo jun. is the son of Hugo, sen., Jacob is his cousin. Hugo, John and Benjamin are Hugo, jun.'s sons.

The assessor having crossed the Wallkill, at what is now Perrine's Bridge, is coming southward on the east side of the stream.

Benjamin Deyo, who is the ancestor of the Bontocoe Deyos,

occupies the house of his father Hendricus, which is known as the Abm. W. Deyo farm in our day.

The three LeFevres, Daniel, Petrus and Johannes, are sons of Isaac, the first of the name at Bontecoe.

Abraham Ean is the son of Jan and grandson of Elias. His farm, which is still owned in the family joined the LeFevre estate on the south as it does, to-day.

Here the assessor makes a break and inserts the name of Nathaniel DuBois, who built the first mill at Libertyville and is the son of Jonathan and grandson of Louis, jun.

Right here should come the names of Petrus and John Hasbrouck, sons of Solomon, which do not appear on the roll until a little later. Petrus owned and occupied what is now the Walsh house at Middletown and John the old stone house of his father, a short distance south, which tumbled into ruins about 1870.

We are now back to the village.

Jacob Hasbrouck, Jr. built at a later date the house where his greatgrandson Abm. M. Hasbrouck now lives, but in 1765 he was living and quite certainly keeping a store in what is now the Memorial House.

Abraham Deyo (2) lived in the homestead in this village, which passed from one Abraham to another and is now owned by Abm. Deyo Brodhead.

Simon DuBois is the son of Daniel and grandson of Isaac the Patentee. He occupied the house now owned by his descendants, Mary DuBois Berry's daughters, which has always been in the family and is the oldest house in the village. Maritje (widow) who is assessed for a small amount is Simon's mother.

Josiah Eltinge owned and occupied the house still called the "Eltinge Homestead," and Roelif J. and Abraham are his

sons.   Here Roelif J. kept a store in Revolutionary times.
Abraham afterward lived in the house about a mile north of
the village, which has ever since been in the family and where
his great grandson S. L. F. Elting now lives.

Andries LeFevre, Jr., who is the last of that line of LeFevres,
lived with his mother Petronella in the old homestead, since
torn down, in the north part of the present church yard.

Winetie Hasbrouck is the widow of Daniel, son of Abraham
the Patentee.   She lived with her six sons directly across the
street from the present church building and the house is still
owned in the family.

Johannes M. Low lived in the house which had come to him
from his father-in-law Hugo Freer, Sn. and this is still standing, being the most northern of the old stone houses on the
street.

The next two names on the list, Abraham Vandemark and
Benj. I. Freer, we can not place.

The next name, Lewis Bevier, puzzles us, as there was no
person of the name at New Paltz.   Possibly the Bevier homestead in this village had not yet been bought by Josiah Eltinge
and belonged to Louis Bevier of Marbletown or Louis of
Wawarsing.

Nathaniel LeFevre lived on the Plains in the house of his
father Jean.   His mother Carolintje and his son Matthew, who
afterward occupied the place, are assessed for small amounts.

Noah Elting is the brother of Josiah.   He lived on the
estate where his father Roelif had lived in his old age and where
Edmund Eltinge lived in our day.

Dominie Moriches Goetchius was the minister of the churches
at New Paltz and Shawangunk from 1760 to 1771, living at
Shawangunk, where he died in 1771.

Lewis DuBois is the Capt. Lewis J. DuBois of Revolutionary

times. His house, a frame building, is still standing, south of the Libertyville ford on the east side of the Wallkill and is now owned by his descendant, Henry L. DuBois.

Abram and Andries LeFevre are brothers and the pioneers at Kettelboro.

The assessor now turns east. The two Terwilligers, Joseph and Jonathan, lived we think on the Plattekill, east of Jenkintown.

Isaac and Joseph Freer owned the next farm on the north. This is the Freer patent and some part still owned in the family.

Petrus Van Wagenen is the ancestor of all the Van Wagenens in New Paltz. He lived in a stone house, still standing but not occupied, about a mile north of Put Corners.

Abraham Donaldson probably lived at Elmore's Corners, as the Donaldson family located there at an early date.

David and Christian Auchmoody are sons of Jeems Auchmoody, the first of the name at New Paltz.

Most of the other names are for small amounts. Some of them we recognize as the ancestors of people in Highland and vicinity: Devoe, Mackey, Palmatier, Pressler, Wisemiller.

Phelick Ransom lived at Highland and was afterward a captain in the Revolutionary army.

Jacob DuBois lived near Tuthill and had in 1757 purchased a tract lying on both sides of the Wallkill including the island at Tuthill. His son Isaac kept his homestead and his son Jacob lived where Gardiner village now is. His old home was a short distance south of Kingston. He was probably the son of Isaac DuBois who was of Kingston and his wife Neiltje Rose, as they had a son Jacob, baptised in 1733. Isaac was the son of Jacob of Hurley, who was one of the seven sons of Louis the Patentee.

Joseph Coddington was the village schoolmaster in those days.

Daniel Deyo lived a short distance north of what is now Ireland Corners and is the ancestor of that branch of the Deyo family. Daniel's father Abm. who resided in this village, still owned the farm in 1765.

CHAPTER XI

THE CONTRACT OF 1744

In this contract the owners of the patent, 34 in all, bind themselves each to the other for fifteen years to pay all assessments made by the twelve men for expenses in defending the claim of title of any owner. The document is in English and is here transcribed *verbatim et literatim*.

Articles of agreement Indented had made concluded and agreed upon This Twenty Third Day of may In the Seventeenth Year of The Reign of our Sovereign Lord George The Second by the Grace of God of Great Brittain France and Ireland King Defender of the faith &c. annoq, Domini 1744 *Between* The Persons Whose names are hereunder Written and Seals affixed and Who Executed The Same In Due form of Law. *Whereas* Edmund Andross Esq. Seigneur of Sansmaraz Lieut. and Governour Generall under his Royal Highness James Duke of York and Albany etc. of all his Territories In America. *By* his Letters Patent bearing Date The Twenty Ninth Day of September In the Year of our Lord 1677 Did Give Ratifye Confirm and Grant, Conformable To an Indian purchase From The Indian Propriators *unto* Lewis DuBois and Partners (That is to say) Christian Duyow Abraham Hasbroucq Andries Lefever, Jean Hasbroucq, Pierre Duyo, Laurens Beveir, Anthony Crespell, Abraham Dubois, Hugo

Frere, Isaac Dubois & Simon Lefever Their heirs and assigns
All That Certain piece of Land Lyeing on The South Side of
the Rondout Creek or Kill *Begining* From the High Hills
Called Moggonck and Now known by The name of The
High Point on The mountains commonly called the Paltz
point From Thence Stretching South East Near The Great
River To a Certain Point or hook Called The Juffrous Hoocke
Lyeing In The Long Reach named by the Indians Magatramis
Being a Little Distance To the Northward from the Place
where the Late Dwelling House of Denis Raelje Deceased
stood where it is Fixed by Virtue of a warrant By Cadwallader
Colden Esq. To him Directed as Surveyor General For the
Province of New York, Then North up along The River to an
Island In a Crooked Elbow, In The begining of The Land
Reach Called Little Esopus Island and by the Indians Raphoes
Then West on the High Hills To a place Called Waratahaes
and Tawarataque and known by The name of Northwest bounds
being at the North End of The mountain and Severall marks
There made, and soe along The Said High Hills South west
To Moggonck or The High Point aforesaid *To Hold* unto Tne
Said Lewis Dubois and Partners Their heirs and assigns For-
ever, *And Whereas* We The Subscribers who Have hereunto
Set our hands and affixed our Seals being owners and Inter-
tested In The aforesaid Pattent or Tract of Land and In order
To Keep and Prepare The Said Tract of Land unto us and our
heirs and assigns Forever, From being Incroached upon by
any Person or Persons Whatsoever we Shall Each of us and
Every one of us, or our heirs Exs. admin. and assigns advance
And Disburs So much money To make a Common Stock To
Defend The before Recited Tract of Land, and Every one
Shall but advance or Disburse So much money according to
The Share proportion or Interest he or She hath in Said Tract

of Land and so according To a Greater and Lesser Quantity
So In proportion *And Whereas* When Such money or moneys
Shall be or must be Disbursed or advanced as often as It Shall
Happen, To and for the Defence of before Recited Patent If
it Should happen To be Disputed by any one of us or our heirs
and Assigns Whether It is Requisite and necessary for any
Such Sum or Sums of money To be Disbursed, It Shall (and
It Is hereby agreed To and between The said Parties) That it
must be Determined Then by the Twelve men or The Major
Part of Them Who are annually Chosen by the Inhabitants of
aforesaid Patent on the First Tuesday in April by Virtue of
an Instrument In writing bearing Date The Twenty first Day
of April annoq. Domini 1728 Reference being Thereunto had
may more fully and at Large appear || *And* That the True
Intent and meaning of the Present Articles be no ways Frus-
trated, it is hereby Further Covenanted, Concluded, Granted
and agreed upon by and between The Said Parties *That
Whereas* union is the Strength of all Copartnerships for their
own Generall and Respective advantage and Safety they Doe
oblidge themselves their heirs and assigns, to defend Joyntly
the Whole tract above mentioned and to Stand In mutuall defence of Each other Lot or Lots farm and Farms against all
Incroachment and Pretences of Right to the Same for Ever
From any Person or Persons Whatsoever For Fifteen whole
and Consecutive years From the Date of these Presents *And
Now* For the True Performance of all and Singular the present articles and every one of them, The Parties to these presents Doe hereby bind Each one to each other and their heirs
Execs. and adms. Respectively In the Penall Sum of Two Hundred Pounds Currant Lawfull money of the province of New
York Payable by the nonperformers To the others || *In Witness*
whereof the parties to these present articles have Respectively

Set their hands and affixed their Seals the Day and year above written.

his	(s.) Antho Slecht (s.)
Matthys x Van Keuren	(s.) Jan Slecht (s.)
mark	(s.) Antoney Crespell (s.)
Hend. Sleight	(s.) Johannes Crespell (s.)
his	Roeloff Eltinge (s.)
(s.) Isaac x Frere (s.)	Yean le Fevre (s.)
mark	Abraham doian (s.)
(s.) Jacob hasbrouck (s.)	Daniel Dubois (s.)
(s.) Isaac le Fevre (s.)	Samuel Bevier (s.)
(s.) Aenrei dieo (s.)	Josia Eltinge (s.)
his	daniel hasbroecq (s.)
(s.) Hugo x Frere Jun (s.)	johannis maty jun (s.)
mark	his
(s.) Jacob Frere (s.)	John T Terpenning (s.)
(s.) Jonas Frere (s.)	mark
(s.) Louis bevier (s.)	Solomons hasbrouq (s.)

Sealed and Delivered In presence of us

Abraham Van Der Merkan

A Hasbrouck $\overline{36}$

memorandum anthony Sleght Jan Sleght, anthony Crespell, Johannis Crespel, Mathias Van Keuren and Hendricus Sleght have signed Sealed and Delivered this within Instrument In presence of us

Jacob Hasbrouck Junr.

A Hasbrouck.

CIVIL GOVERNMENT

In its civil government New Paltz at an early period included not only the entire southeastern portion of Ulster county as it is at present, but a considerable portion of Orange county likewise. From page 23 of Ruttenber's History of Orange county we quote: "Immediately north of Murderer's Creek there was no civil organization until the advent of the Palatines in 1709, when the precinct of the Highlands was erected and attached to New Paltz. The boundaries of the precinct are not stated but the order is understood to have applied more especially to the territory extending from New Paltz to Murderer's Creek, in which district the Palatines of Quassaick were then the principal settlers. At the same time or soon after the constitution of the precinct of the Highlands, and evidently by order of the court the precincts of Maghagh-branch and Shawangunk were constituted, the latter attached to New Paltz. As in the case of the precinct of the High lands no boundaries are given, but from deeds, tax rolls and other papers of record it is clear that the present towns of Montgomery, Crawford and Wallkill were embraced in the limits of the precinct. Under this limited organization the territory which these precincts covered remained until 1743, when by act of Dec. 17 three full precincts, having all the officers of towns and exercising all their duties were established by act of the Assembly."

NEIGHBORHOODS ANNEXED TO NEW PALTZ

The precinct of the Highlands was bounded on the west by the precincts of Wallkill, Shawangunk and the "neighborhoods annexed to New Paltz." These neighborhoods were the Louis DuBois patent, the Guilford patent, the Thomas

Garland patent at Kettelborough and Ireland Corners and the Hugo Freer patent of 1200 acres on a portion of which Zach. Freer lived. The territory of these "neighborhoods annexed to New Paltz" is thus described: "Guilford and several other patents, from the south bounds of New Paltz to the north bounds of Shawangunk precinct and from the foot of the high mountains eastward to the east line of the patent granted to Thomas Garland and by the south and east by the land granted to Hugh Freer and others and to the eastward by an east line from the said Hugh Freer's bounds to the bounds of town of New Paltz."

PAYMENTS OF RENT AND TAXES

During all the Colonial period the payment of rent continued. The following in the Dutch language, among the papers in the Patentees' trunk, is a sample of the receipts given:

Received of the inhabitants of the New Paltz one year's quit rent being thirty-five bushels of good winter wheat delivered to me in Kingston 1710 November 18.   J. hardenbergh.

It is stated that one year the Freers paid the entire quit rent due from the New Paltz people and in return were given a tract of 200 acres at Mud Hook.

Besides the quit rent, which was paid in wheat, taxes for special purposes were levied as shown by the following samples of tax warrant and receipt:

TAX RECEIPT

New York 26 May 1716.

Then Received of Mr. Daniel Duboy & Hugh Frera Jun. Collectors of New Paltz Ulster County the Sume of Eleven

Pounds Fifteen Shillings & 3d Tax & for ye Treasurers Salary Six Shill. Being on ye fifth & Sixth Payment wch. will be payable ye Last Day of this Instant May and ye Last Day of Novem. Next Ensuing on ye £10000 Tax I say Rec by me.

A. D. Peyster.

Recded in the book of Receipts,
No. A Folio 21.

Wm. Nottingham, Clk.

The tax warrant is directed to the assessors of New Paltz dated 1746, and is signed by Jan Eltinge, Jean (or Johannes) Hardenberg, Jr., Johannes De Witt, Abraham Hardenberg, Jacobus Bruyn, Charles Clinton and Cadwalder Colden, Jr., supervisors of the several towns manors and precincts:

"Pursuant of an act of General Assembly of the Province of New York, made in the present Nineteenth year of his majestic Reign, Entitled an act for raising a supply of the sum of thirteen thousand pounds by a tax on Estates Real and Personal for the more effectual fortifying this Colony, etc."

CHAPTER XII

A Short Historical Memorandum

The first attempt at writing anything of a historical nature concerning New Paltz that we have seen is contained in the following paper, written by grandfather Peter LeFever and dated 1830.

One leaf of the original seems to be torn off and the memorandum begins abruptly as follows:

"It appears they settled in what is now called the old village and it is said they all laboured together and cleared their lands at first and afterwards divided the cleared lands by parole, without deed.

On the 25th day of August, 1703, some of the original proprietors were then dead: the survivors met together and conveyed by their deed, bearing the above date, to each Patentee then living his proportion of the cleared land in their possession as the same had been divided by parole, and also his undivided twelfth part of the whole patent; and also conveyed to the legal representatives of the original patentees who were then dead, the full share of their ancestors.

Andries Lefever having died without lawful issue, Simon Lefever being dead, they conveyed to Andries Lefever, Isaac Lefever, John Lefever and Mary Lefever, the three sons and daughter of Simon Lefever, all the lots and parcels belonging to them from their father Simon Lefever and from their uncle Andries Lefever; and also one fifth part of their grandfather's land (Christeyan Deyou, usually called *Grandpere*) as the same had been laid out and divided by parole and then in their possession; together with two twelfth parts and one fifth of a twelfth part of the whole patent of all the lands not yet laid out and divided.

Simon Lefever had been married to Elizabeth Deyou, daughter of the said Christeyan Deyou, called *Grandpere* in the French language, which means grand-father, who had devised to his son Peter and his four daughters each one fifth part of his land. His son Peter was also a patentee.

The widow of Simon Lefever afterwards married Moses Cantine, who was also a French refugee, by whom she had one son, viz. Peter Cantine, Esq., to whom the Patentees gave no share of the land of his mother, who thought he ought to have shared in his mother's land. (Peter Cantine was my mother's father.)

The Patentees afterwards entered into an article in writing to elect at their annual town meeting twelve men to represent the twelve Patentees—one from the descendants of each Patentee, who, to entitle them to that office must be a descendant of such Patentee he represented and a freeholder by heirship in such Patentee's share.

These "Twelve Men," so called, had their by-laws, kept a book and record of their proceedings, made divisions of the whole patent (except some land on the north side of the patent and some other small lots) and entered their proceedings in a book.

These "Twelve Men" were also empowered by another bond, or instrument in writing to defend the boundaries of the patent and to raise money for that purpose from the representatives of the Patentees, according to their several rights.

Shortly after the Revolutionary war it was discovered that the divisions made by the "Twelve Men" were not lawful, and void. They then petitioned the Legislature of the State of New York to confirm such division (which was done by an act of the Legislature) and directed their book, wherein they had recorded their division, to be deposited in the office of the county of Ulster, where it now remains, and a certified copy of the act confirming said division is now in the possession of my son, Daniel.

The "Twelve Men" continued to be elected until about the year 1820. Their coffer, and copy of the book wherein the records of the division is entered, and patent, and sundry records and other patents was left in the care of Ezekiel Eltinge."

MATTERS SUBMITTED TO VOTERS

Rev. Ame Vennema has compiled from papers in the Patentees' trunk the following list of matters submitted to voters during the period of ten years from 1756 to 1766, showing how close was the union of church and State at New Paltz in those colonial days:

In 1756 3 "chimmily Vewers" were elected, and the "fine on ye chimmilis" fixed at 3d.

In 1757 Whether the money received for the collectorship should be applied "on the Highway" or "to the use of the church." The latter was preferred, the amount was 44s., 6d.

In 1758 Whether the money rec'd for the office of Collector should be applied "to the benefit of the church of the New Paltz," or "on the Highway," or "given to the clerk of the New Paltz church for the time being" or "half to the church and half to the clerk."

The result was in favor of the first proposition. Amount 46s.

In 1759 Whether the money received for the collectorship shall be given to the clerk of the church, to the poor, or used for the purchase of a "pall." The result is thus recorded, "By Plurality of Voices it is carried, That the money given for the Collectorship shall be Applyed for buying a Pall for the Precinct of the New Paltz, And there is Bid for the Collectorship the sum of 57 shillings. And Tis Agreed that the Deacons of the New Paltz church shall be Managers for Procuring said Pall as aforesaid, who are to buy said Pall as soon as said money shall come in."

In 1760 Whether the money of the Collectorship should be applied in Part "to a Pall and the Remainder for a Silver Beaker" (chalice) or, in part to a "Pall and the Remainder to a Bare to Cary the Corps of the Dad to the Grave."

The result of the election was that it "be applyd to Bie a Pall and the over Plush to Bie a Silver Beaker to the use and Benefit of the New Paltz Preseinct; and there is Bid for the Collector Ship the Sum of 68s. by Jonathan Terwilliger, and paid."

1761 It was decided by vote that the money of the Collectorship be used to purchase "a Silver Cup for the use of the Reformed Dutch Church at the New Paltz"—

That Sheep may not have free Running but must be kept. The fine for pounding sheep to be not 4d but 3d.

1762 Noe Eltinge was elected for a "Commissioner to Lay out Highway."

Valentine Perkins for "pownder for ye River, and Josaphat Hasbrouck for pownder for ye Paltz."

1763 The money for the Collectorship was "voted to be Applyed to pay the Assessors for their Trouble for the Ensuing Year."

In 1764 It was submitted to the voters "Whether there shall be Five overseers of the Roads, or two."

Whether a Pound shall be made "adjoining the South East side of the Land of Abraham Bevier, at the Orchard."

8

The money of the Collectorship shall go to the Assessors.

1765 Whether Pound Masters shall be elected or "every man be his own Pounder."

It was decided by vote: "That the Poundage of Horses and Horned Cattle shall be 2s. a head."

That the fences be "4 foot 6 inches High, post and Rales Fence, to have 4 Rales."

1766 Of the 25s. rec'd. for the Collectorship it was voted that 3s. be paid to the Constables the residue to the Assessors.

CHAPTER XIII

THE FIRST MANUFACTURING INDUSTRY IN SOUTHERN ULSTER

The brook which now runs so quietly through the northern suburbs of our village is still called the Mill brook, but for many years no mill has marked its course to the Wallkill. However this brook was in by gone days the propelling power of no less than three mills located at different points and built at different times in the history of New Paltz. About a mile north east of the village are the remains of an old saw mill on this brook. The stone dam and a portion of the timbers are still to be seen. The situation is in a romantic glen and the place is well worth a visit. This mill was used in sawing logs as late as 1855.

Half a mile further down the brook, near the present residence of Mr. Wm. E. DuBois, are the remains of another dam. Here there was a grist mill erected at an early date which continued in use until about 1820. Here Isaac DuBois, grandfather of the late John W. DuBois, carried on the milling business shortly after the Revolutionary war, and here the late Nathaniel DuBois of Shivertown carried on the business about 1820. At about that date the mill ceased running and New Paltz people after that time took their grain to the mill at Libertyville or the mill just erected at Dashville.

Still further down this brook, almost directly north of the residence of John Wynkoop, on Mulberry street, may be found the grass grown remains of a much older mill dam, which has recently been rebuilt and a large pond formed and an ice house built. Here in the early days of the settlement the

Huguenot pioneers of New Paltz took their grain to be manufactured into flour. On this spot Daniel Hasbrouck, son of Abraham Hasbrouck, the Patentee, had a mill as early as 1730. In a document of that date, bearing the signature of Hugo Freer, Sen., son of Hugo the Patentee, reference is made to the lane on the north bounds of the old village, "leading to the mill of Daniel Hasbrouck." This property remained in the possession of Daniel Hasbrouck's descendants until quite a recent date. Tradition says that this mill was for the grinding of grain, but there may have been a saw mill connected with it. The brook does not give abundant water power, but probably it furnished all that was needed for the infant settlement. This ancient mill may have been erected quite a number of years previous to 1730, but we have no evidence on that point. First in the history of New Paltz, after the settlement of 1677, came the organization of the church in 1683 and the erection of the church building. Next in importance was the education of the children, and in 1689 and perhaps at an earlier date there was a schoolmaster at New Paltz. The next enterprise to claim attention would naturally be a mill, and we have documentary evidence, amply confirmed by the still remaining earthwork of the dam and by tradition among the descendants of Daniel Hasbrouck, that this was the spot to which in ancient times the New Paltz people brought their wheat to be manufactured into flour.

It was no doubt the first manufacturing industry established in Southern Ulster.

SOLDIERS IN THE COLONIAL PERIOD

The report of State Historian Hugh Hastings comprising volume 1, of the Colonial series contains a complete list of all soldiers in the Colonial period, subsequent to 1700.

The first New Paltz name in point of date is that of Abraham Hasbrouck who received his commission as lieutenant of a company of foot for New Paltz and Kingston August 30, 1685. In 1689 he was appointed as "captain of foot at Ye Palz, Ulster county."

Under the date of 1700 in a foot company appear the names of the following officers: Abm. Hasbrouck, captain; Moses Quantin, lieut.; Lewis Bevier, ensign.

In the list of volunteers to march to the invasion of Canada in 1711 in Captain Wessel Tenbrook's company appear the names of Isaacq Hasbrouck and Jean Lefeber.

In 1715 in the list of the troop under the command of Capt. John Rutzen appear the following: Anthony Crispell, Lowis Dubois, Jun., corporal Louis DuBois, Solomon Hasbrouck, Daniel Hasbrouck, Daniel Dubooy, Philip DuBois, Jacob Hasbrouck.

At the same date in the same regiment in Capt. Vernooy's company (Wawarsing and Rochester) appear the following names: Lieut. David Dubois, Samuel Bevier, Abraham Bevier, Jan Bevier.

At the same date in the same regiment in Capt. Johannes Schepmoes' company for the town of Hurley appear the following: Lieut. Jacob Dubois, Jan Crispell.

At the same date in the same regiment in Capt. Nicholas Hoffman's company for Kingston we find the following: Roeloff Elting, William Elting, Peter Cantyn, Louis DuBois, Jun., Louis Matthyse DuBois, Jan Freer, Johannes Crispel.

In a Dutchess county company under date of 1715 appears the name of Peiter DuBoy.

The next year, 1716, in Capt. Hoffman's company a large number of New Paltz names appear as follows: Sergeant abream deyou, Lieut. Andries Lowerre, insign Lewis Lowies

Jun. aberam de boys, aberam ferer, yakop ferer, hendrick deyoo, elyas yu, kriteyon de you, Ysack leferer, piter daow, Hyge Abaram fere, Ysack fere, Symon ferer, Benjamin du boois, benjamin hasberck, yoel debois, Yan lefever.

The above can quite readily be recognized as the names of the sons of the Patentees by combining the Christian name with the family name in each case. But the spelling is unusually bad.

In 1717 in a list of militia officers for Ulster county the names of the officers for New Paltz and Shawangunk are as follows: Capt. Zach. Hoffman, Lieut. Andries Fever, ensign, Louis Bevier, Jun. The name of Jacob Dubois appears in a list of the Hurley company, in 1717.

In a list of eight companies of an Orange county regiment of foot militia in 1738 Nathaniel Dubois' name appears as captain of the fifth company.

In a list of officers and soldiers in Ulster County militia in 1738 under Capt. Johannes Ten Broock appear the following New Paltz names: corporal Solomon Haesbrock, Jacob Haesbrock, Samuel Bovie, Jan Ffreere, Daniel Dubois, Daniel Haesbrock, Johannes DuBois.

The following of New Paltz ancestry appear in 1738 as foot soldiers of the corporation of Kingston: corporal Nathan Dubois, Jacobus Dubois, Jr., Solomon Freer, Johannes Dubois, Hiskiah Dubois, Gerrett Freer, Jacobus De Ioo, Isaac Dubois.

In the same date, 1738, Lewis Bevier's name appears in the Marbletown company of militia.

At the same date in the Rochester company appear the names of Lieut. Philip DuBois and Josaphat Dubois, Louis Bovier, Jr., Cornelius Bovier, Samuel Bovier, Jr., and Jacob Bovier.

At the same date (1738) in the list of militia of the foot company of New Paltz (which then stretched down into Orange county) under Capt. Zacharias Hoffman, are the following: Sergt. John Freer, corporals, Christian Deyo, Hendrick Deyo, Isaac Lefever; privates, Isaac freer, Jan Une, Jonas freer, James Agmodi, Simon Lefever, Josiah Elting, Abra. Dujo, Cornelius Dubois, Jonathan Dubois, Hendr Dubois, Moses Dujo, Isaac Haasbrouck, Jacob Haasbrouck, Jun., Benja Haasbrouck, Jun., Abra. Bovier, Mathues Bovier, Jacobus Bovier, Isaac Bovier, Abra Lefever, Nathael Lefever, Benja Haasbrouck, Symon Dubois, Isaac Lefever, Junr., Peter Dejo, Huge Freer, Junr., Lewis Sa. Bovier.

In 1758 in the roll of Stephen Nottingham's company appear the following: Jacob S. Freer, Jacob Freer, Wilhelmus Crispel.

Coats of Arms in Huguenot Families at New Paltz

It is highly probable that all of the Huguenot settlers at New Paltz had coats of arms. The count de Vermont, who is a recognized authority on this subject, says that previous to 1789 not only the nobility in France but most families of the "bourgeois" had regularly registered coats of arms recording some distinguished action on the part of the bearer or his ancestors.

Most descendants of the early settlers of New Paltz have taken little interest in the matter of coats of arms and we have not considered it in our province in writing a history of New Paltz from 1678 to 1820 to enter into the subject at any length, because during that period the matter of coats of arms is not alluded to in any records that we have seen or in any tradition that we have heard.

Of late years some interest has been shown in the subject. Many years ago Gen. Geo. H. Sharpe found at Brussels a coat of arms of the Hasbrouck family, a copy of which he brought with him to his home in Kingston. In the Memorial House at New Paltz, among the other relics is a coat of arms of the Bevier family. In the LeFevre family there are, we are told, three coats of arms, one of which belonged to the LeFevres of Paris and the others to certain families of the name in other parts of France. The name Deyo is thought by one authority to be the same as de Joux, which name was borne by a princely family, whose castle and home was in Franche Comté. This is of course mere surmise.

The coat of arms of the DuBois family, as certified by the count de Vermont, is thus described:

Argent, a lion rampant *sable,* armed and langued *gules.* Crest, between two tree stumps: *Vert,* the lion of the shield. Motto—*Tiens ta foy*—(Hold to thy faith).

On page 39 of the DuBois Reunion book, in the paper read at the Reunion, written by Dr. Henry A. DuBois of New Haven, Conn., appears a cut of what is denominated "Original DuBois Arms": *Or,* an eagle displayed *sable,* peaked and clawed *gules.*

Another coat of arms which has a curious history is that which has come down in the family of Abram DuBois, who moved from New Paltz to New Jersey and was the son of Abraham the Patentee and grandson of Louis the Patentee. This coat of arms was found pasted in an old book, published in 1707, which had come down from father to son in this branch of the DuBois family. A greyhound is a prominent figure in the coat of arms. The motto is *"Honestas est optima polita."* The name "Duboys" appears on the coat of arms.

We note, lastly, the coat of arms on the old silver snuff box, which has come down in the family of Solomon DuBois, son of Louis DuBois the Patentee. This box is in itself a very valuable relic. It bears on one side the names of different owners in the DuBois family and dates, the most ancient being 1707. On the other side is a coat of arms. Mr. Patterson DuBois in the DuBois Reunion book says "While the one side of the box may have meant 'nobility' to our ancestor the simple blazon of a name and date (1707) on the other side is our title to the truer nobility of the soul, which our Huguenot fathers have bequeathed us in the annals of an heroic devotion to their faith." Mr. William E. DuBois of New Paltz is now the owner of the box and has placed it with the other relics in the Memorial House.

There will probably always be difference of opinion among the descendants of Louis DuBois the Patentee as to which of the four coats of arms above noted is that of their ancestor. The predilections of the writer would naturally be in favor of that which has come down in the family of his grandmother and the other descendants of Louis' son Solomon.

CHAPTER XIV

TORIES IN THE REVOLUTION

Among the papers of Gen. George Clinton, published by the State in book form, in 1899, appears an account of the proceedings of a general court martial, held at Fort Montgomery, April 30, 1777, and continued several days for the trial of a number of tories who had been captured while on their way to join the British army.

At this court martial Col. Lewis DuBois was president and 15 captains and 2 lieutenants were members, among the number Capts. Hasbrouck, Bevier and Hardenbergh.

It appears from the proceedings of the court martial that a certain Lieut. Jacobus Rose by the offer of a bounty and the assurance that King George would soon win, got together a body of 36 men in the neighborhood of Shokan and Shandaken.

They started to join the British army, traveling by night and taking with them their guns and provisions for 4 to 5 days. They crossed the Esopus and Rondout creeks and the Shawangunk mountains. They came into the precinct of New Paltz at what is now Mountain Rest and passed down the mountain to the ford at Cornelius DuBois' place, now Capt. W. H. D. Blake's. One Wouter Slouter was their guide to the ford.

While crossing the Shawangunk mountain they had been told that scouting parties were out to apprehend them. This was true, for about a dozen or fifteen of the neighbors in New Paltz had got together, placing sentries at the different roads where they crossed the Wallkill—at Peter Deyo's (Tuthill) at Isaac Low's (Libertyville) and at Cornelius DuBois', where Capt. W. H. D. Blake now resides. At the last named place Tunis Van Vliet and Jacob Freer were stationed, sitting under an apple tree, guarding the road leading to the ford.

Rose and his party came upon them suddenly in the night and took them prisoners, then crossed the Wallkill in two canoes, repeated trips being necessary for the purpose. On the east side of the Wallkill the tories were challenged by Lieut. Terwilligar, who was at once fired upon by one of Rose's followers and wounded in the arm. Terwilligar escaped and so did Tunis Van Vliet, who had been taken prisoner on the west side of the stream. Both proceeded to Noah Elting's, and procured horses and a man in order that the news might be sent post haste to Newburgh and our army warned of the approach of the tory band. It is a proof of the strict discipline in our army that Tunis Van Vliet was afterwards arrested and sent to Fort Montgomery for not having more promptly raised the alarm and aroused the rest of the guard, only 150 yards away, this delay on his part, after his escape, giving the tories time to get their whole band across the Wallkill in safety.

Rose and his party traveled on, reaching Alex. Campbell's that night and staying there the next day. The next evening they went to the barn of Arthur McKinney and staid there the next day and night. Here, near Little Britain, they learned that it was impossible to get through our lines. Shortly afterwards they were attacked by 50 of our militia, who had been sent out to meet them. Several of the tories were killed, a large proportion were taken prisoners and a few escaped for the time being.

The court martial, after due consideration sentenced 16 of the tory band, including those who had given them aid and comfort on the route, to be hanged. Seven of the 16 were

recommended for mercy. Subsequently 14 others of the band
received the same sentence, a few of the number being recommended for mercy. The charge against a portion of the number was "levying war against the United States of America"
and with those who had helped them along the route "giving
aid and comfort to the enemies of the State of New York."

This sentence was subject to the approval of the Convention, which met at Kingston May 3d. Gen. Clinton, in a letter
to the President of the Convention says, "The inhabitants are
so much irritated by the conduct of the prisoners in marching
armed in a body to join the enemy that I fear they will soon
take the law in their own hands against them." He urges
that a severe example should be made of those tories. With
a few exceptions the Convention approved the action of the
court martial and no doubt it was promptly carried into effect
so far as Rose and one at least of his companions were
concerned.

On May 5th Capt. John A. Hardenbergh, who was of Guilford, writes from New Paltz to Gen. Clinton that in pursuance of his orders he arrived at home on Saturday evening,
got all the men together he could and scoured the mountain in
search of those of Rose's party who had escaped. They
found two men, hidden under a great rock, who confessed
having belonged to his band. The next day he went to another
mountain where he found the party of Capt. Broadhead who
had also captured three of the band. All the prisoners were
sent under guard to Fort Montgomery.

OLD FRAME HOUSES

Until the time of the Revolution there were few frame
houses built in this part of the country and stone houses continued to be erected until about the beginning of the last cen-

tury. The oldest frame house in this vicinity we believe is that now owned by Henry L. DuBois, near Libertyville. This house in Revolutionary times was owned and occupied by Capt. Louis J. DuBois, son of Jonathan and grandson of Louis Jr. From Capt. Louis J. it passed to his son Louis and from him to his son John L. of whom it was purchased by the present owner, Henry L. DuBois, who is also one of the very large number of descendants of Capt. Louis J. DuBois. The old house has been re-sided and repainted since it was built but the great beams are as of old.

Perhaps the oldest frame house in this village is the one on Huguenot street, directly south of the church yard. This was occupied about 1800 by Lucas Van Wagenen. Another old frame house is the one on the farm now owned by Richard S. Deyo, about a mile north of this village, which was owned by Peter W. A. Freer. On this farm his father Elias and his grandfather Jonas lived, but the latter resided in the stone house on the east end of the farm.

A Famous Old Oak

The old oak tree at the residence of Mr. A. M. Lowe on the Paltz Plains is the largest and no doubt the oldest tree in this part of the county. Mr. Edmund Eltinge tells us that in the old days when regimental training was held on the Plains there were other old oaks a little farther to the west on the brow of the hill. Under these the sutlers' booths were pitched on training days. One of these old oaks was sawed down many years ago. Mr. Eltinge counted the rings in the tree and found there were 478, showing that the tree had attained that great age. The one still standing is probably full 500 years old.

THE FAMOUS OLD OAK ON THE PLAINS

How They Crossed the Wallkill

An ancient document, recently come to light, is of interest as showing how our great-grandfathers crossed the Wallkill, before any bridge had been built at this village. The names which are subscribed to the document we recognize as the great-grandfathers of the New Paltz people of the present day. The document is as follows:

We the Subscribers of these Presents, Do Promise to pay to Roelif J. Eltinge of the Precinct of the New Paltz in the County of Ulster and State of New York, the Respective Sums of money assigned and affixed to our respective names, For the use herein after mentioned, viz. to Build a Skow or flat to ferry across the Wall kill at the town of the New Paltz, where the oald Skow was kept Before, and to be made of good Yellow Pitchpine Wood, Except the Ribs, to be of good White-oak wood 4 by five to lay 9 inches apart, and the Length of Said Skow to be 28 feet, and the Breadth 11½ feet (out Side work) the Botom 3 inches thick, and the Sides 4 inches thick, and 15 inches Broad in the midel, and to rise 4 inches at each end from the main Botom and allso to Provide a good Rope to hall the Said Skow across by, and to fix everything belonging to Said Skow in good order and then to Set the Said Skow With the appurtenances up at publick vendue to the highest Bidder living in the town and the highest Bidder is to be the Ferry man for one year then Next ensuing, and to have the Care thereof and to keep it in order, and to take ferry-age money of all those that have no Right in Said Skow, and those that have not Paid for the Liberty of using it. Except those that are Comeing to, and going from Devine Service in the town of the New Paltz, and Every Subscriber is to have free Liberty to ferry any of his friends or Relation across

With Said Skow Provided he Does not take ferryage money for it, and the money arising by the Sail of the Said Skow or ferry and for the Sail of the Liberty of useing it, is to be applied annually to the Repair of Said Skow and Rope and if not Wanted for that purpose, to be returned to the Subscribers in Proportion to their Subscription, and the Said ferry man is to Provide a good Lock that Whensoever the kill Rises So high, that the Said Skow cannot be used with the Rope he may Lock the Said Skow (in the night) and every Subscriber, and those that have Liberty to use it, Will be obliged to fetch the kee at his house and Return it there again, as soon as possible. In Witness Whereof each of us have hereunto Set our hand this 20th day of Jany 1791.

	£	s	d
Josiah Hasbrouck & Jacob Hasbrouck, Jr	2	0	0
Roelof Josias Eltinge.	2	0	0
Andrias Lefever, Jun.	1	10	0
George Wertz.......	2	0	0
Philip Doyo.........	1	0	0
Abraham Doyo......	1	0	0
Simeon Low........	0	10	0
Daniel Dubis Junr & Joseph Dubois....	2	0	0
Jesais Hasbroucck.	0	8	0
Received of Andries Lefever for			
Christophol Doyo....	0	4	0
Mathusalem Dubois..	0	4	0
Joseph Hasbrouck....	0	4	0
Samuel Bevier.......	0	3	2

	£	s	d
Abraham Eltinge....	0	4	0
Cornelius Dubois Junr	0	4	0
Isaac Dubois........	0	4	0
Mathew Bevier......	0	4	0
Christiaen Doyou....	0	3	0
David Hasbrouck....	0	4	0

1793

	£	s	d
Rec. of Ezekiel Eltinge for being a ferry man	0	14	0
Ezechol Eltinge......	0	6	0
Richard mckinly.....	0	2	0
Isaac Bodeyn (mending chain)........	0	3	0
Simon Rosa	0	3	0
Richard mckinly.....	0	18	6

£ s d

1795

Ezechiel Eltinge chain
and cash.......... 0 11 7
Cash Joseph Has-
brouck 1 0 0
Cash from John Wil-
ketd 0 2 0

1797

Collected by Lucas
Vanwagenen for
ferry man **0 14 0**

────

Total 19 10 3

—

Dr.

1791

Paid to Daniel Dubois. 0 11 8
"   Wm. Coutant. 11 10 0
"   myself for go-
ing to and
crossing to bild
the Skow..... 0 12 0
"   Simon Rose... 0 1 6

£ s d

1794

"   for a Rope.... 6 17 7
"   for mending
chain 0 0 6
"   Peter Lefever,
Jack for tak-
ing the Scow
up 0 3 0

────

Total 19 19 3

1800.

Paid to Ez. Eltinge.. 1 3 9
"   his bond in full
for the rent of
the Scow for the
year 1797 ..... 0 17 0
Paid to Ezekiel El-
tinge 1 3 0
"   to Luke Van-
Wagenen 0 1 0
Scow yet indebted... 0 10 0
Paid to Ezekel El-
tinge 0 10 0

THE SPRINGTOWN MERCHANT OF 1800

The following story dates back to about 1800, when Col.
Josiah Hasbrouck kept a store in what is now the Memorial
House and Ezekiel Elting and his brother-in-law Philip Elting
kept a store in the stone house with a brick front, now the
property of Jesse M. Elting, adjoining his residence. A negro
living at Springtown, had a little store, his goods being kept

altogether in a large chest. He sold molasses by the pint and whatever other articles he had for sale in like proportion. In those days flax seed was one of the principal articles sold by farmers, and purchased by the village merchants. One day our Springtown merchant came to the village and having quite a high idea of his importance as a business man dropped in at Col. Hasbrouck's store, saying that as spring was approaching he thought he would come to New Paltz so that he and Col. Hasbrouck and the proprietors of the Elting store might "put their heads together" and dictate what price they would pay the farmers for their flax seed that spring. But Col. Hasbrouck did not take kindly to the idea of putting their heads together in this matter and the Springtown merchant left his store in a hurry. This story shows that although the slaves were not set free until long afterwards, a negro kept a store at Springtown, even if it was a small one; it shows, moreover, that the organization of a trust in those old days was attended with difficulties.

WASHINGTON IRVING AND MARTIN VAN BUREN

Hon. Andrew E. Elmore, of Fort Howard, Wis., relates the following anecdote concerning two of the Empire State's most prominent citizens of former days, showing that even in the early part of the last century the New Paltz records were known to be of interest:

In 1821, when Mr. Elmore was a lad about seven years of age and his father Job Elmore kept a store at what is now Highland, Washington Irving and Martin VanBuren, afterwards President of the United States, came one day in a carriage from Po'keepsie to examine the old records in New Paltz. The New Paltz turnpike was not yet constructed and the old road was not in first-class condition. One of the horses lost a shoe and the carriage was stopped at a black-smith shop across the street from his father's store to have a new shoe put on. The whip had also lost its cracker, and Mr. VanBuren came over to the store and got a skein of silk and tried to make a new cracker while the blacksmith was shoeing the horse. He did not succeed in making the cracker, but got the silk in a snarl. A bystander who knew him addressed him by name, and told him he had the silk in a tangle similar to that in which he would sometimes get the minds of people in arguing a case in court. Mr. VanBuren was surprised at being recognized and addressed by name, but procured another skein of silk of which the bystander made him a cracker for his whip.

REGIMENTAL TRAININGS

The greatest days of the year at New Paltz in the first half of the last century were the training days. The regimental district included the old town of New Paltz—that is, New Paltz as it was, before being dismembered, including all of Lloyd, about half of the present towns of Esopus and Gardiner, and one-third of Rosendale. Plattekill was also included in the regimental district. Regimental training at New Paltz ceased about 1848. Perry Deyo, of Highland, was the last Colonel. His predecessor was Josiah P. Le-Fevre of this town, and Solomon Elting, father of A. V. N. Elting, was his predecessor. The training ground for a long time was on the Paltz Plains. The regiment consisted of eight companies of infantry, one of light infantry, and one of artillery. The men had to bear their own expenses and provide their own flint lock muskets. There was one company from Kettleborough, one from Springtown, one from Highland, one from Nescatook (now Libertyville).

The last named company was the best.   The Highland
people did not usually turn out very well.

The Brigadier General and staff would inspect the regiment and were usually entertained at the residence of Dirck
Wynkoop, grand-father of Edmund Eltinge.   Mr. Wynkoop
was famous for his hospitality and likewise for his fine
horses.   Under the old oak tree still standing at Mr. Low's,
at the north end of the Plains, a temporary structure would
be set up where refreshments and whiskey were sold.

After the Plains were fenced in, about 1840, training was
held either at Abm. M. Hasbrouck's, north of the village, or
on the other side of the Wallkill.   When Perry Deyo was
Colonel, just before the training days were finally discontinued, he ordered the destruction of a quantity of whiskey,
which had been brought on the ground by a huckster.   Mr.
Deyo was sued by the huckster, but was sustained by the
court, as he had no permission or legal right to sell.

Amusements in the Olden Times

The old folks probably had quite as much fun as their descendants of to-day.   It is related that Isaac LeFever, the first
settler of Bontecoe, went to Albany and ran a foot race, in
which his friends shouted in French, "Courage, Isaac." He
won the race.   Major Isaac, his grandson, skated to Albany
and back in a day; the skates he wore are now in the Memorial House.   It is related that cock fighting was not an unknown sport in the old times.   The widow of Daniel, son of
Abram Hasbrouck, the patentee, lived in the house still standing
directly opposite the brick church.   She had a lot of boys, and
"Wyntje's kitchen" is spoken of as a famous place for cock
fighting.   We are told that the old folks thought nothing of
riding as far as Shawangunk to a husking.   Horse racing on

the Paltz plains, which were not fenced in until about 1820, was a very common sport, especially at town meeting.

The young men doubtless derived much innocent amusement from the races, but there is an old story of a race on the plains which shows that there were some wicked young men in the good old days.

The story dates back to the time of good old Dominie Bogardus, who was pastor of the churches at New Paltz and New Hurley, in 1820. Charles DuBois, of Libertyville, was a prominent man in the church, and his son, Louis, was fond of horse racing, concerning which the dominie remonstrated with Charles. The latter sold his horse to another DuBois, likewise named Louis. Subsequently, by trading, the dominie himself became the owner of the very horse, which he rode on his visits among the congregation, but of course never indulged in racing. Young Louis did not submit in a very christian frame of mind, but bided his time.

The race track for the young men, in those days, was over the Paltz plains, from Peter Elting's, now Edmund Eltinge's, to Andries Deyo's, now Josiah Sprague's place. Young Louis made his plans. The dominie was on his way to the village by the Kettelborough road, after preaching in the afternoon at New Hurley. The young man stationed a few companions, who were doubtless ready for the sport, at Andries Deyo's to wait for the fun. Then coming behind the dominie, likewise on horseback, he shouted at the dominie's horse, who, remembering old times, broke from the control of his driver and away both dashed. The dominie won the race, much against his will no doubt, and much to his chagrin, we may guess, as the young men, stationed at the outcome, swung their hats and shouted, "Hurrah for the dominie." The dominie could not check his horse till he reached the old oak tree, where Mr. Lowe now lives.

CHAPTER XV

THE NEW PALTZ CHURCH

The name Huguenot was not applied in the old days to the church at New Paltz, either by the people themselves or by strangers. It was called the Walloon church; sometimes the French church. The people were called Walloons. Louis DuBois, the leader in the settlement was called Louis the Walloon.

The New Paltz church was peculiar in the respect that for a period of 75 years it owned no authority higher than its own membership, having no subjection to the classis of Amsterdam as had the Dutch churches. The church records, still in perfect preservation, are unique likewise in the fact that they are in three languages—in French for a period of about 50 years, then in Dutch for about 70 years and since 1800 in English.

As New Paltz was settled by people who had left their home on account of religious persecution it was to be expected that religion and the church should occupy a large place in their hearts when they made for themselves a new home in the wilderness. Several of the older settlers at New Paltz brought with them certificates of membership in the churches with which they had united, while sojourning in the Palatinate. Two at least of the Patentees and probably others had Bibles in the French language. When they reached New Paltz on their journey from Kingston and alighted from their wagons one of their number read a psalm. Among the log buildings erected at the outset was one for a church and school house. In 1683, only five years after the settlement, a church was organized. In their purchase of the land of the Indians and their honest payment for it they displayed Christian principle, which had its just reward in the peace and friendship always existing between them and the savages. In the institution of the government of the Dusine or Twelve Men for the division of lands and settling of disputes concerning land titles they showed a feeling of Christian brotherhood, which prevented all lawsuits on that score. It was not the spirit of commercial gain, but the desire to worship God according to the dictates of their own conscience that prompted the Huguenots to leave France. Religious motives led up to the settlement at New Paltz, religious principles controlled it and the exercise of religious duties and privileges formed an important part of the subsequent history of the place.

This condition did not terminate with the first generation. In 1720, though there was no Church Building Fund in those days, a substantial stone church was built. There was no complaint about long sermons, we fancy, among people, some of whom walked several miles barefoot to church in summer and in winter tried to keep themselves warm in church by little foot stoves. During the long intervals when no minister visited New Paltz the journey of 16 miles was made to Kingston, where a large proportion of the children in the early days were baptized.

In writing the history of the New Paltz church it is peculiarly fortunate that all the records are still in existence. The opinion that has been advanced that one book had been lost because but two entries of baptisms are found from 1700 to 1730 is doubtless incorrect, as will be shown hereafter.

The books containing the church records are four in number. The oldest is a small memorandum book of 17 pages, on coarse paper and somewhat yellow with age, but the writing is distinct. This book is altogether in French (with the exception of two entries interpolated at a later date in Dutch), and gives the record of baptisms and other matters while the church was under the charge of the two French pastors, Rev. Pierre Dailie and Rev. David Bonrepos, extending from 1683 to 1700.

The first entry is as follows in the handwriting of Louis DuBois:

"Le 22 de Janv. (Janvier), 1683, monsieur pierre daillie, minister de la parole de dieu, est arive (arrive) au nouveau palatinat. et presca (precha) deux fois le dimance (Dimanche) suivant, et proposa au ceef (chefs) des famille de coisir (choisir) a plus de vois (voix), par les peres de famille, un ancien et un diake (diacre), ce qu il firt (qu'ils firent), et coisir (choisirent) Louys du bois pour ancien et hughe frere pour diake, pour ayder le ministre a conduire les membres de leglise (l'eglise) quil sasemble (qui s'assemble) au nouveau palatinat; lequel furt confirme (lesquels furent con firmes) ensuite dans ladict carge (charge) dancien et diake. Le present liuur (livre) a est faict (a ete fait) pour mestre (metre) les choses quil apatien (qui appartiennent) a la dict eglise."

The translation is as follows:

"The 22d of January, 1683, Mr. Pierre Daillie, minister of the Word of God, arrived at New Paltz, and preached twice on the following Sunday, and proposed to the heads of the families that they should choose by a majority of votes, by the fathers of families, one elder and one deacon, which they did, and chose Louis DuBois for elder and Hugh Freer for deacon, to assist the minister in guiding the members of the church that meets in New Paltz; who were subsequently confirmed in the said charge of elder and deacon. This minute has been made to put in order the matters which pertain to the said church."

THE TWO FRENCH PASTORS

The two French pastors, Dailie and Bonrepos, usually visited New Paltz in the spring or early summer and again in October. The pastorate of the former extended over a period of ten years. His main field of labor was in New York, but he seems to have preached in various Huguenot communities. In 1691 and 1692 we find "Rev. Pierre Daillie of New York" officiating at the baptism of children at the Dutch church in Kingston. His last recorded service at New Paltz is in 1692. Before leaving France he had been Professor of theology in the Protestant seminary at Samur. In 1696 he received a call from the French church in Boston, where he died in 1715, aged about 66 years.

OLD PAPER WITH SIGNATURE OF REV. PIERRE DAILLE

During the period of ten years from 1683 to 1693 the name of no child of New Paltz parentage is found recorded on the church book at Kingston. All were baptized at New Paltz.

From 1696 until 1700 Rev. David Bonrepos visited New Paltz occasionally, baptizing children and receiving members at the table of the Lord. His special field of labor was on Staten Island. Book 1 ends with a marriage in 1702, which, although not so stated, was probably performed by Bonrepos and was his last service here. A long blank in the church records follows, extending until 1729, broken by the record in Dutch of the baptism of two children, not of New Paltz parentage, in 1718, and by the account of the building of the first stone church, which was finished in 1720. It has been supposed that a book containing a record of baptisms and other church services from 1702 to 1729 must have been lost. But an examination of the Kingston church records shows that during this time a large number of children of New Paltz parents were baptised there.

It is altogether likely that during this period of about 30 years no regular minister held services at New Paltz for the reason that the people here had no claims on the Dutch church and probably did not understand that language, while the few French ministers, who had come to this country were now dead or otherwise engaged and there were no French Protestant seminaries on either side of the Atlantic to train others in their stead. Be this as it may the fire still burned brightly on the altar as is shown by the entry on the church book when the first stone church was built, as follows:

"Beni sois Dieu, Quij Le nous a mys a cœur de Luy batir une maison pour y estre adores et servir, et que par sa grace nous Lavon finys en Lan Dix vii; et Dieu veillie que son evangile y soit anouce dean ce ciecle et dedan Lautre y usque au jour D Leternite. Amen."

The translation is as follows:

"Blessed be God, who has put it into our hearts to build a house where He may be adored and served, and that by his grace we have finished it in the year 17 [1717]; and God grant that his gospel may be preached here from one age to another till the day of eternity. Amen."

THE FIRST STONE CHURCH

Next on the church book comes the names of those who assisted in building the first stone church as follows: Mary, widow of Abraham Hasbrouck, now dead; Luoy Bevier (deceased) and at present Samuel and Loui Bevier; Abraham DuBois, Huge Frere, Salomon Duboys, Louys Duboys, Abraham Doyo, Andres LeFevre, Joseph Hasbrouck, Jacob Hasbrouck, Mary Duboys, now dead, and at present Daniel and Philip Duboys, Jean LeFevre, Isaac LeFevre, Ely Un, Chrestiane Doyo, Hanry Doyo, Abraham Frere, Jacob Frere.

It will be noted that Abraham DuBois is the only one of the original Patentees, whose name appears in this list. All the rest were dead.

In 1720 an entry is made in the church book assigning and deeding certain pews to all who had assisted in building the church.

This church stood at the north end of the old graveyard. In 1895, in digging for the foundation for the addition to the residence of Mrs. S. A. LeFevre, the foundation of this old church was found and it was followed up for some distance. This building was the house of worship for the little community till 1773. Then a larger stone church was erected near the site of the present church edifice. The old church of 1717 was then taken down and the stone of which

THE FIRST STONE CHURCH AT NEW PALTZ

it was built drawn to a new site on what is now North Front St., where they were used in building the school house, which was the only public school building in the village until 1874. Then a new brick school house was built and the old stone building was purchased by Mr. John Drake, who remodeled it somewhat and made it his residence. A pen and ink picture of this old church is found in an ancient map, which has come down from the days of the Dusine. It was probably the exact size of the school building, that is about 33 feet square. It had a large window on each of its three sides and on the fourth a capacious door and portico. From the steeple a horn was sounded for religious meetings.

There can hardly be a doubt that religious service of some kind was held at this church each Sabbath even though no minister was present to conduct it. The entry on the church book, at the time of building shows how desirous the people were of having the gospel preached.

There were some 16 or 18 families who assisted in building the church. The records of the Kingston church show that during the period from 1700 to 1730 an average of 5 or 6 children of New Paltz parentage were baptized there, each year. Had there been a minister visiting New Paltz, even two or three times a year, as in the days of the French pastors, very few would probably have been taken on the long journey to Kingston.

REV. JOHANNES VAN DRIESSEN

Rev. Johannes Van Driessen took charge of the church at New Paltz in 1731, or possibly a year or two earlier. He received only £10 a year for his services. His first entries on the church book are in French. In one of these he calls the church here "our French church." Doubtless his services were in that language. Probably but a small portion of his time was spent at New Paltz.

Mr. Van Driessen was educated in Belgium. The church book contains a copy in Latin of a certificate showing that he had been examined in 1727 by the Presbytery of New Haven in the halls of Yale college and had well sustained the examination. In 1736 he accepted a call to the church at Acquackanonk, N. J., and for the space of about 16 years thereafter New Paltz was without a regular pastor, though visited occasionally by ministers from other churches.

From 1700 until 1731 there is no record of officers of the church. At the latter date, when Mr. Van Driessen became pastor, Nicholas Rose and Andries LeFevre were elected elders and Samuel Bevier and Solomon Hasbrouck deacons. In 1733 Louis DuBois, Jr. was elected elder and Christian Deyo deacon. In 1734 Nicholas Rose was again chosen elder; Jacob Hasbrouck was chosen deacon. In 1736 Samuel Bevier was chosen elder and Daniel Hasbrouck deacon. Then there is no further record of church officers until 1750.

Rev. Johannes Van Driessen was not regularly ordained by the Dutch church and 20 years after he came to New Paltz the next regular minister, Rev. B. Vrooman, instituted an inquiry as to whether the members admitted by Van Driessen believed the doctrines of the Reformed church according to the Heidelbergh catechism. During Mr. Van Driessen's pastorate of about five years 19 joined the church and about 30 children were baptized. During the same period about half that number of children of New Paltz parents were baptized at Kingston.

In 1738 a highway, probably the first in this town, was laid out on the east side of the Wallkill for the purpose, as stated in the record, of better enabling the people to get to church at New Paltz and Kingston.

At this time the Dutch language was coming into more general use in New Paltz and a side light is thrown on this fact by the will of Jean Tebenin, the old French schoolmaster in 1730 giving his property to the church with the special request that if the French language should cease to be used the Bible should be sold and the proceeds given to the poor.

After 1736 there is no record of baptisms until 1739 when three are recorded in French by Rev. J. J. Moulinars.

In 1740, in 1741 and again in 1742 Rev. Isaac Chalker officiated at six different times, baptizing 15 persons in all. Each time the record is in English, but it is not to be supposed that the service was performed in that language, which must have been an unknown tongue to nearly all of his hearers.

In 1741 the New Paltz church, and Shawangunk, Rochester, and Marbletown made a call upon Rev. J. Casparus Freyenmoet, who was then preaching at Minisink, but the call was not accepted and the consistory of the Minisink church sent a very indignant letter to the consistory of the Rochester church, reprimanding them for attempting to take away their minister.

From 1742 to '49 the record shows no baptisms and one marriage only, that of Andries Le Fever and Rachel DuBois, Oct. 1745, after three proclamations "in our French Church," at New Paltz. The visiting ministers from the close of Rev. Mr. Van Driessen's to the commencement of the next regular pastorate baptized infants, but except in the case above noted no marriage by a minister is recorded from 1737 to 1751. In 1742 and 1749 marriages are recorded on the church books as being performed by Zacharias Hoffman, Esq., and Cornelius DuBois, Esq. In the latter year the name of

Rev. J. Henry Goetschius appears as baptizing infants and in 1751 he performed six marriages. He was settled over the churches at Schraalenbergh and Hackensack, occasionally coming to New Paltz, receiving members in communion and baptizing infants. In 1750 we find the name of J. C. Freyenmoet, in 1751 that of Rev. Theodorus Frelinghuysen "pastor at Albany" and in 1752 that of Dominie Meynema as performing baptisms.

REV. BARENT VROOMAN

Then at last in 1753 New Paltz has once more a settled minister, Rev. Barent Vrooman, of Schoharie, whose call had been sent to Amsterdam and returned with the endorsement of the Classis. He was the first regularly installed Dutch pastor at New Paltz. He also preached at Shawangunk. His stay was short and in 1754 he accepted a call from the church at Schenectady.

From this date we may consider the Dutch language and the Dutch church established in New Paltz, though in some of the homes the French tongue doubtless lingered a while longer.

In 1751, '52, '53 and '54 no less than 75 persons joined the church on confession of faith and 23 by certificate from other churches. Part of these were admitted by Rev. J. H. Goetschius and part by Rev. B. Vrooman.

The bounds of the New Paltz congregation at this time extended over a territory stretching about ten miles to the south and eight miles to the north, that is from New Hurley on the south to Swartekill on the north. John George Ronk of New Hurley, ancestor of the Ronk family, joined the church in 1750 and Johannes Hardenbergh, of Rosendale, in 1751 and were soon afterwards made officers in the church. A few years afterwards Petrus Ostrander of Platte-kill and Abraham Hardenbergh of Guilford were officers in the church.

In 1752 at a meeting of the consistory it was resolved to elect, beside the governing elders and deacons, two more elders and deacons and this resolution was at once carried into effect.

After Rev. B. Vrooman departed for Schenectady the New Paltz church was dependent on supplies for six years. During that period Rev. J. H. Goetschius, Rev. Theodorus Freling-huysen, Rev. D. B. Meynema and Rev. Johannes Schuneman officiated at different times, baptizing quite a number of in-fants, although none joined the church on confession and but one marriage is recorded in all those years.

BAPTIZING THE CHILDREN AT KINGSTON

During the long intervals while New Paltz was without a minister some of the little children were baptized by visiting ministers, but a great portion were taken to Kingston and the solemn rite was there performed. In the 16 years from the end of Rev. Mr. Van Driessen's pastorate in 1736 to the com-mencement of that of Rev. B. Vrooman in 1752 there were about 85 children of New Paltz parents baptized at Kingston. During a portion of this 16 years, that is from 1742 to 1749, the record shows no baptisms at New Paltz and 59 of New Paltz parentage at Kingston, that is an average of over 7 each year. After 1752 there were few baptisms of New Paltz children at Kingston—only about a dozen in the next ten years. During this time visiting ministers came quite often to New Paltz and the church grew and prospered. It is worthy of note that the Kingston ministers never baptized chil-dren at New Paltz, though their church book shows that they performed that service at Marbletown, Rochester, Shawangunk and Minisink.

The long ride from New Paltz to Kingston was taken probably on horseback. There were no spring wagons until long after that date. The route on the east side of the Wallkill led from one to another of the stone houses, crossing the stream by a scow, just this side of the present Bontecoe school-house. We may suppose that a stop was frequently made at Rosendale, at the residence of Col. Johannes Hardenbergh, whose wife Marie DuBois, was the daughter of Louis DuBois, Jr., of Nescatock. A few miles further north at Bloomingdale we may suppose another stop would be made at the residence of Matthew LeFevre, who moved from our village about 1740 and located there. There may have been a little danger from wild beasts, but there was none from Indians. In passing through the clearings the gates must be opened, as it was not till long afterward that the farmers were required to build a fence on each side of the highway.

CONNECTION BETWEEN CHURCH AND STATE

There was a close connection between church and state at New Paltz in those days as shown by certain records in papers that have come down in the Patentees' trunk, showing what matters were submitted to voters, as follows:

In 1757 whether the money received for the collectorship should be applied on the highway or to the use of the church; the latter was preferred. In 1758 the same question was again decided by vote with the same result. In 1759 it was put to vote whether the money received for the collectorship should be given to the clerk of the church, to the poor, or used for the purchase of a "pall." It was decided to use it for the last named purpose. The next year it was again voted to apply the money received for the collectorship to the purchase of a pall and the overplus for the purchase of a silver cup or beaker for the use of the church. The next year it was again voted that the money received for the collectorship should be applied to the purchase of a silver cup for the church.

REV JOHANNES MAURITIUS GOETSCHIUS

In 1760 the churches at New Paltz and Shawangunk made a call on Rev. Johannes Mauritius Goetschius. He was a native of Switzerland, a younger brother of Rev. J. H. Goetschius, had studied medicine before coming to America, studied theology with his brother at Hackensack, N. J. and had preached two years at Schoharie. The call, which was accepted, stated that from Easter to October he should preach twice each Lord's Day, holding services alternately at Shawangunk and at New Paltz, preaching in the forenoon from some text in the Bible and in the afternoon from the Heidelbergh catechism. The rest of the year he was to preach one sermon each Sunday. He was to administer the sacrament of the Lord's Supper twice in the year at Shawangunk and twice a year at New Paltz and attend to the house visiting once a year. He should have a house, barn, 90 acres of land and a good spring at Shawangunk, where he had his home, and while at New Paltz should be provided with bed, board and quarters. He was to receive an annual salary of £80, one half to be paid by each of the churches. The call was approved by the Coetus in New York.

Rev. Mr. Goetschius continued to minister to the churches at New Paltz and Shawangunk until 1771, when he died at his home in Shawangunk in the 48th year of his age and was buried in the baptistry of the church. Mr. Goetschius practiced medicine as well as preached the gospel. In 1762, during the early part of his pastorate steps were taken looking toward the erection of a new church building at New Paltz, but the plan was not carried out, owing probably to the quarrel between the Coetus and Conferentia parties, which split the Dutch church at New Paltz, as well as elsewhere in America, into two factions and led to the erection of a church building about two miles from our village on the road to the county house by the Conferentia party.

THE CONFERENTIA CHURCH

We have come now to a most exciting period in the history of the Dutch church at New Paltz, as well as elsewhere in America: that is the period of the struggle between the Coetus and Conferentia parties. This strife was due we may say, stating the case broadly, to the same causes that afterward provoked a revolt against the political control of Great Britain. In each of these cases the grievances were not great, but the American child, feeling its ability to walk alone, did not care to pay homage any longer to the mother church or to the mother country.

The Coetus party did not care to own allegiance to any foreign ecclesiastical power.

The Conferentia party held that the church in this country ought to remain subordinate to the classis of North Amsterdam and accused the Coetus party of "despicable ingratitude against their benefactors, who had so long labored for their well being and have exerted so many efforts in behalf of the churches of New York."

The battle raged fiercely among the Dutch churches in America. The consistory of the New Paltz church took sides with the Coetus and the great majority of the people ranged themselves with that party. There was an element, however, respectable in numbers and especially so in means and influence, which sided with the Conferentia. This party was almost altogether of Dutch descent, had moved from Kingston to New Paltz at a considerable period after the first settlement, and few had formally united with the church here. This party comprised the Eltings, the Lows and the Van Wagenens; also Jacob DuBois, who had recently moved from near Kingston, and Hendricus DuBois. The last named was a member of the New Paltz church and may be considered the foremost man in the Conferentia movement. In 1765 he was suspended for provoking schism and secession in the church and refusing to answer after three citations. He was evidently not much frightened and two years afterwards a meeting was held at his house to organize a Conferentia church. Rev. Isaac Rysdyck of Poughkeepsie and Fishkill was the officiating minister.

The following persons, members of the Kingston church, joined the new church organization: Josiah Elting and his brother Noah, Petrus Van Wagenen, Jacob DuBois, Rebecca Van Wagenen, Dirk D. Wynkoop, Magdalena DuBois, Jacomyntje Elting, Sarah Low. On the same day the following joined the church: Petrus, Solomon and Isaac Low, Hendricus DuBois, Debora Van Vliet and Jannitje Houghtaling The next year there were admitted to the church on confession Josiah Elting's four sons: Roelif J., Abraham, Solomon and Cornelius; also various female members of the families of those previously mentioned; also Jacobus Auchmoody.

The new church organization was weak in numbers, but strong in determination and had a house of worship almost completed before the church was organized. This church building was located a short distance this side of the present residence of Capt. W. H. D. Blake, about two miles south of

our village, on the west side of the Wallkill. This church
building was called "Kerk of het Grootstuck" that is in English "Church of the Great Piece," that being the name of the
tract of land on which the church was located and which belonged to Noah Eltinge.   It was usually called the "owl"
church, probably because the neighborhood abounded in owls.
It was a frame building, 30 feet square, boarded without, plas-
tered with clay within, shingle roofed, and containing 20 pews.
It cost about £150.   Josiah Elting and Hendricus DuBois
were the most liberal contributors, each giving about £25.
Noah Eltinge was elected elder and Petrus Van Wagenen
deacon.   Rev. G. D. Cock served for a time as stated supply
for this church.   Then in 1774 Rev. Rynier Van Nest was
called to the pastorate of the church at Shawangunk and
the Conferentia church at New Paltz.   He received as
salary £60 a year from Shawangunk and £20 a year from New
Paltz.

The feud between the Coetus and Conferentia parties in the
Dutch church in America did not prevail many years, but it
was a long time before the two churches at New Paltz were
united.

In 1771 a convention was held in New York, attended by
delegates, ministers and elders from most of the churches, at
which articles of union were drawn up.   The Coetus church
at New Paltz was represented by Johannes Hardenbergh.   The
Conferentia church had no delegate.   The articles of union,
adopted at this convention, left the church in this country practically independent of the mother church in Holland, though
it was provided that if difficulties should arise concerning important points of doctrine or any member be deposed on account
of heresy or misconduct there should be the right of appeal to
the classis of Amsterdam.   Johannes Hardenbergh, delegate

from the old church at New Paltz, signed this agreement and his action was promptly approved by his consistory. The Conferentia party at New Paltz took no action for a long time. Finally in 1783 the spirit of harmony had been restored to so great an extent that at last the "owl" church was abandoned as a house of worship and its members in full harmony joined with the worshipers in the church in this village and its records were preserved with those of the older church. The "owl" church building was taken down and a granary was built of its material by Roelif J. Elting, at his home in this village. During its existence the total number of baptisms registered in this church were 60. There were 2 marriages recorded and 35 persons in all had joined the church. Of this number 19 united with the church in this village May 25th, 1783.

The persons who came in from the Conferentia church were Dirk Wynkoop, Jr. and wife Sarah (daughter of Noah Eltinge) Abraham Elting, David Low, Henry DuBois and his wife Rebecca Van Wagenen and his mother Janiteje Houghtaling, Jacob DuBois and wife, Solomon Low and wife, Magdalena DuBois widow of Josiah Elting, Margaret Hue widow of William Patterson, Maria Low wife of Roelif J. Elting, Cornelius Elting, Jacobus Auchmoody, Ann DuBois, Petrus Van Wagenen and wife Sarah Low.

Having now concluded the history of the Conferentia church we go back twelve years and take up the history of the original New Paltz church.

In March 1771 the pastor, Rev. Mauritius Goetschius died. In October of the same year the Convention was held in New York, which apparently had no immediate effect at New Paltz, though it resulted in the restoration of harmony twelve years later.

The Second Stone Church

In the same year, 1771, though without a minister and without the assistance of the Conferentia party, action was taken toward building a new house of worship. The location of this new church was a few yards south of the site of the present brick church. The land was bought of Petronella Le-Fevre, widow of Simon. The new church building was of stone, much larger than the old church and remained as the house of worship until 1839. The following persons were chosen as the building committee: Abraham Deyo (grandfather of the late Judge Abm. A. Deyo of Modena) Jacob Hasbrouck, Jr. (great-grandfather of Jacob M. Hasbrouck) Simon DuBois (great-grandfather of the late John W. DuBois) Nathaniel LeFevre (great-grandfather of Hon. Jacob LeFevre) Garret Freer, Jr., Abraham LeFevre (great-grandfather of Josiah LeFevre) and Hugo Freer, ancestor of a number of the Bontecoe Freers. The initials of several of these men and the date may still be seen in a large stone under the horse block at the south end of the portico. This was no doubt the corner stone of the building. Abram Deyo was appointed overseer of the work. He was required to give a bond and he kept a strict account of everything. His account book, in the Dutch language, containing a full statement of these matters is in possession of his descendant Abm. Deyo Brodhead, who occupies his house.

A lime oven was erected and lime for making mortar burned on the ground. The masons' helpers were paid 4 shillings a day, a man with a team and wagon was paid 9 shillings a day for carting lime and 10 shillings a day for carting wood; 1 shilling a day was allowed for boarding each workman; authority was given to buy beer for the workmen, also a barrel of rum.

THE SECOND STONE CHURCH AT NEW PALTZ

This church was a substantial, well-proportioned building, with a hipped roof and a cupola from which a bell sounded for religious services. The total subscriptions amounted to only £546, but the sum realized from the sale of pews fully doubled that amount. The list of subscribers comprises 85 names, the Freers being far in advance, with 17 names. The heaviest subscribers were Jacob Hasbrouck, Jr. £55, Abram Deyo £45, Wyntje Hasbrouck £33, Col. Abm. Hasbrouck (Kingston) £30, Hugo Freer £25, Simon DuBois £27.

In the list of subscribers appear the names of 17 Freers contributing £162, 9 LeFevres contributing £130, 8 Hasbroucks contributing £168, 8 Deyos contributing £97, 6 DuBoises contributing £77, 4 Beviers contributing £57, 3 Hardenberghs contributing £32, 3 Terwilligers contributing £32, 5 Ostranders contributing £9, 2 Eans contributing £7, 2 Schoonmakers contributing £11, 2 Lows £15, 2 Vandemarks £17.

There are also on the list of contributors the names of Dr. Geo. Wurts, Petrus Smedes, John York, Teunis Van Vliet, Dennis Relyea, Johannes Walron, Lewis Brodhead and Joseph Coddington. The last named was the village schoolmaster and performed much clerical work connected with building of the church.

Among the names of purchasers of seats, beside those residing in this vicinity were Philip D. B. Bevier of Rochester, David Bevier of Marbletown, Col. Abm. Hasbrouck of Kingston, Isaac Hasbrouck, Jr. of Stone Ridge, Jacobus Bruyn of Bruynswick, Hendrick Smit of Rifton, Col. Johannes Hardenbergh of Rosendale and Dennis Relyea of New Hurley.

The total appraisement of the pews was £2280. The total sum realized at the sale was considerably more, amounting to £2684.

Although the work was commenced in 1771 it was not until 1774 that the pews were sold at public auction.

The old Shawangunk church, with which the New Paltz church had formerly been connected, being now a Conferentia church, the New Paltz church joined with the New Hurley church in 1775 in extending a call to Rev. Stephen Goetschius, which was accepted. He was the son of Rev. J. Henry Goetschius and nephew of his predecessor Rev. Mauritius Goetschius. He was 23 years of age when he came to New Paltz and remained here 21 years—a longer period of service than any of the successors. He was a graduate of Princeton and had studied theology with four eminent divines, including his father. His call stated that New Paltz should receive two-thirds of his services and provide him with house, barn, 60 acres of land, pay £56 10 s. as salary. New Hurley should pay £33 10 s. annually. About ten years afterwards his salary was increased to £114, New Paltz paying two thirds and New Hurley one third.

In the early part of his ministry he boarded with Capt. Lewis DuBois who resided about half way between New Paltz and New Hurley. His daughter Elizabeth he married. In his later years at New Paltz he built the Philip D. Elting stone house, still standing in the northern part of our village. He was the only minister who ever built a house at New Paltz. His pastorate covered the eventful period of the Revolutionary war and the reunion of the Conferentia party with the church. The period succeeding the Revolutionary war was not favorable to the growth of religion owing to the influence of French thought and French skepticism and we may suppose that New Paltz did not entirely escape the contagion. During the long period of his pastorate 102 in all were added to the church, including the 19 from the Conferentia church. Toward the close of his ministry, which ended in 1796, he preached occasionally in English, which he had learned sufficiently for that purpose and which pleased the younger members of his congregation. He is described as a man of deep thought, abundant in labors and holding strongly to Calvinistic doctrines.

A loose slip of paper in the church book dated 1782, shows that Joseph Coddington had been reader and singer in the church and Simeon Low was his successor. The paper, which is a subscription list, commences as follows: "Whereas reading and singing during religious service are not only beautiful, but in accordance with the word of God and the canons of the church, therefore the consistory, after Mr. Coddington for different reasons had resigned, have unanimously elected Mr. Simeon Low and contracted with him for £3 annually."

REV. JOHN H. MEYER

The next minister was Rev. John H. Meier. He was a graduate of Columbia College and had studied with Rev. Dr. John H. Livingston. Mr. Meier was called to the pastorate of the churches of New Paltz and New Hurley in 1799. His call stipulated that he was to preach three-fifths of the year at New Paltz and two-fifths of the year at New Hurley and that the services should be performed one half in Dutch and one half in English. As his salary he received £135, besides a house, barn and 60 acres of land at New Paltz. He was to call on each family in the congregation once in two years. From this time the church records are written in English. He remained only a little over three years, when he received a call from the church at Schenectady. During his pastorate 22 were received as members of the church, 154 were baptized and 88 marriages were performed.

Rev. Peter D. Freligh

The church was without a minister about four years and then a call was made by the two churches upon Rev. Peter D. Freligh, who accepted. He was a graduate of Columbia College, his father and uncle were ministers and he had previously had charge of a church in the northern part of the state. He preached alternately in English and Dutch. He was faithful in catechising the young and his sermons were sound and interesting. He remained until 1815, when he removed to Acquacanock, N. J. During his pastorate 82 persons joined the church and 177 marriages were solemnized.

Rev. William R. Bogardus

Rev. Wm. R. Bogardus was the next minister, his pastorate commencing in 1817. He was a graduate of Union College, Schenectady, and of the Theological Seminary at New Brunswick, N. J. He was a young man when he came to New Paltz. For eleven years he served the churches at New Paltz and New Hurley, riding back and forth on horseback. From 1828 to 1831 he was pastor of the New Paltz church alone. Besides his other qualifications as a preacher and pastor he had the gift of song in a remarkable degree and even in old age would lead in the singing. He is remembered by the old people as an eloquent preacher of the word of God and a faithful and conscientious pastor. His ministry was greatly blessed. During his pastorate 280 joined the church, 696 were baptized and 379 marriages performed. In was during his pastorate that the first great wave of temperance reform swept over the state and Mr. Bogardus was one of its pioneers in Ulster county. When a new barn was erected at the parsonage a pitcher of cold water, flanked with temperance tracts took the place of the strong drink customary on such occasions. In 1831 he accepted a call from the church at Acquanonck, N. J., and in 1856 retired from the ministry.

REV. DOUW VAN OLINDA

The next minister was Rev. Douw Van Olinda. He was a graduate of the Theological Seminary at New Brunswick, N. J., and before coming to New Paltz had been minister at Canajoharie, N. Y. His first service at New Paltz was on the first Sunday in January, 1832, and he remained at New Paltz twelve years. The period of his pastorate was a time of active public enterprise in the town, marked by the building of the New Paltz Academy, the New Paltz turnpike and that portion of the present church building that now constitutes its eastern extension. In the building of the Academy he took a very active part and may we think be considered the prime mover. He was possessed of much executive ability. His sermons were preached without any notes. In 1839 the brick church was built to take the place of the old stone church which had been the house of worship for more than 60 years. The congregation was now too large for this old church building.

After due consideration it was decided that the new church edifice should be of brick. Its dimensions were as follows: length 66 feet, width 54 feet, height 26 feet. It was modeled after the church of New Hackensack in every respect except the steeple. The portico, with its pillars, and the vestibule, likewise the steeple and clock were constructed as they remain to the present day. A basement was made under the edifice in which prayer meetings and Sunday school have since been held. The stones of the old church went into the basement and foundation walls and so did the stones of the LeFevre house, which until that time had occupied what is now the northern part of the churchyard. The bell of the old church went into the school house and a new one, costing $375, was presented to the consistory by the citizens of the place and this, with its mellow tones, still continues to summon the worshipers to the house of God.

In 1844 Rev. Douw Van Olinda resigned his position as pastor and took charge of a church at Fonda, N. Y.

CHAPTER XVI

Old County Records at Kingston

In the county clerk's office at Kingston is a box containing a number of ancient papers.

Among the most interesting and valuable of these old papers is the Proceedings of the Board of Supervisors from 1710 to 1731, inclusive, written in English, in a plain hand.

It appears from this document that in 1710 there were only five towns in the county: Kingston, Hurley, Marbletown, Rochester and New Paltz. Before the close of this record in 1731 the number of towns in the county had greatly increased and included New Windsor and other places in what is now Orange county and also what is now Delaware county. The only business performed by the supervisors in those days, as appears from this record, was the auditing of bills against the county. Most of these bills were for bounties for killing wolves. Solomon DuBois of Poughwoughtenonk killed 12 wolves in one year and for a number of years was the champion wolf slayer in the county. Possibly a number of these wolves were caught in the trap now in the Memorial House, which caught the last wolf in this town and was at the time the property of Josiah DuBois, great-grandson of Solomon.

The county treasurer in 1710, as appears from this record, was Jean Cottin, who after serving the New Paltz people for many years as their schoolmaster, moved to Kingston, married the widow of Louis DuBois the Patentee, long carried on the mercantile business and when he died left his property to the church. Monsieur Cottin was county treasurer for several years and on two or three occasions, when the county was in debt a little, he advanced the needed sum. He charged for his services one year £2.

Roelif Elting, the ancestor of the New Paltz Eltings, had not yet moved from Kingston and represented that town in the Board of Supervisors in 1711 and 1712.

Col. Henry Beekman, who with Capt. Garton represented the county in the colonial legislature in 1710, brought in to the supervisors "an account of wine expended the third and fourth days of October last when his Excellency the Governor was in Kingston to the value of at least £3." The supervisors did not allow this bill, thinking no doubt that if he was disposed to feast the Governor he should not ask the county to pay the bill.

The next year, in 1711, Col. Beekman is allowed a charge of £5 for a present to the Esopus Indians. In 1713 Major John Hardenbergh is allowed £1 16 shillings for a present to the Indians and Frederick Van Vliet is allowed £1 for five days spent in going to the Indians. In 1714 he is allowed a charge of 10 shillings for going to the Indians.

In 1714 Abraham DuBois, the last survivor of the Patentees, represented New Paltz in the Board of Supervisors. Evert Wynkoop represented Kingston, Matthew Ten Eyck represented Hurley and Capt. Thomas Garton Marbletown. This year the Supervisors decided that they would pay Col. Henry Beekman for his expenses in coming and going, while he was serving as representative in the colonial legislature, but not for the time while there. Col. Beekman asked that if the charge were not paid by the king if it might be promised by the Supervisors, but they decided that it was not "cognizable" so far as they were concerned.

11

In this year, 1714, appears the first charge for laying out highways. The next year Joseph Hasbrouck of Guilford, Capt. Egbert Schoonmaker and Arion Gerison bring in a charge as commissioners for laying out highways. In the same year the Supervisors voted £100 for repairing court house and jail.

In 1716 Solomon DuBois of New Paltz killed no less than 12 wolves, for which he is allowed £7 4 shillings as bounty by the Supervisors. In previous years he had also headed the list as the foremost wolf killer in the county. In 1712 there were 21 killed in all, of which number 6 were slain by Solomon DuBois, 1 by his brother Abraham DuBois, 2 by Louis Bevier and 1 by Moses Cantain, who, about 1704, moved from New Paltz to Ponckhockie. In 1713 Solomon DuBois headed the list with 6 wolves killed and in 1714 he slew 5 and no other person more than 2. In 1717 he slaughtered 4 wolves, but this number was excelled by Jacobus Swartwout, who killed 6. Wolves appear to have been more numerous at New Paltz than elsewhere. The names of Daniel DuBois and Hugo Freer, Jr. appear among those killing wolves in 1717. The Dubois brothers, sons of Louis the Patentee, especially distinguished themselves as wolf hunters, the names of David DuBois of Rochester and Jacob of Hurley appearing on the list in 1717. In the latter case however the record says "killed by his negro."

The different towns in the county were represented in the Board of Supervisors in 1710 as follows: Kingston, Edward Whitaker; Hurley, Capt. Mattys Ten Eyck; Marbletown, Capt. Charles Brodhead; Rochester, Capt. Jochim Schoonmaker; New Paltz, Left. Solomon DuBois.

All the Supervisors with one exception are set down with their military titles.

The different charges against the county allowed by the Supervisors in 1710 are as follows:

Col. Beekman, services as representative £27			os	od
Capt. Garton, services as representative	27		0	0
Jean Cottin, county treasurer.........		2	9	0
David DuBois, killing 2 wolves.......		1	4	0
Gerrit Decker,	1	"	0	12	0
Cornelius Litts,	2	"	1	4	0
Jacob Vernooy,	1	"	0	12	0
Solomon DuBois,	2	"	1	4	0
Philip DuBois,	1	"	0	12	0
Peter Jansen,	2	"	1	4	0
Severyn Tenhout	1	"	0	12	0
Jan Werts,	3	"	1	16	0
Louis Bevier,	2	"	1	4	0
Aaron Genton,	1	"	0	12	0
Jacob Barentse, for ringing the bell...		2	5	0
William Nottingham, services as clerk.		9	15	6
Mattys Slecht		0	13	6
Bernardus Swartwout, 1 years service				
as messenger and 1 load of wood....		4	6	0
Total £95			2s	6d

In 1711 in addition to the usual charges Mattys Mattyson is allowed £5 for "making carriages for ye great guns."

In 1717 the towns were represented in the Board of Supervisors as follows: Kingston, Major Johannes Wynkoop; Hurley, Nicholas Roosa; Marbletown, Charles Brodhead; New Paltz, Joseph Hasbrouck; Rochester, Lieut. David DuBois.

In addition to the regular charges for wolf killing, etc., Evert

Wynkoop is allowed 12 shillings for half of vat beer for the Assessors and Tunis Tappan is allowed a charge for meat, drink and house room for the Assessors.

In the older books in the County Clerk's office are several records of matters of interest to New Paltz people as follows:

COULD NOT BUILD A CHURCH BY TAX

In 1716 an agreement was made by the New Paltz people to erect a new church edifice and this action was duly recorded in French in one of the old record books. Afterwards it was concluded that this agreement was not legal; so the church was built by voluntary contribution. The entry on the county record is marked "Cancelled," and four years later appears the following entry in English, signed by Abraham Deyo: I, Abraham Deyo, having caused a certain writing, made by the major part of the inhabitants of the town of the New Paltz concerning the building of a common house for the worship of God and other uses for the town, to be recorded and by experience have found that the said writing is and may be a breach of ye peace of said town, concerning said town house and ye building thereof, I do hereby order and direct the said writing to be cancelled on record as if it had never been.

WILLS OF EARLY NEW PALTZ PEOPLE

The oldest books of record have a few wills of New Paltz people, jumbled in with deeds and other legal papers. Among these wills are the following: of Louis Bevier the Patentee, in Dutch, dated in 1722; of Abraham Deyo, son of Pierre the Patentee, in French, dated 1725; of Andre LeFevre, eldest son of Simon LeFevre the Patentee, in English, dated in 1738; of Cornelius DuBois of Poughwoughtenonk, dated 1780; of Dan-

iel LeFevre of Bontecoe, dated in 1784; of Jacob I. Hasbrouck
of Marbletown, dated in 1818.

Other valuable ancient records concerning New Paltz people
in the County Clerk's office are quit claims, given by the children of Louis DuBois the Patentee to each other for their
shares in their father's estate in 1706; an acknowledgment,
dated in 1714, from Louis Bevier of Marbletown and his wife,
Elizabeth Hasbrouck, that they had received certain property
from Jacob Hasbrouck, Andre LeFevre and Louis DuBois,
executors of Jean Hasbrouck the Patentee; a deed, dated in
1704, from Moses Cantain of Kingston and Mary, his wife, to
Mattys DuBois.

The most interesting of these old records in our estimation
is a deed of gift, dated in 1705, from Anthony Crispell the
Patentee to his daughter Elizabeth, wife of Elias Uine (Ein),
of four lots at New Paltz: the first located on the south side
of the Paltz creek, between the Bontekous kill and a lot of the
heirs of Simon LeFevre; second lot lying on the south side of
Bontekou's kill, in an elbow called in Dutch ———— in heyning;
the third lot lying on the north side of the Paltz creek, between
a lot of Isaac DuBois and a lot of the heirs of Simon LeFevre,
on the side of the farthest Bontekou; the fourth lot lying on
the north side of the Paltz creek, opposite the house of Abraham Freer, in a half moon. This deed of gift further provides
that after the death of Elias Uine and his wife, Elizabeth Crispell, the property shall go to their descendants forever and shall
never be sold to strangers, but that it may be sold to descendants
of the said Anthony Crispell.

The foregoing record is specially interesting to the writer
because Bontekous kill, still known by that name, is the brook

in which, when a small boy he would stop to fish on his way home from school. The Eins still own and occupy the first mentioned of the four lots and the LeFevres still own and occupy the adjoining farm, on which Isaac, son of Simon the Patentee, located probably about 1718.

But the greatest value that attaches to this record is the fact that it shows that Abraham Freer, second son of Hugo the Patentee, as early as 1705 had moved from the village and built a house five miles north, near the northern bounds of the patent, directly across the Wallkill from the piece of lowland still called the Half Moon and owned by the Eins until about 1880. On this spot, about 200 yards south of the Bontecoe schoolhouse and about half a mile south of Perrine's bridge, still stands an old stone house, which may be the identical house built by Abraham Freer.

CHAPTER XVII

Signers of the Articles of Association

The descendants of all persons who signed the Articles of Association are admitted to membership in the Daughters of the American Revolution and other patriotic societies of the pres· ent day. The Articles of Association were adopted on the 29th day of April, 1775, ten days after the fight at Lexington, by the "Freemen, Freeholders and Inhabitants of the City and County of New York," and copies of the document were transmitted to all parts of the province of New York for signers. The language of these Articles of Association was very bold and shows a spirit of determined opposition to British tyranny. In the various towns in Ulster county most of the people signed the document. The heading was as follows:

ARTICLES OF ASSOCIATION

"Persuaded that the salvation of the rights and liberties of America depends, under God, on the firm union of its inhabitants in a vigorous prosecution of the measures necessary for its safety, and convinced of the necessity of preventing the anarchy and confusion which attend a dissolution of the powers of government, we, the Freemen, Freeholders, and Inhabitants (of the City and County of New York), being greatly alarmed at the avowed design of the ministry to raise a revenue in America, and shocked by the bloody scene now acting in the Massachusetts Bay, do, in the most solemn manner, resolve never to become slaves; and do associate under the ties of religion, honor, and love to our country to adopt and endeavor to carry into execution, whatever measures may be recommended by the Continental Congress, or resolved upon by our Provincial Convention, for the purpose of preserving our Constitution, and opposing the execution of the several arbitrary and oppressive Acts of the British Parliament, until a reconciliation between Great Britain and America on Constitutional Principles (which we most ardently desire) can be obtained; and that we will in all things follow the advice of our General Committee, respecting the purpose aforesaid, the preservation of peace and good order, and the safety of individuals and private property."

In New Paltz a meeting was held of which Nathaniel DuBois was chairman and Joseph Coddington was committee clerk. There were in all 218 signatures in this town to the Articles of Association.

The names of the men, descendants from early settlers at New Paltz, appear in the document as follows:

Abraham Deyo, Abraham Deyo, Jr., Simon Deyo, Simon Deyo, Jr., Christophel Deyo, Philip Deyo, Jonathan Deyo, Daniel Deyo, Henry Deyo, Jr., John B. Deyo, Johannes Deyo, Jr., Peter Deyo, Christeyan Deyo, Benjamin Deyo, Nathaniel DuBois, Louis T. DuBois, Jacob DuBois, Hendricus DuBois, Cornelius DuBois, Daniel DuBois, Isaac DuBois, Cornelius DuBois, Jr., Simon DuBois, Hendricus DuBois, Jr., Methuselem DuBois, Benjamin DuBois, Abraham DuBois, Andreus DuBois, Jr., Daniel DuBois, Jr., Andries LeFevre, Jr., Andries LeFevre, Jonathan LeFever, Isaac LeFever, Abraham LeFever, Daniel LeFevre, Matthew LeFevre, Solomon LeFevre, Nathaniel LeFevre, Petrus LeFevre, John LeFevre, Jr., John LeFevre, Roelif J. Elting, Abraham Elting Cornelius Elting,

Solomon Elting, Petrus Bevier, Samuel Bevier, Solomon Bevier, Jacob Bevier, Zacharias Hasbrouck, Jacob Hasbrouck, Jr., Petrus Hasbrouck, Joseph Hasbrouck, Benjamin Hasbrouck, Jr., Josaphat Hasbrouck, Jesaias Hasbrouck, Jacobus Hasbrouck, David Hasbrouck, Garret Freer, Jr., Petrus Freer, Simon Freer, Daniel Freer, Jr., Hugo Freer, Jr., Isaac Freer, Benjamin Freer, Jacob T. Freer, Paulus Freer, Jonas Freer, Jonas Freer, Jr., Joseph Freer, Johannes Freer, Daniel Freer, Johannes Low, Solomon Low, Jehu Low, Johannis M. Low, Isaac Low, Simeon Low, David Low, John A. Hardenbergh, Elias Hardenbergh, Peleg Ransom, John McDaniel (McDonald), Wm. Hood, Abraham Ein, John Terwilliger, Joseph Terwilliger, George Wirtz, Derrick D. Wynkoop, James Done, Abraham Donaldson, James Auchmoutie, Thomas Tompkins, Jedediah Deur, Zophar Perkins, Oliver Grey, Leonard Lewis, John Stevens, Daniel Fowler, Daniel Woolsey, Alexander Lane, Abm. Vandermerken, Michael Devoe, Richard Tompkins, William Reeck, Johannis Walron, Petrus Van Wagenen, Ebenezer Perkins, Johannes Eckert, Nathaniel Potter, Daniel Diver, Samuel Johnson, Ralph Trowbridge, and others whose names we do not recognize but who were probably residents in the territory in Esopus and Lloyd, then a part of New Paltz.

People of New Paltz ancestry signed the document in other towns of the county as follows:

Kingston—Joshua DuBois, Jeremiah DuBois, Jacobus DuBois, Samuel DuBois, William DuBois, Hezekiah DuBois, Johannis N. DuBois, David DuBois, Hezekiah DuBois, Jr., Johannes J. DuBois, Johannes DuBois, Elias Hasbrouck, Abm. A. Hasbrouck, Solomon Hasbrouck, Col. A. Hasbrouck, A.

Hasbrouck, Jr., Samuel Freer, Jan Freer, Solomon Freer, John Freer, Jacob Freer, Gerrit Freer.

Hurley—Johannes DuBois, Jacob DuBois, Jr., Hugo Freer, Jacob Freer, Jr., Benj. H. Freer, Hugo J. Freer, Jonathan Freer, Jecimia Freer, Samuel LeFevre, Simon LeFevre, Jacob LeFevre, Coenradt LeFevre.

Marbletown — Coenradt DuBois, David Freer, Philip B. Freer, Jacob S. Freer, Severyn Hasbrouck, John Hasbrouck, Isaac Hasbrouck, Jr., Joseph Hasbrouck, Jr., Jacobus B. Hasbrouck, Jacob J. Hasbrouck, Jacob I. Hasbrouck, Jacob Hasbrouck, Philip B. Bevier, David Bevier.

New Marlborough—Lewis DuBois, Henry Deyo, Senior.

Rochester, including Wawarsing — Jonas Hasbrouck, Johannes Bevier, Simon Bevier, Benjamin Bevier, Andrew Bevier, Abraham Bevier, Jacob Bevier, Coenradt Bevier, Solomon Bevier, Jesse Bevier, Josiah Bevier, Isaac Bevier.

CHAPTER XVIII

New Paltz in the Revolution

The volume published by the State in 1898 entitled "New York in the Revolution," contains the names of about 40,000 soldiers from this State. The list as published in the volume mentioned is unsatisfactory in not saying what towns the companies were from.

There were four Ulster Co. Regiments of militia.

The First Ulster county Regiment was sometimes called the Northern Regiment, and was drawn mainly from the northern part of the county. Johannes Snyder was colonel.

There are more New Paltz names in the Third Regiment, John Cantine of Stone Ridge, colonel, than in any other organization.

In the Fourth Ulster county regiment, appear also a large number of New Paltz names. Jonathan Hasbrouck of Newburgh, was colonel of this regiment, but owing to his ill health it was most of the time commanded by Lieut-Col. Johannes Hardenbergh, Jr., of Swartekill.

As to the names appearing under the head of "Land Bounty Rights," the following explanation is given: Toward the close of the war of the Revolution a bounty of "Land Rights" was offered to officers and men for two regiments to be raised for the defense of the state. A master or mistress who should deliver an able bodied slave to serve was entitled to one Right. By the act of 1778 each militia regiment was divided into classes of 15 men. When soldiers were needed to complete the regiments of the Line, otherwise known as Continentals, each class must within nine days furnish a man fully armed and equipped. If a class furnished a man it was entitled to a money bounty; afterward a land bounty was added.

There is no evidence from the state documents to show that the men who signed the Land Bounty Rights ever saw active service and Comptroller Roberts has published their names for whatever they may be worth. He says additional proof is required to show that any of the names that appear in the Land Bounty Rights are of men who actually served in the army. We find a large portion of the names that appear under the heading of "Land Bounty Rights" also appear in the names of the militia as elsewhere published.

It is not possible to tell from these records, as published, whether the men whose names are given below resided in New Paltz or other parts of the county, but their ancestors were New Paltz Patentees, the Eltings excepted:

1ST ULSTER COUNTY REGIMENT

Lieut., Anthony Freer.

Abm. Crispell, Jacob Crispell, John T. Crispell, Peter T. Crispell, Peter J. Crispell, Benj. Crispell, John J. Crispell, Jacobus DuBois, James DuBois, Wm. DuBois, David DuBois, James DuBois, Jr., James DuBois, Jeremiah DuBois, Johannes DuBois, John DuBois, John I. DuBois, John J. DuBois, John T. DuBois, Matthew DuBois, Robert DuBois, Wm. DuBois, Hendrich Elting, John Elting, Peter Elting, Peter Elting, Jr., Wm. Elting, Garret Freer, Abm. Freer, Benj. Freer, Hugo Freer, Jeremiah Freer, Jeremias Freer, Johanis Freer, Jonathan Freer, Peter Freer, Samuel Freer, Jacobus Hasbrouck, Daniel Hasbrouck, Jacobus Hasbrouck, Jr., John Hasbrouck, Jonathan Hasbrouck, Solomon Hasbrouck, Conrad LeFevre, Jonathan LeFevre.

LAND BOUNTY RIGHTS

Capt., Simon LeFevre.

Abraham DuBois, Cornelius DuBois, Hezekiah DuBois, Jacob DuBois, Johannis DuBois, Jr., Peter DuBois, Samuel DuBois, James DuBois, Joshua DuBois, Jacob Freer, Petrus Freer, A. Hasbrouck, Jr., Abraham Hasbrouck, Elias Hasbrouck, John Hasbrouck, Jr.

2ND ULSTER COUNTY REGIMENT

Capt., Matthew DuBois.

LAND BOUNTY RIGHTS

Isaac DuBois.

3RD ULSTER COUNTY REGIMENT

Capt., John Hasbrouck.

Lieuts., Jacobus Hasbrouck, Cornelius DuBois, Daniel Freer, Joseph Hasbrouck, Josiah Hasbrouck. Ensign, Levi Deyo.

Abm. Bevier, Abm. Bevier, Jr., Benj. Bevier, Cornelius Bevier, Jacob Bevier, Conrad Bevier, Matthew Bevier, Nathaniel Bevier, Petrus Bevier, Abm. Crispell, Henry Deyo, John Deyo, Simon Deyo, Abm. B. Deyo, Levi Deyo, John Deyo, Abraham Deyo, Jr., Ezekiel Deyo, Daniel Deyo, Isaac Deyo, Andrew DuBois, Asaph DuBois, Conrad DuBois, Daniel DuBois, Daniel DuBois, Jr., Hendricus DuBois, Henry DuBois, Isaac DuBois, Jacob DuBois, John DuBois, Jacobus DuBois, Mathusalem DuBois, Nathaniel DuBois, Wessel DuBois, Abm. Elting, Isaac Freer, Thomas Freer, Jacob Freer, Jr., Jacob J. Freer,

Jacob S. Freer, John I. Freer, Paulus Freer, Peter Freer, Joseph Freer, Sol. Freer, Jr., John Hasbrouck, Jonas Hasbrouck Solomon Hasbrouck, Benj. Hasbrouck, John Hasbrouck, Jr., Severyn Hasbrouck, Andries LeFevre, Noah LeFevre, Jonathan LeFevre, Solomon LeFevre, Matthew LeFevre, John LeFevre.

LAND BOUNTY RIGHTS

Andries Bevier, Benj. Bevier, Jr., David Bevier, Elias Bevier, Jacob Bevier, Jr., Johan. Bevier, Jr., Ph. D. Bevier, Samuel Bevier, Simon Bevier, Abm. Deyo, Henry Deyo, Jr., Levi Deyo, Luke Deyo, Simon Deyo, Abm. Deyo, Benj. Deyo, Christopher Deyo, Daniel Deyo, Hendricus Deyo, Johannis Deyo, Jr., Jonathan Deyo, Philip Deyo, Solomon Deyo, Andries DuBois, Cornelius DuBois, Garrit DuBois, Jonathan DuBois, Joseph DuBois, Louis J. DuBois, Samuel DuBois, Tobias DuBois, Abraham Ean, Rœlif Eltinge, Abm. Eltinge, Cornelius Eltinge, Ezekiel Eltinge, Hendricus Eltinge, Jr., Josiah Eltinge, Jr., Noah Eltinge, Thomas Eltinge, Benjamin Freer, Daniel Freer, Daniel Freer, Jr., Isaac Freer, Isaac Freer, Jr., Jeremiah Freer, Johannis Freer, Jonas Freer, Petrus Freer, Simon Freer, Solomon Freer, Jerry Freer, Jr., Nathaniel LeFevre, Abm. LeFevre, Andries LeFevre, Andris LeFevre, Jr., Daniel LeFevre, Isaac LeFevre, Jacob LeFevre, Johannes LeFevre, John LeFevre, Matthew LeFevre, Nathan LeFevre, Peter LeFevre, Jr., Petrus LeFevre, Philip LeFevre.

4TH ULSTER COUNTY REGIMENT

Cols., Jonathan Hasbrouck, Johannes Hardenbergh.
Quartermaster, Cornelius DuBois, Jr.
Capts., Louis J. DuBois, Jacob Hasbrouck, Jr.
Lieuts., Andries Bevier, Joshua DuBois, Abm. Deyo, Jr.,

Anthony Freer, Petrus Hasbrouck, Matthew LeFevre, Simon LeFevre.

Ensigns, Mathuselem DuBois, Nathaniel DuBois, Daniel Bevier.

Abm. Bevier, Cornelius Bevier, Daniel Bevier, Jonas Beviei, Nathaniel Bevier, Andries DuBois, Hezekiah DuBois, Jona- than DuBois, Nathaniel DuBois, William DuBois, Andries DuBois, Jeremiah Freer, John Freer, Conrad LeFevre.

LAND BOUNTY RIGHTS

Johannis Bevier, Jonathan Bevier, Hendricus Deyo, Louis DuBois, Wilhelmus DuBois, Petrus Eltinge, Benjamin I. Freer, Benj. T. Freer, Elisa Freer, Joannis Freer, Martinis Freer, Cornelius Hasbrouck, Isaac Hasbrouck, Jonathan Has- brouck.

In the Fourth Orange County Militia, Col. John Hathorn, Joseph Hasbrouck of Guilford was Lieut.-Col. John, Solo- mon and Noah LeFevre, all of Kettleborough, served in this regiment.

In the Albany County Militia appear the names of Lieut.- Col. Cornelius DuBois and Capt. Benjamin DuBois of Catskill.

John Freer was colonel of the 4th Dutchess Co. Regi- ment.

Peter and Simon Freer served in the 5th Dutchess Co. Regiment.

Abm. Freer, Jr., and Thomas Freer served in the Dutchess Co. Minute men.

In the 5th Regiment of the Line or Continentals Louis DuBois was colonel, Philip DuBois Bevier and David DuBois were captains.

Berthold Fernow, custodian of the department of manu- scripts at the state library at Albany published in 1888 as complete a list as could then be obtained of New York Revolutionary officers and soldiers.

In the list we find the following names of people who were of New Paltz lineage:

Jonathan Hasbrouck, Col., 4th Regiment, Ulster county militia.

Abraham Hasbrouck, Lieut. Col., 1st or Northern Regiment, Ulster Co. militia, October 25, 1775; Col. same Regiment elected February 13; Commander February 20, 1775.

Elias Hasbrouck, Captain 3d Regiment New York Line, June 28, 1775; Captain of a company of Rangers in 1777.

Zachariah DuBois, Major Cornwall Regiment Orange County militia.

Simon LeFevre was reappointed 1st Lieutenant, 7th Company, 1st (or Northern) Ulster county Regiment, May 28, 1778, Captain same Company, vice Gerardus Hardenbugh, resigned October 23, 1779.

The following commissions at the dates given were issued to Lewis DuBois, of Marlborough.

Lewis DuBois, Captain, 3d Regiment N. Y. Line, Dutchess county Company, July 3, 1775; Captain, 4th Ulster county militia Regiment South District New Marlborough Precinct, Sept. 20, 1775; Major, N. Y. Line, Feb. 9, 1776; Colonel 5th Regiment, N. Y. Line, June 25, 1776, resigned Dec. 22, 1779, upon reduction of regiment.

THIRD REGIMENT, ULSTER CO. MILITIA.

COMMISSIONS ISSUED OCT. 25, 1775.

1st Company—Captain, Lewis J. DuBois; 1st Lieutenant, John A. Hardenbergh; 2nd Lieutenant, Matthew LeFevre; Ensign, Mathusalem DuBois.

2d Company—Captain, Jacob Hasbrouck, Jun.; 1st Lieutenant, Abram Deyou, Jun.; 2d Lieutenant, Petrus Hasbrouck; Ensign, Samuel Bevier.

Third Company, no names given.

COMMISSIONS ISSUED FEB. 21, 1778.

Jacob Hasbrouck, Jun., promoted Major, Vice Joseph Hasbrouck, Lieutenant Colonel, February 21, 1778.

1st Company—Captain, John Hardenbergh; 1st Lieutenant, Jon'n Terwilliger; 2d Lieutenant, Daniel Frere; Ensign, Levi Deyou.

2d Company—Captain, Abr'm Deyou; 1st Lieutenant, Petrus Hasbrouck; 2d Lieutenant, Samuel Bevier; Ensign, Joshuah Hasbrouck.

COMMISSIONS ISSUED FEB. 17, 1780.

Second Lieutenant, Josiah Hasbrouck vice Bevier, declined; Ensign, Petrus Bevier.

In Col. John Cantine's Regiment, 3d Ulster Co. militia, 2d New Paltz Company served Jonathan LeFevre, John LeFevre, John A. LeFevre, Matthew LeFevre, Philip LeFevre, all privates. Noah LeFevre was Sergeant in Brodhead's Co., Hathorn's Regiment, Orange Co. militia.

CHAPTER XIX

Col. John Cantine of the Third Ulster County Militia was ranking officer in 1778 in the Rondout Valley, which was then the frontier and exposed to attacks from the Indians, who would travel hundreds of miles to obtain scalps and plunder and spare neither age nor sex. Col. Cantine lived near Stone Ridge. His father, Peter Cantine, was a native of New Paltz; his brother Matthew was a member of the Council of Safety; his sister Catharine was the wife of Daniel LeFevre of Bontecoe. There were more New Paltz men in this regiment than in any other. The First and Second companies were officered altogether by New Paltz men.

Joseph Hasbrouck of Guilford was lieutenant colonel in this regiment; Jacob Hasbrouck, whose residence was in what is now the Memorial House in this village, was a captain in this regiment and afterwards a major; his son Josiah in 1780 received a commission as second lieutenant in this regiment. In this regiment also Abraham Deyo, who lived on Huguenot street, where Abm. Deyo Brodhead now lives, was captain of the Second company; Petrus Hasbrouck, who lived about three miles north of this village, was first lieutenant. In the First company Lewis J. DuBois, whose house is still standing on the east side of the Libertyville ford, was captain; John A. Hardenbergh of Guilford was first lieutenant; Matthew LeFevre of the Plains was second lieutenant; Mathusalem DuBois of Nescatack was ensign. Matthew LeFevre's brothers John and Jonathan were privates in the Second company and likewise their cousins, John A. and Philip LeFevre of Kettleboro.

Col. Cantine's Letters to Gen. Clinton

From letters to Gen. Clinton, which are now published, it is evident that his own regiment and the First Ulster Co. Regiment, sometimes called the Northern Regiment, which was commanded by Col. Johannes Snyder, were both stationed in the northwestern part of our county.

The time when these letters was written was about a year after the surrender of Burgoyne at Saratoga, after which there were no important battles in this state. But, as will be noted from the letters, the First and Third Ulster County regiments, commanded respectively by Cols. Snyder and Cantine, were required at these stations on the western frontiers of Ulster and Orange counties, Col. Cantine being in command, not only of his own regiment, but of all detachments of militia in actual service on the frontier, including, not only the two Ulster county regiments mentioned, but detachments from the regiments of Colonels Woodhull, Hathorn, Newkirk, Hasbrouck and Tusten. These were all Ulster and Orange county men. They were all needed to protect the frontiers from the attacks of tories and Indians. Their task was especially disagreeable, because it was not known at what moment a force of savages might swoop down on the scattered habitations.

In a letter to Gen. Clinton, written July 11th, 1778, Col. Cantine says:

"The men from Ulster County are posted, 40 at Mememacoting, 130 at Hunck, 80 at Great Shandaken, and at Little Shandaken the whole of Col. Snyder's regiment, which Returns I have Not as yet had. The Whole Will amount to about 400, a Number Quite Sufficient, I believe, to Defend posts at present where the proportions But Equal out the Different Regiments. This moment I am informed by Col. Newkark that Several of the Orange County men are on their Way to Peenpeck and Minsinck. I have sent Detachment from the Different posts to the Delaware. With orders to act against those who are taken an active part against us as Enemys, Leaveing others Unmolested, excepting those In whose possession the goods robbed from the Inhabitants of the frontiers Should Be found.

Have also at the unanimous request of the inhabitants of Lurienkil, Naponagh, Warwasinck and the Southern part of Rochester, Changed my post from Lackawack to this place (Honck Falls), finding it much more Convenient for keeping out Scouts and patroling parties, as the Woods on Both Sides of Lackawack are Exceeding Rof that it is Impossible to keep out Scouts at any Distance there. By the Last Returns of Col. Newkark, of the Orange County at Peenpeck and Minisinck, there where about Ninety men (that is) Eleven from Col. Woodhull's, fifty-nine of Col. Heathorne's, twenty of Col. Tusten's."

MONEY PROMISED WHEN HE WAS APPOINTED AT NEW PALTZ

In a letter written at Rochester, Aug. 19, Col. Cantine says:

"I would Not have Changed my post from Lagawack to Hunk if It had Not Been at the Unanimous Request of the Inhabitants Concerned. Not But I judge that Lagawack would have answered the purpose as well as Hunk (Except) that of Keeping out Scouting parties mentioned in my Last and the additional Expense of getting up supplys for the Regiment.

The Little money I was able to advance was soon Expended in Supplying the Regiment and Col. Newkark makeing Application to me for money in favour of the men he had employed to provide for the party at Peenpack and Minisinck till Such Time as it would be in the power of the Commissary to Supply them and that he could Buy much Cheaper for Cash; and as Your Excellency may Remember of Signifying at the time of my appointment, at ye New Paltz, to give me an order on the treasurer for that purpose, I haveing my promises, on the Exspective of Being Supplyed In that manner and therefor would have been glad to have Received the order. But as it would take us out of the Common Course of Business I Shall Endeavor to Do without it.

MURDER BY INDIANS

In a letter, from Col. Newkirk, forwarded to Gen. Clinton by Col. Cantine, it is stated that about 20 Indians and one McDonald, a Tory, had come to the house of one Brooks, took the whole family, 11 in all, as prisoners, murdered and scalped one who was wounded and carried off the rest.

ESCAPED FROM INDIAN CAPTIVITY

Another letter from Cantine to Clinton relates the wonderful story of the capture and escape of George Andries and Jacob Osterhout, who were captured by the Indians under a Mohawk chief and were carried almost to Fort Niagara; then at night while the savages slept Andries made a desperate attempt for liberty, got an ax with which he killed the three Indians who composed the party together with two squaws, who escaped. Andries and Osterhout got back to Ulster county in 19 days, almost starved. With the letter to Clinton is enclosed the affidavits of Andries and Osterhout, giving a full account of their escape from Indian captivity.

Paying His Men

In regard to paying his men Col. Cantine writes:

Your Excellency will readily conceive that the making of monthly pay abstract for this Regim't will be attended with many Difficulties, when you consider that the monthly Detachment of the Different Regim'ts, of which this is composed, Do commence at Different Days. I, therefore would be glad to Draw a Sum of money in order to pay off the different companies as their time expires, making an abstract of the whole at the time when I shall be Discharged, and then account for the sum drawn.

Cowardly Behaviour of Orange County Militia

In a letter written from Marbletown to Gen. Clinton, Aug. 28, 1778, Col. Cantine says:

I also had Information of the Unsoldierly Behaviour of the troops at them posts, which Caused my Going their to inquire into the matter which, haveing Done, I found that also to Be true. Capt. Miller, of Col. Heathorn's Regiment, haveing evecuated his post, on the freevilous Report that two Indians haveing Been Seen By some of his Scouts, which had Been out a few miles into the woods. He went off in Such a Hurry as to leave his Bread in the oven and his Beef in the well. Notwithstanding he was in a fort which, with the men he had in it, might In my opinion have Been Defended against five hundred men. Lieut. Tryon, of Col. Ellison's Reg't, Hearing that the enemy was back of Jacob Dewitt's mill at the time Mr. Brooks' family was tacken, Run of, saying Every man for himself and God for us all, and went of with the greater part of his company, not Returning till the next day—if my information is Right. The conduct of these 10 men appeared so scandalous that I could not avoid laying them under Errest and ordered them to Repear at the court martial at Goshen on the 25th instant.

200 INDIANS REPORTED—MAN SHOT

The guard from Shandaken haveing fetch Down the Inhabitants of Packatacan with some of their Effects, Returned on the Evening of the 26th Instant. Petter Hendrics, who left their, Came down Immediately after them with the following information that Harmania Dumon was going to his place at Pancatack and meet the guard Comeing from there about five miles from it. Dumon proceeded on to his house, Loaded his wagon with his effects, and on his Return about two miles from his house was shot through the Belly. Peter Hendrics further Says that there was two Hundred of the Enemy and few Cattle that Seame to have Been Left was all taken.

TIME OF SOME OF COL. JONATHAN HASBROUCK'S MEN EXPIRED

As the time of Capt. Conklen—who Lays at that post—of Colo. Hasbrouck's Regim't, is Expired to Day and No Relief is yet Come to that place, I, with the advice of Coll Pawling, Called some of my own Regim't to fetch down Dumon as well as to Distroy ye provision on that place agreeable to yours on the 22d.

GEN. CLINTON REPLIES

In a letter to Col. Cantine, written at Poughkeepsie, Sept. 6th, 1778, Gov. Clinton speaks of the recent burning of three houses and the killing and taking prisoners of men on the frontier and says:

This Mischief, if I understand the Geography of the Country

and am not mistaken as to the particular Situation of the above
.Persons' Habitations, might have been prevented had your
Guard occupied the first Post at Lackawack.

PLUNDER BY THE MILITIA

Gen. Clinton says moreover in another letter :

I am much surprised to learn that the Parties of Militia
which have been sent out to the settlements on the Delaware to
remove the Cattle and Effects from thence and thereby prevent
their serving as Supplies to the Enemy, have considered what
they have brought off as Plunder and accordingly appropriated
the same to their own use.   Upon what principle or by what
authority this is done you best know.   This is contrary to every
Idea of Justice and good Policy and will be productive of much
Mischief is certain.   I am bound, therefore, to call upon you to
exercise your Authority as Commanding Officer of the Detachments of Militia in actual Service on the Frontier of Ulster
and Orange Counties not only to prevent the like abuses in
Future, but to have the past to be rectified as far as may be
in your Power.

I am fully convinced that we are not to have Peace on our
Frontier until the Straggling Indians and Tories who infest it
are exterminated or drove back and their Settlements destroyed.
If, therefore, you can destroy the settlement of Acquago it will
in my opinion be a good Piece of Service.

Shortly afterwards in September Clinton writes to Col.
Cantine that he has received a petition from inhabitants of
Marbletown, asking that a guard be stationed on the frontier
of that town to scout north and south and stating that he
favored granting the petition provided he (Col. Cantine) approved it and could spare the men.   He advises him to confer
with Judge Pawling in reference to this matter, asks his opinion

as to the number of men needed to proceed against the Indian town of Ocquago and says that he approves of offering a reward of $100 for the capture of Middagh and Parks, through whose agency much mischief had been done.

A week afterwards Còl. Cantine writes to Clinton that he had received information, supported by affidavits, that Brant the Indian leader, was on the war path, with a force, variously estimated at from 200 to 450, that he has visited German Flats and Unadilla and it was reported would strike a blow somewhere in this quarter. As his men are not acquainted with the woods he asks for authority to employ one or two spies to go as far as the Delaware and give timely notice of the coming of Brant's savage warriors; he thinks that 600 or 700 men would be needed to attack the Indian town of Ochquago. He adds: But as my Regt. now Stands it is not in my power to undertake an Expedition of that nature, as the Reliefs are Comeing and going every week in the month. I have consulted with Judge Pawling But he thinks it will not answer with militia, as they are called out in classes, as many are men you can not depend on unless the number be greater than I mentioned.

On the 21st of October Gen. Clinton writes to Col. Cantine that Gen. Washington has sent him information, corroborating that from other sources that the Senecas and other tribes of Indians are prepared to attack the settlements. He considers Minisink in the most imminent danger and says that Col. Cortlandt's regiment is on the way from Peekskill to Rochester and that his brother's whole brigade will probably be sent out for duty on the frontier; but as it will be some time before they arrive a greater proportion of militia should be called into the service.

On the 22nd of November Gen. Clinton writes to Cantine from Po'keepsie that he had received a letter from Col. Cortlandt (who it is evident had then arrived with his regiment) that it would now be safe to allow the militia in actual service on the frontier in Ulster county to return home except about 70 to be stationed as follows: 2 officers and 25 men at Shandaken, 1 officer and 10 men at Yeugh's creppelbush, 1 officer and 10 men at Queens kill, 2 officers and 20 men at Mamakating. Gen. Clinton says: As I am extremely desirous of making their Duty as little burthensome as may be consistent with the safety of the frontier settlement, it is therefore my desire that you dismiss for the present all but the above number.

Next on the file is a letter dated Dec. 13, from Capt. Wm. Johnson, who was a Mohawk chief, and three other chiefs, threatening vengeance in case the people on the Delaware above Econack were molested.

April 21st, 1779, W. Malcolm writes to Gen. Clinton from Minisink that as his regiment has been incorporated with Spencer's all his officers except two or three have resigned and he shall do so too; moreover that the frontier is now unprotected; worst of all about 40 savages have attacked Lacawack and burned the place and houses within 13 miles of the River.

On the 25th of April Col. Cortlandt writes from Rochester to Gen. Clinton that he had received orders from Gen. Washington to march his regiment immediately to Minisink and he supposes he will go to Wyoming; his absence will leave the frontier unprotected.

Two days later, April 27th, 1779, A. De Witt, John Brodhead and 64 other citizens, writing from Rochester, send a petition to Gen. Clinton stating that Col. Cortlandt (who had been protecting the frontier) had received marching orders from Gen. Washington and asking that a sufficient guard might be furnished to protect them from the savages.

On the 29th of April Clinton writes to Cortlandt wishing

him an agreeable march and stating that he had ordered a fourth part of Col. Cantine's and a fourth part of Col. Snyder's regiments to occupy the posts that he (Cortlandt) now holds, until he can relieve them by the levies intended for the defense of the frontier, not yet completed.

On the 4th of May Col. Cortlandt writes to Gen. Clinton that just as he was marching his regiment he received an account of the burning of several houses at the Fantine kill. He marched to intercept the enemy, whom he saw, but could not surround, as they were on a mountain when discovered. They had burned four houses and killed 6 persons and perhaps 3 or 4 more. They had not killed any of the soldiers, nor had the soldiers been able to kill any of the Indians, though they exchanged shots with them at a long distance. The Indian band was thought to number 30 or 40. As he (Cortlandt) was under the most pressing orders to march with all expedition he forwarded this letter by express. He said in closing that Col. Cantine had gone to Lackawack and that he thinks not over 50 of the men whom Gen. Clinton had ordered had as yet arrived, although more might come the next day.

In this attack the Indians murdered Mrs. Isaac Bevier and her sister Mrs. Michael Sax and others, some 8 in all. A number of neighbors fled across the mountain to Shawangunk.

The next day Gen. Clinton writes to Cortlandt that he had ordered out one fourth of Hardenbergh's regiment and one fourth of McCloughry's regiment to join Cantine and a like proportion of the three northern regiments of Orange county to such posts on the frontier of that county as the commanding officers shall deem best; the same day Clinton writes to Cantine that he has ordered one fourth of Hardenbergh's regiment and one fourth of McCloughry's regiment to march immediately and put themselves under his command.

Indian Villages Destroyed

In the summer of this year Gen. Clinton's advice that it was necessary in order to have peace on the frontier that the Indian settlements should be destroyed was fully carried out. Gen. James Clinton with five New York state regiments united with Gen. Sullivan and routed the Indians under their celebrated leader Brant, near Elmira, with little resistance; then burned their villages and destroyed all food supplies. In this expedition into the Indian country in what is now central New York Col. Lewis DuBois bore an important command.

Still Another Attack on Wawarsing

In 1781 another and the last attack was made on the Wawarsing settlements, a large force of Indians being fitted out at one of the northern forts under command of one Coldwell. Five or six houses at Wawarsing were burned by the savages. The inhabitants defended themselves with great bravery. A force of about 400 men, under Col. John Cantine, started the next day in pursuit, but gave up the chase without capturing any of the savages.

A full account of the Indian forays in Wawarsing was published in pamphlet form in 1846 by a member of the Bevier family.

Capt. Abm. Deyo's Men

Among the old papers preserved in the Deyo family at New Paltz, is a pay roll dated Sept. 19th, 1778, and signed by 23 men, acknowledging that they had "received of Capt. Abraham Doiau our respective wages and billeting money for one month's term of duty at the Frontiers. (parts of months of July and August, 1778)."

Among the 23 signatures are those of Isaac DuBois, whose home was the Old Fort on Huguenot street and Zachariah Hasbrouck, who lived in the old stone house, across the street from the Reformed church. The name of Abraham Ean of Bontecoe also appears among the signers.

These men were certainly with Col. Cantine. They were apparently called out for one month only and then allowed to return to their homes. From one of Cantine's letters to Clinton it is evident that the different companies from various regiments came in at different times.

CHAPTER XX

HISTORY OF FARMING AT NEW PALTZ

The history of farming in Ulster county practically begins at about the time of the settlement of New Paltz in 1678. Kingston was settled about a score of years earlier, but we have reason to believe that trading with the Indians for furs, was until about this time one main occupation of the people, though wheat was grown to quite an extent.

The Indians of the Atlantic States raised corn, beans and pumpkins and the savages who came on board the vessel of Hendrick Hudson as he sailed up the North River traded with the crew for corn and beans. Do any of my readers as they make or eat the soup of sweet corn usually called "ogreeches" ever consider the origin of the word? It is not English or Dutch or French. But undoubtedly both the name and the dish itself were from the Indians. We have not found any one outside of Ulster county who knows what ogreeches means.

In the grant of the patent of New Paltz by Gov. Edmund Andross we find that he required from the patentees the payment of an annual rental of "five bushels of wheat, payable at the Redoubt at Esopus to such officers as shall have power to receive it." Wheat, then, was the staple product of the early settlers. One of the first sales of land in this vicinity, of which we have any record was in 1699, when Antoine Crispell, one of the Paltz Patentees sold to Louis Bevier, another of the Patentees, his share (one twelfth part) of the land already divided in the immediate vicinity of this village. The price paid was 140 schepels of wheat. Wheat then was not only the staple crop but, to some extent, the substitute for money in commercial transactions.

In another sale of land at New Paltz in 1693 we find the payment made partly in wheat and partly in flax seed.

The annual rental of five bushels of wheat for the tract of about 36,000 acres, included in the Paltz Patent, was, we are told, always paid promptly and it is related that the Freers for paying the rent, one year, without help from the other members of the little colony, received a tract of land at Mud Hook in the north-west bounds of the patent. Even this small matter of five bushels of wheat may have seemed no trifle to the handful of settlers during the first few years, when but a small clearing had been opened in the wilderness.

The progress of agriculture and the growth in population were very slow in the century that elapsed from the first settlement until the time of the Revolution. Here and there, along the streams, the sons and grandsons of the early settlers, at Kingston and New Paltz located and opened clearings.

About 1720 Jacob Freer, Hendrick Deyo and Isaac LeFevre, son of Simon LeFever the Patentee, located some 4 or 5 miles north of this village in the neighborhood still called Bontecoe. Abraham Freer, son of Hugo, located there previous to 1705. The land in that locality was famous, in those days, for the production of wheat.

The land at the first settlement was of course, all owned in common. There were divisions of land, in the Patent, at least two different times.

There was little sale of land in those old colonial days and the price was almost nominal. When Matthew LeFever moved from this village and located at Bloomingdale, in the present town of Rosendale, about 1740, he paid $700 for 700 acres of land. The farm lately owned by Abm. V. N. Eltinge along the turnpike, directly east of this village, was purchased by his great-grandfather, Roelif J. Elting, about the time of the Revolution, for $2.50 an acre, and tradition still preserves the fact that he thought he was compelled to pay an exhorbitant price. In the early part of the present century, good upland in the towns of Marbletown and Rochester has been sold at less than 10 cents per acre. About 1830 good lowland in this county was worth $50 an acre. The farm of Lewis H. Woolsey consisting of 180 acres was purchased by his father about 1820 for $4000 —that is about $22 an acre. In the old days, shortly after the Revolution, there was little buying or selling of land or any thing else. The people manufactured their own clothing, out of flax and wool of their own raising, made shoes (few boots were worn) out of leather, tanned, to a great extent, by themselves, out of the hides of their own cattle. They raised their own grain. One of the chief employments of the young women was spinning. Agricultural implements were few in number as compared with the present day.

We must confess that as a general rule, the old people were not, apparently, inclined to over work themselves. Had they been bent in that direction the cellars of the old houses might have been dug deeper so that one would not have been obliged to stoop so much in entering them. To clear up a piece of forest to obtain a new field for planting, was quite an undertaking in the old days and an old story is still related that the owners of a clearing at the little falls in the Wallkill, about half a mile above our village, would bravely resolve, year after year, to clear up another patch of forest for planting but that finally they would give up the undertaking and again "plant the *Voltje*" (as the old field was called), which passed into a sort of proverb.

With the early settlers game and fish formed a considerable

part of the means of subsistence and the remains of some ½ a dozen ell-weirs are to be seen, in the Wallkill, between this village and Libertyville.

Slavery as it existed here and at the south in the old times doubtless prevented the whites from exerting themselves as they do at the present day. In 1755 there were 80 slaves, above the age of 14, owned in the precinct of New Paltz and Solomon DuBois and Abram Hardenburgh, who were the largest slave owners, each owned 7 slaves. An old gentleman in an adjoining town tells us that his grand-father owned about 20 slaves and that they did not do any more work than a few persons would do at the present day. It is related, that when the slaves became free in 1827 and the farmers' sons had to do the hard work themselves, which the slaves had formerly done at New Paltz, some of them died, as was thought from overwork, to which they had not been brought up.

Let us picture a farm scene at New Paltz in the colonial days, just before the Revolution. The farmer with his sons, and one or two of his daughters has been in the field husking corn, for it is an October day and the sun is setting, as the farmer jogs along homeward with his load of husked corn, and yoke of oxen, which his negro slave is driving. On the way they have taken good notice whether the colts and young cattle were to be seen, for in those days the stock was branded and ran at large in the woods and particularly good care must be taken of the sheep for up to the time of the digging of the D. & H. Canal, in 1826, the wolves would come on their long, stealthy marches from the wilds of Sullivan and work havoc among the flocks in the valley of the Wallkill. But our farmer is unloading his corn, which is carried up the stairs to the loft of the dwelling, which in the olden times served as a granary, and night settles down on the quiet scene.

13

The Poor Soil of Kettleborough

The traditions all agree that when the first settlers, Abram and Andries LeFevre, first located at Kettleborough, about 1740, the gravelly soil of that locality was considered very poor. But a new era was brought about in Ulster county about the time of Revolution, when the ravages of the Hessian fly made wheat growing unprofitable and corn became the popular crop. The corn from the valley of the Wallkill was marketed at Capt. Swart's, on the Strand, now called Rondout.

Clover and Plaster the First Commercial Fertilizers

The introduction of clover and plaster formed a great event in the history of farming in this region. This must have been very soon after the Revolutionary war, and they were first introduced in Kettleborough. The story goes that the sons of Abm. LeFever one of the two pioneer brothers in that locality bought the plaster at the Strand (Rondout) at the extraordinary price of $30 a ton and the clover seed at Newburgh at the high rate of $20 a bushel. But the investment proved a good one. The result was marvelous. People came a distance of over 20 miles to see the clover. Andries LeFever, the pioneer of Kettleborough, then a very old man, had not approved the large expenditure by his nephews in their new fangled farming, but when he came and gazed on the clover, he said that "now the reproach would be taken away from Kettleborough" and so it was. From that day to this Kettleborough soil has been considered as good as any in the county.

Ancient Names of Clearings on the Wallkill

At the close of the Revolutionary war very little of the upland in this town was cleared. The place had been settled over a century but the woodman's ax had found no sufficient incentive to destroy the forests except upon the lowland, along the Wallkill. One of the peculiarities of the old people was to give names to the small tracts of cleared land. These names were handed down from father to son and have only died out in the common speech of the people during the present generation. A very few can still tell the names of these tracts. The piece of lowland, just across the Wallkill from our village, on the left hand side from the present highway was called *Pashemoy*. This we believe included two fields, as the fences were of late. The piece of lowland just across the Wallkill on the right was called *Pashecanoe*. The lot on the left of the highway near Perry Deyo's was called *Tri Cor*. The tract on the other side of *Tri Cor* was called *A venyear*. Where the road forks to go to Butterville another tract of three or four fields was called *Rumpause*.

Up the stream, where the little falls still is, a cleared field on the east side was called the *Falls*. On the east side of the Wallkill, a short distance above the mouth of the Plattekill an old clearing is still called *Yonkers Hook*. On the west side of the creek the place where Mr. Blake now resides was called *Poughwaughhononk*. A little farther up, the next clearing, near where Libertyville now is was called *Nescatock*. Still farther up the Wallkill the next settlement, where the Hasbroucks located at an early date, was called *Guilford,* which name it still bears. Going down the stream again, the lot where the Normal School building now is, was called by the old people *Kill Bogert,* or Creek Orchard. West of the Church in this village, a tract was called *Ver Maucoslandt*. A tract of about 30 acres on the west side of the Wallkill near what is now the Jonas F. Atkins place was called by the old people *Humpho,* a name still applied to the brook, near by. Still farther down the stream four different tracts of good land in the bends of the Wallkill were called *Bontecoe, Klina Bontecoe, Grote Bontecoe* and *Bontecoe* in *Haning*. Still farther down, near Mud Hook, a tract was called *Sponza Zee,* or Spanish Sea. Again farther down the Wallkill, about one-fourth of a mile above Perrine's Bridge, a tract of about ten acres of very fertile lowland is called the *Half Moon* in a document dated 1705. This tract is still known as the Half Moon. It was owned by the Ean family from about 1705 until almost the present time.

Racing Horses

In the beginning of the last century fine horses were raised in this vicinity. These horses were, to a great extent, of Diomed, Durock and Messenger stock and were noted for their endurance as well as speed. An old gentleman, lately living in this village, at the age of 86, tells us that when he was a young man, he, with three others, raced their horses, all the way from this village to Perrine's Bridge and back by the Springtown road, a distance of over 12 miles. The Paltz Plains, which were in those days, unfenced and lying in common were the favorite racing grounds for young men, and many were the contests of speed, especially on election day.

Depression Among the Farmers

The war of 1812 was followed by a long period of great depression in farming. In an inventory taken about 1830 we find the highest price for a horse $80, the next highest $50, and a two year old colt $30. A yoke of oxen was valued at $40. The best cows at $15, other cows from $10 to $14. 28 sheep and lambs were inventoried at $35. Such were the prices in those days.

The Implements Used by Our Forefathers

The tools used by the farmers in the old times were blacksmith made, or made by the farmers themselves. The plows used by the old people had wooden mouldboards with steel shares. The harrows had wooden teeth. The introduction of the iron mouldboard plow marked quite an era in the history of farming, in Ulster county. But at first, this innovation was looked on with suspicion and the story is told that the farmers feared that the iron mouldboard plows would hurt their land. A Marbletown man tells a good story of the purchase of an iron mouldboard plow by a farmer and the interest with which its work was watched by a neighbor as it smoothly turned over the furrow of Marbletown lowland. The neighbor gazed and scratched his head, then exclaimed "Jakey, Jakey, do you think it will be good." Then continued, "Jakey, Jakey, don't you think it will hurt the wheat." Such was the distrust with which the iron mouldboard plow was greeted, and coming down to our own time, we may note that the introduction of the mowing machine, about 1855, was likewise viewed with apprehension, on the ground that it would injure the roots of the grass.

The New Paltz Turnpike

The New Paltz Turnpike was constructed, about 1830, and proved a great blessing to the farmers of the Wallkill Valley. Capt. Abram Elting was, at that time, and had been for some years previous, running a sloop from New Paltz Landing to New York. With the greatly improved facilities for getting produce to the landing as soon as the turnpike was built, the farmers, in all this region, became more prosperous. In those days flax seed was one of the chief articles, sent to New York by the farmers in this section. But the culture of flax was gradually abandoned. Dairying came to the front and the shipment of butter, calves, poultry and pork to New York became the leading industries with the farmers.

The building of the D. & H. Canal in 1826 made a fine market for oats. The culture of wheat had been abandoned long before; rye had taken its place, and rye bread was used altogether in farmers' families. It is within the memory of men now living when the first barrel of wheat flour was sold by a village merchant in this place.

CHAPTER XXI

New Paltz Village and Town in 1820

There were in the village in 1820 twenty dwellings, two stores, two hotels, two cake and beer shops, one blacksmith shop, one schoolhouse and one church.

Commencing on the northern limits of the village the house now owned and occupied by Abm. M. Hasbrouck, was owned by his grandfather Jacob J. Hasbrouck, who at about this time gave up this house and farm to his son Maurice and moved to Bontecoe, where he built a brick house and spent the remainder of his days on the farm now owned by his grandson Luther Hasbrouck. Coming on toward the village the stone house of Philip D. Elting was occupied by Roelif Elting, father of Ezekiel and Brodhead Elting, who lived and died at Port Ewen, and Daniel Elting, late of Ellenville. The parsonage was occupied by Dominie Bogardus. Where now is Huguenot Hall stood a house, part stone and part frame, occupied by Jeremy Low. Just north of the churchyard, as it is at present, was the blacksmith shop of Mr. Kilby, father of Jas. and Eb. Kilby. In the northernmost of the old stone houses on Huguenot street Mr. Selleck had a harness shop at about this time. Directly across the street in the north part of the present church yard stood an old stone house, owned and occupied by Andries DuBois. This was the original LeFevre house and was torn down when the brick church was built. The old stone church then occupied the site of the present brick church, which was built in 1839. The stone house of Isaiah Hasbrouck directly across the street from the church was owned and occupied by his grandmother "Mowche" Hasbrouck, who was a widow. The house next the churchyard on the south was occupied by Mrs. Lucas Van Wagenen, a widow, mother of Benj. Van Wagenen and great grandmother of Easton Van Wagenen. She sold cake and temperance drink. The Mary DuBois Berry place was owned and occupied by her father Daniel DuBois. The old stone house directly across the street was owned by Ezekiel Elting, and occupied by his son Jacob Elting, who afterwards moved to Clintondale. The house of Abm. D. Brodhead was owned by his great-grandfather Judge Abram A. Deyo, and occupied by Richard Hardenbergh, who leased the farm. His son Jacob, afterwards one of the most distinguished men in the state, was born in this house at about this time.

A few yards farther south, on the corner of the street, a shoemaker's shop and a harnessmaker's shop were located. There has been no building there for many years.

Across the street the building of Mrs. S. A. LeFevre, still sometimes called the "white store," was occupied for mercantile purposes by Cornelius Bruyn who afterwards went to Kingston and was for a long time the head of the Ulster County Bank. His brother DuBois Bruyn was with him in the store a portion of the time. Josiah DuBois, grandfather of William E. DuBois, lived directly across the street, in what is now the Memorial House. In this building he had formerly kept a store with his father-in-law, Col. Josiah Hasbrouck. Col. Hasbrouck had removed to the Plattekill. Mr. DuBois had given up the mercantile business and was occupying the building simply as a dwelling. Shortly afterwards Mr. DuBois removed to Pough-woughtenonk and built the brick house, now occupied by Capt. W. H. D. Blake, where he resided until his death. Passing by the old graveyard the stone house with a brick front now owned by Jesse M. Elting, was occupied as a residence by Ezekiel Elting, grandfather of Jesse Elting. The north room was used as a store. This building was erected in 1800.

Ezekiel Elting was probably the most extensive man of business in this place in 1820. He carried on the mercantile business in this building in partnership with his brother-in-law, Philip Elting, and in partnership with another brother-in-law, Peter LeFevre of Bontecoe he built the grist mill at Dashville in which his daughter, Mrs. Dinah Brodhead, carried on business for a long, long time afterwards. Geo. D. Freer of Libertyville has told us that, about 1825, when he was a small boy and lived with his father near Perrine's Bridge, he would drive the cows to pasture on a lot which his father owned a short distance north of the Simon LeFevre farm. Sometimes he would see Ezekiel Elting, then an old man, going with his team of gray horses from his residence at New Paltz to the mill at Dashville. He would take grain sometimes for the farmers to accommodate them and occasionally would deliver the flour, when on his return.

Across the street, lived a Mr. Jackson who employed two or three men in the business of making hats in a shop a little nearer the Wallkill. The Academy was not built until about 13 years afterwards. Just below the Academy grounds were the remains of the old bridge across the Wallkill, but at that time a scow was the only means of transportation across the stream. Not long afterwards the bridge was erected at its present location. Passing on to the locust grove, near the present bridge, Dr. Jacob Wurts lived in the house torn down about 1875. The next house farther south was that in which the Wurts family lately lived, which was occupied by tenants.

Going on still south there was no house until the Plains were reached. There Nathaniel LeFevre lived in the stone house torn down about 1885 by A. V. N. Elting. The Plains were all unfenced, lying in commons.

Coming back to the village Main street was not yet laid out. People crossing the Wallkill came around by the "white store" and up North Front street. The hotel property, corner of North Front and Chestnut streets, was occupied then and for a long time before and afterwards as a hotel by Samuel Budd, who likewise carried on the wagon making business. About 1858 this old building was replaced by the present structure. Chestnut street was not laid out until many years afterwards, when Solomon Elting, father of A. V. N. Elting, bought the *"scaup way,"* sheep pasture, and laid out the present street, and also the street that divides the property of J. J. Hasbrouck and Abner DuBois.

The old stone building now occupied by John Drake as a residence, was a school building then, as it continued to be until a recent date. The school at that time was taught by Moses Dewitt, father of D. M. Dewitt of Kingston. About the same time Burr Dewitt, a brother of Moses, also presided as a pedagogue and taught the young idea how to shoot. Adjoining the school house on the east, "Cookey John" Freer lived in the house torn down about 1880. "Cookey John" sold cakes, cider, etc. On the other side of the street was a frame tenant house.

Passing up the street where Mrs. Oscar C. Hasbrouck now lives, Jacob Terwilliger, an uncle of Nelson, resided. He afterwards moved to Ohio. There was no other building in this part of the village except what is now the Steen hotel property. Here a hotel was kept by Angevine Latten. Mr. Latten or his wife owned the land in the vicinity of the Huguenot Bank. Where Elias Coe's tenant house now stands in the rear of the trolley depot were several tall hickory trees.

Springtown in 1820

In 1820 Springtown was about as much of a village as New Paltz, each numbering about 20 houses. In those days the main thoroughfare from north to south ran through Springtown and this gave it great advantage over New Paltz. The stage line, which before the day of railroads, was a very important interest, ran on the west side of the Wallkill and stopped at Springtown. Here lived Judge Jonathan DuBois, who was county judge in 1821 and probably the most prominent man in the town at the time. At Springtown there was a scow and directly across the Wallkill, perhaps 100 yards from the railroad bridge, was a tannery carried on by Wm. McDonald. From this a road ran eastward and intersected the Middletown road near the Ean residence. About 1820 Ulster county had an agricultural society, of which —— DeWitt, of Rochester, was President, and at least one fair was held at Springtown.

In those days many droves of cattle and sheep and some horses would come from the north and the region about Lake Champlain and would pass through Springtown on their way to the New York or Philadelphia market. There was no ferry at Kingston or Poughkeepsie large enough to take droves of cattle across the river. The Poughkeepsie ferryboat was so small that a farmer going to that place had to unhitch his horses from the wagon. When the wind was not favorable the ferryman had to depend on his oars for motive power. This was before the days of the horse boat.

But to return to Springtown. Of course the numerous droves of stock made considerable business for the people along the line, in feeding man and beast. Accordingly we find no less than six houses of entertainment or taverns, between New

Paltz and Rosendale, by the Springtown road, as follows:
Frederick Stokes at what is now the Beaver place, Roelif Has-
brouck, Ezekiel Low and Abm. Traphagan, in Springtown;
Abm. DuBois in the old stone house about two miles north of
Springtown and Wm. Delamater at this end of the Rosendale
Plains. From this to Rosendale there were no houses.

Houses North of Our Village in 1820

Going north from the present corporate bounds of our village the first place was that of Philip Elting, who owned the
place now the residence of his grandson Sol. L. F. Elting.
Philip Elting was a man of extensive means and beside farming carried on the mercantile business in this village in partnership with Ezekiel Elting, who was his double brother-in-law,
each having married the other's sister. The next place on the
present highway was that of Elias Freer, who left a numerous
family of children, the last survivor of whom in this vicinity
was Peter W. A. Freer. Elias' father Jonas lived on the
eastern end of the same tract at Shivertown, in a stone house,
occupied in our day by his grandson Stephen Freer. Next to
the Elias Freer place came the farm of Joseph DuBois, afterward the Moses P. LeFevre farm. Next on the north came
the brick house now owned by the Terpenings. This is by
far the oldest brick house in the town. It was built in 1786
by Josiah Elting, brother of Philip, and in 1820 was occupied
by Abm. J. Elting, son of Josiah. Near the house stood a
saw mill, which was taken down about 1870. Going on to the
north we come next to the Ean place, still owned in the family.
The old stone house, still occupied as a residence, has on its
corner stone the initials E. E. (Elias Ean) and R. H. B. (Roelif
Hasbrouck) also the date of building, 1789. From Elias Ean,

senior, the farm descended to his son Elias and then to James
Ean. A curious feature of this place was the large stone oven,
6 or 8 feet square, which stood on a rock, directly across the
street from the house, and which was taken down some years
ago. When the bread was ready for baking it had to be taken
across the street to this oven.

From the Ean place a road ran westward to the McDonald
tannery and the scow ferry at Springtown. Nearly half way
on this road was the old stone house of Solomon Hasbrouck,
son of Abraham the Patentee. From Solomon the place
passed to his son John, then to John's son John and finally
became the property of the Eltings, who owned the farm adjoining. Charles Elting, brother of Abram J., occupied this
old stone house in 1820, but afterwards built a frame house
where his grandson Watson has lived of late. The old stone
house tumbled into ruins about 1860. Near by is an old barn
and a large graveyard in which a large number of the Middletown people of those days were buried. A little farther north
stands a stone house with slate roof, built not long before the
Revolution for Petrus Hasbrouck and afterwards occupied by
his son Samuel. This was in 1820 the home of Wm. W. Deyo,
whom the writer best remembers as superintendent of the Middletown Sunday school, thirty years later. Returning to the
present highway, 'Squire Philip Hasbrouck had a blacksmith
shop about 1820, which continued in use until about 1855.
The old Middletown school house, replaced by the present
structure about 1855, was a small, unpainted frame building,
a little north of the present location. The house just south
of the school house was owned a short time previous to 1820
by Elias Bevier, whose wife was the daughter of Petrus Le-
Fevre of Bontecoe. They moved west.

Northeast of the Middletown school house, on the farm of

his father-in-law John Waldron, lived Lawrence Hood, the ancestor of the Hood family. He died before his father-in-law, leaving two sons, John and Isaac. The farm passed from John Hood to his son Jesse, whose son lately owned it. Isaac owned the farm a short distance north.

BONTECOE IN 1820

Bontecoe has not changed so much since 1820 as some other parts of the town. At that time there were a number of Freers located on the northern bounds of the Paltz patent on both sides of the Wallkill. A little farther south were several members of the Deyo family, descendants of Hendricus Deyo. The southernmost of these farms was that of William Deyo. Next came the LeFevre tract. Grandfather Peter LeFevre occupied the old stone house still standing, which had come to him from his father Daniel. Besides carrying on the farming business, grandfather was a justice of the peace and was usually called 'Squire. The office was of considerably more importance than at the present day. Besides trying many important cases he performed duties now restricted to lawyers, such as the drawing up of wills. There was no lawyer in New Paltz until about 1870.

The next old stone house, also still standing, was that of grandfather's cousin, Major Isaac LeFevre, who built the house and resided in it for some time, but removed to Esopus at about this date. He was a noted surveyor and about all the work in that line in this part of the country was done by him. Next to the LeFevre tract came the Ean farm, then owned by Peter Ean. Crossing Bontecoe kill, there was a school house on top of the hill at about this date.

THE OLD LIBERTYVILLE MILL AS IT IS TO-DAY

LIBERTYVILLE IN 1820

In 1820 and until a much later date Libertyville was known by its old Indian name, Nescatock. Here Chas. DuBois long carried on the milling business and was a prominent man. At that time there were about as many people in the Libertyville neighborhood as at present and nearly all were DuBoises— descendants of the two brothers, Solomon and Louis, Jr., the original settlers there.

The mill at Libertyville was probably the first running by water power, in this portion of Ulster county, except the one in the Mill brook north of our village. Still there was not much difference in the date of the erection of the Libertyville mill and the one at Tuthill. The Libertyville mill was built before 1790, by Nathaniel DuBois, who was a bachelor, and from him it passed to his nephew Charles. The mill-house was rebuilt in 1804. At first there was no dam across the stream, but after the draining of the Drowned Lands, in Orange county the water in the stream got so low, in summer, that a dam had to be built. Nearly all the Paltz farmers brought their grain to the Libertyville mill and would some- times wait for it to be ground, sitting, in cold weather, by the blazing fire in the cellar kitchen, eating apples and drinking cider.

OHIOVILLE IN 1820

The New Paltz turnpike was not constructed until about a dozen years after this time. Going east from our village in 1820, the first house was that of Dr. Bogardus, where Jona- than Deyo now lives. Directly across the street lived John Terwillegar. Simon Rose, grandfather of Daniel Rose of this village, occupied the stone house now the home of Jacob

Champlin. A little further on the farm house, in which Levi Wright long resided, was occupied by Jacob Halstead and an old man named Van Aken, who wore knee breeches. Where Milton B. Hasbrouck now resides was a house and blacksmith shop where John DeGroodt carried on business. Just this side of Ohioville a hotel was kept by Henry Cronk. Ohioville in those old days was called H—l town, a name which stuck to the place until Moses Freer came back from Ohio and called it Ohioville.

HOUSES SOUTH OF OUR VILLAGE IN 1820

Passing on to the south from the present corporate limits of our village we have noted the old LeFevre house, built by Jean, son of Simon the Patentee, torn down about 1880. The next house in 1820 was that of Andries Deyo, now the Sprague place. This house was built in Revolutionary times by Andries Deyo's father, Philip. Andries had a large family of sons and daughters, of whom Solomon Deyo of this village is the only survivor.

Next to the Andries Deyo farm came the Edmund Eltinge farm of our day, which was owned in 1820 by Edmund's father, Peter Eltinge, who in 1826 built the present fine brick residence to take the place of the old stone house, which had burned down. The place came to Peter Eltinge from his father-in-law, Gen. Derick Wynkoop, who died about 1820.

Going on to the south there comes next the Cornelius Du-Bois, senior, tract of land, which requires some explanation. Cornelius DuBois, senior, of Poughwoughtenonk, son of Solomon, had left a landed estate of about 3,000 acres, lying on both sides of the Wallkill, and he had left a most singular will providing that his son, Cornelius, junior, should have the entire

14

real estate during his life time, but that after his death his other children or their heirs should have their proper share. Cornelius' estate included on the east of the Wallkill the tract now comprising the farms of Lewis H. Woolsey, Wm. F. Du-Bois, Solomon DuBois and C. L. Van Orden. Cornelius, senior, had a large family of daughters. When, after the death of Cornelius, junior, the division of the property was made, what is now the Woolsey farm fell to the share of the daughter Sarah, who had married Jacob Hasbrouck of Mar-bletown. The Hasbroucks sold the place to a man named Peltz, who sold it to Elijah Woolsey, about 1825, at the rate of about $22 an acre.

The farm now owned by Wm. F. DuBois was also a part of the Cornelius DuBois estate and passed in the division to the share of a daughter Catharine (in Dutch Tryntje), who had married Col. Jonathan Hasbrouck of Newburgh. It passed from her to her daughter Rachel, who married her cousin Daniel, son of Col. Abraham Hasbrouck of Kingston, and located at Wallkill, Orange county. Jonas DuBois, grand-father of the present owner, bought of Daniel Hasbrouck and wife of Orange county, in 1830, 102 acres, constituting most of the present farm. The place was all in woods with no build-ings and the price paid was $2,000 for 102 acres.

What is now the Solomon DuBois farm, 160 acres, in the division of the Cornelius DuBois estate fell to the share of the daughter Jemima, who had married Andries Bevier of Wa-warsing. Jacob G. DuBois purchased it of the Beviers about 1829, paying about $20 an acre. There was a house on the place occupied by Joachim Schoonmaker.

The next farm, now owned by C. L. Van Orden, has had a singular history from the fact that it has passed in each gen-eration for a century from one family to another in the female line and three of its owners were named Leah. In the division of the property of Cornelius DuBois, senior, this tract fell to the share of his daughter Leah, who had married Cornelius Wynkoop of Hurley. It passed to their daughter Leah, who married Dr. Dewitt of Rochester. Dr. Dewitt's daughter Jane married Henry Hornbeck, also of Rochester, and they came to live on the place. In the next generation it became the property of their daughter Leah, who married Alfred Deyo. About 1830 Henry Hornbeck built the house, which at the time was considered the finest residence between Goshen and New Paltz.

We have come now on the Kettelboro road to the LeFevre tract of 1,000 acres, originally a part of the Garland patent. The old stone house now owned and occupied by Nathaniel Deyo, was the residence in 1820 of Noah LeFevre, grandfather of Josiah LeFevre of this village. It came to Noah from his father Abraham, and it passed from Noah to his son Jonas.

What is now the Jansen Hasbrouck place was in 1820 occupied by John LeFevre, son of the pioneer Abraham. It passed from John to his son Matthew and then to Matthew's son John M., who is now living at Peekskill with his son Matthew J.

The next farm, now owned by J. Elting LeFevre of Highland, was owned in 1820 by his great-grandfather, 'Squire Johannes LeFevre, who built the present large frame house about 1816, intending it for his son, Andries J. The latter died in 1817 and 'Squire Johannes moved into the house himself, where he lived until his death, about 1840. The farm afterwards became the property of Andries J.'s son, Cornelius D., from whom it passed to the present owner.

The next farm was owned in 1820 by Jacobus LeFevre, a nephew of 'Squire Johannes. Jacobus built, about 1815, the frame house still standing. After Jacobus' death the farm was sold to divide his estate and became the property of Garret LeFevre and subsequently of John H. Wurts.

Next comes the farm, now owned by Albert Decker, which was owned in 1820 by Lewis LeFevre, a brother of Jacobus above mentioned. The house burned down about 1838 and was replaced by the present residence.

We have come now to the Deyo tract of 500 acres, which like the LeFevre tract was a portion of the Jas. Garland patent. The Daniel Bevier farm of our day was owned in 1820 by Daniel A. Deyo, father of Thomas J. Deyo of Wallkill.

Next comes the old stone house of Daniel Deyo, who was the ancestor of the Deyo family in this neighborhood. This house was occupied in 1820 by Jonathan, father of Dr. Abm. Deyo.

We have now come to Ireland Corners and to the southern boundary of the town of New Paltz as it was before the town of Gardiner was created.

BUTTERVILLE IN 1820

The neighborhood, now known as Butterville, about two miles west of this village, was not settled until about 1812. The old Dutch name of the locality was *"Oleynuit"* (Butternut), and was doubtless bestowed on account of the number of butternut trees in that region. Afterwards, on account of the number of members of the Society of Friends who settled in that region, it was called "The Quaker Neighborhood." The name, Butterville was given to the locality by S. D. B. Stokes in selecting a name for the Sunday school which he and others had organized in that locality.

One of the first settlers in this region was Abram Steen, the father of our informant, Peter Steen. He was the son of Michael Steen, who emigrated from Holland and settled near the Swartekill, in Esopus. Michael's sons were Jacob, Abram, Matthew and Thomas. Abram was the only one of these who located permanently in this vicinity. He married a Freer from Bontecoe and purchased the land on which he located at Butterville of Major Isaac LeFevre. At that time the country all the way over the mountains to the Philip Ayres place, near the Clove, was in woods.

At about the same time that Abm. Steen built his house a number of the Society of Friends located in the neighborhood. Mr. Peter Steen's recollections of these neighbors, as they were about 1820, were as follows:

Rowland DeGarmo, father of Wm. H. DeGarmo, late of Rondout, came from Dutchess county and located where Henry Vanderlyn afterwards lived. Here he long carried on the tanning business on quite an extensive scale. Merritt Moore, who afterwards moved to Poughkeepsie, lived on what was afterwards the S. D. B. Stokes place. Next came the houses of Isaac and David Sutton, who were brothers and also came from Dutchess county. Matthew DuBois lately lived on the place of Isaac and Mr. Holmes on the place of David Sutton. Isaac was the father of Isaac S. and Henry P.; David was the grandfather of Thomas Sutton of this village.

Gideon Mullenix came from Dutchess county, we believe. His house was the only one of stone. He resided where Timothy Benjamin lived of late. Wm. Minard came from Esopus. He lived on the clay hill, in a house torn down about 1845. Benj. Wood lived near Libertyville, on a place owned of late by Daniel I. Hasbrouck. Increase Green lived on the place lately occupied by Samuel A. DuBois. David Dickinson was another of the early settlers and lived in a log house.

Under Bontecoe Point lived Abel A. Ayers, where his father, Thomas, lived before him on a tract purchased of the Beviers in 1808 and here Abel's son, Thomas, afterwards lived. Benj. Roberts, father of the late William B. of Clintondale, lived on the other side of the mountain, just above the Clove.

DeGarmo, the Sutton brothers, Moore, Mullenix, Minard, Wood, Dickinson, Green, Ayres and Roberts were all Friends.

James Pine came some time after the first settlement from Honk Hill. He was also a Friend.

There was no school house at Butterville until about 1830. Before that time, Mr. Steen tells us, his brothers went all the way to a private school on the other side of the mountain where Philip Ayres of late lived.

About 1825 the road was laid out across the mountain from Butterville to Wessel Brodhead's near Alligerville. The state road was laid out from Peter D. LeFever's through Canaan to be out of the reach of high water in the Wallkill. It went through Butterville to Libertyville.

Abm. Steen, the father of our informant, carried on the nursery business quite extensively about 1830. He raised his own stock of apple, pear, peach, plum and cherry trees. At first he supplied only the neighbors, but there were few nurseries at that time and as its fame spread he supplied trees to parties in Orange, Sullivan and Dutchess as well as in Ulster counties. Once a customer came all the way from the Shaker commuity, near Albany, and took a large load of trees. Peter Steen did a great portion of the grafting for his father. About 1860 the nursery business was discontinued.

The Friends' meeting house, at Butterville was built about 1820. Besides those in the neighborhood, a family named Ballou would come all the way from Greenfield in Wawarsing to attend the meetings. The land on which the meeting house was built was given for the purpose by

Gideon Birdsall of Plattekill Valley. Abel Ayres was the only person residing in the neighborhood who frequently spoke in meetings. Speakers would come from other places. The division between the Orthodox and Hicksite parties made considerable feeling in the meeting.

All the people in the neighborhood were Friends except Abram Steen, Jonas Freer, Martinas Freer and a few others.

PLUTARCH IN 1820

In all the Plutarch neighborhood there were only two clearings in 1820. One of these was the home of Abm. J. Deyo, whose stone house, built in 1812, was quite certainly the last stone house built in New Paltz.

This section of our town was called by the old people Grawhow (in English Great Ridge), a name by which it is still sometimes called.

INDUSTRIES IN THIS TOWN IN 1820

Northeast of our village at about that time Isaac DuBois, grandfather of Isaac DuBois of Ohioville, had a grist mill where Wm. E. DuBois now lives. This mill of Isaac DuBois did but a small business, there being insufficient water.

In the old times hats were not all made in large factories as at present, but in smaller quantities. A man named Jackson carried on the hatting business for a time, in a shop across the street from the old graveyard, and had three or four men working for him. After a while he failed. Samuel Hasbrouck's oldest brother carried on the hatting business at Highland. At one time a man named Kellogg carried on the hatting business, about a mile north of the village.

At Rifton there was a carding and fulling mill, about 1810, before the grist mill was built at Dashville. Farmers would bring their wool there to have it carded and then their wives and daughters would weave and spin it. Some women would go from house to house as spinsters.

In those old days some farmers would tan their own sole leather, but the upper leather was manufactured at the tannery. About 1812 Wm. McDonald, a Scotchman, had a tannery and residence on the east side of the Wallkill, about 200 yards below the present railroad bridge at Springtown. A millstone still marks the site, but the buildings have disappeared and the land passed into the possession of Roelif Hasbrouck and subsequently of Charles Eltinge. McDonald's wife was a Krom, from Marbletown. After a while he sold the tannery and located just south of Perry Deyo's residence, on the road to Libertyville, where he built a house.

About 1815 Rowland DeGarmo, father of Wm. H. DeGarmo, came from Dutchess county and settled at Butterville, where he started a tannery and carried on an extensive business. In those days oak bark was used exclusively for tanning. He would send around his teams to the farmers at butchering time and gather up hides, which he would tan on shares.

In those days John Hait, father of Thad Hait, carried on the tanning business in Plattekill. There was a tannery at Centerville, and another which carried on a large business at the lower toll-gate on the Turnpike. Now there is not a tannery in Southern Ulster.

TEACHERS ABOUT 1820 AND EARLIER

We have found among the old papers information concerning only one schoolmaster during the Dutch-speaking period in New Paltz, that is from about 1750 to 1800. This was

Joseph Coddington, who was probably the ancestor of the Coddington family in Ulster county, though we have no information on that point. Joseph Coddington's name first appears on the church book in 1758, when he and his wife, Catharine Vandemark, had a child, Sarah, baptized. At different dates the baptism of other children are recorded. When the second stone church was built in 1771 Joseph Coddington performed a great amount of clerical work, every item of which is set down minutely in the church book and for which he charged £12 19s. In a document dated 1781 Jonathan LeFevre, grandfather of Hon. Jacob LeFevre, and his brother John leased for ten years to Joseph Coddington, schoolmaster, without any rent except payment of taxes, lots No. 15 and 199, being a portion of the 1,529 acres granted by letters patent to Noah Eltinge and Nathaniel LeFevre and being within the neighborhood annexed to New Paltz. Mr. Coddington was at that time becoming advanced in years and had probably concluded to give up his school, which must have been in the old stone building, now the John Drake residence, and end his days as a farmer. We have no further information concerning Joseph Coddington, nor have we any information concerning teachers at New Paltz in the period succeeding the Revolutionary War.

ALEXANDER DOAG

One of the most noted teachers in the Kettleborough neighborhood and elsewhere in southern Ulster in the early part of the last century was Alexander Doag. He was a Scotchman, educated at the University of Edinburgh and taught at Kettleborough for a considerable period, about 1815. Although a man of fine education he was a slave of the drink habit. Each morning, on arriving at the schoolhouse he would take a drink from a bottle in his desk. In his latter years fortune frowned upon him and he ended his days in our county poorhouse.

Gilbert C. Rice

A man of different type from Alexander Doag, at least so far as his habits was concerned, was Gilbert Cuthbert Rice, a young Irishman, who taught in different schools in this vicinity at about the same time as Doag. Rice was only about sixteen years of age when he commenced teaching in the Bontecoe neighborhood. He was a youth of great energy and determination, and, although his severity in school would not be tolerated at the present day, yet after teaching at Bontecoe he taught at Kettleborough and, perhaps, elsewhere in this part of the country. He was a Catholic in religion, but that did not prevent him from attending Protestant church service.

Miss Ransome

One of the first lady teachers in this part of the country was Miss Ransome, who taught the Kettleborough school for a long period, about 1825. Afterwards she married Henry G. DuBois and removed to Ohio. She was a lady of great tact and was greatly liked by the children and parents. She taught the girls to work embroidery as well as to understand the mysteries of arithmetic, geography, etc. The mother of the editor of the *Independent* had a sampler, which she worked when a little girl at school under Miss Ransome's guidance, and which a granddaughter now cherishes among her treasures. Very well, too, do we remember mother's advice when we started out as a lad of sixteen to teach a country school, that we should imitate Miss Ransome's method of governing a school, by judicious praise, which was indeed in striking contrast with the severity of her predecessor, Mr. Rice.

SKY TOP

This cut shows the lower portion of Sky Top, the south west corner of the Paltz Patent, called by the Indians Moggonck and by the old people Paltz Point. This cut shows also the Great Crevice and Table Rock, called by the old people Ephriam's Point.

PART II

HISTORY OF THE OLD FAMILIES OF
NEW PALTZ

CHAPTER XXII

THE FAMILY OF LOUIS BEVIER, THE PATENTEE

By Louis Bevier of Marbletown

When in 1628 the last of the Huguenot strongholds was taken by Richelieu, the Minister of Louis XIII, and some of the disheartened leaders in the Huguenot ranks abjured their faith and reentered the Church of Rome, the outlook of Protestantism seemed dárk and gloomy indeed.

But the mass of the Huguenots still held fast the doctrine of the Reformation until the oppression and exactions of an unfriendly and unscrupulous government became unendurable. Then those in the northern provinces of France took refuge in the adjoining Protestant lands.

Thus it came to pass that the Walloons escaped from their oppressors to the Palatinate. This movement began as early as 1640 and continued until 1670, and even later, and it was during this period that many of those Huguenots, who afterwards settled at New Paltz, found a temporary home in the Palatinate.

They all seem to have applied themselves to those industrial pursuits to which they had been accustomed at home, and thus became a valuable element among the people with whom they were sojourning.

In the Palatinate at the following dates, were:

Louis DuBois and family, 1659, at Manheim.
Jean Hasbrock and family, 1672, at Manheim.

Christian Deyo and family, 1675, at Mutterstadt.

Abm. Hasbrouck (probably), 1675, (his wife born at Mutterstadt).

Louis Bevier and wife, 1675, at Frankenthal.

Simon and Andre Lefevre, (probably) at Manheim.

Anthony Crispell, (probably) 1660.

The names in the above list with those of Hugo Freer, Abraham and Isaac DuBois and Pierre Deyo make up the twelve "Patentees," and it is reasonably certain that all of them were in the Palatinate just before their departure for Wiltwyck. It is certain that all of them were in Wiltwyck when, under the leadership of Louis DuBois, they secured the Patent from Gov. Andros in 1677.

In 1678 these men with their families proceeded to occupy the land and to build shelters for their families upon it on the site of the village, which, by general consent, they now named New Paltz, in fond remembrance of their first place of rest in exile from their native land.

Now the task of clearing and improving the land was begun, while title was held in common, no general division being made until 1703. The fact that no serious misunderstanding arose during nearly a quarter of a century of such joint occupancy should redound to the credit of this amicable and peace-loving community.

These settlers soon organized a French church at New Paltz in 1683, with Louis DuBois as elder and Hugo Freer as deacon, and having Dr. Daille as minister until 1696.

After a time they enjoyed the pastoral care of the ministers of the Reformed Dutch church of Kingston.

Louis Bevier, one of the twelve patentees named above, was born at Lille about 1648. In early manhood he embraced the doctrines of the Reformation, and, with his ardent temperament, he soon drew down upon himself so much opposition, and eventually persecution, that he could no longer remain in safety at home, so, with some Huguenot friends, he took refuge in the Palatinate, and settled near Frankenthal, in which vicinity he remained until 1675. In the meanwhile he connected himself with a Protestant church of that place, and in 1673 he married Marie Le Blanc, a member of a family of Huguenot refugees from his native place.

In 1675, being desirous to emigrate to New York in order to rejoin his friends and relatives who had preceded him, he obtained from the pastor of the church in Frankenthal a certificate stating that he and his wife were members in good and regular standing, and commending them to other churches of like faith.

Dated, Frankenthal, March 5, 1675.

H. Lucasse, Pastor.

William Gosse,
Andre Le Blanc,
    Witnesses.

The descendants of almost all of these Paltz Huguenot families have similar certificates still in their possession.

After coming to New York Louis Bevier remained with relatives until 1677, when he united with the other patentees in purchasing from the Indians the land for which they afterward obtained the Patent.

From the spring of 1678 he, with his fellow Patentees, remained here without any marked change for many years, and his children were born and reared in the faith of their parents, all of them being active in the maintenance of the

Protestant church, first in New Paltz and later in the several communities where they afterward settled.

In 1710, his wife being dead, Louis Bevier proceeded to London and procured his "Denization" papers qualifying him as an English citizen. He then went to France where, as tradition reports, he met with a rough reception, but, notwithstanding this, it is highly probable that his business was in part satisfactorily adjusted and that he recovered at least some of his property.

Coming home again to New Paltz he bought lands in Wawarsing upon which his sons Jean and Abraham settled, and he likewise bought the land at Marbletown upon which his son Louis settled in 1715.

Meanwhile his son Samuel occupied his lands at New Paltz, where he himself remained in his declining years, his other son, Andries, being in some manner disabled, remained with him, and his only living daughter was married to Jacob Hasbrouck, and settled at New Paltz.

Realizing that his end was near, on May 2, 1720, he disposed of all his real and personal estate by will, dividing it equally among his six children, deferring only so far to the custom of the times as to give to Jean one pound extra for his birthright.

A short time after this he died and was buried at New Paltz; his will was admitted to probate July 4, 1720.

Louis Bevier's children were:

1. Maria, born July 9, 1674, died in infancy.
2. Jean, born Jan. 2, 1676, married Catharine Montanye.
3. Abraham, born Jan. 20, 1678, married Rachel Vernooy.
4. Samuel, born Jan. 21, 1680, married Magdalena Blanshan.
5. Andries, born July 12, 1682, single, died 1768.
6. Louis, born Nov. 6, 1684, married Elizabeth Hasbrouck.

7. Esther, born Nov. 16, 1686, married Jacob Hasbrouck.
8. Solomon, born July 12, 1689, died in infancy.

The names of the children, with the dates of their birth, are found in the original record as made in French apparently by Louis Bevier himself on a fly-leaf of an old folio Bible still in our possession.

JEAN BEVIER

Two of the daughters of Jean Bevier perished with their families in the attack on the settlement at Fantinekill, made by the Indians under Brandt in 1779. These were Elizabeth, who had married her cousin, Isaac Bevier, son of Samuel, and Johannah, the wife of Michael Sax. The surviving descendants of Jean Bevier afterwards removed to the west.

Some years ago, in digging down the foundation of the old Bevier house near Napanoch, the fragments of a boy's diary were found in a recess which formed part of the chimney. These records were written by Cornelius, a son of Captain Andries Bevier, nephew of the murdered women. The translation is given below as it was sent to me:

"Went to Warwarsing with a load of rye to mill for father. Stopped at the tavern, took a drink and got some tobacco. Some of Captain Cortland's soldiers were there and drinking hard; some got drunk and they had to take their guns away; two of them tackled Tewn Osterhoudt because he wouldn't treat, but they were so drunk he throwed both of them and choked one of them pretty badly.

"Went to the fort with some potatoes. Sam went with me. Heard that Indian tracks had been seen above Honk Falls. Coon Bevier said he could overturn any living Indian, and hoped they would try and catch him.

"All woke up by guns. Heard them shoot towards Fantinekill. After breakfast saw smoke that way, like a building. Heard there were Indians. Jesse's dog came down here, and after a while Captain Cortland's soldiers came up and father went with them, with all the men toward Fantinekill and left us all alone. We heard them shoot after they had been gone about an hour and we heard the Indians yell, and then we all started for the mountain. Sam and I took the silver mugs, the spoons and some money, and started for the mountain. More than twenty people came with us because we knew the path over, and they all carried their best things with them. We stopped by the spring and looked down, and saw the fire at Mike Sock's and heard them shoot at Jesse's. Black Bob came up to us on the path. He said he had run from the Fantinekill, and that the Indians had killed them all. We all started on foot as we could go, and went along the mountain to Maratanza Pond, and then hid all the silver and other things we could in the sand, and then Sam and I went over to the home of Mentz and rested. Mrs. Mentz gave us some milk. They were all scared. When we got to the pond, we went to the edge of the rocks and looked again. All the fire was out except John Bodley's house, which smoked yet; we thought we could hear some shooting, but not sure. We went over to Shawangunk and told the people. Sam and I were barefooted and outran most of the others until I hurt my foot in the burnt wood above Napanoch and it made me lame. In the night some of our folks came over; and said that the Indians had gone, and that some of the people were lost in the mountains.

"I went back over the mountain and rode part of the way on a horse, as my foot was lame. We went down to Fantinekill and found the houses burned except Jesse Bevier's, which was partly burned, but the soldiers drove the Indians off.

"They had killed all Mike Sock's family before the soldiers came. It looked terrible around there."

ABRAHAM BEVIER

Some of the descendants of Abraham Bevier have remained in Wawarsing to the present day, represented in the fourth generation by Andries, who was a captain of militia and prominent in the business of the town; and by Conrad, who also served in the militia and was a member of the Legislature in 1777. In the fifth generation Dr. Benjamin R. Bevier was a widely-known physician of Napanoch and he is followed by his son, Dr. Benjamin Rush Bevier. Other descendants of Abraham removed to neighboring towns, and to various points in the west and south.

One of his grandsons went to New Paltz, another to Shawangunk, while still another removed to Oil Creek, Penn. In the fifth generation the family was still more widely scattered, five sons of Captain Andries Bevier removed to Owasco, N. Y., and his daughter Rachel married Henry J. Brinkerhoff of Mansfield, Ohio, and is the grandmother of Gen. Rœlif Brinkerhoff. One of the sons, Abraham J. Bevier, removed to Stark county, Ill., another to Fairfax, Va. Johannes, the son of Cornelius, went to western New York and his children later removed to Wisconsin and Illinois.

In the sixth generation we find Dr. Matthew Bevier of Owasco, Richard Brodhead Bevier of Gardiner, Abraham A. Bevier of Napanoch, Rev. Johannes Hornbeck Bevier, at one time editor of the *Christian Intelligencer.* John Hardenbergh Bevier of Bath, Ill., Dr. Wm. Bevier of Denning, Ulster county, N. Y., Benjamin Bevier of Wilcox, Penn., Simon Bevier of Auburn, N. Y., and A. L. R. Bevier of Stark county, Ill.

SAMUEL BEVIER

Samuel Bevier, the son of Louis the immigrant, remained on the old homestead at New Paltz and his father made his home with him until his death in 1720.

Of his children Abraham, Jacob and Philip settled at New Paltz, Abraham being an Associate Judge of that town. Johannes moved to Shawangunk where he was a prominent citizen and a leading elder in the church. Isaac removed to Rochester and his widow and two sons were killed by the Indians. Five grandsons of Samuel Bevier removed to western New York, being followed in the next generation by many more of the family, so that there are very few of Samuel's line now living in Ulster county. This branch of the Bevier family is represented in the seventh generation by Orville D. Bevier of New York city and by Mrs. Henry A. Temple of St. John, N. B.

LOUIS BEVIER

Louis Bevier, the second of the name, settled in Marbletown in 1715 on the land purchased for him by his father of Peter Van Leuvan. He married Elizabeth Hasbrouck, daughter of Jean Hasbrouck of New Paltz, and died in 1753. His only child, Louis, was born April 29, 1717. He was a noted surveyor and also served as Supervisor of his town. He married, in 1745, Esther, daughter of Philip Du-

HOUSE OF LOUIS BEVIER AT MARBLETOWN

Bois of Rochester, he died in 1772. Of this third Louis his cousin Abraham Hasbrouck writes:

"My cousin, Louis Bevier, departed this transitory life the 29th day of September, at two o'clock in the morning and in the year of our Lord 1772, aged 55 years, 4 months, 19 days, and rests in the Lord until his coming. He was a good husband, a tender father, a good master, a kind neighbor, a true friend to liberty, a pillar in the church at Marbletown and elsewhere, an honest gentleman. He was endowed with a good share of knowledge, he was a comely man of middle stature, strong of body. He died of an apoplectic fit in the night, very suddenly, before his wife and children could come to him to see his exit."

Louis Bevier, the third, had two sons that survived him, David and Philip.   David, the grandfather of the writer, remained on the Marbletown homestead where I now reside; while Philip removed to Rochester. Philip served as a Member of the Assembly in 1777 and was a colonel in the regular army during the Revolution. His only son, Dr. Louis D. B. Bevier, was a prominent physician, and died in 1851, leaving no heirs.

David Bevier, at the age of 29 years, was an adjutant in a regiment of militia under Col. Levi Pawling, later he was one of the Committee of Safety.   He married, in 1778, Maria, daughter of Abraham Hasbrouck of Kingston, and in deference to her wishes the family ceased using the French language and adopted the Dutch.

David Bevier had two sons, the elder Louis and the younger Joseph. For the latter he purchased a farm at Catskill, but he afterwards sold this place and returned to the town of Olive, in Ulster county, where he resided till his death in 1840. Joseph had but one son, David, whose sons, Joseph and Hasbrouck, are settled in Olive, while his youngest son, Charles, removed to Minnesota.

The elder son, Louis, father of the writer, remained at Marbletown where he married Maria Eltinge, daughter of Cornelius Eltinge of Hurley. He was a captain in the war of 1812 and died in 1826. His only son is the writer of the present sketch.

This line is further represented in the seventh generation by Louis Bevier, Jr., Professor of Greek in Rutgers College, New Brunswick, N. J., and in the eighth generation by Louis Bevier third, still a minor.

GENEALOGY OF THE BEVIER FAMILY

1. LOUIS BEVIER, MARRIED IN 1673, MARIE LE BLANC

2ND GENERATION

Marie, born July 19, 1674, died in infancy.

Jean, born Jan. 29, 1676, married April 14, 1712, settled at Wawarsing, died 1745. Catharine Montanye.

Abraham, born Jan. 20, 1678, married Feb. 18, 1707, settled at Wawarsing, died 1774. Rachel Vernooy.

Samuel, born Jan. 21, 1680. Settled at New Paltz, died 1746. Magdalena Blanshan, daughter of Matthese Blanshan.

Andries, born July 12, 1682, unmarried, settled at New Paltz, died 1768.

Louis, born Nov. 6, 1684, married May 6, 1713, settled at Marbletown, died Feb. 10, 1753. Elizabeth Hasbrouck, daughter of Jean, born Feb. 25, 1685, died June 10, 1760.

Esther, born Nov. 16, 1686, married Nov. 7, 1714. Jacob Hasbrouck, son of Jean.

Solomon, born July 12, 1689, died young.

2. Jean Bevier, Married Catharine Montanye

3rd generation

Marie, born March 7, 1713, died in infancy.

Elenora, born May 23, 1714, settled at Minnisink. Benjamin Rolscher.

Elizabeth, born Feb. 10, 1717, married 1751, settled at Wawarsing, died 1779. Isaac Bevier, son of Samuel, born Dec. 25, 1714.

Johanna, born May 15, 1720, married April 23, 1753, settled at Wawarsing, died 1779. Michael Sax.

Esther, born Oct. 18, 1722, married May 4, 1748. Solomon Westbrook, settled at Minnisink.

Louis J., born Oct. 18, 1724, unmarried, settled at Wawarsing, died 1812.

Jesse, born May 11, 1729, married, settled at Wawarsing, died 1803. Elizabeth Hoffman.

Johannes, born June 18, 1727, died in infancy.

3. Jesse Bevier, Married Elizabeth Hoffman

4th generation

Blandina, born 1762, settled at Wawarsing. William Bodley; 3 children baptized—Wawarsing records.

David, born April 1, 1764, settled at Wawarsing. Sally Gier.

Catharine, born Aug. 1, 1765, settled at Kerhonkson. Benjamin Depuy, Jr.; 8 children baptized.

John, born Nov. 30, 1758, married Feb., 1792, settled at Jackson county, Indiana. Martha Green of Reddington.

Lea, born Sept. 16, 1771, married April 9, 1792. William W. DeWitt; 4 children baptized.

4. David Bevier, Married Sally Gier

5th Generation

Mary White, born June 17, 1806.

Charles, born July 4, 1808.

Elizabeth Hoffman, born Sept. 20, 1810.

4. John Bevier, Married Martha Green

Caty, born Jan. 27, 1794.

Ann Elizabeth, born Nov. 5, 1795, married DeWitt Depuy, settled at Rochester.

Some of these two families moved to Jackson county, Indiana.

2. Abraham Bevier, Married Rachel Vernooy

3rd Generation

Louis, born 1708, unmarried, died in 1750.

Anna, born May 7, 1710, died in infancy.

Cornelius, born Jan. 20, 1712, unmarried, died in 1770.

Samuel, born Aug. 28, 1715, married June 10, 1739, settled at Wawarsing, died 1774. Sarah LeFevre, daughter of Andries, born March 1, 1719.

Jacob, born Sept. 29, 1716, married Feb. 23, 1751, settled at Wawarsing, died 1800. Anna Vernooy.

Abraham, born Jan. 10, 1720, died aged 19 (see will).

Maria, born Jan, 21, 1722, married June 20, 1745. Benjamin DuBois, son of Daniel, settled at New Paltz.

Johannes, born April 26, 1724, married first Aug. 9, 1747, second Sept. 18, 1764, Wawarsing, died 1797. First, Rachel LeFevre, daughter of Andries, born June 23, 1728. Second, Elizabeth VanVleit, nee Gonzales.

Benjamin, born May 7, 1727, married Dec. 13, 1760, died 1803. Elizabeth Van Keuren, born July 29, 1726, daughter of Tjerck Matthysen and Maria Ten Eyck.

Daniel, unmarried, died 1786.

3. SAMUEL BEVIER, MARRIED SARAH LeFEVRE

4TH GENERATION

Andries, born April 14, 1742, married June 21, 1764, settled at Wawarsing, died 1800. Jacomyntje DuBois, born April 21, 1745, daughter of Cornelius DuBois.

Abraham, Jr., born Nov. 18, 1746, settled at Shawangunk. Maria DuBois, born April 20, 1746, daughter of Jonathan.

Maria, born Oct. 17, 1750, married April 23, 1772. Cornelius G. Vernooy, Rochester.

Rachel, born Oct. 17, 1750, married April 19, 1776. Johannes A. DeWitt, Rochester.

Maria and Rachel were twins.

Matthew, born 1744, married Dec. 2, 1769, Shawangunk. Jacomytje Bevier, born Sept. 28, 1744, daughter of Abram S.

Elizabeth, born Feb. 18, 1753, married. Arthur Morris, Rochester.

Cornelia, born Jan. 21, 1755, married, first Dec. 9, 1774. First, Matthew Newkirk, Hurley. Second, Peter Bevier, Chenango.

3. JACOB BEVIER, MARRIED ANNA VERNOOY

4TH GENERATION

Jenneke, born Jan. 16, 1752, died in infancy.

Abraham, born July 19, 1753, married, Wawarsing, died 1825. First, Margaret LeFevre, born Oct. 26, 1752, daughter

of Abraham LeFevre.   Second, Abagail Vanderbilt.   Third,
Sarah Vernooy, widow.

Sarah, born Aug. 28, 1755, married.   Cornelius Bevier, son
of Johannes.

Rachal, born Feb. 10, 1759, died young.

Elizabeth, born 1762, unmarried, died 1828.

Anna, born May 12, 1765, married.   John J. DuBois, born
Aug. 4, 1751, son of Johannes DuBois and Judith Wynkoop,
Hurley.

Catherine, born July 28, 1768, married Nov. 8, 1796.   Peter
Jansen, born Nov. 16, 1755, Marbletown.

3. JOHANNES BEVIER, MARRIED, 1ST RACHEL LEFEVRE;
2ND CORNELIA VERNOOY

4TH GENERATION

Maria, born 1750, married, Auburn, John L. Hardenberg,
2nd wife, Martha Brinkerhoff.

Sarah, born June 16, 1752, married, Mamakating.   Manuel
Gonsaulus.

Andries LeFevre, born March 20, 1754, died young.

Simon Bevier, born April 29, 1756, married Dec. 11, 1790,
Wawarsing.   Maria Bevier, daughter of Benjamin, born Oct.
16, 1768.   Elizabeth Cantine.

Conrad, born May 7, 1758, Napanock.   Elizabeth Roosa.

Cornelius, born 1760, Wawarsing, died 1790.   Sarah Bevier,
daughter of Jacobus, Cornelia Vernooy.

Cornelia, born 1762, Chenango, N. Y.   Petrus Bevier, born
April 8, 1753, son of Philip.

Jacob J., born June 1, 1766, married Aug. 6, 1786, Leurenkill.   Margaret DeWitt.

Daniel, born Dec. 17, 1768, married Nov. 19, 1791, Oil Creek. Sarah Bevier, daughter of Abraham Bevier, Jr.

Abraham, born March 11, 1770, married Dec. 11, 1793, Leurenkill. Jennike Vernooy.

BENJAMIN, MARRIED ELIZABETH VANKEUREN

4TH GENERATION

Benjamin, born 1762, married 1790, Wawarsing. Leah Roosa.

Maritje, born Oct. 16, 1768, married Feb. 1, 1790, Wawarsing, died 1792. Simon Bevier, born 1756, son of Johannes; 2nd wife, Eliza Cantine.

4. ANDRIES BEVIER, MARRIED JACOMYNTJE DUBOIS

5TH GENERATION

Sarah, born Aug. 1, 1765, unmarried, settled in Owasco.

Samuel, born Oct. 25, 1766, married, settled in Cayuga county. Elizabeth Bevier, born 1768, daughter of Abm. Bevier.

Cornelius, born April 27, 1769, married, settled in Cayuga county. Susan Nottingham.

Wilhelmus, born May 10, 1771, married Jan. 11, 1801, settled at Wawarsing. Annatje Hoornbeck, born May 29, 1771.

Lewis, born Dec. 4, 1773, married Oct. 20, 1805, settled at Wawarsing, died 1838. Garretje VanKeuren.

Abraham A., born July 28, 1776, married Aug. 8, 1801, settled at Wawarsing. Ann Perrine.

Marjritje, May 30, 1779, unmarried, Owasco.

Jannet, born Aug. 30, 1781, died in infancy.

Josiah, born Feb. 9, 1785, married, Owasco. 1st, Hannah

Brinkerhoff. 2nd, Leah Bevier, born March 23, 1787, daughter of Conrad Bevier.

Rachel, born March 1, 1791, married. Henry J. Brinkerhoff, Mansfield, Ohio.

4. ABRAHAM BEVIER, MARRIED MARIA DuBOIS

Elizabeth, born Nov. 20, 1768, married. Samuel Bevier, born Oct. 25, 1766, son of Andries.

Sarah, born Sept. 9, 1770, married Nov. 19, 1791. Daniel Bevier, born Dec. 17, 1768, son of Johannes, Oil Creek.

Samuel, born Jan. 4, 1772.

Rachel, born May 7, 1774.

Jonathan, born May 27, 1776.

Nathaniel DuBois, born Sept. 13, 1777, Shawangunk.

4. MATTHEW BEVIER, MARRIED JACOMYNTJE BEVIER

5TH GENERATION

Abraham, born Jan. 8, 1772.

Sarah, born July 9, 1775.

Samuel, born Nov. 7, 1777.

Margaret, born July 13, 1780.

Cornelius, born Nov. 19, 1784.

4. ABRAHAM BEVIER, MARRIED, 1ST MARGARET LeFEVRE, 2ND ABBY VANDERBILT, 3RD SARAH VERNOOY

5TH GENERATION

Andries, born Oct. 28, 1780, married Feb. 18, 1805, settled in Gardiner, died Jan., 1845. Mary Deyo, born Dec. 2, 1785, died April 19, 1858.

Maria, born Feb. 10, 1783, married July 18, 1802, settled at Wawarsing. Andries I. LeFevre, born Oct. 5, 1777.

Rachel, born Oct. 25, 1785.

Lena, born Nov. 16, 1787, married.   Simon Muller.

Cornelia, born May 6, 1790.

Marjrietje, born Aug. 11, 1791, unmarried.

Abagail, born Nov. 17, 1794, married.   David McKinstry.

4.   CONRAD BEVIER, MARRIED ELÍZABETH ROOSA

5TH GENERATION

Benjamin Rosa, born Sept. 10, 1782, married, settled in Napanoch, died in 1865.   Catharine Ten Eyck, daughter of Richard Ten Eyck.

Matthew, born Oct. 2, 1785, married, settled in Bath, Ill. Cornelia Hardenburgh.

Lea, born March 23, 1787, 2nd wife of Josiah Bevier, son of Andries Bevier, Owasco.

Lucas, born April 2, 1792, unmarried.

Maria, born July 18, 1795, married.   Simon Bevier, born March 5, 1788, son of Cornelius, Wawarsing.

Jane, born March 19, 1799, married.   Moses C. Depuy, Rochester.

4.   CORNELIUS BEVIER, MARRIED, 1ST SARAH BEVIER, 2ND CORNELIA VERNOOY

5TH GENERATION

Sarah, born April 20, 1777, married, Wawarsing.   Jacob Hermance.

Johannes, born Oct. 15, 1784, married Aug. 14, 1808, Lackawack, died Feb. 22, 1842.   Elizabeth Tearhout, July 31, 1792.

Conrad, born April 2, 1786, married, Lackawack.   Sarah Vernooy.

Simon, born 1788, Wawarsing, died April 23, 1846.   Maria Bevier, born July 18, 1795, daughter of Conrad.

4. SIMON BEVIER, MARRIED, 1ST MARIA BEVIER, 2ND ELIZABETH CANTINE

5TH GENERATION

Simon, born Oct. 3, 1792, died in infancy.

Samuel, born Oct. 3, 1796, married, Oil Creek. Maria Van Wagenen.

Magdalena, born April 9, 1798, unmarried, Buffalo.

Peter, born March 4, 1802, married Jan. 1, 1828, Drowned Lands. Elizabeth Terwilliger; no children.

Elijah, born Dec. 5, 1805, married, Owasco, Onondaga county, Elizabeth Bevier.

Rachel, born Aug. 1, 1808, married, Wawarsing. Peter Cantine; no children.

Maria, born March 7, 1811, married. Stephen Dewitt, Western New York.

Andrew, born Sept. 20, 1813, married, Western New York. Martha J. Shaver.

Margaret, born Feb. 14, 1816, married. Andries Dewitt, Ohio.

4. JACOB J. BEVIER, MARRIED MARGARET DEWITT

5TH GENERATION

Johannes Dewitt, born Sept. 14, 1787, Leurenkill.

Cornelius, born Feb. 26, 1791.

Alexander, born Sept. 14, 1792.

Richard Brodhead, born July 10, 1796.

Daniel.

Matthew.

Nathaniel.

Simon.

Catharine.

Leah.

4. DANIEL BEVIER, MARRIED SARAH BEVIER

5TH GENERATION

Maria, born Feb. 24, 1793.

Johannes, born Nov. 13, 1794, Oil Creek.

4. ABRAHAM J. BEVIER, MARRIED JENNEKE VERNOOY

5TH GENERATION

Jenneke, born Sept. 30, 1794, married. John A. Snyder, Ellenville.

Elizabeth, born April 20, 1796, married, Wawarsing; 1st, Moses Bevier, son of Benjamin; 2d, Charles Shultz.

Nathan, born Feb. 11, 1798, married, Lafayette, Stark county, Ill. Sarah Brannen.

Maria Vernooy, born May 28, 1800, married. Daniel Elmore.

Jacob Hoornbeck, born Oct. 29, 1802, died in infancy.

Jacob Hoornbeck, born Aug. 15, 1805, married, Fairfax county, Va., died Dec. 6, 1888. Sarah Devine.

Sarah Vernooy, born March 5, 1811, married. Silas Gillett, Illinois.

4. BENJAMIN BEVIER, MARRIED LEAH ROOSA

5TH GENERATION

Elizabeth, born Sept. 16, 1790, married. Luke Dewitt, Owasco.

Jannetje, born May 9, 1795. Jophat Hoornbeck, Rochester.

Levi, born July 22, 1797, died young.

Moses, born Oct. 18, 1799, married, Ellenville, died Nov. 22, 1828. Elizabeth Bevier, born April 20, 1796. (2d husband Chas. Schultz.)

Lewis, born Oct. 25, 1802, married, Wawarsing. Gertrude Smeedes; no children.

Maria, born Jan. 15, 1805.

Ann, born Oct. 25, 1807.

Tjerck, born ———, married ———, died 1830. Sarah Dewitt, daughter of Reuben Dewitt.

2. SAMUEL BEVIER, MARRIED MAGDALENA BLANJEAN

3D GENERATION

Solomon, born May 13, 1711, died in infancy.

Matthew, born June 28, 1712, died 1746.

Abraham, born June, 1713, married Jan. 3, 1742. Settled at New Paltz, died 1796. Margaret Elting, born May 18, 1718, daughter of Rœlof Elting.

Isaac, born Dec. 25, 1714, married 1751, settled at Wawarsing. Elizabeth Bevier, born Feb. 10, 1727, daughter of Jean Bevier.

Jacobus, born April 29, 1716, married 1740, New Paltz. Antje Freer.

Margaret, born June 30, 1717, married June 17, 1737, Bloomingdale. Matthew LeFevre, born April 10, 1710, son of Andries.

Maria, born Oct. 5, 1718, married Abraham LeFevre, born March 25, 1716, son of Jan LeFevre.

Louis S., born Jan. 10, 1720, died young.

Esther, born Jan. 8, 1721, married. Cornelius L. Brink, Shawangunk.

Johannes, born Sept. 9, 1722, married Sept. 2, 1749, Shawangunk, died 1796. Magdalena LeFevre, born Oct. 11, 1724, daughter of Simon.

Philip, born Feb. 9, 1724, married July 10, 1748, Tryntje Low. 2nd husband Adriance Newkirk, of Hurley.

3. ABRAHAM BEVIER, MARRIED MARGARET ELTINGE

4TH GENERATION

Sarah, born June 25, 1744, married Oct. 25, 1765. Petrus Hasbrouck, born Aug. 20, 1738, New Paltz.

Jacomyntje, born Sept. 28, 1746, married Dec. 2, 1769. Matthew ᵈ Bevier, born 1744, son of Samuel, Shawangunk.

Solomon, born Dec. 4, 1748, married, died Nov. 10, 1810. Elenor Griffin, born Dec. 22, 1745, died Aug. 12, 1820.

Katrintje, born Oct. 19, 1750, married Jan. 24, 1762. Mathusalem DuBois, born May 23, 1742, son of Ephriam.

Rœlof Eltinge, born May 16, 1753, died young.

Maria, born March 18, 1755, married. Isaac Hasbrouck, born April 13, 1746, son of Daniel.

Abraham A., born Oct. 29, 1758, married, Chenango, died 1817. Maria Freer.

Magdalen, married Nov. 9, 1766. Mattheus Decker, Shawangunk.

Esther, died young.

3. ISAAC BEVIER, MARRIED ELIZABETH BEVIER

4TH GENERATION

Katrintje, born April 28, 1752, married. Abraham Jansen, Leurenkill.

Solomon, born March 20, 1754.

Josiah, born Aug. 10, 1756.

The two above persons were killed by Indians in 1779.

Magdalena, born June 24, 1759, unmarried.

Eliza, born April 17, 1763, died young.

3. JOHANNES BEVIER, MARRIED MAGDALENA LEFEVRE

4TH GENERATION

Cornelia, born Aug. 30, 1750, died young.

Jonathan, born Jan. 28, 1752, unmarried.

Magdalena, born Nov. 25, 1753, married 1783. Jan Hoffman, Shawangunk.

Nathaniel, born April 17, 1756, married, Shawangunk. Catharine Dewitt, daughter of Dr. Andries Dewitt.

Jonas, born July 26, 1758, Shawangunk. Maria Dewitt.

Cornelia, born Jan. 25, 1761, married Nov. 7, 1786. Noah LeFevre, born Oct. 29, 1754, son of Abraham.

3. PHILIP BEVIER, MARRIED TRYNTJE LOW

4TH GENERATION

Catharine, born April 9, 1749, unmarried, New Hurley.

Magdalena, born Jan. 13, 1751, married. Abraham DuBois, born Feb. 15, 1749, son of Benjamin.

Petrus, born April 28, 1753, married. Cornelia Bevier, born 1762, daughter of Johannes.

Sarah, born April 23, 1755.

Elias, born April 25, 1756.

Sara, born Jan. 22, 1758.

4. SOLOMON BEVIER, MARRIED ELEANOR GRIFFIN

5TH GENERATION

Abraham Solomon, born June 27, 1774.

Rœlof, born Jan. 21, 1776.

John, born May 8, 1777, married, 1st Hannah Smith on Jan. 22, 1804, 2nd Margaret Anable on March 22, 1826.

Margrietje, born Jan. 15, 1779.

Caty, born Aug. 17, 1780.

Charity, born Jan. 31, 1781.

Nelly, born Nov. 27, 1783.

Noah, born April 25, 1785.

Maria, born Oct. 20, 1787.

ABRAHAM A. BEVIER, MARRIED MARIA FREER

5TH GENERATION

Isaac, born Oct. 29, 1784.

Rœlof Eltinge, born Dec. 28, 1785.

Abraham, born April 13, 1787.

Thomas, born Nov. 29, 1788.

Thomas, born Dec. 29, 1790.

Zacharias, born March 6, 1796.

All the above were born in Broome county, N. Y.

3. JACOBUS BEVIER, MARRIED ANTJE FREER

4TH GENERATION

Samuel, born Nov. 9, 1740, married, settled in Chenango. Rachel Auchmoody.

Jacob, born 1742, died in infancy.

Antje, born June 3, 1745, married. Benjamin Hasbrouck, born Jan. 31, 1748, son of Daniel.

Jacob, born Feb. 1, 1747, married, New Paltz. Maria York.

Matthew, born June 24, 1748.

Magdalena, born Dec. 23, 1749, married Jonas Freer.

Simeon, born Jan. 28, 1752.

Elias, born March 28, 1753, married, New Paltz and Broome county, N. Y. Sarah LeFevre, born June 5, 1763, daughter of Peter LeFevre.

Sarah, born July 30, 1755, married Johannis Freer.

Maria, born Jan. 24, 1758, married, second wife. Benjamin Hasbrouck, born Jan. 31, 1748, son of Daniel.

Jannetje, born Jan. 31, 1761, married. John York, New Paltz.

4. SAMUEL BEVIER, MARRIED RACHEL AUCHMOODY

5TH GENERATION

Maria, born Dec. 7, 1774.

Jacobus, born Sept. 8, 1776.

Antje, born Aug. 11, 1778.

Cornelius, born Feb. 6, 1780.

Josiah, born July 12, 1782.

Lydia, born Aug. 25, 1784.

Christian, born Sept. 1, 1786, married March 20, 1810. Magdalena Freer.

All the above were born in Chenango, Broome county.

Maria, born July 3, 1789.

Eliza, born Aug. 27, 1791.

3. JACOB BEVIER, MARRIED MARIA YORK

5TH GENERATION

Maria, born July 2, 1775, died in infancy.

Maria, born Oct. 18, 1776, married. Ambrose Mitchel.

Jacobus, born June 30, 1778, married, New Paltz. Mary Yandel.

Isaac, born March 27, 1780, married Dec. 2, 1802, New Paltz, died Oct. 3, 1820. Mary York, died Aug. 8, 1859.

Catharine, born Jan. 23, 1782, married, Luther Sawtell.

Ezekiel, born July 23, 1784, married March 22, 1810, died April 22, 1869. Helen Van Bumble.

Jonathan, born Aug. 17, 1786, married March 17, 1811. Judith Low.

Jeremiah, born May 11, 1789, married April 30, 1812, Esopus. Wyntje Smith.

Henry, born Nov. 25, 1791.

4. ELIAS BEVIER, MARRIED SARAH LeFEVRE

5TH GENERATION

Petrus LeFevre, born 1786.

Elizabeth, born Jan. 18, 1788.

Antje, born Dec. 15, 1789.

Maria, born Sept. 27, 1791, married Dec. 29, 1814. Gerrit Newkirk.

Reuben, born Dec. 4, 1793.

Magdalena, born March 7, 1796.

Jennike, born July 4, 1798.

Lydia, born Jan. 25, 1801.

Johan Vernooy, born March 20, 1804.

Samuel, born July 13, 1806.

4. NATHANIEL BEVIER, MARRIED CATRINA DEWITT

5TH GENERATION

Sarah, born Oct. 21, ——.

Magdalena, born April 28, 1790, married March 30, 1812. Charles Elting, born March 30, 1792.

Jane Vernooy, born Feb. 24, 1792, married. Abraham Elting, born March 30, 1792.

Elizabeth Lynot, born Oct. 12, 1795, married May 28, 1814, died Nov. 25, 1835. Henry Deyo, born March 30, 1792.

4. JONAS BEVIER, MARRIED MARIA DEWITT

5TH GENERATION

Magdalena, born Sept. 15, 1794.

Neeltje, born Sept. 15, 1796, married Feb. 3, 1818. Silas Winfield, Shawangunk.

Johannes Dewitt, born Feb. 28, 1798, died young.

Jonathan, born July 20, 1800, married Dec. 10, 1825, died ———, 1829. Hannah LeFevre.

Nathaniel, born Feb. 25, 1804.

Stephen, born April 19, 1806.

Lea Dewitt, born Feb. 16, 1808.

Jane Newkirk, born Dec. 5, 1810, married. Annanius Winfield.

4. PETRUS BEVIER, MARRIED CORNELIA BEVIER

5TH GENERATION

Catrintje, born June 12, 1785.

Philippus, born Oct. 31, 1787.

Rachel, born Jan. 8, 1789.

Mattheus, born Nov. 29, 1790, Chenango, N. Y.

2. LOUIS BEVIER, MARRIED ELIZABETH HASBROUCK

3RD GENERATION

Louis, born April 29, 1717, married Oct. 24, 1745, Marbletown, died Sept. 29, 1772. Esther DuBois, born June 20, 1718, daughter of Philip DuBois, died Oct. 7, 1790.

3. LOUIS BEVIER, MARRIED ESTHER DUBOIS

4TH GENERATION

David, born Nov. 27, 1746, married Jan. 27, 1772, Marbletown, died June 17, 1822. Maria Hasbrouck, born July 7, 1751, daughter of Abraham Hasbrouck, died Nov. 29, 1816.

Elizabeth, born June 9, 1749, married March 4, 1773. Joseph Hasbrouck, born March 4, 1744, son of Abraham, Guilford, died Feb. 26, 1808.

Philip D. B., born Dec. 28, 1751, married Dec. 29, 1782, Rochester, died April 18, 1802. Ann Dewitt, born Oct. 20, 1862.

Louis, born Aug. 15, 1754, died in infancy.

Esther, born Dec. 23, 1755, died in infancy.

4. DAVID BEVIER, MARRIED MARIA HASBROUCK

5TH GENERATION

Louis, born Feb. 13, 1779, married Jan. 6, 1807, Marbletown, died Oct. 25, 1826.   Maria Eltinge, born March 9, 1785, daughter of Cornelius Eltinge.

Abraham Bourbon, born March 30, 1781, died May 5, 1782.

Joseph, born Nov. 1, 1703, married, Olive, died 1840. Catharine Hasbrouck, daughter of Jacobus B. Hasbrouck.

Philip, born Dec. 11, 1785, died Oct. 25, 1791.

Catharine, born Sept. 29, 1789, married Jan. 18, 1815. Stephen Stilwell, New Paltz.

Esther, born Aug. 6, 1791, died Nov. 20, 1791.

4. PHILIP D. B. BEVIER, MARRIED ANN DEWITT

5TH GENERATION

Esther, born Jan. 8, 1785, married Jan. 30, 1810, died Aug. 30, 1871.   Philip Hasbrouck, born Oct. 22, 1783, son of Joseph Hasbrouck, New Paltz.

Hilletje, born Feb. 14, 1788, died July 25, 1788.

Rachel, born Jan. 18, 1786, married April 30, 1809, died

Feb. 2, 1858. Thomas R. Hardenburgh, Woodburn, Sullivan county, died May 14, 1869.

Elizabeth, born Jan. 18, 1790, unmarried.

Maria Ann, born Feb. 2, 1791, married, Port Jarvis. Rev. Cornelius C. Eltinge, born May 12, 1793, son of Cornelius Eltinge.

Henrietta Cornelia, born Nov. 22, 1792. James Hasbrouck, son of Joseph Hasbrouck, New Paltz.

Louis DuBois, born June 3, 1794, married June, 1839, Rochester, died March 31, 1851. Charity Hoornbeck.

Hylah, born Aug. 3, 1795, New Paltz. Levi Hasbrouck, son of Josiah Hasbrouck, died March 7, 1861.

Sarah Amelia, born March 23, 1797, married, died Oct. 18, 1861. Cornelius Bruyn, born June 16, 1789, died April 23, 1873.

5. LOUIS BEVIER, MARRIED MARIA ELTINGE

6TH GENERATION

Maria, born Sept. 21, 1807, married, died Aug. 1, 1878. Rev. Cornelius L. Van Dyck, born Jan. 5, 1804, died Sept. 13, 1866.

Blandina, born Oct. 1, 1809, unmarried, died June 21, 1889.

Catharine, born Nov. 11, 1811, married, died March 29, 1868. Oliver G. DuBois, son of Derick DuBois.

Jane, born April 26, 1814, married, died March 29, 1883. Edgar Hasbrouck, born Feb. 25, 1814, son of I. S. Hasbrouck, died July 15, 1854.

Esther Gumaer, born July 6, 1817, died Oct. 15, 1877. G. W. Basten, son of Geo. Basten.

Magdalena DuBois, born Jan. 23, 1820, died Feb., 1897. Willet S. Northrop, died Aug., 1895.

Louis, born Aug. 21, 1822, married, Marbletown. Catharine

Van Dyck, born March 29, 1824, daughter of Lawrence C. Van Dyck, died Jan. 24, 1885.

Elizabeth, born Dec. 10, 1824, married. Peter Van Dyck.

5. JOSEPH BEVIER, MARRIED CATHARINE HASBROUCK

6TH GENERATION

Mary Ann, married. Russell Holmes, Catskill and Olive.

David, born Aug. 10, 1818, married, Olive, died Sept. 11, 1866. Deborah Lockwood, born June 28, 1820, died April 2, 1887.

Catharine, unmarried, died 1840.

Eleanor, married, second wife, Russell Holmes.

CHAPTER XXIII

THE DEYO FAMILY AT NEW PALTZ

Two New Paltz patentees, Christian and Pierre, bore the name of Deyo and were father and son. They were among the last of the twelve to set foot on the soil of the New World, where Anthony Crispell, Louis DuBois and his sons and the two LeFevre brothers had already resided for some years. In 1675 Pierre Deyo was still in the Palatinate as is shown by his certificate of good standing and church membership from the noted pastor Amyot. This precious relic which has come straight down in the Deyo family is now in the possession of Mr. A. D. Brodhead. It is in the German tongue, is in a good state of preservation and a translation is as follows:

This is to certify that Peter Doio and Agatha Nickel both in honor living in Curr Pfaltz, Mutterstadt, circuit of New-stadt, have been united in marriage, the intent of such marriage having been announced three times from the pulpit, that they are members of the Reformed church and as far as we know the same are well behaved people. Mutterstadt, Curr Pfaltz, 21 Jan., 1675. Jacob Amyot, Pastor.

Louis DuBois was the man who discovered New Paltz and was the leader in the settlement, but Christian Deyo was called "Grandpere" or grandfather in the old documents and was, in fact, the grandfather of most of the children of the youthful settlement. Christian's son Pierre was a patentee, likewise his four sons-in-law, John and Abraham Hasbrouck, Simon Le-Fevre and Abraham DuBois. The youngest of the patentees,

Isaac DuBois, married Maria, daughter of Jean Hasbrouck and granddaughter of Christian Deyo. Christian Deyo had grandchildren born on the other side of the Atlantic and one of his granddaughters, Esther Hasbrouck, who was born in the Palatinate, married in 1692, Peter Gumaer, one of the earliest settlers of Minisink, so already at that early date New Paltz became the cradle of the surrounding country.

Before ending his days, Christian Deyo saw his family all settled around him at New Paltz, the three unmarried daughters who came with him to the new world having become the wives of Abraham Hasbrouck, Simon LeFevre and Abraham DuBois.

Christian Deyo was quite certainly an old man at the time of the settlement of New Paltz and lived only about ten years afterwards. His will, which is recorded in Book A, in the County Clerk's office at Kingston, is as follows:

In ye name of God, amen. Ye first day of February, Anno Dom., 1686-7 (the fractional form showing the date according to the Old and New Style), Christian Doyou, of ye New Paltz, in ye County of Ulster, being sick in body and of good and perfect memory, thanks be to Almighty God, and calling to remembrance the uncertain state of this transitory life and that all flesh must yield to death when it shall please God to call, I do make, constitute, ordain and declare this my last will and testament in manner following, revoking and annulling by these presents all and every testament in manner following:

I will, first, that all my just debts be paid within convenient time after my decease by my executors, as named. I give to my son Peter Doyou fiftyrix dollars, that my son was indebted to me and then to share equally with all of the rest of my children of my estate and further I do give to my son's son,

Christian Doyou, forty pieces of eight and a small gun and then I do hereby give unto my five children all ye rest of my estate of lands, housings, chattles and movable goods, to them, their heirs, executors and assigns forever, as witness my hand and seal, in Kingston, ye day and year above written and I do desire that my corpse may be buried at ye New Paltz.

Ye mark of
CHRISTIAN DOYAU.

Signed, sealed and delivered in presence of

Nicator Depew,
William DuMont,
Jno. David,
Humphrey Davenol.

It will be noticed that the will does not mention any executor, and perhaps it was owing to this singular omission that the estate was settled by the heirs as appears by a writing in French of which the following literal translation was made by Frank Hasbrouck of Poughkeepsie.

The twenty-fourth October 1687 we the undersigned have agreed that which follows, that is, that to terminate the difference which we might have for the inheritance of our father me abraham assebroucg will receive thirty pieces of eight [dollars] from Mr. Bekman upon that which he owes to our father christian doyeau and me abraham dubois will receive also from said bekman twenty-eight pieces of eight and from my brother-in-law pierre doyeau fifty-five bushels of good winter wheat because of what comes to me of my part of the negro of our father from the said pierre doyau and me Jean assebroucg should receive from Abraham assebroucg ten bushels and from abraham dubois eleven bushels and we

Pierre doyau Jean assebroucg and Simon le fevre will receive
from said bekman the surplus of said thirty pieces of eight
and of said twenty pieces of eight which are due [word oblite-
rated] the abraham assebrouc and habraham dubois the surplus say I which the said bekman owes to our father christian
doyau we the under-named pierre doyau ian assebrouc and
Simon le febvre will share it equally as also the twenty-five
pieces of eight which vallerem dumont owes to our father christian doyau and that which is due for the rest by the other
debtors of our said father except that the said abraham assebrouc and abraham dubois should be able to claim nothing in
the said debts and it is agreed that if there are any complaints
from any of those interested in the inheritance of our father
because of what things have been done or what could be done
each of us five heirs will pay our part of it and if the said re-
payments arise from the complaint of any one of us that one
alone shall pay the said penalty.

	pierre doyo
Marque de	Simon lefebvre
Abraham hasbrouck	Jean assebrouc
Abraham duboi	

PIERRE THE PATENTEE

There is an old tradition that Pierre Deyo the Patentee, only
son of Christian Deyo, died while on an expedition to find a
route from New Paltz to the River, and that long afterwards a
buckle of a truss that he had worn was found at the foot of a
tree and that this was the only clue to his mysterious fate.
This story is told by Josiah R. Elting in his genealogical record,
but it is probable that the Pierre who died on the way to the

River was Pierre, son of the Patentee of the same name. This Pierre grew to man's estate but left no children, as Josiah R. Elting says concerning the Pierre who died looking for a route to the River.

Pierre the Patentee left four sons, Christian, born in Palatinate in 1674; Abraham, born at Hurley in 1676; Pierre, baptized at New Paltz in 1683 and Henricus baptized at New Paltz in 1690; also two daughters, Mary and Margaret; the first born in 1679, married Jacob Clearwater, settled at Bontecoe and had a son, Abraham, christened at New Paltz in 1699.

The very oldest paper in the Theodore Deyo collection is a bond given by Pierre Deyo the Patentee, in 1681, and is in English as follows:

Kingestowne, 26th April, 1681.

I under written Peter dolliaw of ye New Palse doe owne to stand indebted unto mee Thomas Dellavoll ye sum of fifty two Sch. wheatte, wch I doe oblige my self to pay this next year now cominge on, whereunto I have sett my hand to be delivered at ye water syde. Pierre doyo.

On the back of this paper is indorsed,

Kingstowne, 26th April 1681 Peter doliou of ye New Palse his obligation for 52 Sch. wheatte to be paid this winter coming on.

There is also the further indorsement.

Kingstowne 23d Jan. 168$\frac{1}{2}$.

Recd of ye sed Peter Doliaw ye contents of this bond, say recd by mee John Fontaine for my master.

Thomas Delavoll.

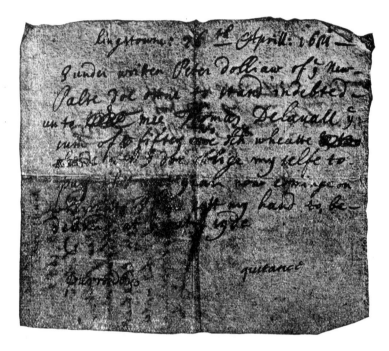

ANCIENT DOCUMENT WITH SIGNATURE OF PIERRE DEYO, THE PATENTEE.

CHRISTIAN, SON OF PIERRE THE PATENTEE

Christian settled without doubt in the Springtown neighborhood, where his descendants have since lived and where his descendants James E. and Matthew Deyo now reside. In the will of his grandfather Christian is specially remembered by the bequest of a small gun. Christian was married at New Paltz in 1702 to Marytje DeGraff (in French LeConte). It is somewhat singular that the marriage is recorded on the church books both at New Paltz and Kingston. On the New Paltz church book the quaint record is as follows: "Christian Doyo and Mary LeConte were married in this town of Paltz (Pals, sometimes also called Le Palle)."

Christian's name appears in the list of taxpayers in 1712, in the list of soldiers in Capt. Hoffman's company in 1716, in the list of those who built the first stone church in 1720, in the list of freeholders in 1728 and in the list of slaveholders in 1755. His name appears as deacon in the church at New Paltz in 1733 and in 1765 as an elder.

Christian left only two sons of whom we have any record, Moses and Jacobus; also a daughter Mary, who in 1731 married Jeems Ackmoidi, a Scotchman and ancestor of the Auchmoody family.

Christian's son Jacobus moved to Kingston and we shall give his history hereafter. Moses who was born in 1706 married in 1728 Clarissa Stokhard and lived in a frame house, torn down about 1820 about a mile north of Springtown. Moses' name appears in the list of New Paltz soldiers in 1738. He and his wife Clarissa Stokhard joined the church at New Paltz in 1752. In the tax list of 1765 we find the names of Moses and his sons, Christian, Jr., and Johannis, Jr., all residing in the Springtown neighborhood. (On the same list we find the names of Johannis and Christopher Deyo, sons of Hendricus and cousins of Moses, as residing in the same locality.)   Christian, Jr., who was born in 1732, married Elidia Terwilliger in 1762. We have no account of his brother Johannis. The sons of Christian, Jr., and Elidia Terwilliger were Josiah, born in 1763; Jonathan (in Dutch Yoane), born in 1766; Moses, born in 1768, and Matthew, born in 1777. Jonathan and Matthew married and resided in the neighborhood. We have no account of Moses, and none of Josiah except that he married Catharine Blanshan and had a daughter Maria, who married Martinas Freer and moved with him to western New York. Romeo H. Freer, attorney general of the State of West Virginia, is their grandson.

Jonathan married Catharine Ean of Bontecoe, a sister of Peter Ean. From Jonathan the homestead descended to his son Christian, who occupied it during his life and was the last to bear the honored name of the eldest of the New Paltz Patentees.

From Christian the farm descended to his sons, James E. and Matthew, who now till the land that has been in the family so many generations.

Years ago the house burned and the family papers were lost. It is, therefore, not possible to give as full a history of the family as could otherwise be done.

JACOBUS DEYO

We will now go back to Jacobus, son of Christian and brother of Moses, who left his home at Springtown and went to Kingston. In 1724 he married, at Kingston, Janitje Freer. Both are set down at that time as residing at New Paltz. They had several daughters and one son Jacobus, born in 1732; also a son Peter. Jacobus' name does not appear on the records at New Paltz, but in 1738 it is found in the list of foot soldiers of Kingston, from which it is evident that he moved to that place. Afterwards he or his widow moved to Dutchess county and in the Poughkeepsie church records appears the following entry: "Janitje Freer, widow of Jacobus DeJoo, born at New Paltz, married April 22, 1754, to Richard Gryn, born at Oswego." The son Jacobus was 22 years old when his mother married again. Jacobus the younger is thought to have resided at Nine Partners, Dutchess county. His son William, who was born about 1775, lived at Ghent, Columbia county and so did William's son Richard. Jacobus has a number of descendants at Saratoga Springs, Binghamton and elsewhere; among others, Hon. Israel T. Deyo, of Binghamton; Prof. M. L. Deyo, of Albany, and Mr. E. J. Taylor, of Saratoga Springs.

ABRAHAM DEYO, SON OF PIERRE THE PATENTEE

Abraham, the second son of Pierre the Patentee, was born at Hurley, October 16, 1676, as shown by a slip from an old family record in French, in an old Dutch Bible in the possession of Mr. Abm. Deyo of this village. Abraham married Elsie Clearwater in 1702 and occupied the homestead in this village. He died in 1725, leaving one son, Abraham (2) and two daughters, Marytje and Wyntje. Marytje married Isaac Freer and Wyntje married Daniel Hasbrouck. Abraham (2) being the only son, kept the homestead in this village. It is uncertain whether it was he or his father who built the stone house which is still standing and which has come down from one Abraham to another almost to the present time, though remodeled a generation ago and altogether transformed in 1894 by its present owner and occupant, Mr. Abm. Deyo Brodhead.

The name of Abraham Deyo (2) appears in an agreement with twenty-seven other owners of land, authorizing the Duzine to fix title to lands. In another paper in the Patentees' trunk

THE OLD DEYO HOUSE IN THIS VILLAGE

appears the statement that at the time of signing the agreement Abraham was under age but acknowledged the signature as his voluntary act. Abraham married Elizabeth DuBois, daughter of Isaac, the Patentee. In a tax list of 1765 we find his name as one of the largest property owners in the precinct. He left a family of five sons—Abraham, Daniel, Simeon, Jonathan and Philip; also one daughter, Mary, who married Nathaniel LeFevre of Kettleborough. Four of Abraham's sons married LeFevres. All five of the brothers have descendants living in Ulster county. It is related by the old people that Abraham was a weakly man and that his wife, Elizabeth, who is called in Dutch Batche, was a woman of masculine strength and spirit and for this reason was called "Captain Batche."

It is stated that on one occasion one of their slaves, having been guilty of impudence, she struck him a blow which broke his arm, and there being no doctor in the place she sent him to Kingston to have his arm set. Another instance of Captain Batche's spirit and physical endurance is the fact that she stood in the mow and pitched hay the day before her son Daniel was born. From 1751 to 1766 Abraham represented the family name of Pierre Deyo in the deliberations of the Duzine. It appears that Abraham owned a tract of land on the south side of the Paltz patent all the way from the top of the mountain to the Hudson river. The houses of three of his sons, Philip, Jonathan and Simeon, were built on this tract, Jonathan taking land on the west side of the Wallkill, Philip living on the Paltz Plains and Simeon locating a short distance south of Highland. Jonathan's son Daniel afterwards located on this tract likewise, his house being located on South street in the present town of Lloyd.

We have said that Abraham (2) left a family of five sons. These were Abraham (afterwards called Capt.), who kept the homestead in this village; Daniel, who located at Ireland Corners and is the ancestor of the Gardiner and Shawangunk Deyos; Simeon, who located at Highland where he has descendants living; Jonathan, who lived on the place now owned by Miss Smedes on the other side of the Wallkill about a mile south of the village; and Philip, who lived in the house now owned and occupied by Josiah Sprague on the Paltz Plains.

CAPT. ABRAHAM DEYO

Capt. Abraham Deyo kept the homestead in this village. He was twice married. His first wife was Elizabeth LeFevre, who left one son, Simon, who died when he was about forty years of age, leaving no children. Capt. Abraham married as his second wife Maria LeFevre, widow of Isaac LeFevre of Bontecoe. She had several children by her previous marriage and continued to reside with them at Bontecoe in the old stone house on the banks of the Wallkill. As the fruit of the marriage with Captain Abraham Deyo she bore one son, and died not long afterwards. The infant (who afterwards became Judge Abm. A. Deyo, of Modena) was carried on a pillow, after the death of his mother, to the residence of his mother's brother, Johannes LeFevre, at Kettleborough. Of Capt. Abraham's record in the Revolutionary war we find that he was commissioned first lieutenant in the second New Paltz company, Third Ulster County regiment, October 25, 1775, and commissioned captain of the second company February 21, 1778.

SOLDIERS IN CAPT. ABM. DEYO'S COMPANY

An original document giving the names of a portion of Capt. Abraham Deyo's company in the Third Regiment of Ulster County Militia in the Revolutionary war follows:

We whose names are hereunto written do hereby acknowledge to have received of Captain Abraham Doiau our respective wages and billeting money for one month's term of duty at the Frontiers (part of months of July and August, 1778), we say received respectively in full by us this 19th day of September, 1778.

Isaac DuBois.

Ezekiel Deyoo.

Zacharias Hasbrouck.

John Terwilliger, Jr.

Josiah Terwilliger, Jr.

Henry Pontinear.

Aurt Terwilliger.

Wm. Sergeant.

Nathaniel Wallters.

his

Benjamin   Sluyter.

mark

his

Frederick   Hyms

mark

Johannes Spratt.

Abraham Ean.

his

Martynes   Griffin.

mark

Jonathan VanWagenen.

Robert Hass.

his

John   York.

mark

Benjamin Freer.

Peter Bevier.

Jacob Krom.

John Nees.

Wm. Dewitt, Jr.

Jacobus Dewitt.

Capt. Abm. Deyo's great-great-grandson, Abm. D. Brodhead, has in his possession his sword, epaulets and pistols, which have always remained in the family. Capt. Abraham's tombstone, which stands in the old graveyard in this village, bears this inscription: "Capt. Abraham Deyo, who departed this life Sept. 12th, 1808, aged 69 years, 6 months and 15 days." There is only one other tombstone in the graveyard bearing a military title in its inscription.

When the stone church which preceded the present brick edifice was built in 1771, Capt. Abm. Deyo had charge of the work, and the papers relating to its building, which are in the Dutch language, are in the possession of Mr. Abm. D. Brod-

head. For a long time after the death of Capt. Deyo the old
homestead in this village was occupied by Richard Hardenbergh, father of Senator Jacob Hardenbergh, who was born
in this house. Judge Deyo occupied the old house for a time
and afterwards lived at Modena. He married Margaret,
daughter of his cousin, Abraham Deyo of Ireland Corners, and
left two sons, John B. and Abm. A., Jr. Judge Deyo was a
prominent citizen, a man of extensive means and Supervisor
of the town of Plattekill for a long period. His son, Sheriff
Abm. A. Deyo, moved into the old stone house in this village
when he married and continued to reside there until he was
elected sheriff and went to Kingston. Sheriff Abraham had
one son, who was also called Abraham and was the sixth of
that name in a direct line. He died at the age of about fourteen, in Kingston, while his father was sheriff, a few months
after the family moved from this village in 1858.

DANIEL DEYO

Daniel, the second son of Abm. (2), married Margaret Le-
Fevre; after her death he married Catharine Dewitt, of Wawarsing, who left no children. He located at Ireland Corners,
where his father purchased for him, in 1763, a tract of 500
acres, being a part of the Garland Patent. The deed for this
tract is in possession of Andrew L. F. Deyo.

According to the tradition in the Deyo family, this land at
the time of the purchase was occupied by J. G. Ronk, who had
built a house and set out an orchard on the place. Not having
a good title, he gave up the property and moved to the New
Hurley neighborhood to a tract which he had purchased a
dozen years before and where he afterwards resided. During
the Revolutionary war Daniel did some service as a teamster,
going on one occasion with a load of arms to the patriot army
which was stationed near Philadelphia.

HOUSE OF DANIEL DEYO NEAR IRELAND CORNERS.

Daniel Deyo's sister, who had married Nathaniel LeFevre, occupied the adjoining farm on the north, known in modern times as the "Sing" LeFevre place. Daniel left a family of three sons, Abm., Nathaniel and Jonathan; also two daughters, Elizabeth, who married Moses DeWitt and moved to Chemung county, and Mary, who married Simon DuBois of Wallkill. Daniel divided his land among his three sons, each taking about an equal part. Abraham, the oldest son, married Ann Brodhead, sister of Congressman John C. Brodhead. Abraham lived in a frame house still standing on what is now known as the Daniel Bevier place. He left one son, Daniel A., and two daughters, one of whom married Judge Abraham Deyo of Modena, and the other married Andrew Bevier and left a family of four sons—Daniel, Richard, A. Deyo and Dr. DuBois. Daniel A. Deyo lived for a time on his father's homestead and then sold it to Daniel Bevier and moved to Chicago, where he purchased the paw paw grove, near the city. This he afterwards sold and returning to the east purchased a farm near Balmville, three miles north of Newburgh. This property at Balmville increased greatly in value with the growth of Newburgh, as it commanded a fine view of the river. Part of it was sold after his death for a large sum. Daniel A. Deyo was three times married. His first wife, Elizabeth Elting, left but one son, Abm. D., of Tuthill; his second wife, Nelly LeFevre, left two sons, Johannes and Brodhead, and one daughter, Cornelia; his third wife, Arabella Hallock, left a son, Thomas J. of Wallkill, and two daughters.

Jonathan Deyo, son of Daniel, the first settler at Ireland Corners, married Mary, daughter of John Charles Hardenbergh of Rosendale. He occupied all his days the old stone house of his father, which is still standing. He left a family of five sons, John H., Dr. Nathaniel, Barzillai and Dr. Abraham, and two daughters, Jane H. and Mary. The latter married Oscar Noyes. The son, Nathaniel, located at Newburgh, where he practiced medicine and there his son John is still engaged in the same profession. Another son, Robert E., is a prominent lawyer in New York City, his office being at 115 Broadway.

Nathaniel, the third son of Daniel Deyo, owned and occupied the house now the residence of his grandson, Andrew L. F. By his first wife, Leah DeWitt, he had three sons, Daniel, Jonathan N. and John. By his second wife, Catharine Hardenburgh of Marbletown, he had one daughter, who married Thomas K. Jessup of Newburgh. The elder son, Daniel, became a doctor, but died a young man and left one son, Alfred. Jonathan N. kept his father's homestead, which he occupied all his days. John located in Shawangunk.

SIMEON DEYO

Simeon, the third son of Abraham (2), was baptized February 13, 1743. He married Antje Low and located about a mile south of the present village of Highland, opposite the old burying ground and just south of the mill pond. Here about 1780 he built a stone house as his residence and had a farm of about 250 acres. Simeon left a family of three sons, Jacob, Abraham and Joseph. The first named, who was born in 1775, married Ruth Smith and lived about half a mile south of the present village of Highland in a house now occupied by Mrs. Lake. This house when built was considered the finest in that section of country. Jacob was at one time colonel of militia and was usually called colonel. His children were Anna, Nathan, Mary Ann, Sarah, Simeon, Eleanor, Anning S., Hiram C. and Oliver Hazard Perry. The last named became a minister, living for many years at Asbury Park, N. J. From him we have our information concerning this branch of the family. Simeon's son Abraham became a doctor and married Catharine DuBois. He died not long after marriage, leaving one daughter, Electa, who married Philip Elting of Highland. Simeon's son Joseph married Julia Kelsey. They left a large family of sons and daughters as follows: Reuben, Simeon, Abraham, Monroe, Delilah, Eleanor and Rowena. All of these married.

Jonathan Deyo

Jonathan Deyo, fourth son of Abraham (2) married Mary, daughter of Daniel LeFevre of Bontecoe. Jonathan lived a short time on the Paltz Plains. But the lands of his father being divided by lot, Jonathan's share fell on the west side of the Wallkill, and he took the farm now owned by Miss Smedes. His house was of frame and must have been one of the first of that material built at New Paltz. This house was torn down in 1850. Jonathan left a family of three sons, Abraham J., Daniel L. and Peter, and three daughters, Elizabeth, who married Henry DuBois; Catharine, who married Wilhelmus DuBois, and Cornelia, who married Josiah Hasbrouck of Marbletown. Jonathan's son, Abraham J., married Maria Deyo and moved to what is now the Cold Spring Corners neighborhood. He lived for a while in a log house, and about 1812 built the stone house in which he afterwards resided and which was probably the last stone house built in this town.

The country about Cold Spring Corners or Grahow, as it was formerly called, was almost an unbroken wilderness then, but there were no Indians and few wild animals, though at a later date Mr. Andries Deyo informs us he has seen deer pasturing on the winter grain. The stone for the house came from the Bear Vly and the mortar used in laying up the wall came from a field near by. The Pang Yang settlement was only about a mile to the east, but it was not until a later period, when others moved in, that the Pang Yang people acquired a reputation for thieving. At that time the residents there were poor but honest people living in thatched log houses.

Daniel L., the second son of Jonathan Deyo, married Jane LeFevre. They lived on South street, which was then called Quaker street in the present town of Lloyd, where their sons, Jonathan and John L. afterwards lived.

Peter, the youngest son of Jonathan Deyo, married Cornelia Elting. Peter kept his father's homestead, now the Miss Smedes' place. He afterwards bought of Isaiah Hasbrouck, father of Daniel I. Hasbrouck, the farm adjoining on the north, where his son Ira afterwards lived and his grandson Perry afterwards resided.

Philip Deyo

Philip Deyo, the youngest of the five brothers, sons of Abraham (2), married Gertrude LeFevre of Kettleborough and lived on the Paltz Plains where is now the Josiah Sprague farm. The house, part frame and part stone, and still standing, was built in the time of the Revolutionary war and it is related that nails were so exceedingly difficult to obtain that a visit was made to Kingston after that place was burned by the British and from the ruins nails were obtained for the new house. Philip Deyo was a man of great intelligence and we have this saying of Josiah DuBois, "Philip Deyo knew enough to be President of the United States." Philip had a family of seven daughters and only one son, Andries, who was the youngest of the family. He married Catharine Elting and kept the homestead. Six of the daughters married as follows: Elizabeth married Simon LeFevre, Maria married Abraham J. Deyo, Elsie married Andries Bruyn, Catharine married Andries El-

THE HOUSE OF HENDRICUS DEYO AT BONTECOE.

ting, Sarah married Solomon LeFevre, Cornelia married Jacob G. DuBois.

THE FAMILY OF HENDRICUS DEYO, SON OF PIERRE, THE PATENTEE

Hendricus Deyo, youngest son of Pierre, the Patentee, was baptized at Kingston, October 12, 1690. He married at Kingston, December 31, 1715, Margaret Von Bummel, who was baptized at Kingston in 1693. They located at Bontecoe, about four miles north of this village. The house, probably built by Hendricus, but perhaps by his son Benjamin, is still standing on the east bank of the Wallkill and is, we think, the most antique and interesting in appearance of all the old houses of that period. The homestead was bounded by the Freers on the north, and by the LeFevres on the south, and came down in the Deyo family almost to the present day, the last owner of the Deyo name being Ezekiel I. Deyo, son of Abm. W. Deyo.

In the old graveyard in this village stands an ancient tombstone which is quite certainly that of Margaret Van Bummel, wife of Hendricus Deyo, son of Pierre, the Patentee. The inscription on this tombstone has proved quite as puzzling as the hieroglyphics of Egypt, but the key, when found, unlocks the mysterious inscription quite as satisfactory as does Champollion's key the ancient hieroglyphics.

The inscription is as follows:

Anno
1747
de 21 FI
is M. V. B. M.
E. D. H. O. S.
H. D. I.

TOMBSTONE OF MARGARET VAN BUMMEL, WIFE OF HENDRICUS DEYO

It must be remembered that the New Paltz people in 1747 used the Dutch language. The first three lines are the date, the fourth line the initials of the person buried. The letters of the fifth line are the initials of the Dutch words *"In Den Heeren Ontslapen"*—"In the Lord Asleep." The final line gives the initials of the husband's name, Hendricus DeIoo. We have seen the name Deyo written DeIoo. This explanation of the inscription is corroborated by the following extract from Rev. Dr. Anson DuBois' history of the DuBois family at Catskill, as found on page 62, as follows: "Cornelius (DuBois') record of his own wife's death is peculiarly devout: it is thus in Dutch, *"Ano 1778, Mert 27, is myne vrow in Den Heeren Ontslapen."* We would read it in English, "March 27, 1778, Now is my wife sleeping in the Lord."

In the above record, as given by Rev. Dr. Anson DuBois, it will be noted that the same order is observed as on the tombstone: first the date, then the statement as to who is here buried, then the pious epitaph.

Learned persons have puzzled over this inscription. Much credit for its satisfactory solution is due to Mrs. Ralph LeFevre.

Hendricus Deyo (1) left a large family of children as follows: Debora, Peter, Jr., Isaac, Benjamin, Johannes, Christoffel, Hagetea, Hendricus, Sara and David. Debora married Peter Ostrander and settled with him near New Hurley. Peter, Jr., born in 1718, married Elizabeth Helm in 1745 and settled near Tuthill, where we find him a large taxpayer in 1765. Isaac, born in 1723, married Agatha Freer. We know nothing further concerning him except that a son, David, was baptized in 1765. Christoffel, born in 1728, married Debora Van Vliet and located at Springtown. Their son David, baptized in 1758, married Rachel Ean. Rev. Paul T. Deyo is their grandson. Johannes, born in 1726, married Sarah Van Wagenen in 1756 and located at Springtown. Hendricus (2), born in 1731, married Elizabeth Beem at Kingston October 13, 1753.

We have no connected genealogy of the family of Hendricus (1) except of the three sons: Peter, Jr., Benjamin (who kept the homestead at Bontecoe) and Hendricus (2). We will take up first the line of Peter, Jr. But we must say that our information concerning him is not complete.

In a tax list of 1765 we find Peter, Jr., located at what is now Tuthill and one of the original grants of land in the present town of Shawangunk was to Peter Deyo and son. We have not learned as yet who were Peter, Jr.'s children, but Lucas Deyo, who lived in 1820 in the house of Philip LeFevre in the Kettleboro neighborhood, was a son. Lucas' wife was a Van Kleeck of Poughkeepsie. They had a large family of boys as follows: Ezekiel, Peter, Evert, Francis and Tjerck. Lucas Deyo had a brother, who was the father of the late Jacob Deyo of Tuthill. We do not know his name.

Hendricus (2), who married Elizabeth Beem, is buried in the old Presbyterian graveyard at Highland. We do not know where he lived. He had only two children who married, the rest probably dying when young. Those two were Hendricus (3), who was baptized at Shawangunk in 1754, and Joseph, who was baptized at Kingston in 1765. Of Joseph we have no further account. Hendricus (2) must have ended his days with his son, Hendricus (3), at the river, as a tombstone in the old Presbyterian graveyard bears the inscription: "Henry Deyo died Dec. 12, 1805, Æ 74." This is the oldest grave marked by a tombstone having a legible inscription and this graveyard is the oldest in the town of Lloyd.

Hendricus (3) (in English Henry) located in the present town of Lloyd. He married Phebe Woolsey and long carried on the milling business at the Shadagee. His residence, however, was not at the Shadagee, but about two miles south of the present village of Highland in a stone house still standing on the west side of the road leading from Highland to Modena, a short distance south of the old Presbyterian graveyard. Henry (3) left a family of six sons and two daughters, all of whom married and left families. The sons were Joseph H., Henry, John W., Thomas, Elijah and Harvey. The daughters were named Clorine and Elizabeth. The former married Elidia Watkins.

Hendricus' (3) large landed estate was divided among his sons.

His sons, Joseph and Henry, occupied adjoining farms, on what is now the Highland and Modena turnpike. Joseph married Jane Deyo, daughter of Wm. Deyo of Bontecoe. Joseph's property passed to his son, Wm. H. Deyo, who rebuilt and greatly enlarged the house. The place is now occupied by Geo. C. Brown, who married Wm. H. Deyo's daughter. Jos. Deyo's other sons were Noah and George, who settled in Illinois, and Ennis, who settled near Clintondale.

Henry Deyo's farm adjoined that of his brother Joseph on the north. Henry married Elizabeth L. Bevier. They had a large family of ten children, as follows: Caroline, Luther, Phebe, Alvah, Elmira, Delia Ann, Emily, Julia, Theora, Elizabeth. All of them married. Caroline married Dewitt Ransom and after his death Alden J. Pratt; Luther married Frances E. Pratt; Phebe married Abm. Deyo; Alvah married Lydia Chambers; Elmira married Philip D. LeFevre; Julia married Philip LeRoy; Delia Ann married Andrew LeFevre; Emily married Josiah Elting; Elizabeth married Abm. E. Hasbrouck.

Hendricus' son, John W., married Annie Beesmer. He owned what has been of late years George W. Pratt's mill and here he carried on the milling business for a long, long time.

His children were Phebe Ann, Henry, Woolsey, Emeretta and Livingston. Phebe Ann married ——— Goodrich; Emeretta married Barton Weed; Livingston married ——— Saxton.

Thomas, son of Hendricus, married ——— Elting, daughter of John Elting. He was never engaged in farming. For a time he attended to his father's mill at Shadegee. At one time he was engaged in the brick manufacturing business and likewise had a store at Pell's dock in partnership, we believe, with his brother-in-law, Daniel Woolsey. By his first wife Thomas Deyo had one son, Maurice W., from whom we have a great portion of the information contained in this sketch. By his second wife, Deborah Brown, Thomas Deyo had several children, as follows: Samuel, Margaret, Mary Ann, George and Heckaliah.

Elijah, son of Hendricus (3), was born at Highland in 1798 and died in 1831. He lived, we believe, in the town of Plattekill. Elijah married Patty Thomas. Their children were Henry, who lived at Clintondale; Theron, who also lived at Clintondale and afterwards at Highland, and Philip T., who has lived for nearly thirty years at Binghamton and from whom we have this information concerning his family.

Harvey, the last son of Hendricus, married Ellen Tooker and had three children, Charles, Anna and Maria.

Going back now to the homestead at Bontecoe, Benjamin, son of Hendricus (1), kept the homestead. He left four sons, William, Abram, Benjamin and John (called Hons in Dutch).

William lived in what has been of late years the Oscar Tschirkey place. He married Sarah, daughter of Roelif J. Elting of this village, and left a large family of sons and daughters, as follows: William W., Abm. W., Cornelius, Ezekiel, Roelif, Maria, Jane, Sarah, Bridget, Catharine and Rebecca. All of these married.

Benjamin lived near Springtown. He was the father of DeWitt Deyo of Springtown, and Tjerck and David of Middletown. Abram lived on what is now the Evert Schoonmaker place. He married his cousin, a Freer, and had but one child, who left no children. John lived part of the time on the Abm. W. Deyo place; part of the time on the Evert Schoonmaker place and also in the stone house east of the Bontecoe schoolhouse. His wife was Catrina Kritsinger. His sons were Stephen, Benjamin I., John, Levi, Moses and Christian of Rochester.

CHAPTER XXIV

The DuBois Family at New Paltz

Louis DuBois, the leader of the Huguenot settlers at New Paltz, was born at Wicres, near Lille, in the province of Artois (in French Flanders), October 27, 1626. The farm of his father Cretien is still pointed out.

Louis moved to Manheim, on the Rhine, the capital of the Palatinate or Paltz, a little principality, now incorporated in Baden, and there he married Catharine Blanshan, the daughter of Matthew Blanshan, a burgher residing there.

To Louis DuBois and his wife there were born a numerous family of children, as follows: Abraham, Isaac, Jacob, Sarah, David, Solomon, Louis, Matthew. Other children died before reaching mature years. Of these children Abraham and Isaac were born at Manheim and the rest in Ulster county. Manheim was at that time a refuge for the Protestants from the neighboring parts of France, and Baird in his "Huguenot Emigration," says that the LeFevres, Hasbroucks, Crispells, etc., were associated with Louis DuBois at Manheim. The exact date of the emigration to America and the name of the ship are not known, but the time was certainly between 1658 and 1661. At the latter date he was residing at Hurley, and his third son, Jacob, was presented for baptism at the church at Kingston, as still shown by the church register, that being one of the earliest entries. In 1663, June 10, Hurley and part of Kingston were burned by the Indians, and the wife of Louis DuBois, with three children, were among those carried away captive. Three months afterwards an expedition under Captain Crieger recovered the captives, surprising the Indians at their fort, near the Hogabergh, in Shawangunk. According to the tradition the discovery of the lowlands along the Wallkill during this expedition led to the settlement at New Paltz in 1678.

Louis DuBois was the first elder of the church here, and the first entry in the church register commencing in 1683, still in existence, is in his hand writing. In 1686 Louis DuBois returned from New Paltz to Kingston, where he bought a house and resided ten years, until his death in 1696. This house stood at the north-west corner of John street and Clinton avenue, near the late residence of F. L. Westbrook.

About two years before Louis DuBois moved from Kingston to New Paltz his brother Jacques came to America. He died soon after, in 1676. His descendants located in Dutchess county.

Not long before his death Louis deeded to his youngest son, Matthew, a certain tract of land in Kingston. The original document is in the possession of Mr. Julius Schoonmaker and is as follows:

To all Christian people To whom this Shall or May Come Lowies dubois of Kingston in ye County of ulster and Catharina his wife Sendeth greeting.

Whereas the said Lowies duboys and Catharine his Wife for Divers good Causes and Considerations them thereunto moving but more & Especially for and Inconsideration of a Certaine Summe or quantity of One thousand and five hundred Schuypples of Wheat to them in hand payd before the Ensealing and Delivery of these presents by Matthew duboys Jongest Sunn of them the said Lowies duboys & Catharina his Wife have Bargained, Sold, alienated enfeofed, assigned and Settover, and by these presents doe Bargain, Sell, alienate Enfeofe assign and Settover unto the Said Matthew Duboys the Right halfe of ye Certaine tract or parcell of Land Situate, Lying & being uppon hooly peece betwixt the Land of Hyman & Jan Roos and the Land of Lammert huylandss and now in the possession of Jacob duboys.   Likewise a house, barne & lot of ground in ye towne of Kingstowne betwixt the housing & ground of Coll. Henricus Beekman & Saloman Duboys.   Likewise a small piece of pasture Land to ye east side of the towne of Kingstowne afous'd betwizt ye ground of sd Henricus Beekman and Wessel Ten Broeck;   To have and to hold the said tract or Parcel of Land, house and lot of ground and pasture Land unto the Said Matthew Duboys his heirs and assigns and to the Only proper use benefit and behoofs of him the Said Matthew Duboys his heirs and assigns for ever, and the Said Matthew Duboys to Enter in peaceable possession of ye Said Land When hee shall Come to ye age of one & twenty years, and the house, pasture Land, &c., O—after the Decease of them the Said Lowies Duboys and Catharina his Wife have hereunto Sett their hands and Affixed their seals.

In Kingstowne this 22d day of February, 1695-6.

> Lowies du boys, (seal)
> Catharina duboys. (seal)

Signed, Sealed and Delivered in the presence of

> Jan Burhans,
> Marttys Slecht,
> W. D. Myer.

In the presence of Me

Jacob Rutsen.

The last will of Louis DuBois, as recorded in the Surrogate's office of the County of New York, is in Dutch, dated March 26, 1694, and was proved July 13, 1697. A previous will is as follows, made at the time of his removal from New Paltz to Kingston:

In the name of God, Amen, the one and thirtieth day of March, Anno Domini, 1686, I, Louis Du bois, of the New Paltz in the County of Ulster, being both sound in body and of good and perfect memory, thanks be to the Almighty, and calling to remembrance the uncertain Estate of this transitory life, and that all flesh must yield unto death whom it shall please God to call; doe make, constitute, ordain and declare this my last will and testament, in manner following: Revoking and annuling, by these presents, all and every testament and testaments, will and wills, hertofore by me made and declared either by word or writing, and this to be my last will and testament. Imprims: I will that all my just debts shall be paid within a convenient time after my decease, and what there shall be found afterwards belonging to my Estate, shall be equally dealt among my children! but my two oldest sons desiring to have each of them a part of the land of the New Paltz, more than the other sons by reason their names are upon the Patent, but they will be content to deale equally with my other children, whether in land, houses, or any other sort of goods whatsoever belonging to my said Estate, as well as the lands of the Paltz that I have bought for me and after my death and their mother's decease, shall be dealt equally amongst them, (to wit,) Three parts lying and being situated in the New Paltz, but if they (to wit) my two eldest sons will each of them have a part of the land lying in the New Paltz, they may have it after myn and their mother's death, with condition they shall pay for the said land with all the interest of the same, unto the

other of my children, and shall not inherit any of the other
land, houses, or any other sort of goods belonging to my said
Estate, but them that have house lots and have built thereon,
shall keep the same upon condition that the other of my children shall have so much land instead thereof, in such convenient places as may be found most expedient for them in
any place belonging to my said Estate.   Myn wife, their
mother, shall have the ordering of the Estate, that is to say, to
have the profits and perquisites of the same, so long as she re-
maineth the widow, but in case she cometh to remarry, that she
shall have the one right half of the whole Estate, either lands,
houses, or any other goods or chattels, whatsoever belong to
my said Estate, and the other half shall be amongst the children aforesaid, equally dealt, except my two eldest sons, which,
if they will have the Lotts above mentioned, must pay for the
same with the interest of the said land, and shall have no other
part in my said Estate, that is my last will and testament and
no other, in witness whereof I have hereunto set my hand and
seal the day and year first above written.   LOUYS DU BOIS.

Signed and sealed in presence of

> Arent Tennisson,
> Dirck Schepmoes.

Entered upon record 19th May, 1686.

> Examined per John Ward,
> D'p't Cl'k.

Louis was not only a very extensive land owner but a money
lender likewise, and the writer has in his possession several
receipts in his handwriting and with his signature for loans
repaid to Louis in his later years.

RECEIPTS WITH SIGNATURE OF LOUIS DU BOIS, THE PATENTEE

Some time after her husband's death, and when she was about
63 years of age, Louis' widow married Jean Cottin, a very
worthy Huguenot, who kept a store at Kingston and had been
previously the schoolmaster at New Paltz.

In the year 1703 we find recorded in the church book at
Kingston the following interesting entry in the list of baptisms, under date of September 5th:

"Rachel ———— after profession of her faith she received
the sacrament of holy baptism, aged 17 years. Besides the
points required of her in the formula of baptism she also
promised the congregation to serve her mistress Catharine
Cottyn faithfully and diligently until the death of her mistress
and after that to serve her master Jan Cottyn and after that
she shall be at liberty and free."

The old Dutch dominie, who recorded all this in the church
book, performed a valuable deed for history and for the descendants of Louis DuBois, the Patentee. Usually the church
record contained simply the name of the child baptised, the
parents, and sponsors; but here we have the evidence that the
woman who, in her early married years, saved her life by
singing a psalm, while the savages were preparing to burn
her at the stake, now in her old age manumitted her negro
woman. This is perhaps the very first recorded instance in
this country of the freeing of a slave.

Louis DuBois, the Patentee, had been dead seven years;
after his death his widow had married that good old French
merchant of Kingston, Jean Cottin, who when he died left all
his property to the church. The families of her seven sons,
Abraham, Isaac, Jacob, David, Solomon, Louis, Jr., and Matthew, were living at New Paltz, Rochester, Hurley and Kingston, but it was to none of these that her negro girl should go

as a slave. Mrs. Cottin was an old woman. It was not to be supposed in the course of nature that she or her husband could live many years. In all probability by the time the negro girl reached the age of 25 she became a free woman by the act of her mistress.

We have said that Louis' sons were Abraham, Isaac, Jacob, David, Solomon, Louis and Matthew.

Of these sons Matthew settled in Kingston, where his descendants still reside. David located in the town of Rochester, where he left a line of descendants. Jacob settled on a farm of his father in old Hurley, where he left a large family, and his second son, Louis, settled in Monmouth county, N. J., and was the father of Rev. Benj. DuBois of Revolutionary fame. Patterson DuBois of Philadelphia is of Jacob's line. The other four sons, Abraham, Isaac, Solomon and Louis, Jr., remained at New Paltz. Although Isaac was only about 18 years of age and his brother Abm. hardly 21, they were both associated with their father as members of the 12 patentees of New Paltz in 1677.

DOCUMENT WITH SIGNATURE OF ABRAHAM DU BOIS, THE PATENTEE

CHAPTER XXV

ABRAHAM DuBOIS, THE PATENTEE

Abraham DuBois married Margaret Deyo, daughter of Christian Deyo, the Patentee. They left a family of children, the eldest of whom, also named Abraham, was baptised in 1685. He settled in the County of Somerset, N. J. There was but one other son, Joel, who died in 1734 and left no family. One daughter of Abm. DuBois, the Patentee, married Roelif Elting, the first of the name at New Paltz; another daughter, Katharine, born in 1693, married Wm. Donalson and located in Lancaster county, Pennsylvania. Another daughter, Leah, married Philip Ferrie and moved with him to Lancaster county, Pa., where her father had obtained a patent for 1,000 acres of land. Another daughter, Rachel, married her cousin, Isaac, son of Solomon DuBois, and likewise moved to Lancaster county, Pennsylvania.

Abm. DuBois was the last survivor of the 12 patentees of New Paltz, a fact that is stated on his tombstone, which is still standing in the old graveyard in this village. He died in 1731.

Among the old records at Albany is an abstract of the will of Abm. DuBois, survivor of the New Paltz Patentees. The will, which was probated in 1731, mentions the wife Margaret, the sons Abraham and Joel, the daughters Sara (wife of Roelif Eltinge) Leah (wife of Philip Ferree) Rachel and Catharine. The will disposes of land on the Raritan in New Jersey, on the south side of the Paltz River (Walkill) at New Paltz, at Canistoga and house and lot at New Paltz; also personal property.

The executors are the son Abraham and the son-in-law Roelif Eltinge. Daniel DuBois is one of the witnesses.

Edmund Eltinge had in his possession two ancient documents relating to Abram DuBois and his children. One of them is an inventory containing a "true and perfect description of all ye goods, rights and credits of Joel Dubois, late of the county of Ulster in ye province of New York, deceased, taken by Abraham DuBois of ye county of Summerset, in the province of New Jersey, husbandman, the only brother and administrator of the said Joel DuBois, deceased, this twenty-first day of June in the eight year of his magisty's reign, anno dom, 1734."

The other paper in Mr. Edmund Eltinge's possession was a release from the heirs of Abraham DuBois, the Patentee, to Roelif Elting and wife, dated A. D. 1732 and signed by

> Wm. Donaldson,
> Katharina Donaldson,
> Rachel Douboys,
> Abraham Duboys,
> Lea ferrie,
> Joel Duboies,
> Philip ferrie.

Captain R. C. DuBois, of Washington, D. C., in 1890 visited New Paltz to gather material for a history of the family of Louis DuBois, and in particular the descendants of his son Abram, the last survivor of the New Paltz Patentees, on his return stopping in Somerset county, N. J., where Abram, son of the New Paltz Patentee of the same name, removed and located.

Capt. DuBois says:

I found the old stone house of Abm. DuBois, son of the New Paltz Patentee, still standing and occupied, looking as if it might withstand the heavy hand of centuries yet to come. It stands within the shadow of the mountain from the heights of which Washington watched the movements of Lord Howe and the British in the attempts of the latter to reach Philadelphia. I found also that two of the grandsons of Abram the Second were in the service and on the right side.

Another grandson made the first dies for the mint at Philadelphia. Thus one of the descendants of Louis and Abram DuBois helped to lay the foundation for the U. S. Mint, which was not established until about nine years later.

TOMBSTONE OF ABRAHAM DU BOIS, THE PATENTEE

CHAPTER XXVI

THE FAMILY OF ISAAC DUBOIS, ONE OF THE NEW PALTZ PATENTEES

Isaac DuBois, the second son of Louis, was the youngest of the New Paltz patentees. He was born at Manheim about 1659. He was about two years old when his parents came to Kingston, and about eighteen years old when they came to New Paltz. In 1683 he married, at Kingston, Mary, daughter of Jean Hasbrouck, the Patentee. Seven years afterwards he died "at his home in Paltz," as is briefly stated in the church book, leaving two sons, Daniel, born April 28, 1684, and Philip, born in 1690; another son, Benjamin, having died young. Daniel's baptism is the first one recorded on the old French church book at New Paltz. Of the son Philip we have no further account except that he married Esther, daughter of Peter Gumaer of Minnisinck, settled at Rochester and left no son. One daughter, Esther, married Louis Bevier of Marbletown. Daniel married, June 8, 1713, Mary, daughter of Simon LeFevre, the Patentee.

The following release from Mary, widow of the Patentee, to her son Daniel is found among the old papers in the family:

Know all men by these presents that I Mary Dubois of the new Paltz in County of Ulster widdow and Relict of Isaac Dubois late of the same place deceased for divers good Causes me thereunto moving but more and Especially for a Competent sume of good and Lawful money to me in hand paid by my son Daniel Dubois of the new paltz aforesaid have given granted Released devised and forever quit claimed and do

hereby Release and forever quit claim unto the sd Daniel
Dubois his heirs and assigns forever all my right title claim
interest and demand whatsoever which I now have or might
could or ought to have of out in or to all and singular the real
estate of lands and buildings situate and being within the
bounds and limits of the township of new paltz which did
belong unto my said deceased husband in his lifetime to have
to hold the same unto the said Daniel Dubois his heirs and
assigns forever to the sole and only proper use benefit and
behoof of him the said Daniel Dubois his heirs and assigns
forever In witness whereof the said Mary Dubois hath hereunto putt her hand and seale in the new paltz this fourteenth
day of February, annoy Dom. 1718-9.

Mary Dubois,
her M mark.

Sealed and delivered In the presence of us,

    Solomon dubois,
    Louis bevier le jun,
    W. Nottingham.

DANIEL, SON OF ISAAC

In 1705 Daniel built the old stone house or fort which is still
standing, with its iron figures, showing the date of erection,
and the port holes in the eastern walls for safety against Indian attacks, and the window high up on the western wall.
We find Daniel's name in the list of freeholders in 1728; also
in the release from the proprietors of the Paltz Patent to Solomon DuBois, in 1729. Daniel died in 1755. His tombstone
in the old graveyard in this village bears simply the date and
the initials D. D. B.

THE OLD DU BOIS HOUSE OR FORT IN THIS VILLAGE

Among the old family papers is found a will of Daniel, in French, dated in 1729. The writing is very plain and legible. Another will, in English, is dated 1747 and is as follows:

In the Name of God amen the twelve day of September in the year of our Lord Christ one thousand seven hundred & forty seven I Daniel Dubois of the new palyes in the County of Ulster and province of New York being sick of body but sound memory and understanding Praised be God for it Calling to mind the mortality of my body and knowing that it is appointed for all men once to die and being Desirous to Settle things in order Do Revoke all former wills and Testaments by me in any ways and manner before this time made named willed Devised and bequeathed Ratified and Confirm this and no other to be my last will and Testament That is to say Principaly and first of all I Give and bequeath my Immortal Soul into the hands of almighty God my Creator that Gave it hoping by the meritorious Death and passion of Jesus Christ my sole Saviour and only Redeemer to Receive pardon and full Remission for all my Sins and my body to the Earth from whence it Came to be buried in Christian Like & Decent manner at the Discretion of my Executors herein named & nominated nothing Doubting but I shall Receive the same again at the General Day of Resurrection by the almighty power of God, and as touching such worldly Estate as it hath pleased God to bless me with in this world I give Devise and Dispose of the same in the following manner and form Imprimis I do order and appoint that my Just and Honest Debts be by my Executors within Convenient time paid and satisfied Item it is my will and order that my two sons Benjamin and Isaac Dubois Shall have as good an outfit as my Son Simon has had Item I give and Bequeath unto Maritie my dearly beloved wife all my whole Estate real and personal during her natural Lifetime and after

her decease to be divided among my children as Shall be hereafter ordered and mentioned in this my last will and Testament
Item I give and bequeath unto my eldest Son Benjamin Dubois
his heirs and assigns for Ever first out of my stock of horses
one horse the choice of all my horses in Consideration as being
my eldest son on which account he shall not have or pretend
to have any thing more by any ways or pretences whatsoever
Item I give and bequeath unto my Three Sons all the rest of
of my stock of horses to be Equally divided amongst them share
and share alike Item I give and bequeath unto my four children all my Remainder and Remainders of all my Estate Real
and personal to be equally divided amongst them share and
share alike Each and equal fourth part of all my Estate that
is to say to my Son Benjamin Dubois his heirs and assigns for
Ever one fourth part of my Estate to my son Simon Dubois
his heirs and assigns for Ever one fourth part of my Estate
to my son Isack Dubois his heirs and assigns for Ever one
fourth part of my estate to my daughter Elizabeth wife of
Abraham doyoe to her heirs and assigns for Ever one fourth
part of my estate Item it is my will and order that if any of
my children shall come to die without having any Lawful
children then that share or fourth part shall be divided into
Three equal Shares amongst the rest of my children to them
their heirs and assigns for Ever and in case any of the Brothers
or Sisters being dead and Leaving children behind them their
children shall have their fathers or mothers share shall be
divided amongst the Children share and share alike Item I
do order constitute and appoint my wife Marietie and my four
children as follows — Benjamin Dubois Simon Debois Isack
Dubois and my daughter Elizabeth doyoe above named to be
my Executors of this my last will and Testament and that
every part and parcel hereof may be performed and fulfilled

TOMBSTONE OF DANIEL DU BOIS IN OLD GRAVE YARD IN THIS VILLAGE

In witness whereof I have hereunto put my hand and seal the day and year above written.

Signed sealed published pronounced and declared by the Said Daniel DuBois to be his last will and testament In the presence of

    Samuel Bevier

    daniel hasbrouck   Daniel Dubois [s]

    Charles Brodhead

    Josia Eltinge.

SIMON DUBOIS

Daniel left three sons, Simon, Isaac and Benjamin, and one daughter, Elizabeth, who married Abraham Deyo (2) and lived with him in this village. We know nothing further concerning Isaac. Simon married Catharine LeFevre and kept the homestead of his father. Benjamin married Maria Bevier and lived either at Springtown or in the stone house still standing on the farm adjoining the Peter D. LeFevre place on the south. In the list of slaveholders, in 1755, Simon DuBois is mentioned as the owner of three male and three female slaves and Benjamin the owner of three slaves. In the tax list of 1765 we find Simon assessed for £42 and Benjamin for £29. We find Simon's name as one of the Duzine in 1772. The old homestead in this village has remained in the possession of Simon's family until the present day. We have in our possession an ancient paper, being the official record of the town election at New Paltz, in 1749, which was held at the house of Simon DuBois, and contains his signature. It is endorsed "Paltz election 1749, filed May 2d." It is in English and a transcript is as follows:

At the annual election of the freeholders and Inhabitants of the township of the New Paltz on the first Tuesday of April

Annoq: Dom: 1749 the following persons were duely chosen and elected by a plurality of Voices of said towns freeholders to serve the said town in the soovrall offices which they were chosen is as followeth V't:

Constable—Jacobus Bovier.

Supervisor—Abraham Hardonborgh.

Assessors { Evort terwellego.
{ Josias Eltinge.

Collector—Noah Eltinge.

Surveyors of Highway—Petrus Low.

Overseers of the Poor { Abraham Rosa.
{ Abraham Lesfover.

Fence Viewers { Josias Eltinge.
{ Isaac Freer.
{ Hendrikus Dubois.

The Election was Koop By me the under Written Simon Dubois as Constable Pme.   Simon Dubois.

There are a number of other papers of Simon DuBois that have come down in the family until the present day and have been stored in the old trunk for perhaps 150 years. Simon Dubois' sons were Joseph, Daniel (called Velche), who kept the homestead in this village; Isaac and Andries, the two latter being twins. Simon also had one daughter, Cornelia, who married Josaphat Hasbrouck, and another daughter, Mary, who married Jacobus Rose.

Daniel married Catharine Bessimer. They had no children. The old homestead in his day is described as an old-fashioned one-story house with a basement, the entrance to which was directly off the street. An old gentleman informs us that when he was a boy there was no fire in the church on Sundays and it was customary for people to have foot-stoves to keep warm while attending Divine service. At the DuBois house a good fire of hickory wood was kept burning on Sunday morning that people might have good coals to put in the foot-stoves.

Isaac, son of Simon and brother of Daniel, married Rebecca Deyo. They lived for a time at what has been of late years the Wm. E. DuBois place, where they had a grist mill. They then moved to Chenango county, but not liking the country there moved back to Ulster county. It is related that Mrs. DuBois in going to Chenango, aided by pushing on the wagon at different places, and in returning was so desirous of getting back to Ulster county that she lent her aid in the same manner. After coming back from Chenango Isaac built what is now the Nathan Townsend house at Centerville, where he lived a long time and ended his days. This house was built of stone, but has been since sided over.

In the Revolutionary War Isaac served as a private in Capt. Abraham Deyo's company in the Third Ulster County Regiment. Isaac DuBois left four sons: Joseph, who lived on South street in the town of Lloyd and afterwards moved to Michigan; Simon, who kept his father's homestead, now the Nathan Townsend place at Centerville; Daniel who took the place of his uncle Daniel in this village; and Henry I., who lived at Ohioville. Simon, at Centerville, was twice married. By his first wife he had one son, Abraham, who sold the house to Nathan Townsend and bought a farm in the Grahow neighborhood. By his second wife, whose maiden name was Poyer, Simon had two daughters.

Daniel DuBois always lived in the homestead of his fathers in this village which had come to him from his uncle Daniel. He married Magdalene Hasbrouck. Daniel's children were John W., Daniel, Melissa, who married Benjamin Relyea, and

Mary, whose heirs now own and occupy the old homestead. Daniel rebuilt the old stone house, but the walls of the lower portion of the house have been left unchanged and the port holes in the eastern and northern walls remain to the present day.

ANDRIES DUBOIS

Isaac's twin brother, Andries, located at Highland where he had a mill, now the Philip Schantz mill. His wife was Mary Deyo, sister of his brother Isaac's wife. Andries was a stone mason and with his own hands built the stone house in which he lived and which is still standing. Andries left but one son, Joseph, who died in the army in the war of 1812, leaving one daughter, who married Daniel Tooker of Marlborough. Andries had four daughters: Phebe, married Job G. Elmore; Ellen, married Reuben Deyo; Elizabeth, married Samuel Duncan; Rachel, married Arthur Doren and kept the mill, and Catharine, married Dr. Deyo and after his death Isaac Craft.

Hon. Andrew E. Elmore, of Fort Howard, Wis., was born in the old stone house of his grandfather, Andries DuBois, and was named for him. From Mr. Elmore we have our information concerning this branch of the family. At the age of eighty-one Mr. Elmore visited the National capital, and on his return stopped at Highland to visit his old home. He likewise drove to New Paltz to see friends and to take another look at the old DuBois house, the house of his mother's ancestors, and in the attic of which, before it was rebuilt, he had slept when a child.

JOSEPH DUBOIS

Joseph, the youngest son of Simon and brother of Daniel, Isaac and Andries, married Mary Hardenburgh and lived about two miles north of this village on what has been known of late years as the Moses P. LeFevre place. Joseph had one son, Hardenburgh, and one daughter who married Daniel Bevier of Ireland Corners. Hardenburgh kept store for a time, about 1830, in what is now the Huguenot bank building.

BENJAMIN DuBois

We will now go back to Benjamin, grandson of Isaac the Patentee and son of Daniel. Benjamin left his brother Simon in possession of the homestead in this village and located on the other side of the Wallkill in the Springtown neighborhood. His wife was Maria Bevier. Benjamin's children were Daniel, who married Catharine LeFevre; Anna, who married Peter Freer; Abraham, who married ———— Bevier, and Samuel, who married Jane LeFevre. All located in the town of New Paltz as it then existed, and in the Springtown neighborhood their descendants lived,—some of them till the present time. Benjamin's oldest son, Daniel, married Catharine LeFevre and lived in the old stone house adjoining the Peter D. LeFevre place on the south, and here his only son, Abraham, lived after him. A little story that dates back about 100 years illustrates the customs of those times. Daniel's cousin Isaac, son of Simon, had come to visit him. Each had a horse of which he was proud and each claimed that his own horse was the better of the two. So to settle the question the two cousins, both of whom were then old men, decided to have a test on the ice on the Wallkill at once. The horses were hitched up forthwith, but the question as to which had the better horse was never settled as one horse fell into an air hole and was drowned.

Abraham, who was Daniel's only son, married Anna Le-Fevre of Bloomingdale. He died in middle age. His sons were Daniel A., Simon L., Benjamin and Samuel. Abraham had a daughter who married Maurice Hasbrouck, another married Alexander Elting and another married Mathusalem Wurts. The two last named moved to the vicinity of Auburn in western New York. The fourth daughter, Margaret, remained unmarried and was the last survivor of the family.

CHAPTER XXVII

SOLOMON DuBOIS, SON OF LOUIS THE PATENTEE

Solomon DuBois was born in 1670, while his parents resided in Hurley. He married, about 1692, Tryntje Gerritson, who was the daughter of Gerrit Cornelissen. Solomon built his house near where Capt. W. H. D. Blake now resides. He died in 1759 at the great age of 89 years. We do not know where he is buried. Solomon was a man of much influence, was an officer in the New Paltz church, occupied civil trusts, and accumulated much landed property not only at New Paltz, but in Greene county and at Perkiomen, Chester county, now Lancaster county, Pa. Louis DuBois, the Patentee, received June 2, 1688, from Gov. Dongan, a patent for a large tract of land, on which his sons Solomon and Louis Jr. located, lying on both sides of the Wallkill. Solomon's house, built on this tract, was quite probably the first house built outside of the village. From a tax list laid by the provincial government, which included a tax on chimneys, it appeared that Solomon's house had two chimneys.

Outside of our village there is no place in Southern Ulster of more interest to the antiquarian than this farm occupied by Capt. W. H. D. Blake. This neighborhood was called by our grandfathers by the Indian name of Poughwoughtenonk. Here, on the patent granted to Louis DuBois, his sons, Solomon and Louis, Jr., lived. Here stood the Conferentie church just before the Revolution. Across the Wallkill, at the mouth of the Plattekill, was the last Indian village in this vicinity. The homestead of Louis DuBois, Jr., who resided a short distance south, was broken up and passed out of the family long, long ago. The site of the house even can not be determined. But the homestead of his brother Solomon descended from generation to generation of DuBoises till about 1880.

Josiah DuBois is still well remembered. He lived to be 87 years of age and in his olden days loved to tell of the days of our forefathers. The writer has still a very distinct recollection of a visit to Uncle Josiah's home in his early childhood and of the stories he told of the old times and old people. Even to the present day a considerable portion of the stories of the olden times are related on the authority of Josiah DuBois.

The homestead at Poughwoughtenonk has passed out of the possession of the DuBois family, but it has a worthy owner in Capt. W. H. D. Blake, who seems to possess all the love of the ancient traditions of Josiah DuBois, who in 1822 built the brick house in which Capt. Blake now resides.

Near the bank of the Wallkill a short distance up the stream is the cellar of the house of Solomon DuBois. The knocker on the door always bore the initials S. D. B. From Solomon this house passed to his son, Cornelius, Sr., who left a rather singular will, providing that his only son, Cornelius, Jr., should have all his real estate during his life time, but after his death his six sisters or their heirs should have their share. The landed estate amounted to about 3,000 acres, lying on both sides of the Wallkill. One of the daughters of the first Cornelius, named Sarah, had married Jacob Hasbrouck of Marbletown. Under the arrangement for the division of the Poughwoughtenonk estate her son, Dr. Cornelius Hasbrouck, the father of Mrs. Peter Barnhart, deceased, of New Paltz, became the owner of this old house, which was torn down in his time.

Solomon left a family of four sons and four daughters.

The sons were Isaac, who settled at Perkiomen, Pa., Benjamin, who settled at Catskill, and Cornelius and Hendricus, who settled on their father's estate in Ulster county. Solomon's daughters married as follows: Jacomyntje married her cousin Barent, son of Jacob; Sarah married Simon Van Wagenen, New Paltz; Helena married Josiah Elting of New Paltz, and Catharine married Peter Low of New Paltz.

The name of Solomon DuBois appears with the title of lieutenant in the documentary history of New York, Vol. III, page 972, and he is credited with active military service.

Solomon's son Isaac, who settled at Perkiomen, Lancaster county, Pennsylvania, married his cousin Rachel, daughter of Abraham, the Patentee. They left no sons, but had a family of four daughters, Catharine, Margaret, Rebecca and Elizabeth. One of the descendants of Isaac DuBois is Mr. Samuel E. Gross of Chicago, who has shown himself one of the warmest friends of the New Paltz Huguenot Memorial Society.

Solomon's son Benjamin married, in 1721, Catharine Suylant and settled at Catskill in what was then a portion of Albany county about 1727.

They had a large family of children, several of whom were born before their location at Catskill. The sons were Petrus, Benjamin, Solomon, Huybartus, Cornelius and Isaac.

The DuBois family flourished at Catskill. But it is not the purpose of this book to trace the fortunes of the New Paltz families outside of Ulster county.

A carefully-written history of the descendants of Benjamin DuBois of Catskill has been published by one of their number, Rev. Dr. Anson DuBois, who is spending an honored old age at Newburgh.

We resume now the thread of our narrative concerning the family at Poughwoughtenonk.

REV. DR. ANSON DU BOIS

The matter of making good the title of Louis DuBois, Jr., and Solomon DuBois to the tract, on which they resided, as far as any possible claims by the proprietors of the Paltz patent were concerned, was perfected in 1729, as shown by an ancient quit claim in possession of the late Edmund Eltinge in which it is stated that for the sum of sixpence the owners of the Paltz patent release unto Solomon and Louis DuBois all claims upon the tract granted unto Louis DuBois, of Kingston, deceased, by Thomas Dongan, late Governor, lying on both sides of the Paltz river and extending from the lands of said Paltz to the lands of James Graham and John Delavoll. (That is the Guilford Patent.) This document is signed

Jacob Hasbrouk,	Solomon Hasbroucq,
Daniel Hasbroucq,	Isaac lefevre,
Daniel DuBois,	Jan een,
Samuel Bevier,	Abraham Doiau,
Andre lefevre,	Louis bevier,
jean lefevre,	his
	Hugo X ffrear.
	mark

(These names are interesting as showing the quaint orthography of those days, showing also who were the Dusine in 1729.)

THE DESCENDANTS OF SOLOMON DUBOIS
AT POUGHWOUGHTENONK

Solomon DuBois, as we have stated, left two sons, Cornelius and Hendricus, who settled on the ancestral acres. The former married Margaret Houghtaling. He inherited 3,000 acres from his father's estate which was called Poughwoughtenonk, and here he resided. He left a family of three sons, Wilhelmus, Josiah and Cornelius, and six daughters. The last named son was the only one who married and outlived his father.

In Solomon's will, which was made in 1756 and admitted to probate in 1759, he gives to his four granddaughters, children of his son Isaac, all the land at Perkiomen, Pa., to his son Benjamin his land at Catskill, but requiring him to pay £100 divided equally between his daughter Helena, wife of Josiah Elting, and the children of his daughter Catharine, wife of Peter Low. The will gives the son Cornelius the lands occupied by him on the patent granted to his father and likewise a moiety of the New Paltz patent, but requires him to pay £100 to his sisters or their heirs. The will gives to the son Hendricus the lands in his possession within the patent granted to the testator's father, Louis DuBois, the Patentee, also a moiety of the New Paltz patent, but requires him to pay £100 to his sisters. The testator provides, moreover, that if any of his children or grandchildren shall commence a law suit against other of his children on account of dissatisfaction with the will they shall forfeit their share of the estate. The sons, Benjamin and Hendricus, and John Elting of Kingston are appointed executors of the will.

The six daughters married as follows: Janitje married Major Jacob Hasbrouck of New Paltz, Catharine married Col. Jonathan Hasbrouck of Newburgh, Rachel married Col. Lewis DuBois of Marlborough, Leah married Cornelius Wynkoop of Hurley, Sarah married Jacob Hasbrouck of Marbletown and Jacomintje married Andries Bevier of Wawarsing. Cornelius, Jr., occupied his father's homestead. In the Revolutionary war he served as quartermaster in the 4th Regiment of Militia, of which his brother-in-law Jonathan Hasbrouck of Newburgh, was colonel. He married Gertrude Bruyn. He left one son, Josiah, who married, and a family of daughters, who married as follows: Jane married Jacob Hardenburgh of New Paltz, Margaret married Abm. J. Hardenburgh of Shawangunk, Sarah married John N. LeFevre of Kettleboro, Hannah married Andries J. LeFevre of Kettleboro, Mary married Wm. McDonald of Wawarsing.

Josiah DuBois in his younger days carried on the mercantile business in what is now the Memorial House in this village in partnership with Col. Josiah Hasbrouck, whose daughter, Elizabeth, he married as his first wife. About 1822 he left New Paltz and moved to the ancestral acres where he erected the fine brick house, still standing, and here he lived until his death in 1868, at the great age of 87 years. After the death of his first wife he married Catharine Winfield, of Peconosink in the town of Shawangunk. The children by the first wife were Sarah, who married Rev. Mr. Easton, and Pamela, who married Abner Hasbrouck. The children by the second wife were Elizabeth, wife of Dr. Isaac Reeve; Gilbert, Edward, Josiah, Antoinette and Jane, wife of Dr. William Pierson.

HENDRICUS DuBOIS

Going back now to Hendricus, the other son of Solomon, we find that he married Janetje Houghtaling. He lived on what is now known as the Capt. Jacob M. DuBois place. Hendricus had a family of four sons, Solomon, Philip, Mathusalem and Henry (sometimes called Hendricus), and four daughters, Catharine, Leah, Rachel and Dina, all of whom married as follows: Catharine married Matthew DuBois, Leah married Christopher Kiersted, Rachel married John A. Hardenburgh and Dinah married Abram Elting.

In the building of the Conferentia church, which was situated near the residence of his brother, Cornelius, Hendricus

DuBois and Noah Elting were the most liberal contributors and in the organization of this church Hendricus took a very active part, a meeting being held at his house August 29, 1767, for the purpose of organizing this church. Both Hendricus and Cornelius were men of large means.

The family of Hendricus DuBois were noted for their great size, and the saying is still remembered of an old negro man named Frank, who lived to be about 100 years of age, that more large people had come out of his house than out of any other house in the country.

Three of Hendricus' sons, Solomon, Mathusalem and Henry, served in the Revolutionary war. The first named had his knee injured in some way in the army and remained lame. His knee would click as he walked, for which reason he was sometimes called "Clinker." Their brother Philip kept a public house at Libertyville, and his widow, whose maiden name was Anna Hue, continued it after his death in Revolutionary times. Methusalem was a captain in the army and was stationed at Newburgh. In "New York in the Revolution" his name appears as ensign in the 4th Ulster County Militia. He was twice married, his first wife being Gertrude Bruyn and his second Catharine Bevier. We have more stories concerning Mathusalem than of almost any man of that period, although we have no account of the battles in which he was engaged. After the war he was usually called "Old Captain." He lived in a house part wood and part stone, torn down about 1830, on the place lately owned by his grandson, Zachariah. The sword which he carried in the army came down to his grandson, Peter W., of Libertyville, who allowed it to be taken to Indiana by one of the family. In those days there was much game in the country, and it is related that Captain Mathusalem was coming afoot to church (of course we mean the Confer-

entia church near Mr. Blake's present residence), when he saw
a deer lying asleep by the side of a log, and that he seized the
deer, and though a little dog that was with him kept snapping
at his legs, while busy, he took out his pocket knife, with which
he dispatched him. He did not go to church that day, but carried the deer home. While Captain DuBois was stationed at
Newburgh the Indians burned Wawarsing, and it was thought
that they would cross the mountains. It is related that an old
colored woman in the place kept a pot of water boiling for two
or three days, in order to give the redskins a warm reception,
but they did not come.

Captain Mathusalem had two sons, Wilhelmus (father of
Peter W.) and Philip (father of Zach.), by his second wife.
By his first wife he also had two sons, Abram, who went west,
and Cornelius, who lived where his grandson, the late Henry
M., resided.

A short distance from the residence of the "Old Captain"
was that of his brother, Henry (or Hendricus), who was an
adjutant in the patriot army in the regiment commanded by
Lewis DuBois of Marlborough. His wife was Rebecca Van
Wagenen. Their children were Garret, Mathusalem, Mary,
Jane and Rebecca. Garret lived where Garret L. DuBois lately
lived, on the east bank of the Wallkill. Mathusalem lived
where his father and his grandfather had lived before him and
his son, Capt. Jacob M., lived after him. Jane married Z.
Freer, the father of Henry D. B. Rebecca married her cousin,
Cornelius, father of Mathusalem and grandfather of Henry M.,
who occupied the old homestead, where his father and his
grandfather lived before him.

CHAPTER XXVIII

The Family of Louis DuBois, Jr., Son of Louis
the Patentee

Louis DuBois, Jr., was born in 1677, and in 1701 married Rachel Hasbrouck. He settled on a portion of the same tract as his brother Solomon, which had been granted by patent to their father, the original Louis. Where Louis, Jr., built his house we do not know, but it was somewhere on the County House plain a little south of his brother's. The locality where Louis, Jr., located was called until quite recently by the Indian name of Nescatack, changed in modern times to Libertyville. In an ancient document the name of Louis, Jr., appears with the title of Captain, but we have no information as to any military service performed by him. Louis DuBois, Jr., left three sons, Jonathan, Nathaniel and Louis. He also had threee daughters, Maria, Mary and Catharine. The first named married Johannes Hardenburgh of Rosendale.

Solomon and Louis DuBois, Jr., sold to Roelif Eltinge, in 1726, the land where Edmund Eltinge resided and the original deed was still in Mr. Eltinge's possession. It read as follows:

To all Christian people to whom this present writing shall or may come. Lewis DuBois and Solomon DuBois, both of the New Paltz, for divers, good causes and considerations, them thereunto moving, have remised, released, and forever quit-claimed and by these presents for themselves and their heirs do fully, freely, clearly, and absolutely remise, release and forever quit-claim unto Roelif Elting, of the same place, yeoman, in his full and peaceable possession and to his heirs and assigns, forever, all such right, estate, title, interest and demand, forever, as they the said Lewis DuBois and Solomon DuBois, had or ought to have, of out, or in, to all that certain tract or parcel of land which, lying and being at the New Paltz aforesaid, on the west side of the Paltz Kil on the grant, piece now in possession of the said Roelif Eltinge and likewise all the land on the east side of the said Kill, now in possession, of the said Roelif Eltinge, together with the house, barn, orchards, pastures and all and every thing appurtenances, thereunto belonging or in any wise appertaining to have and to hold the above remised and released premises, with all and every the appurtenances, thereunto belonging unto the said Roelif Eltinge, his heirs and assigns, forever, so that neither, they the said Lewis DuBois and Solomon DuBois nor their heirs, nor any other person from, by or under them, shall claim, challenge or demand any right, title or interest into or to the premises or any part thereof.

Feb. 4, 1726-7.

Witnesses :—

> Jregan Tappen,
> Geo. vanWagonen.

Acknowledgement signed by Abraham Gaasbeck Chambers, Judge of the supreme court of common pleas.

Gil Livingston, Clerk.

There seems to have been some misunderstanding as to the

exact boundary between the Paltz patent and the DuBois patent occupied by Louis and Solomon, and Mr. Samuel B. Stillwell had among his papers, a document in the hand writing of the late Josiah DuBois, and copied in 1850 by him from the original, bearing date in 1729 and establishing the line as follows:

Pursuant to his excellencies warrant dated the 13th day of November last to me directed, I have by the mutual consent and agreement of Solomon DuBois and Lewis DuBois, owners of a tract of land adjoining to the south bounds of the lands of the New Paltz and of Abm. DuBois, Jacob Hasbrouck, Daniel Hasbrouck and likewise other proprietors and owners of the said New Paltz, surveyed the south bounds of the lands of the said New Paltz as follows, viz: Beginning at a certain high point in the hills lying on the west side of the New Paltz River and from thence runs south thirty-five degrees east to a stone set in the ground on the east side of the highway, and at the west end of a small gully, which falls in the Paltz River and lyes between the fence of the lands of the said New Paltz and the lands of the said Solomon DuBois and Lewis DuBois which stone was allowed by both parties to have been placed there as a mark of the boundaries between the land of the said Solomon and Lewis DuBois and the lands of New Paltz and from the said stone down the said gully two chains and 46 links to the Paltz river, then crossing the said river runs from the opposite side thereof south 56 degrees and 40 minutes east to the south side of Geffrow's hook and the north east corner of John Barbour's land on Hudson River. Given under my hand, this 7th day of April in the second year of his majesty's reign, Anno Dom. 1729.

Copy — — Caldwallader Colden, Jr.

P. S. The stone referred to is marked on the north side
P. L. (meaning I think Paltz limits) on the south side D. D. B.
There are more such stones on the same line, on the east side
of the Wallkill, if not lost.

Louis, Son of Louis, Jr.

The pamphlet published in 1860 by Robert Patterson DuBois,
of New London, Penn., and Wm. E. DuBois, of Philadelphia,
containing the history of a number of the descendants of Louis
DuBois, the Patentee, has only this to say about Louis, Jr.,
and his descendants:

"Louis, who was born about 1677. Having received information from some of his descendants, we can speak more fully
in regard to this line. It appears that Louis was married to
Rachel Hasbrouck in 1701. How many children they had is
not known, only that there was one son named Louis, who was
born about 1717, married Charity Andrevelt and settled in
Staten Island. This last Louis had six children, viz., Louis,
Matthias, Augustus, John, Charles and Elizabeth. Matthias,
the second of these, who was born in 1747 and died in 1820,
had by his first wife, Catharine Carshun, Mary, Louis, Daniel,
Matthias and John; and by his second wife three daughters,
Ann, Lockley and Susan. He removed with all his family,
about the year 1792, from Staten Island to Nanticoke, Broome
county, N. Y., where several branches of his family now reside.
In 1847 John, the only surviving child of Matthias' first wife,
was living in Tioga, N. Y., and about 70 years of age. He was
the father of twelve children, most of whom lived in Tioga
county, N. Y., and two, viz., John and Matthias, were living
in Williamsport, Pa. It was through this last named and his
father that these facts were procured."

Jonathan, Son of Louis, Jr.

Jonathan, son of Louis, Jr., married Elizabeth LeFevre, daughter of Andries LeFevre. They probably occupied the house of his father, but we have no testimony on that score except that they lived in that same neighborhood. They had a family of three sons, Louis J., Andries and Nathaniel, and three daughters, Rachel, Cornelia and Maria. Cornelia married Cornelius Vernooy and Maria married Abm. Bevier and both settled in the New Hurley neighborhood.

The will of Jonathan, which was made in 1746 and admitted to probate in 1749, gives to his eldest son, Louis J., his large Dutch Bible as a birthright; it gives to his wife Elizabeth all his estate during her widowhood, but in case she should marry again she is required to give to the children all the estate except one negro girl and such cows and household goods as she had when she married; after his wife's marriage or death he gives to his eldest son, Louis J., all his land on the south east side of the Paltz river, but he is required to pay to his brothers, Andries and Nathaniel, and to his sisters, Rachel, Cornelia and Maria, £250 current money of New York, to be equally divided between them; to the youngest son, Jonas, the will gives all the land on the north west side of the Paltz river, but he is required to pay to his brothers, Andries and Nathaniel, and his sisters, Rachel, Cornelia and Maria, the sum of £450. In case the wife shall die or marry before the sons, Louis and Jonas, come of age the farms shall be rented by the executors and the proceeds applied to the bringing up and educating the children; to the four sons are bequeathed all horses, wagons and farming utensils, and to the three daughters all household goods and furniture. All the residue of his estate is divided equally between the sons and daughters. The testator's brother, Nathaniel DuBois, and his brother-in-law, Johannes Hardenburgh, and Wessel Brodhead are appointed executors. The will is witnessed by Cornelius DuBois, Evert Terwilliger, Jr., and J. Bruyn.

We have no farther account of Jonathan's son Jonas. He probably died young.

Jonathan's son Andries married Sarah LeFevre, of New Paltz village, and settled at Wallkill, in those days sometimes called New Hurley, where his brick house is still standing and was the first house of brick in this part of the country.

Andries' sons were Simon L., Sen., Jonathan and Andries. He had one daughter, Elizabeth, who married Johannes Le-Fevre, of Kettleborough, and another daughter, Elsie, who married Philip LeFevre, of Kettleborough. Andries, son of the Andries who built the brick house, moved to New Paltz village and occupied the old LeFevre homestead here, which stood in the north part of the present church yard. This property came to him from his uncle, Andries LeFevre, who left no children. When the present brick church was erected, in 1839, this LeFevre house was torn down. Andries moved to Put Corners into the stone house now owned by Mr. Jacob Champlin. His sons were Louis, who occupied his father's residence; Nathaniel, who located at Shivertown, and Jonathan, who lived just north of this village. The descendants of Simon L., Sen., still reside at Wallkill. He had but one son, Simon L., Jr.

Nathaniel DuBois, son of Jonathan and grandson of Louis, Jr., did not marry. He built the first mill at Libertyville. Jonathan's son, Louis J., lived in Revolutionary times where Henry L. DuBois lately resided. His wife was Catharine Brodhead. The house in which they lived is still standing and is probably the oldest frame house in this part of the country.

HOUSE OF CAPT. LOUIS J. DU BOIS

It has been re-sided, but the great beams are as of old. It has always been in the possession of the DuBois family. Louis J. was commissioned as captain of the 1st New Paltz company of the 3rd Ulster County Regiment, October 25, 1775. We have no account of the service that he rendered in this capacity to the patriotic cause during the Revolutionary war. He has a great number of descendants in this vicinity. Louis J.'s children were as follows: Wessel, Jonas, Charles, Louis, Jonathan, Elizabeth and Anna.

Wessel, the eldest son, has no descendants here. He lived in a house, torn down long ago, on the present C. L. Van Orden place. His son Jonathan lived on the other side of the mountain. Eli DuBois, of Ellenville, and ex-supervisor Louis, of Denning, were grandsons of Wessel.

Jonas lived where Louis L. DuBois now resides. He had ten children, of whom ex-supervisor George, of this town, was the last survivor. The other children were L. Nathaniel of Walden, Louis I., LeFevre, James, Wessel, Deyo, David Eliza, wife of Anthony Crispell, and Maria, wife of Jacob Ostrander.

Charles carried on the milling business at Libertyville and was a prominent and highly respected man. His children were Stephen G., Catharine, wife of Abiel Hand, Rebecca, Henry, Louis, Derick W., Jacob and Zacharias. The two last named settled in Michigan.

Jonathan lived in Springtown. He was elected county judge in 1821. Jonathan's children scattered. Two sons, John and Brodhead, settled in Michigan. Another son, George, became a minister and was located at Tarrytown. Three daughters became the wives of Benjamin Van Wagenen, Derick W. Elting and Alexander Hasbrouck.

21

Louis located in the mountains. His children were Coe, Katy Ann and Rachel.

Elizabeth married Rev. Stephen Goetchius, who was pastor of the church at New Paltz from 1775 to 1796. They left a family of children.

Anna became the second wife of Jacob J. Hasbrouck. They left a large family of children.

Altogether the grandchildren of Louis, who grew up, numbered about fifty.

About 1870 the descendants of Louis DuBois held a picnic in the grove on the bank of the Wallkill, on the farm now owned by Louis L. DuBois, and the attendance was very large.

NATHANIEL, SON OF LOUIS, JR.

Nathaniel DuBois, son of Louis, Jr., located at Blooming Grove, now Salisbury Mills, in Orange county. Nathaniel's wife was Gertrude Bruyn, whom he married in 1726. He left three sons, Lewis, Zachariah and Jonas, and three daughters, one of whom, Rachel, became the wife of Andries LeFevre, one of the two brothers who were the first settlers at Kettleborough. Another daughter, Hester, became the wife of Col. Jesse Woodhull.

Nathaniel's son Lewis settled in Marlborough and his house, which is still standing, was the first house on the river front. He served in the army during a great portion of the Revolutionary war, including the invasion of Canada, where he was promoted from captain to major and he afterwards became colonel of the 5th Continental Regiment, receiving his commission November 17, 1776. His tombstone is still pointed out in the graveyard of the old Presbyterian church at Marbleborough. He died in 1812.

Nathaniel's son Zachariah also rendered service in the Revolutionary war as a major and was taken prisoner when the British captured Fort Montgomery.

HOUSE OF COL. LEWIS DU BOIS AT MARLBOROUGH

CHAPTER XXIX

MILITARY SERVICE OF COL. LEWIS DUBOIS

The following account of the service and military career of Col. Lewis DuBois during the Revolutionary war was written by Mr. Robert E. Deyo, of New York:

During the summer of 1775 there was great excitement in the Province of New York over the proposed expedition for conquering Canada. The troops from New York were commanded by General Montgomery. One of the regiments was the Third of the New York line, whose colonel was James Clinton, a brother of Gov. George Clinton. Of one ot the companies of this regiment Lewis DuBois was captain. His commission was issued June 28, 1775. On August 21 the muster roll of his company was returned and filed. The term of enlistment was for six months. This company was known as the Dutchess Company, and its officers were: Captain, Lewis Dubos; first lieut., Elias Van Benschoten; second lieut., Andrew T. Lawrence; vice, Cornelius Adriance, resigned.

Mr. Ruttenber says: "These regiments were more especially recruited for the invasion of Canada, a popular craze at that time which did much to fritter away the resources of the colonists and yielded no other return than the development of capacities for leadership and experience in the service. It was a severe school, but men marched to it with a shout. They were well armed and uniformed. * * * The Third or Ulster Regiment had gray coats with green cuffs and facings. Their breeches and waistcoats were of Russia drilling, the former were short (to the knee) and the latter long (to the hips).

Their stockings were long (to the knee) of coarse woolen homespun, low shoes, linen cravats and low-crowned, broad-brimmed felt hats.

"The New York regiments were brigaded under General Montgomery and were with him in all his movements. At Point aux Trembles, on the 1st of December, the entire force under his command had dwindled down to about 900 effective men. In fruitless attempts to force an entrance into Quebec, three weeks were wasted and then an assault made. Montgomery, at the head of his New York men, descended from the Plains of Abraham in the neighborhood of St. John's and St. Louis gates and Cape Diamond bastion. At the narrowest point under Cape Diamond the British had planted a three-gun battery. On the river side was a precipice, and on the left rough crags of dark slate towered above them. The guard at the battery in front stood ready with lighted matches. Montgomery halted a moment to reconnoitre and then into the jaws of death charged the 900 over heaps of ice and snow. When within forty paces of the battery, its fire was opened on the advancing column and a storm of grape shot swept the narrow pass and continued for ten minutes. Montgomery and both his aids and several privates were killed—the unwounded living fell back."

After this repulse our little army lay before Quebec all of the winter of 1775-6. Of what occurred we know but little. While in the field Lewis DuBois was raised from captain to major. General Benedict Arnold wrote to the President of Congress a long letter dated from "Camp before Quebec, 1 February, 1776." In this among other things he states the reason why a certain Major Brown should not be promoted and ends up by saying: "This transaction, Colonel Campbell, Major Dubois and several gentlemen were knowing to."

This extract is only important as showing that on February 1, 1776, he was already a major. On March 8, 1776, he was made a major in Col. John Nicholson's regiment raised in Canada out of the four New York regiments which originally went there, the term of their enlistment, being for only six months, having expired.

General George Clinton writes in 1776:

"Major Dubois is highly recommended to Congress as well by the general officers, as the Committee who lately returned from Canada. I wish and believe young Richard Platt may be properly provided for in the (new) regiment. He was with Major Dubois and Capt. Bruyn at Point Lacoy at the engagement between our people and a number of Canadians in which the latter was defeated, and behaved well as Major Dubois can testify."

At the same time that Lewis Dubois was in Canada with Montgomery, he was second major in Col. Jonathan Hasbrouck's militia regiment. The other officers were: Lieutenant-colonel, Johannis Hardenbergh, Jr.; first major, Johannes Jansen, Jr.; second major, Lewis DuBois; adjutant, Abraham Schoonmaker; quartermaster, Isaac Belknap. This regiment was organized September 2, 1775. The commissions of the officers were dated 25th of October, 1775.

At the time of the return of the expedition which went to Canada, there were four regiments of the line enlisted for three years or during the war, existing in the State of New York. It was determined to raise a fifth. The preliminary step seems to have led to a clash of authority between the Continental Congress and the Provincial Congress. On the 26th of June, 1776, John Hancock, president of the Continental Congress, wrote a letter to the Provincial Convention in which was enclosed a notice that Lewis DuBois, major in the Canada service, was commissioned June 25, 1776, by the Continental Congress, with instruction to raise a regiment for three years or during the war, to be the Fifth Regiment of the New York line, and that the Continental Congress had, on June 26th, appointed the other officers for the regiment as follows:

Lieutenant-colonel, Jacobus S. Bruyn; major, William Goforth; captains, David DuBois, Elias Van Benschoten, Thomas DeWitt, Isaac Wool, Philip D. B. Bevier, Richard Platt, Albert Pawling, Cornelius T. Jansen.

First lieutenants, James Gregg, Aaron Austin, Jonathan Piercy, Evans Wherry, Garret Van Wagenen, Henry Vandenburg, Nathaniel Conklin, Henry Dodge.

Second lieutenant, 1st Company, Dan. Gano; surgeon, John Coates, and adjutant, Henry DuBois.

Commissions were to be given as soon as the full complement of men had been raised.

In the letter which enclosed this list, President Hancock says: "You will perceive by the enclosed resolves which I do myself the honor of transmitting in obedience to the commands of Congress, they have appointed not only the field officers in the regiment to be raised in your colony, but likewise a number of subalterns. The reason that induced Congress to take that step, as it is a deviation from rule, should be particularly mentioned. I am therefore directed to inform you, that in consequence of their being furnished with a list of officers who had served in Canada, they had been enabled to appoint, and in fact have only appointed, such as were recommended and appointed by the Provincial Congress of your Colony, and have served faithfully in the last summer campaign and through the winter. It is apprehended therefore that the Congress have only prevented (forestalled) you in their appointments and that the same gentlemen would have met with your approbation for their services to their country; added to this the last intelligence from Canada showing our affairs to be in the most imminent danger rendered the utmost dispatch necessary, that not a moment's time might be lost.

"The other officers of the battalion I am to request you will be pleased to appoint and exert every nerve to equip the battalion as soon as possible. As an additional encouragement the Congress have resolved that a bounty of ten dollars be given every soldier who shall enlist for three years."

Of the officers named, Richard Platt, Aaron Austin, Jonathan Piercy, Garret Van Wagenen and Dan Gano, resigned because they considered themselves slighted by the positions assigned them. In addition, the Provincial Convention considered that the Continental Congress was unwarrantably interfering.

In the proceedings of the Provincial Convention, November 21, 1776, the committee appointed to carry into execution the resolves of Congress relative to the new arrangement of officers, reported through Robert Yates, chairman, that they had completed an arrangement of officers for the four battalions ordered to be raised in this State, and further that in forming their report so far as the officers of Col. DuBois' regiment are concerned in it, your committee considered that they were entitled to no other rank than what they held prior to their appointment in that regiment, which was done without the recommendation or intervention of the Convention of this State, contrary to the uniform practice in all similar cases and in prejudice of other officers of higher rank and equal merit. That your committee were constrained by those principles to omit Col. DuBois' name in the present arrangement. That Col. DuBois has been well recommended to this committee as an exceeding good officer capable of commanding a regiment with credit to himself and advantageous to his country.

That from the quota of this State being assessed as low as four battalions, many good officers will be unprovided for. That sundry applications have been made to your committee for commissions by young gentlemen of fortune and family, whose services your committee are under the disagreeable necessity of declining to accept.

That your committee are clearly of opinion that another battalion might be raised in this State, and they therefore earnestly recommend it to the convention to use their influence with the General Congress to obtain their permission and order for that purpose, and that Col. Dubois command the said battalion so to be raised and to have the rank of fourth colonel of New York forces.

Thereupon it was, among other things,

"Ordered, that a letter be written to the Hon. the Continental Congress requesting their approbation of the resolutions for raising a fifth battalion in this state to be commanded by Col. Louis Dubois, and another letter to General Washington requesting his countenance to that measure."

These efforts were successful.

The Fifth Regiment was finally organized with the following officers:

Louis Dubois, colonel; Jacobus Bruyn, lieutenant-colonel; Samuel Logan, major; Henry Dubois, adjutant; Nehimiah Carpenter, quartermaster; Samuel Townsend, paymaster; John Gano, chaplain; Samuel Cook, surgeon; Ebenezer Hutchinson, surgeon's mate.

Captains, Jacobus Rosecrans, Jas. Stewart, Amos Hutchins,

Philip D. Bevier, Thomas Lee, Henry Goodwin, John F. Hamtrack, John Johnston.

First lieutenants, Henry Dodge, John Burnett, Patten Jackson, Thos. Brinkley, Henry Pawling, Samuel Pendleton, Francis Hanmer, Henry Vandenburgh.

Second lieutenants, Samuel Dodge, Alex. McArthur, John Furman, Samuel English, Daniel Birdsall, Ebenezer Mott, James Betts.

Ensigns, Henry Swartout, John McClaughry, Edward Weaver, Jacobus Sleight, Thomas Beynx, Abraham Lent, Henry J. Vandenburgh.

The commission of Col. Dubois was dated November 17, 1776. While the Fifth Regiment was forming he was too zealous to remain inactive. The British were then in possession of New York. The Patriot army was in the vicinity ot White Plains. On the 28th of January, 1777, William Duer, in a letter to General Washington, dated from camp in Westchester county, says:

" * * Col. Dubois who has come down with the York militia as a volunteer and who has repeatedly offered his service to destroy King's bridge, will, I fear, return to-morrow, despairing to see anything effectual done."

Early in 1777 the Fifth Regiment was ordered to garrison duty at Fort Montgomery. On April 30th of that year a court martial, of which Col. Lewis Dubois was president, was there convened by order of Brig.-Gen. Geo. Clinton, for the trial of all such persons as should come before them charged with levying war against the State of New York within the same, adhering to the King of Great Britain and owing allegiance or deriving protection from the laws of the said State of New York. This court recommended that eleven men who were tried before them should be hanged. Others were acquitted or designated for milder punishment.

We shall not recapitulate the incidents which led up to the assault on Fort Montgomery by the British, nor to the details of that fight. These are accessible in any good history. With regard to Col Lewis Dubois' share in this fight, Mr. Ruttenber says:

"His services in the army were held in high esteem by his contemporaries; Col. Dubois' (Fifth) regiment was especially the regiment of this (Newburgh) district both in its membership and in its services. It was stationed in the Highlands in the spring of 1777 and was there when Forts Clinton and Montgomery were taken by the English forces in October of that year. Through a mistaken conclusion arising from the fact that they were clothed in hunting shirts such as farmers' servants in England wear, its dead in that action were ranked as militia by the British. The facts are that the brunt of the desperate and heroic resistance which was made fell on Col. Lewis Dubois' regiment, shared by Lamb's artillery. The returns of Col. Dubois' Fifth as they stand on its roll book, are: taken prisoners, Lieut. Col. Jacobus Bruyn, Major Samuel Logan, Quartermaster Nehemiah Carpenter, Captain Henry Goodwin, Lieutenants Alex. McArthur, Patten Jackson, Henry Pawling, Solomon Pendleton. Second Lieuts. Samuel Dodge, John Furman, Ebenezer Mott. Ensigns Henry Swartout, John McClaughry, Abm. Leggett. Sergeant Henry Schoonmaker. "Missing in action" is written against the name of ninety-six of the privates or not less than one-third of the whole strength of the regiment at that time. These men did not run—they were overwhelmed. While all of them were not killed, many were, and their bodies pierced by the bayonet for no gun was fired by the assaulting column—found resting place in the waters of "bloody pond," where in the succeeding spring, with an arm, a leg or a part of the body above the surface they presented the scene which Dwight describes as 'monstrous.' "

In this engagement Col. Dubois received a bayonet wound in the neck, as appears by a letter from Gen. Putnam to Gen. Gates, hereafter quoted from. This shows the desperate character of the fighting.

The course of those who escaped appears quite clearly from an account of it by Rev. John Gano, chaplain of the regiment, who wrote:

"The dusk of the evening, together with the smoke and rushing in of the enemy, made it impossible for us to distinguish friend or foe. This confusion gave us an opportunity of escaping through the enemy over the breastwork. Many escaped to the water and got on board a scow and pushed off. Before she had got twice her length we grappled one of our row-galleys into which we all got and crossed the river. We arrived safe at New Windsor, where, in a few days after we were joined by some more of our army who had escaped from the forts."

Gen. Clinton, writing to Gen. Washington, says:

"Many officers and men and myself having the advantage of the enemy by being well acquainted with the ground, were so fortunate as to effect our escape under cover of the night after the enemy were possessed of all the works."

It is not true, as often asserted, that Col. Lewis Dubois was taken prisoner at Fort Montgomery. Maj. Zachary Dubois, of Col. Jesse Woodhull's regiment of Orange county militia, a brother of Col. Lewis Dubois, was taken a prisoner and removed to New York. Some glimpse of what happened to the Major after his capture is had from the following documents.

MEMORANDUM OF ZACHARIAH DUBOIS OF CAPTURE AND IMPRISONMENT

Monday the 6th Oct. 1777, then I was taken prisoner at Fort Montgomery and kept there till the eighth day, then I was taken aboard the Archer ship, a transport, there kept till the tenth, then taken to the old City Hall, there kept till the twelfth, then taken to the Provost, there kept till the 1st day of November, then got on parole on Long Island, Bedford, till the ———, then moved to New Utritch, and there staid till the twenty-eighth, then they sent us on board the transport ship Judith, and there kept till the 10th day of December, then to our old quarters at New Utritch, etc.

PAROLE

I, Zachariah Dubois, of Goshen, in the Province of New York, having leave from General Sir Henry Clinton, to go out of this city in order to effect the exchange of myself for Maj. Thomas Moncrief, do hereby pledge my faith and word of honor, that I will not do or say anything contrary to the interest of his Majesty or his Government, and that if the exchange of the above person for myself cannot be effected within twenty days, I will return back to my captivity in this city.

Given under my hand in New York, this fourth day of August, 1776.

Witness: Thos. Clark.

Zachariah Dubois.

A true copy, John Winslow,

D. Com. Prs.

DISCHARGE AND PAROLE

This is to certify that Zachariah Dubois, Major in Colonel Woodhull's regiment of militia in the state of New York, and made prisoner by the enemy at the reduction of Fort Montgomery, was this day regularly discharged for Maj. Moncrief, in the service of the King of Great Britain.

Elizabethtown, Aug. 6, 1778.

Jno. Beatty,

Com. Gen. Pris'rs.

After the first shock of defeat the disaster was found not to be serious as at first supposed. General Putnam, writing to General Washington under date of Fishkill, 8 October, 1777, says:

"I have the pleasure to inform you that many more of our troops made their escape than what I was at first informed of. Colonel Dubois who is one of the number, this day collected near 200 of his regiment that got off after the enemy were in the Fort."

General Putnam, writing to General Gates from Fishkill, eleven o'clock a. m., 9 October, 1777, says:

"Colonel Dubois, who had a wound with a bayonet in his neck, has mustered near 200 of his men, who were with him in the action, many of whom have slight wounds with bayonets and swords but are in high spirits."

From General Putnam, Governor Clinton obtained Col. Webb's brigade and with them crossed the river to New Windsor, Orange county, on October 8th, the second day after the battle. On the same day Governor Clinton wrote to the Legislature from his headquarters at the house of Mrs. Falls, which still stands in Little Britain Square, that "not more than eleven officers of Col. Dubois' regiment are missing, 200 of his men including non-commissioned officers, have already joined me at this place; many more of them may be hourly expected as we have heard of their escape."

By alarms and signal guns the militia that had not been in the action were brought together and by the time the British had destroyed the obstructions to the navigation of the river a respectable force was again under the Clintons' command on the west shore. On the eastern side Putnam was protecting the army stores at Fishkill and at points above.

While the British were removing the obstructions to navigation and awaiting the return of a reconnoitering party which started up the river on the 11th, General Clinton was collecting his little force at New Windsor.

On the 10th, one Daniel Taylor was arrested near the camp. He was a bearer of a message from the British General Sir Henry Clinton, to Burgoyne, then sorely pressed by General Gates at Saratoga, although Sir Henry was not aware of Burgoyne's sorry plight.

"The letter from Clinton to Burgoyne," writes General George Clinton, "was enclosed in a small silver ball of an oval form about the size of a fusee bullet, and shut with a screw in the middle. When he was taken and brought before me he swallowed it. I mistrusted this to be the case from information I received and administered to him a very strong emetic calculated to act either way. This had the desired effect; it brought it from him; but though closely watched he had the art to conceal it a second time.

"I made him believe I had taken one from Capt. Campbell, another messenger who was on the same business; that I learned from him all I wanted to know, and demanded the ball on pain of being hung up instantly and cut open to search for it. This brought it forth."

The contents of this letter are as follows:

"Fort Montgomery, Oct. 8, 1777.

"*Nous y voici* (here we are) and nothing now between us but Gates. I sincerely hope this little success of ours may facilitate your operations. In answer to your letter of the 28th Sept. by C. C. I can only say I cannot presume to order, or even advise for reasons obvious. I heartily wish you success. Faithfully yours,

"Gen. Burgoyne. H. Clinton."

Dr. Moses Higby, residing at New Windsor, administered the emetic which afforded such convincing proof of Taylor's employment. Many interesting facts concerning the curious personality of the doctor will be found in Eager's History of Orange County.

On October 14th, a general court martial met for the trial of Taylor by order of General Clinton. The following document from the "Clinton papers" gives the names of those constituting the court and is an official record of the proceedings:

"At a general court martial held at the Heights of New Windsor the 14th of October, 1777, by order of Brigadier General George Clinton, whereof Colonel Lewis Dubois was President:

Major Bradford,	Capt. Galespie,
Maj. Huntington,	" Conklin,
Capt. Savage,	" Wood,
" Watson	" Hamtramk,
" Wyllis,	" Lee,
" Ellis,	" Huested.

(In Eager's Orange County, it is stated that John Woodworth was Judge Advocate.)

"Daniel Taylor, charged with lurking about the camp as a spy from the enemy, confined by order of General Clinton, was brought before said court, and to the above crime the prisoner plead not guilty, but confessed his being an express from Gen. Clinton to Gen. Burgoyne, when taken. And that he had been employed as an express also, from Gen. Burgoyne to Gen. Clinton, and was taken in the Camp of the Army of the United States, near New Windsor, by Lieut. Howe. Taylor likewise confessed his being a first Lieutenant in Capt. Stewart's Company in the 9th regiment of the British Troops, and but one man in company when taken. The prisoner plead that he was not employed as a spy, but on the contrary was charged both by Gen. Clinton and Gen. Burgoyne not to come near our camp; but meeting accidentally with some of our troops in British uniform, he was thereby deceived and discovered himself to them.

"The court after considering the case, were of the opinion that the prisoner is guilty of the charge brought against him and adjudged him to suffer death, to be hanged at such time and place as the General shall direct.

A true copy of the proceedings:

Test.   Lewis Dubois, Col.
                                        President."

When the little army of Governor Clinton moved down the Wallkill on the 15th, to save Kingston, Taylor was taken along, his name appearing every day in the guard reports. A general order issued on the morning of the destruction of Kingston, determined his fate.

It was not, however, carried into effect on the 17th, as directed; no doubt the attention of the troops was taken up with matters at Kingston. He was still under guard on the morning of the 18th, after which his name ceases to trouble the officer in charge.

In a MS. journal kept by a person in Clinton's force, probably a chaplain, is this entry:

"October 18th, Saturday, Mr. Taylor, a spy taken in Little Britain, was hung here. Mr. Romain and myself attended him yesterday, and I have spent the morning in discoursing to him, and attended him at the gallows. He did not appear to be either a political or gospel penitent."

Tradition has it that Taylor was hanged on an apple tree near the village of Hurley.

Having anticipated somewhat, in order to keep the story of the capture, trial and execution of Taylor together, we must now go back. The British reconnoitering party, which started on the 11th of October, ascended the river to within three miles of Poughkeepsie and returned in safety, having burned several buildings and old vessels along the shore. The report favored an advance of the whole force which accordingly started from Peekskill October 14th.

On October 15th, at nine o'clock a. m., General George Clinton wrote to Kingston from Headquarters near New Windsor that twenty sail of the enemy's shipping had been discovered in the river below Butter Hill (Storm King). After speaking of matters which need not here be recapitulated, the letter proceeds as follows:

"Since writing the above the enemy's fleet consisting of thirty sail have passed Newburgh and with crowded sail and and fair wind are moving quick up the river; the front of them are already at the Danskammer. There are eight large square-rigged vessels among them and all appear to have troops on board. My troops are parading to march to Kingston. Our route will be through Shawangunk to prevent delay in crossing the Paltz (Wallkill) river. I leave Col. Woodhull's, Mc-Claughry's and part of Hasbrouck's regiment as a guard along the river. * * * I will be with you if nothing extra happens before day; though my troop cannot."

What a thrilling sight it must have been to see thirty vessels, eight of them square-rigged, crowded with troops whose gay uniforms vied with the gaudy splendors of an American autumn sailing in a compact mass with colors flying, sails distended, waves dancing and sparkling as the great flotilla moves through Newburgh Bay and Danskammer Point. This is a picture over which the imagination lingers, especially with those whose good fortune it has been to have seen at the corresponding season, the georgeous ampitheatre within which this scene was set.

The force which moved with Geo. Clinton in his effort to prevent the burning of Kingston was about 1,000 men, composed of the skeleton regiments of Cols. Lewis Dubois, Webb, Sutherland and Ellison, with a part of Hasbrouck's, and what remained of Lamb's artillery. Only a portion of the advance guard got near enough to Kingston to behold the village in flames and the enemy retiring to his shipping.

The British reached the landing place for Kingston on the evening of the 15th, the town being burned on the 16th. On the way up they fired their cannon at the houses of known rebels on either shore. Attention was paid to the house of Col. Dubois, which, although not in sight of the river, was within easy cannon shot of it, the firing point being selected from the mouth of a brook emptying into the river, which was within close range of the house. This cannonade was harmless, but that the intention of the firing party was serious is evidenced by the cannon balls which have from time to time been dug out of a bank of earth a short distance west of the house. One of these, weighing 24½ pounds and the heaviest among a large collection, is now deposited at Washington's Headquarters in Newburgh.

General Clinton's little army was still at Hurley on October 20th, as appears by the report of the Officer of the Day.

Ruttenber says:

"During the winter of 1777-8, Dubois' regiment was in barracks at Fishkill. Its condition there was deplorable. In January, 1778, General Putnam writes, 'Dubois' regiment is unfit to be ordered on duty, there being not one blanket in the regiment. Very few have either a shoe or a shirt and most of them have neither stockings, breeches or overalls. Chastellux writes that many were absolutely naked, being only covered by straw suspended from the waist. The losses in stores at Fort Montgomery brought on this destitution very largely. It did not continue long after Putnam called Gov. Clinton's attention to it.'"

"In July, 1778, the five New York regiments were brigaded under Gen. James Clinton."

This brigade took a very active part in the expedition against the Indians in the western part of this State in 1779. General Sullivan with the main body of the army, which did not include Clinton's brigade, started from the vicinity of Easton, Pennsylvania, and penetrated the wilderness to the vicinity of Elmira. Gen. Clinton's force included, besides his own brigade, some regiments from other states, the whole command amounting to about 1,600 men.

The roster of the Fifth New York regiment on this expedition was as follows:

Lewis Dubois, Col.
Henry Dubois, Adjt. and Col.
Henry Dodge, Adjt. and Lieut.
Michael Connolly, Paymaster and 2nd Lieut.
James Johnston, Q. M. and Ensign.
Samuel Cooke, Surgeon.
Ebenezer Hutchinson, Surgeon's Mate.
James Rosekrans, Capt.
John F. Hamtranck, Capt.
John Johnson, Capt.
Philip DuBois Bevier, Capt.
James Stewart, Capt.
Henry W. Vanderburgh, Lieut.
Daniel Birdsall, 2nd Lieut.
James Betts, 2nd Lieut.
Barthal Vanderburgh, Ensign.
Francis Hanmer, Ensign.
Henry Vanderburgh, Ensign.

About the middle of June, 1779, Clinton, in order to join Sullivan, began transporting his force from the Mohawk river by the way of Canajoharie and Springfield to Lake Otsego, the headwaters of the Susquehanna.

On this part of the trip we catch a glimpse of Col. DuBois in the following extract from the diary of Lieut. Beatty of the 4th Penna. Line, part of Clinton's force.

Monday, June 28, 1779. "This day the Col, and a number of officers with myself went to see Col. Dubois and his officers who were encamped at Low's Grove on the upper landing, found them all very well and they provided a very good dinner for us suitable to the place and time, there was about fifty officers dined together. After dinner we had a song or two from different officers and returned home a little before sundown. We were all very sociable at dinner and spent our time with the officers very agreeable."

Clinton remained at Lake Otsego from the 3d of July to the 9th of August awaiting orders from Gen. Sullivan. When these orders came Clinton moved forward and effected a junction with Sullivan. In organizing for the fighting and devastation which followed, the hazardous position of commanding the right flank was assigned to Col. Dubois, who had under him two companies of the German battalion and 200 picked men in addition. The army of Sullivan far outnumbered that of the Indians under the celebrated Chief Brant, aided by a few British regulars and tories. The enemy made but one serious effort to check the invaders. Behind a hastily constructed rampart, in the vicinity of Elmira, they made a stand, but were soon driven away. In this engagement Col. Dubois participated. The victorious army then turned northward, and carried out the purpose of the expedition by burning many villages and destroying all food supplies. It was a work of devastation, and many there be that say the measure was unnecessarily harsh. Be that as it may, the power of the Indians in this State was broken by this expedition of Gen. Sullivan.

Lewis Dubois resigned his commission as colonel December 29, 1779. This seems to have been brought about by the dwindling of all the regiments in the New York brigade, for in the subsequent year the 1st and 3rd regiments were consolidated into one regiment, known as the 1st, under Col. Van Schaick, and the 2nd, 4th and 5th and Col. Livingston's regiment into another, known as the 2nd, under Col. Philip Van Cortlandt.

There remains for consideration such information as could be gathered concerning the descendants of the children of Col. Lewis Dubois.

1—Nathaniel Dubois, his first child, died April 18, 1788, in the 30th year of his age. He left one daughter, Hannah, who was his only child. Nothing is known of her history.

2—Wilhelmus lived and died on the tract of land near Marlborough village, given to him by his father's will. It ran from the village to the road known as West street and along the latter. His wife was Mary Hudson. They had four children, John, Cornelius, Elizabeth and Nathaniel.

John married Rebecca Wygant and had four children, William, Matthew Wygant, Maria and Ann Eliza.

Cornelius had three wives and ten children, Mary, Elizabeth, Sarah, Deborah Ann, Jane, Caroline, Charlotte, Daniel Asa and Ann Amelia.

Elizabeth married John W. Wygant and had seven children, William D., Asa, Cornelius, Ostrom, Mary Jane, J. Ward and Elizabeth.

Nathaniel married Deborah Ann Bloomer and had eleven children, Fletcher, Charles Augustus, Elizabeth Wygant, Mary Louisa, Eugene, Hudson, Emma, Ann Amelia, Theron, Luther and Dallas.

3—Mary, the first daughter, married Asa Steward. She was living in the town of Minisink as late as 1811. She had two daughters, Elizabeth and Margaret.

4—Rachel, the first daughter by his second wife, married Cornelius Low, by whom she had one daughter, Cornelia, born

March 5, 1792. Rachel Low died November 6, 1793, in her 23rd year.

Nothing is known of the career of her daughter, Cornelia Low. Cornelius Low is said to have been a prominent man of Kingston and to have taken up, with others, large tracts of land in Wawarsing.

5—Lewis (4) was born December 20, 1774, and was baptized at New Marlborough by Rev. Samson Occum. He was married to Annie Hull, daughter of Nathaniel Hull, January 3, 1809. She was born February 15, 1787. He died August 22, 1831. His children were as follows:

Rachel Margaret, born October 1, 1809, married to Lewis W. Young June 28, 1827. She died at Newburgh March 21, 1890. Her children were Juliet, Henrietta and Jas. Henry.

Lewis (5), born June 28, 1811, married Jane Thorn. He died December 11, 1854. He had one child, a son named Charles, who died about 1870, leaving issue.

Amanda, born January 25, 1813, married Samuel Harris in 1831. She died October 25, 1875. Mr. Harris purchased the Dubois homestead at a partition sale held in 1842, and his son William now resides on it. The children of Samuel Harris and Amanda Dubois Harris were Francis, Emily, Ida, Jessie and William.

Melissa, born May 20, 1814, married William C. Goddard and died March, 1892. She lived in Brooklyn, New York, after her marriage. Her children were Edward, William, Emily and Adeline.

Nathaniel Hull, born December 27, 1815. He had two children, a son Solomon, who died in infancy, and a daughter, Julia Ferris. He is still living at Marlborough, Ulster county.

Elizabeth, born June 1, 1817, died August 17, 1819.

Daniel Lockwood, born August 29, 1819, died July 6, 1862. Never married.

Clementine Williams, born June 4, 1821, married January 14, 1845, to Reuben H. Rohrer, of Lancaster, Pa., where she lived and died. Her children were four sons, Dubois, Reuben S., Leland and Mifflin.

Cornelia Bruyn, born November 9, 1822, married May 6, 1840, to Nathaniel Deyo, M. D. She died at Newburgh, December 16, 1876. Her children, who lived to maturity, were Evelina, Robert Emmet, Frank DeWitt, Nathaniel Dubois, John, Van Zandt and Cornelia Ann.

Daniel Lockwood (2), born August 29, 1819, died July 6, 1862, unmarried.

Anna, born November 18, 1826, married June 16, 1851, to Henry E. Leman, of Lancaster, Pa., where she died April 22, 1873. Her children were Henry E., Samuel W., Adelia, Lewis D. and James C.

Marcus Dougherty, born June 4, 1828, now living at New Windsor, Orange county, unmarried.

6—Margaret, born January 29, 1776, and was baptized at New Marlborough by Rev. Mr. Carr from Goshen. She died May 6, 1855.

She married Daniel Lockwood about 1790 and had—

Rachel Lockwood, born August 26, 1792, and died December 29, 1793.

Lewis D. Lockwood, born August 8, 1794; died May 3, 1874.

Daniel Lockwood, born August 8, 1797.

Eli T. Lockwood, born April 14, 1800; died January 27, 1848.

Charles Lockwood, born November 17, 1802; died July 1, 1829.

Nathaniel D. Lockwood, born February 6, 1804; "was drowned on fast day," January 12, 1815.

Daniel Lockwood, the first husband of Margaret Dubois, died November 27, 1804.

On August 25, 1814, she married Gen. Nathaniel Dubois, the son of her uncle Zachary, and had—

Isaac Dubois, born July 12, 1815; died August, 18, 1876.

Edwin Lockwood Dubois, born October 2, 1817; died February 5, 1860.

THE OLD FREER HOUSE AT NEW PALTZ

CHAPTER XXX

THE FREER FAMILY AT NEW PALTZ

The Freer family of New Paltz and elsewhere in the United States is descended from Hugo Freer, one of the New Paltz patentees.

Hugo was one of the last of the little band to arrive at Kingston. There is no mention of his name previous to the purchase of the New Paltz patent from the Indians in 1677. He probably had just arrived in the country at that time. He was accompanied by his wife, Mary Haye, and their three eldest children, Hugo, Abraham and Isaac.

In the papers that have come down to the present time there are more in the French language among the descendants of Hugo Freer than of any of the other Patentees, which seems to indicate that he had not been very long absent from his native country when he came to New Paltz.

When the church was organized at New Paltz in 1683 Hugo Freer was chosen deacon, and in 1690 he was elder in the church. This would show that he was a man of known piety and excellent standing among the brethren in the little community.

Most of the other settlers at New Paltz were related by marriage. But neither Hugo the Patentee nor any of his children married New Paltz people. A good portion of the children and grandchildren of Hugo the Patentee married and settled outside the bounds of the New Paltz patent, going to Kingston, to Dutchess county and elsewhere. Still among his numerous descendants many remained at New Paltz.

During the first century after the settlement there was perhaps no family that furnished a larger proportion of eminent men than the descendants of Hugo Freer the Patentee.

The Freers of colonial days had means and piety as well. The Bontecoe Freers, cultivating the lowlands on the Wallkill in the great bend of the stream, above Dashville Falls, would walk barefoot five miles to church at New Paltz in summer, putting on their shoes when near the village. But when the time came to put up the new stone church in 1772, the Freer family contributed considerably more than one-fourth of the whole amount needed, and two of the name served on the building committee.

Tradition states that one year the Freers paid the whole amount of the quit rent due from the New Paltz settlers to the colonial government and in return received 200 acres of land at Mud Hook, near the north west corner of the New Paltz Patent.

In the Revolutionary war the Freers furnished a large number of officers and men, the list including Col. John Freer and Capt. Jacobus Freer of Dutchess county and Lieuts. Daniel Freer and Anthony Freer of Ulster, also about a score of private soldiers.

At the commencement of the last century Samuel Freer of Kingston was for many years a noted newspaper man, editing the *Gazette*. If not the very first, he is at least the best remembered editor of the first quarter of the last century. He used to carry his papers on horseback to his patrons at New Paltz and elsewhere, and it is related that when asked if he had news to tell would answer in Dutch, "Always news when the paper comes."

In the second war with England, Capt. Zachary Freer of New Paltz served as a captain, his regiment being stationed on Long Island.

The Freers left the village at an early date. Not a single tombstone bearing the name or initials of any member of the family is to be found in the old graveyard here. The old homestead in this village passed from Hugo Freer, senior, son of the Patentee, to his son-in-law, Johannis Low, whose descendants occupied it for a long time.

The Freers scattered widely during the colonial period, and for that reason it has been difficult to trace their history. The family was most numerous at Bontecoe. The old graveyard there is probably next to that in this village the oldest in the Patent. Among the Bontecoe Freers the name of their ancestor Hugo was continued from generation to generation, but has now died out and the last Hugo in this vicinity died at his home at Bontecoe at a good old age about 1850.

In the old days it was not customary for laymen to take part in the services in church. It is stated that the only man to raise his voice in public prayer in the New Paltz church at about 1820 was Jonathan Freer of the Ohioville neighborhood.

None of the Freers of the early days were merchants, as far as we know, and none of them made or sold whiskey, that we are aware of.

The Freer homestead in this village is the northernmost of the old stone houses on Huguenot street. It is still occupied as a residence, is in a good state of repair and has not been changed much since the olden times, except that the great beams have been cut down and there is no longer a great fireplace. The house is about 40 feet in length and 35 in width, including a small, frame addition in the rear.

Hugo Freer, the Patentee, was twice married, his first wife being Mary Haye and the second Jannitje Wibau. The children of Hugo, the Patentee, were: Hugo, Senior, Abraham,

Isaac (who died when 18 years old), Jacob, Jean, Mary and Sarah. The first named daughter married Lewis Viele of Schenectady, and the other married Teunis Clausen Van Volgen of the same place. The three eldest sons of Hugo, the Patentee, located at New Paltz and Jean moved to Kingston.

Mary, the daughter of Hugo the Patentee and wife of Lewis Viele of Schenectady, sold her one-sixth part of her father's estate to her brother Hugo for £83, as is shown by a document dated 1710, which among many other papers of Hugo Freer, Senior, has come down to the present day and is now in the possession of the writer.

Jean Freer, son of the Patentee, who had located at Kingston, also sold to his brother Hugo, Senior, his share, one-sixth part, of the estate of their father. The sale was made in 1713 and the price paid was £80.

HUGO, SENIOR, SON OF HUGO, PATENTEE

Hugo, Senior, eldest son of the Patentee, was married in 1690 to Mary LeRoy, by Rev. Pierre Dailie.

In June, 1715, Hugo, Senior, and his sons, Hugo, Junior, Isaac and Simon, who moved to Dutchess county, obtained a patent for 1,200 acres of land about three miles south east of this village and near the Paltz patent. On this tract Isaac located and it has come down in his family to the present day.

Hugo, Senior's, name appears in the list of those who built the first stone church, in 1720, and he and his eldest son, Hugo, Junior, are assigned seats in the church. In the list of freeholders in 1728 appear the names of his sons Hugo, Junior, and Isaac.

From the "New Paltz Orders" in 1710 it is evident that Hugo, Senior, resided in the northern part of the village. The exact location and other facts are set forth in a release granted to his 13 children in 1732 as follows:

This indenture made the 29th day June, in the sixth year of the reign of our sovereign, George the second, by the grace of God, of Great Britain France and Ireland, king, defender of the faith, &c., Anno Domini, 1732, between Hugo Freer senior, of the New Paltz, in the county of Ulster and province of New York, yeoman, of the first part, and Hugo junior, Isaac, Simon, Jonah, Mary wife of Isaac LeFevre, Sarah wife of Evert Terwilliger, Esther wife of John Terpening, Catharine wife of Isaac Van Wagonen, Dina wife of Michael Van Kleeck, Rachel wife of Hendrick TerBoss, Janitje, Rebecca (afterwards wife of Johannes Low) and Elizabeth all of them sons and daughters of Hugo Freer senior of the other part, witnesseth, that in consideration of the sum of five shillings, current money of New York to him in hand paid by the said 13 children he hath granted to the said 4 sons and 9 daughters all that certain lot of land in the New Paltz Patent, near the north end of the town (village) of New Paltz, on the east side of the street, being bounded to the west by the street aforesaid, to the south by the house lot of Daniel Hasbrouck, to the east by Andries Lefever, to the north by the said Andries Lefever and the street aforesaid, together with all buildings, houses, barns, stables, yards, gardens, orchards and other improvements; also all that other certain piece of land lying and being within the limits and bounds of the New Paltz, bounded to the east by the said street, to the south by the house lots of Daniel DuBois, to the west by the said lots in Wassamakos land, and to the north by lot of Mattys Sleght, and also all that other lot or piece of ground being a lot which the said Hugo Freer senior hath purchased of Anthony Crispell, deceased lying on the east side of said street, being bounded to the west by the street aforesaid, to the south by a lot of Andries Lefever, to the east by the said Andries Lefever and to the north by a lane that leads to Daniel Hasbrouck's mill; also all that certain lot lying in the great pature within the bounds of the patent of New Paltz bounded on the west by the road that leads to Walravens bourey, to the south by a lot of John Terpening, to the east by the Paltz common or undivided lands, and to the north by a lot of Daniel DuBois, and also all that four-sixth the parts of him the said Hugo Freer, senior of the one-twelfth part of the undivided lands there now are lying undivided and in common within the limits and bounds of the Patent of New Paltz aforesaid, which was granted by the said letters patent unto Hugo Freer, deceased, together with all ponds, pools, etc., etc., * * yielding and paying therefor unto the said Hugo Freer senior his heirs or assigns the rent of one pepper corn only on the first day of May next ensuing if demanded. * * * *

Hugo Freer, Senior,
his mark.

The most extensive and interesting collection of papers in archaic French that has come down to the present day is that once the property of Hugo Freer, Senior, which has come down in the family of his son Jonah, and passed from father to son in that family.

An Ancient and Interesting Letter

Perhaps the most interesting document in the Freer collection of ancient papers is a letter written in 1699 to Mrs. Hugo Freer, Sen., by her uncle, Jean Giron of Quebec, now framed in glass

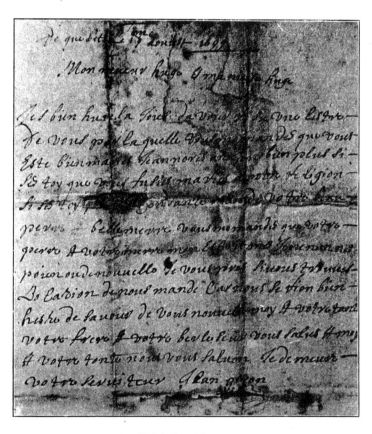

LETTER FROM JEAN GIRON TO HUGO FREER, SR., AND WIFE

and deposited in the Memorial House. Through the kindness of Mr. Alfred LeRoy Becker of Buffalo we are enabled to publish a full translation. Mr. Becker writes concerning this letter:

"It is addressed to 'My nephew Huge and my niece Huge' by which the writer means Hugo Freer, Sr., son of the patentee, and his wife, Marie Anne LeRoy, whom he married, according to the record of the New Paltz church, June 7, 1690. The letter was written nine years later, but news of the marriage had apparently only just reached the writer. The letter is written in a fair if cramped hand, but it shows an almost total lack of knowledge of how to spell, so that it has been extremely difficult to make the translation which is given herewith.

De quebet Le tme aouiest 1699.

Mon niueur (neveu) huge Et ma niesse huge.

Jes (J'ai) bien hu (eu) de la Joies davoier resu une lestre De vous par laquelle vous memandes que vous Este bien maries Jeannoris (J'en aurais) ancore (encore) bein plus si ses toy (c'estoit) que vous fusies maries a notre religion si sestoy (c'estoit) p * * * * * (hole in MS. Should "par le" be supplied?) Constanteman (consentment) de votre beauperre Et bellemerre (.) vous me mandes que votre perre Et votre merre mon EsCrit (m'ont escrit) mes Je ne nannes poien ou (Je n'en ai point eu?) de nouuelle (.) Je vous pris (,) si vous trouues Do Cazion (D'occasion) de nous mande Car nous serion bien hesze (aise) de savoier de vous nouuelle (,) moy Et votre tante (.) votre frere Et votre berleseur (belles-oeur) vous salus Et moy Et votre tante nous vous saluon Je demeure votre seruiteur   Jean giron.

Translation.

Quebec, August 17th, 1699.

My nephew Huge and my niece Huge:

I have indeed been rejoiced to have received a letter from you by which you inform me that you are well married. I should be still more rejoiced if it was that you were married in our religion, if it was by the consent of your father-in-law and mother-in-law. (That is, if by the consent of Hugo Freer's father and mother, she was married to him according to the forms of the Catholic church.) You inform me that your father and mother have written me, but I have had no news of them whatever. I beg of you, if you find occasion, to write to us, for we should be very glad to have news of you,—your aunt and I. Your brother and your sister salute you and your aunt and I, we salute you. I remain, your servant,

Jean giron.

"Jean Giron came from France to Canada and bought a farm on the River St. Charles, near Quebec. He married one of three orphan sisters who came to New France in this year, Madeleine Des Chalets. He was from Creances, bishopric of Coutances, in Manche, the long finger with Cherbourg at the tip which points from the north of France into the English Channel. In the same year Simeon Le Roy, who was a master carpenter, bought land next to his brother-in-law on the River St. Charles. He remained in Quebec until 1679 or later, but in 1681 he had removed to Montreal. While he was in Canada he appears to have been a Catholic, for all his children were baptized by the priests. In 1682 he was in Albany, and thereafter he lived in Kingston, where he was as late as 1701. In 1704, however, he probably left there and he was a witness at the baptism of one of his grandchildren on Staten Island, in 1706 or 1707. Through his son Francis he was the head of the Le Roy family, originally of Dutchess county, and through his son Leonard, or "Jonar" as the Dutch called it, corrupting the French sound, he was the head of the "Laraway" family, originally of Schoharie county. All of his children, except Jean, who is mentioned in the letter and remained in Canada, married either Huguenots or Hollanders and became Protestants."

In the will of Hugo Freer, Senior, which was written in 1728, a number of years before his death, he appointed his brothers, Abraham, Jacob and Jean, and his friend, Aart Van Wagenen, as executors.

Nearly all of the Freers in this vicinity are descended from Hugo, Senior. His brother Jean went to Kingston. His brother Abraham lived in New Paltz, as we have stated, for a time, but his sons scattered, one going to Dutchess county and another to Minnisink. The remaining brother of Hugo, Senior, Jacob, located on the west side of the Wallkill, near the Bontecoe school house and his descendants lived in that locality and on the Rosendale Plains.

The sons of Hugo, Senior, located as follows: Hugo, Junior, near the north borders of the patent; Isaac on the 1,200 acre tract obtained by patent; Jonah at "Kleyne Bontecoe," at the present R. V. N. Beaver place, near Springtown. Simon went to Dutchess county. The sons of Hugo, Senior, married as follows: Hugo, Junior, who was born in 1691, married, in 1715, Bridgen Terpening; Isaac, who was born in 1693, married, in 1723, Mary Deyo, daughter of Pierre the Patentee; Jonah married, in 1727, Catharine Stokhard, who was born in

Germany. Simon married, in 1720, Mariten Wamboon at Kingston. The sons of Hugo Freer, Junior, who married Bridgen Terpening and located at Bontecoe, near the present school house, were Hugo, who married ——— Van Aken; John, who married Hagetta Deyo, in 1749; Benjamin, who married Elizabeth Terwilliger, and Garret, who married Maria Freer, in 1748. In the list of taxpayers in 1765 we find the names of Hugo Freer, Junior, and his sons, Hugo, John, Benjamin and Garret. The three first named lived at Bontecoe. Neither Benjamin or John left children. Garret is the ancestor of Ezekiel Freer of the Grahow neighborhood. Hugo lived in the Jeremiah Freer place of modern times.

In the list of soldiers in the Revolutionary war appear the names of Hugo, John, Garret and Benjamin Freer in the First or Northern Regiment.

In the subscription list for the building of the second stone church at New Paltz, in 1772, appear the names of Hugo, John, Benjamin and Garret Freer, Jr. Hugo Freer subscribed £25, being one of the largest subscriptions made. Hugo Freer and Garret Freer, Jr., were members of the building committee.

The last Hugo at Bontecoe, who wrote his name Hugo B., died about 1850 and was the son of the Hugo above named and grandson of Hugo, Jr. He lived in the house, part stone and part frame, a short distance southwest of the Bontecoe school house. He inherited the farm from his uncle, Benjamin, who, as we have said, left no children.

All of the Bontecoe Freers are not of this line, a considerable portion being descended from Jacob Freer, son of Hugo the Patentee, who owned land on the west side of the Wallkill on the north bounds of the Patent and probably located there some years before his nephew, Hugo, Junior.

Isaac, Son of Hugo, Senior

Isaac, the second son of Hugo Freer, Senior, married Mariten Deyo and located on the tract of 1,200 acres where Zach. Freer, deceased, lived. Isaac's name appears in the list of Captain Hoffman's Company in 1716, also in the list of soldiers enrolled in this town in 1738. His old stone house was burned down about 1880. It is said that his house at first consisted of one room only, others being afterwards added. The sons of Isaac Freer (1) were Isaac, born in 1734, and Daniel, Jr., born in 1743. He had several daughters. Isaac Freer and his wife Maritje united with the church at New Paltz in 1752. Isaac's son Isaac married Hester Jansen. Daniel married, in 1765, Annitje Deyo. In the Revolutionary war Daniel was lieutenant in the First Company, Third Regiment Ulster County Militia, and the names of Isaac and Thomas Freer appear as privates in the same regiment. In the list of subscriptions to the building of the second stone church, in 1772, appear the names of Isaac Freer for £15, Daniel Freer £2.15 and Daniel Freer, Jr., for £10. The sons of Isaac Freer and Hester Jansen were Thomas, born in 1760; Isaac, born in 1765; Zacharias, born in 1769. The last named kept the old homestead and married Rachel DuBois, daughter of Hendricus DuBois of Noscatack. Their children were Thomas, Henry D. B., Johannes, Isaac and Maria. In the war of 1812 Zacharias Freer was a captain, his regiment being stationed in Long Island. Zacharias held the old stone homestead of the family and from him it passed into the possession of his son, Henry D. B. It was burned about 1880 and whatever old papers were in the house were lost in the fire.

JONAS, SON OF HUGO, SENIOR

Jonas, son of Hugo, Senior, married Catharine Stokhard, who was of German birth, and lived at "Kleyne Bontecoe," near Springtown, on what is now the R. V. N. Beaver place; Jonas' name appears in the list of soldiers in this town in 1738. In the tax list of 1765 he is set down for £25, which indicates that he was in pretty comfortable circumstances for those days. In his will, executed in 1775, Jonas disposes of his property as follows: after providing for his widow, Catharine, he gives to his son, Jonas, the farm on which the son then lived on the east side of the Wallkill. This passed from Jonas (2) to his son Elias, and then to Elias' sons, Stephen and Peter W. A. Jonas (1) in his will gives to his son Simon the tract on which the testator lived at Kleyne Bontecoe; to his sons, Johannes and Elisa, land on the Swartekill, in the town of Newburgh, which he had bought of John Preevost. This was on what is now called South street, in the present town of Lloyd. To his remaining son, Petrus, is given in Jonas' will the place on which he lived, which was purchased of Christian Deyo, and £60 of money. Petrus moved to Dutchess county.

We have not traced the history of this branch of the family further, except in the case of Johannes (in English John), who located near the present Clintondale depot on land which his father had bought of John Preevost. He wrote his name Johannes, Jr. His wife was Sarah, daughter of Abm. Bevier, of New Paltz. . His second son, Martinas, born in 1762, emigrated, about 1800, to western New York and subsequently to Ohio. Attorney-General Romeo H. Freer, of Harrisville, West Virginia, and Attorney Charles Freer, of Warren, Ohio, are grandsons of Martinas.

The most extensive collection of ancient papers that we have found anywhere has come down in the family of Jonas Freer. This collection includes letters, wills, receipts, deeds, etc. Some of the papers are in English, some in Dutch and many in French. Quite a number are dated previous to 1700. One, dated in 1691, bears the signature of Rev. Pierre Daillie, the first pastor of the New Paltz church; another, dated in 1699, bears the signature of his successor, Rev. David Bonrepos. There are in the collection three papers, in French, in the hand writing and bearing the signature of Louis DuBois the Patentee, who died in 1696. Another paper, in English, dated 1710, is in the handwriting and bears the signature of Roelif Eltinge, the first of the line at New Paltz, but at that time still residing in Kingston and already a Justice of the Peace. Other papers bear the signatures of the Patentees Abraham Hasbrouck and Louis Bevier; another has the signature of Moses Cantine, ancestor of the Cantine family. One of the most interesting papers is a tax list of the precinct in 1712, in English, which shows that four of the Patentees were living at that time, namely, Louis Bevier, Abraham Hasbrouck, Jean Hasbrouck and Abraham DuBois. A number of these papers have been framed in glass and placed in the New Paltz Memorial House. The most ancient papers in the collection were once the property of Hugo, Sen. Two letters, both in French, are addressed to him personally: one, dated in 1699, congratulates him on his marriage; the other, written 20 years later, speaks of the shipment of peas and other farm produce. When Hugo, Senior, died these old papers were taken to the residence of his son Jonas at Kleyne Bontecoe, who added to the collection whatever valuable papers he had of his own.

From Jonas Freer these papers evidently passed into the possession of his son Jonas (2), who lived where his son Elias and his grandson Stephen afterward resided. In each generation such papers as were considered valuable were added to the collection.

Jonas (2) left four sons: Elias, Simeon, Joshua and Jonathan, Jr. He also left three daughters that married, becoming the wives of Philip Schoonmaker, Abm. P. Schoonmaker and Archa P. Van Wagenen.

ABRAHAM, THE SON OF HUGO THE PATENTEE

We will pass now to the history of Abraham, son of Hugo the Patentee. Abraham married, in 1694, Aagien Titesort. In 1705 he resided at Bontecoe, south of the present schoolhouse, opposite the piece of lowland called the Half Moon. Abraham's name appears in the list of those who built the first stone church, in 1720. In the list of freeholders, in 1728, his name does not appear. He probably moved away, as we find in 1723 that he transferred his two seats in the church to his brother, Hugo, Senior. Abraham's sons were Hugo Ab., Abraham, Jr., Solomon, William and Philip. Hugo Ab. married Marytje Dewitt, at Kingston, in 1720. His name appears as a soldier in Captain Hoffman's company in 1716. Solomon married Claritje Westvaal and located at Minnisink.

Solomon's son Johannes married Hester Lounsberry. His family Bible, dating back to 1749, was in the possession of his great-great-grandson, Nathan M. Freer, late of Chicago.

Johannes' son, John J., was a soldier in the Revolution and died at New Paltz in 1828. The Bible afterwards came into the possession of John J.'s son, Elias, who died at Lockport, Ill., in 1868, and then passed into the possession of his son, S. C. Paine Freer, a prominent citizen of Chicago and father of Nathan M. Freer, lately deceased.

William, son of Abraham, married, in 1729, Maryanette Van Kuykendall of Minnisink. He is set down as living at

New Paltz. Their sons were Benjamin, Jacob and Abraham. Philip moved to Dutchess county, and in 1735 married Catharine Scharp of Claverack. Abraham, Jr., in 1720, married, at Kingston, Janitje Degraff. He then lived at New Paltz. In 1734 he married at Poughkeepsie (where he evidently then resided) as his second wife, Johanna Louis, widow of Peter Van Bome. They had a son, Johannes (in English John) baptized in 1739. This is undoubtedly the Col. John Freer who commanded the 4th Dutchess County Regiment in the Revolution. Abraham, Jr., had another son, Thomas, baptized in 1747, in Poughkeepsie. The Freer family increased in numbers in Poughkeepsie, and a portion of that city was called Freertown down to modern times. At Rhinebeck also the names of a number of Freers are recorded in the church record.

JACOB, SON OF HUGO THE PATENTEE

Jacob Freer, son of Hugo the Patentee, was born in 1679. He married, in 1705, Aritje Van Wagen. He owned land at Bontecoe, in 1730, on the west side of the Wallkill, adjoining the tract belonging to the Eans and still known as the Half Moon, and he probably lived there. His name appears as one of those who built the old stone church at New Paltz in 1720; also as one of the soldiers in Capt. Hoffman's company in 1715, and as one of the freeholders in the town in 1728. Jacob's sons were Abraham and Isaac (twins) ; Jacob, born in 1742; Daniel and Cornelis. The son, Jacob, Jr., lived in the same neighborhood. His name appears on the tax list of the precinct of New Paltz, in 1765, for £12. In the building of the second stone church at New Paltz, in 1772, Jacob Freer, Jr., contributed £12 and Jacob J. Freer £3 10s. In 1775 the name of Jacob Freer, Jr., appears as one of the consistory of the New Paltz church. His wife was Sarah Freer.

JEAN, SON OF HUGO THE PATENTEE

Jean, the youngest son of Hugo Freer, the Patentee, was born in 1682. He married Rebecca Van Wagenen about 1707. He was a resident of Kingston in 1720, as is shown by a bond given by him to his brother, Hugo, Senior, in that year, now in possession of the writer. Jean's name does not appear in the list of those who built the first stone church at New Paltz in 1718, nor in the list of freeholders of the town in 1728. He doubtless moved to Kingston when a young man and continued to reside there.

The children of Jean Freer and Rebecca Van Wagenen were Sara, born 1708; Gerrit, born 1711; Jannitje, born 1714; Marytje, born 1716; Jacob, born 1719; Rebecca, born 1726.

Gerritt's name appears on the list of foot soldiers in Kingston, in 1738. He married, in 1735, Elizabeth Van Vliet. They had one son, William.

Jacob married, in 1754, Annitje Van Aken of Kingston. In the record on the church book Jacob is said to have been of Wagondahl (the old name for Creek Locks). The children of Jacob Freer and Annitje Van Aken were Jan, born in 1755; Jacob, born in 1758; Peter, born in 1760; Gerrit, born in 1765; Annitje, born in 1776.

Gerritt married, in 1786, Gertje Van Vliet. Both are set down in the marriage as then residing in Kingston. They resided at New Salem, where their son, John G., afterwards lived and carried on the milling business.

The children of Gerritt J. Freer and Geritje Van Vliet were Selitje, born in 1787; Lidia, born July 3, 1791; Jan (in English John), born March 29, 1793; Blondini, born 1796; Gerrit, born in 1798; Cornelia, born in 1811; William, born in 1804.

John wrote his name John G. He married Dina Rose and resided on the farm of his father at New Salem. He was en-. gaged with his father in the milling business in his early years near New Salem, in the town of Esopus, and also owned the Eddyville ferry. In 1826 he built a stone house still standing.

THE ABRAHAM HASBROUCK HOUSE IN THIS VILLAGE

CHAPTER XXXI

THE FAMILY OF ABRAHAM HASBROUCK, THE PATENTEE

Abraham Hasbrouck, the Patentee, has a numerous line of descendants in Ulster, Orange and Dutchess counties.

The two brothers, Abraham and John (in French Jean) Hasbrouck (or Broecq, as the name was sometimes written), were natives of Calais. Like others of the Paltz patentees, they emigrated to Manheim, in the Palatinate, which was in those days the great harbor of refuge for the Huguenots flying from persecution in France. Abraham Hasbrouck, likewise, probably resided in Holland. Quite certain it is that he lived for a time in England and served in the English army. He received his commission as lieutenant of a company of foot for New Paltz and Kingston, August 30, 1685. In 1689 he was appointed as "captain of foot at Ye Paltz, Ulster county."

Under the date of 1700 in a foot company appear the names of the following officers: Abm. Hasbrouck, captain; Moses Quantin, lieutenant; Lewis Bevier, ensign.

In the records of the Kingston church, under date of 1676, appears the following marriage entry: "Abraham Hasbroocq of Calis and Maria Deyo (of) Moeterstat in Duyslant."

Before coming to New Paltz, and while residing at Hurley, he was appointed Justice.

Tradition states that Abraham Hasbrouck served in the English army with Gov. Edmund Andross, and that it was owing to his influence with the Colonial Governor that the Huguenots obtained the grant of so large and fine a tract of land at New Paltz.

In the diary of Col. Abraham Hasbrouck of Kingston, who was a grandson of Abraham Hasbrouck the Patentee, it is stated that his grandfather left Mannheim, where he resided with his father, went to Rotterdam and thence to Amsterdam, where he embarked for England in April, 1675. From England he sailed to Boston, from thence he proceeded to Esopus, where he found his brother Jean, who had come to America three years before.

Quite possibly Abraham may have served in the English army and then gone back to his home in Mannheim before he left that place for the new world. Abraham reached Esopus in July, 1675. The next year he married, at Hurley, Maria Deyo, daughter of Christian Deyo, a young woman with whom he had been acquainted in the Palatinate and who was one of the passengers with him on the passage across the ocean to America.

Abraham died March 7, 1717, in an apoplectic fit. His wife died March 27, 1741, in her 88th year. They left a family of five sons, Joseph, Solomon, Daniel, Jonas and Benjamin, and one daughter, Rachel, who married Louis DuBois, Jr.

Joseph married Ellsje Schoonmaker and located at Guilford. Solomon married Sarah Van Wagenen and located about 1½ miles north of this village. Daniel married Wyntje Deyo and kept his father's homestead. Jonas probably died young. Benjamin married Jannitje DeLong and moved to Dutchess county.

The home of Abraham the Patentee, in this village, was built directly across the street from the present Reformed (Dutch) church. The old stone house, still standing, was possibly built by Abraham, but perhaps by his son Daniel, in whose line it has come straight down. There is no date on the old stone house to mark the time of its erection. Like other of the ancient houses in this village, it had formerly a sub-cellar, which has been filled in during the last century.

The house is about sixty feet in length and thirty in width. It has evidently been erected at different times, the northern part at a later date than the other portion. There are initials on the stones at the northeast and southwest corners of the building, but so worn by the elements that it is impossible to decipher them. This house has not been modernized since its erection. The chimney in the north end is built in the wall. There is a cellar kitchen in this portion of the building. One or two rooms have been finished off in the loft. It is one of the most antique in appearance of the old houses in our village. It is still occupied and still a comfortable house.

Daniel, Son of Abraham the Patentee

Daniel, born in 1692, kept his father's homestead in this village. We find his name in the list of freeholders in 1728, also in the list of slave owners in 1755. He did not marry until in 1734, when 42 years of age. His wife was Wyntje Deyo, daughter of Abm. Deyo of this village, who was the son of Pierre Deyo the Patentee. Daniel had a large family of sons and daughters and the name Daniel has been handed down in this branch of the Hasbrouck family until the present day. Daniel died in 1759. His widow long survived him and continued to occupy with her six sons the old stone house, still standing, opposite the Reformed church. Daniel Rose, who is a descendant of Daniel Hasbrouck, has in his possession an abstract of his will, dated January 26, 1754. The will gives to each of his sons, Jonas, Josaphat, David, Isaiah, Benjamin and Zachariah, one-sixth of his property; to the daughter, Elsie, who married Peter Smedes, three milch cows and £200 of New York currency. The will directs that the widow shall retain possession of the property, both real and personal, as long as she remains a widow, but that if she marries again she shall give up possession of the property to the children. In the tax list of 1765 we find the property all assessed to Wyntje Hasbrouck, and she was one of the wealthiest residents of the community. The old homestead in this village passed into the possession of Daniel's son, Isaiah, who married Mary Bevier, who, like her mother-in-law, was left a widow with a large family of children. The children of Isaiah Hasbrouck were Ezekiel, Isaiah, Josiah, Noah, Elsie and Mary. The last named, who did not marry, owned the old homestead until her death, about 1880. The brothers, Isaiah and Josiah, settled in Sullivan county. Noah lived where his son-in-law, Abm. R. DuBois, afterwards resided.

From Mary Hasbrouck the old homestead passed into the possession of Isaiah Hasbrouck, who now owns it.

Josaphat, another of the sons of Daniel Hasbrouck, married Cornelia DuBois. They have but one descendant of the male line living at the present day, that is Daniel A. Hasbrouck of this village, who is the only great-grandson. However, Josaphat and his wife, Cornelia DuBois, left three sons, Zachariah, Simon and Andries. The two first mentioned did not marry and lived in the Clintondale neighborhood in the house still owned by the family with their brother, Andries, who married Elizabeth Hasbrouck. Zachariah lived to a vigorous old age and is well remembered by the people of the present generation.

Jonas, another son of Daniel, lived on the other side of the mountains and married Catharine DuBois; he left three sons, Josaphat, who married ——— DuBois; Daniel, who married Margaret Schoonmaker, and Isaiah, who married Elizabeth

Westbrook and lived where Perry Deyo lately resided. Daniel I., of Gardiner, is their son.

Daniel's son David married Maritje Houghland. They lived in what is now the Lewis H. Deyo house, near Butterville. They had but one son, William, who did not marry. David died March, 1806, and is buried in the southwest portion of the old graveyard in this village. In the same portion of the graveyard and enclosed in an iron railing, are the graves of his nephews, Daniel and Isaiah, and their wives, Margaret Schoonmaker and Elizabeth Westbrook, the last named of whom died in 1864, aged 75 years. This was the last interment in the old graveyard.

Zachariah, another of the six sons of Daniel Hasbrouck and Wyntje Deyo, married Rachel Waring. They had a son, John.

Benjamin, the remaining one of the six sons of Daniel Hasbrouck, married Mary Bevier. They lived on the farm now owned by their grandson, Daniel Rose, about one mile from this village on the Modena road. Benjamin left but one son, Daniel B., who kept the homestead, and one daughter, who married Peter Rose. Daniel B. left no children.

SOLOMON, SON OF ABRAHAM THE PATENTEE

Solomon was born in 1686 and married Sarah Van Wagenen in 1721. They lived in a stone house about 1½ miles north of this village and a quarter of a mile east of the Springtown bridge. This house, after being unoccupied for many years, tumbled into ruins about 1860. There is a barn near by and about 100 yards south is a large old graveyard. Solomon had a large family of sons as follows:

Abraham, Jr., Jacobus, John, Daniel, Simon, Petrus and Elias. Of Abraham, Jr., Daniel and Simon we have no account except that the first named married Rachel Sleight.

Jacobus' son Benjamin owned what is known as the Simon L. DuBois farm near Springtown. He gave a life estate in the farm to his son Abraham, who was the grandfather of John H. Hasbrouck and Milton B. Hasbrouck.

Of Petrus, John and Elias we have quite a complete record.

Petrus lived in the old stone house now owned by Mr. A. Neal, at Middletown. This house was built for Petrus; his wife was Sarah, daughter of Abm. Bevier. In Revolutionary times Petrus was second lieutenant in the second company of New Paltz militia, serving in Col. Johannis Hardenburgh's regiment, which regiment served from October 25, 1775, till 1782 and saw much fighting.

Petrus' children were Rœlif, who lived at Springtown; Simon, who lived in the old homestead and died unmarried; Samuel, who married Lydia Crispell and inherited the old homestead; Jeremiah, who married a Bruyn and moved to Elmira; Mathusalem, who married Maria Deyo and moved to Binghamton; Solomon, who married Magdalen LeFevre and lived at Centerville; Abram, who married Mary Blanshan and lived on what is now the John Morey farm at Bontecoe. Rœlif, the eldest son, was twice married. His first wife was Jane Elting. They had four children—all girls, Sarah, who married Wm. W. Deyo; Catharine, who married Jacob Rose; Dinah, who married Jonathan LeFevre; Magdalen, who married Daniel DuBois.

Rœlif's second wife was Maria DeWitt. They had three sons, DeWitt, Clinton and Charles B. The last named long carried on the mercantile business in this village in the building afterwards occupied by his nephew, Oscar C. Hasbrouck.

Petrus' son Samuel was the father of Miss Cornelia Hasbrouck and Mrs. Elihu Schoonmaker of this village, from the latter of whom we have our information in regard to this branch of the Hasbrouck family.

Elias Hasbrouck, the brother of Petrus Hasbrouck, moved to Kingston, where he engaged in the mercantile business, his store being located on the corner of Wall and Main streets, opposite the First Reformed church. Elias commanded a company of rangers in the Revolutionary war and saw much active service. He was with Gen. Richard Montgomery in the attack on Quebec, in which Montgomery lost his life. He named one of his sons Montgomery in honor of his old commander and to his son, as well as all other sons of his old comrades who were named for her husband, Gen. Montgomery's widow made a present of a gold ring. This ring passed from Montgomery Hasbrouck to his daughter, Mrs. ——— Keator, who long resided with her son-in-law, Mr. Chas. Drake, in this village, and preserved the ring as a precious heirloom. From her we have full information of the family of Elias Hasbrouck. When the British burned Kingston, in the time of the Revolutionary war, the store of Elias Hasbrouck was consumed.

After the war he went to Shandaken Valley, in Woodstock, where he bought a piece of land at what is now Lake Hill. Elias Hasbrouck's wife was Elizabeth Sleight of Esopus. They had a family of two daughters and five sons, Elias, John, Daniel, Montgomery and Peter. The last named moved to Kingston. The other brothers all settled on the tract purchased by their father in Woodstock, where they had farms adjoining each other. Two of Montgomery's sons, Daniel, late of Modena, and John W., of Middletown, Orange county, have taken an active interest in the family history.

Going back now to John, the brother of Elias and Petrus, we find that he kept the homestead of his father, Solomon— that is the old stone house, afterwards owned and occupied by

Charles Elting, standing a few rods west of the late residence of Jas. Ean, which tumbled down about 1860.

John Hasbrouck left two sons, John and ———. John was the only one who married. John's wife was a daughter of Wm. McDonald, a Scotchman, who had a tannery about where the eastern end of the Springtown railroad bridge now is. John and his wife had four sons, Andrew, William, Philip and John. Andrew and William emigrated in their youth, the last named, we believe, to Florida. John went to Indiana and left a large family of children. Philip resided in the neighborhood all his life, his residence being directly across the street from the school house. For a great number of years he held the office of justice of the peace and was usually called "'Squire." He had three sons: Washington, Peter and Evert. The first named was a very prominent educational man, was the founder of the Hasbrouck Institute at Jersey City and was for a number of years principal of the New Jersey State Normal school at Trenton.

This ends the history of the descendants of Solomon, son of Abraham Hasbrouck, the patentee.

JOSEPH, SON OF ABRAHAM THE PATENTEE

We will now proceed to the history of Joseph, the eldest son of Abraham the Patentee, who was born in 1684. Joseph Hasbrouck, and his wife, Ellsje Schoonmaker, are buried in the graveyard in this village, but for a great number of years they have had few descendants permanently residing in the town of New Paltz. Nevertheless none of the New Paltz Huguenots have left a more honored line of descendants and none have taken greater interest in the history of the place.

Joseph and his wife, Ellsje Schoonmaker, were married in 1706. They located at Guilford, on a tract of 2,000 acres,

TOMBSTONE OF JOSEPH HASBROUCK IN THE OLD GRAVE YARD IN THIS
VILLAGE

which had been granted by patent in 1685 to James Graham and John Delavall. The original parchment is now in the possession of Joseph Hasbrouck, Jr., who is the owner and occupant of the farm where his father, Joseph L., his grandfather, Col. Joe., and his great-grandfather, Gen. Joe., lived before him. Gen. Joe.'s father, Col. Abraham, lived in Kingston in Revolutionary times and his father is the first Joseph in the line.

The parchment, on which the grant of the Guilford tract is written, is in a good state of preservation. About 1860 the family residence was burned down and a number of papers burned, but this patent being in the safe was preserved.

The following is a copy, the quaint spelling of certain words being given as in the original:

"Thomas Dongan, Lieutenant Governor and vice admirall of New Yorke and its dependencyes under his majesty, James the Second, by the Grace of God of England, Scotland, France and Ireland, King, Defender of the faith, Supreme Lord and proprietor of the colony and province of New Yorke and dependencyes in America. To all to whom this shall come sendeth greeting.

Whereas Phillip Wells, esquire, surveyor general, hath by virtue of my warrant, bearing date the 16th day of December, one thousand six hundred and eighty-five, surveyed and laid out for James Graham and John Delavall, a certain tract of land, being situate and lying upon both sides the Walls River, of the New Palls and known by the Indian name Nescatock and now by the name of Guilford, in the county of Ulster beginning on the east side the river and att the south end of a small island, off the mouth of the River Chauwangung and stretching into the woods by a line of marked trees, east, south-

east, five degrees and thirty minutes, southerly fifty one chains
and a halfe and then in length north by east six degrees and
forty five minutes easterly one hundred and ninety chains and
then in breadth to the River west, northwest, five degrees and
thirty minutes northerly, by a line of marked trees, fifty one
chains and a half to the pauls River and so crossing the River,
to a tree marked with three notches, and a cross on them,
standing off the mouth of a small run and so continues by a
line of marked trees, fifty one chains and a halfe over a small
hill and then in length south southwest two degrees and thirty
minutes westerly, one hundred and seventy six chains, to a tree
marked, near the River Chauwangung and from thence east,
southeast to the said River and so by the River to the aforesaid
small island, including the said island, containing in all wood-
land and meadows two thousand acres as by the Rowenty of
the survey Remaining on record in the secretary's office may
more fully and att large appear : NOW KNOW YEE that I,
the said Thomas Dongan, by virtue of the power and authority
to me devised from his most sacred majesty, and in pursuance
of the same have given, granted, ratified, released and con-
furred, and by these presents, do give, grant, ratify, release
and confirme unto the said James Graham and John Delavoll,
all the aforesaid tract and Parcell of land and Island lying and
being scituated within the limitts and bounds aforesaid, together with all the woods, underwoods, timber, swamps, meadows, pastures, fields, islands, waters, lakes, ponds, Rivers, Rivu-
lets, Runns, Creeks, Quarries, Mines, Mineralls, ffishing, hunting, hawking, ffowling and all other Royalties, Proffits, Com-
moditites, hereadaments to the said tract and parcell of land,
island and premissess with their appurtenances, belonging or
in any wise appertaining (silver and gold mines only excepted)
to have and to hold all the aforecited tract and parcell of land

Island and premises with all and everything appurtenances, unto the said James Graham and John Delavall, their heirs and assigns, to the sole and proper use, beneffitt and behoof of them the said James Graham and John Delavall, their heirs and assigns, forever, without any lett, hindrance or molestation, to be had or Reserved upon (word illegible) or joynt tenancy or survivorship, any thing contained herein to the contrary in any wise, notwithstanding, to be holden of his most sacred majesty, his heirs and successors in free and comon Soccage, according to the tenure of east Greenwich, in the county of Kent, within the Realms of England yielding, rendering and paying therefor yearly and every year, unto his said majesty, his heirs and successors or to such officer or officers as shall be empowered to receive the same on the five and twentieth Day of March, att the city of New Yorke six bushels of good, winter, merchantable wheat, as an acklowledgment or quit rent, in lieu of all services and demands whatsoever.

In Testimony, whereof, I have caused these presents to be recorded in the secretary's office and seale of the province to be hereunto affixed, this eleventh day of September, Ann Dom one thousand six hundred and eighty six, and in the second year of his majesty's reign.

THOMAS DONGAN.

Recorded in the Secretary's office for the province of New York in Liber W. S. book of Pattents begun 1684, pages 546, 547, 548.   G. I. SPRAGUE, Sec.

May it please your honor, the attorney-general hath perused this patent and finds nothing contained therein prejudicial to his majesty's interest.   JA. GRAHAM.

Exam. August, 1686.

We do not know very much about the first Joseph Hasbrouck, except that he was one of the Justices of the County
of Ulster in 1722, and his name is mentioned in a record of
that date as having proceeded with two other Justices and an
Indian to locate definitely the southwest corner of the Paltz
patent at Moggonck.

The diary of Joseph's son, Col. Abraham Hasbrouck, says
he was "a gentleman much respected by those with whom he
was acquainted and he served in several public stations in
Ulster county.   He was very affable and agreeable in company,
eloquent in speech, spoke French, Dutch, and very tolerable
English."

Joseph Hasbrouck is buried in the old graveyard in this village and the stone which marks his last resting place bears
the oldest date of any in the graveyard.   It is of brown sand
stone, such as was used at that period.   At the top of the
stone is an angel's head and wings.   The inscription is as
follows: "Here lyes the Body of Joseph Hasbrouck, Esq.,
aged 40 years, 3 months and 18 days, deceased, January 28,
172¾."   The fraction ¾ marks the date in Old Style.   By
the side of this grave is another similar stone with the inscription: "Here lies interred the Body of Ellsje Hasbrouck,
widow of Joseph Hasbrouck, Esq., deceased ye 27 day of July
1764, aged 78 years, 8 months and 3 days."

Joseph's widow, as will be noted by these inscriptions, outlived her husband forty years.   We may suppose the stones
were put up by her sons after their mother's death.   Quite
certainly no gravestones of brown sandstone were used in the
graveyard here at so early a period as 1723.

At just what date Joseph Hasbrouck moved from his father's
home in this village and located at Guilford we can not say.
It was probably shortly after his marriage in 1706.

In our previous sketches of the early settlers of New Paltz we have noted various instances of a widow being left at a comparatively youthful age with a large family on her hands. We have noted the additional fact as appearing in the early history of New Paltz that, where there was a large family of sons the record of the mother was that of an exceedingly able woman.

Joseph Hasbrouck's wife lost her husband when she was about thirty-seven years of age, and was left with ten children on her hands, while her oldest, Abraham, was only about seventeen years of age. It requires little imagination to see that this woman, in the wilderness five miles from the little settlement at New Paltz, with no houses on the way except those of Louis DuBois, Jr., on the county house plains, and Solomon DuBois, where Mr. Blake now lives, must have had a dreary time, and had she not possessed a brave heart, would have succumbed to the hardships of the environment. But she did not give up the fight nor move back to New Paltz. She raised her family of six sons and four daughters. In her later years, when neighbors increased, she kept a store in the house. Nine of her children married. Her family scattered widely and rose to eminence.

The sons of Joseph Hasbrouck and his wife, Ellsje Schoonmaker, were Col. Abraham, who married Catharine Bruyn and located in Kingston; Isaac, who married Antje Low, widow of John Van Gasbeck, and located a short distance east of old Shawangunk church; Jacob, who married Mary Hornbeck and moved to Marbletown; Benjamin, who married Eledia Schoonmaker and located at what is now the Borden residence at Wallkill; Cornelius, who did not marry; Col. Jonathan, who married Catharine DuBois and located at Newburgh. There were also four daughters, all of whom married.

COL. ABRAHAM, SON OF JOSEPH

The oldest son, Abraham, married Catharine Bruyn, daughter of Jacobus Bruyn, who lived a few miles south of Guilford, and in 1735, fourteen years after the death of his father, moved to Kingston and left the other children to help their mother to carry on the farm. We may consider that the boys who were left at home under care of their mother did good service in clearing up the forest land, for in 1765, one year after her death, we find the farm assessed to Abraham, the oldest son (who had bought it) at a higher rate than any other farm in the whole precinct of New Paltz.

For thirty-one years Abraham carried on the mercantile business in Kingston. In 1776 his store was destroyed by fire. He then moved, and in his later years had his residence in the large stone building, well remembered by people of the present generation as Schryver's Hotel, on East Front street, destroyed by fire about 1876. He is usually called "Colonel," but was not engaged in active service in the Revolutionary army, being an old man when the war commenced. He was a lieutenant-colonel of militia, was for twenty years member of the Provincial Assembly and was a member of the State Senate in 1781.

In 1775 he was elected colonel of the 1st Northern Ulster County Regiment and the next year was elected commander. During a long term of years he kept a diary, which contained more authentic information probably than any other record of that time in the county. This diary is quite a large volume and is now in the possession of the family of his great-grand-daughter, Mrs. Geo. H. Sharpe. Col. Abraham Hasbrouck, though residing in Kingston, continued to take a great interest in the affairs at New Paltz, and in the feud between the Hasbroucks and the Eltings, which formed so important a part of the history of those times, he bore quite a conspicuous part.

The origin of the feud was, as nearly as we can ascertain, the attempt on the part of Noah Elting and Nathaniel LeFevre to obtain from the Colonial government a patent for 3,000 acres of land lying on the south of the Paltz patent. This was strongly opposed by Col. Abraham Hasbrouck and others in behalf of the balance of the Paltz people, alleging that the original Paltz patent covered a part of this tract. To make the fight more bitter an action was commenced against Noah, who resided where the late Edmund Eltinge lived, and it was claimed that the land he occupied and which his father purchased of Solomon and Louis DuBois, Jr., in 1726, was also a part of the Paltz patent and that therefore his title to it was not valid. Finally the matter was settled without coming into court. In 1755 Col. Abraham, together with Louis Bevier of Marbletown and Jacob Hasbrouck, obtained a grant of 2,000 acres of land south of the New Paltz patent and in the neighborhood of the present Clintondale depot.

Col. Abraham Hasbrouck of Kingston left four sons, Joseph, Daniel, Jonathan and James. The oldest son, Joseph, when he became a man moved back to the old homestead at Guilford. Daniel located at Wallkill, Orange county, and left two sons, neither of whom married, and four daughters.

Jonathan lived in Kingston and is well remembered as "Judge Jonathan," and was the father of Hon. A. Bruyn Hasbrouck, than whom Ulster county has had no more honored son. James occupied his father's house, subsequently the Schryver hotel property, at Kingston.

We will now go back with Col. Abraham's son, Joseph, to the homestead at Guilford. Having been placed by his father on the farm he worked it on shares for several years. In 1773, when thirty years of age, he married Elizabeth Bevier. Joseph

was a brigadier-general of militia and is usually spoken of as
"General Jo." During the Revolutionary war his farm was a
depot of supplies for the federal army stationed at New Windsor and other places and these supplies were forwarded as
needed. The book with his account of these transactions is
still in possession of the family at Guilford. During the Revolutionary war he was lieutenant-colonel in Col. Cantine's regiment. His title as general was probably for militia service
after the war. He was a member of the Assembly in 1786
and a member of the State Senate in 1793-96. He died in 1808.

Gen. Jo. left one daughter and a large family of sons as
follows: Abraham, Louis, Daniel, Joseph, Philip, James and
Luther.

The oldest son, Abraham, who was born in 1775, moved to
Rondout when a young man, and for half a century carried on
a general mercantile business, being known among his old
neighbors in Southern Ulster as "Abraham Hasbrouck of the
Strand." He was in the freighting business, as well as the
mercantile business, accumulated a large amount of property,
and was a member of Congress in 1813-15. His wife was
Helena Jansen. Their children were Jansen, Helena, wife of
Henry Sharpe and mother of Gen. George H. Sharpe; Elizabeth, wife of Dr. Richard Elting; Catharine, wife of Judge
G. W. Ludlum; Maria, wife of Robert Gosman. Jansen, the
only son, was a very prominent citizen of Rondout and until
shortly before his death was president of the Rondout bank.

Besides Abraham "of the Strand," the other sons of "General
Jo." of Guilford, as we have said, were Louis, David, Joseph,
Philip, James and Luther. Louis located at Ogdensburgh,
where his descendants still live.

David became a doctor and settled in Utica. He left at
least two sons, William and John L., the latter the well-known

New York merchant. Gen. Jo.'s sons Philip and Luther married, but left no children. Philip lived where his nephew, Philip B., now lives in Gardiner. The two remaining sons, James and Joseph, located in the vicinity, Joseph retaining the old homestead at Guilford and being sometimes called "Colonel Jo." James lived west of the Guilford church. His surviving sons are Louis of Libertyville and Philip B. Col. Jo., who kept the old homestead, left a family of four sons, Abner, Oscar, Dr. Alfred, who settled in Poughkeepsie, and Joseph L., who kept the old homestead.

About 1850 fire destroyed the old stone mansion, and some of the ancient papers, but a portion of the most valuable ones were in the safe unharmed. A brick house of modern pattern took the place of the stone house. On the death of Joseph L. Hasbrouck the property came into the occupancy of his only surviving son, Mr. Joseph Hasbrouck, Jr.

Louis Hasbrouck (son of Joseph, son of Abraham, son of Joseph, son of Abraham the Patentee), who settled at Ogdensburgh, was born April 22, 1777, and was baptized May 11, 1777, at Shawangunk by Rev. Regnier Van Niest. He was educated at Princeton and graduated in 1797. He studied law in the office of Josiah Ogden Hoffman in New York city and was admitted to the bar in 1801. Shortly afterwards he removed to Ogdensburgh, N. Y. He was the first County Clerk of St. Lawrence county, Postmaster of Ogdensburgh, Member of the Legislature and State Senator. He died August 20, 1834.

He married Catharine Banks, daughter of Justus Banks. They had several children, of whom one son, Louis, born in 1814, and two daughters, Sarah Sophia and Louisa, married. One daughter, Jane, is still living. Louis, the second of the name at Ogdensburgh, was twice married. His first wife was

25

Louise Seymour Allen and his second wife was Sarah Maria
Hasbrouck, daughter of Levi Hasbrouck of New Paltz. By
the first marriage there were three children, two of whom, a
son and daughter, are now living—the son, who is named Louis,
being a prominent lawyer at Ogdensburg. By the second marriage there were three children, two of whom, Levi and Laura
Maria, are still living.

Isaac, Son of Joseph and Grandson of Abraham the Patentee

Isaac Hasbrouck, second son of Joseph and grandson of
Abraham the Patentee, was born March 12, 1712, and in 1766
married Antje Low, widow of John Van Gaasbeck, settled in
Shawangunk about a mile south of Tuthill and built the house
still standing, owned by Richard Hardenberg and his children
for seventy years. His lands joined the Wallkill on the east
for nearly a mile and extended west to where the Shawangunk
church stands and probably extended a little farther to the
Shawangunk kill. When the Shawangunk church was organized in 1737 he gave the land where the building stands.

Isaac Hasbrouck was Supervisor of the town of Shawangunk in 1751 and 1752.

Isaac and his wife had three children—Joseph I., Elsie and
Jane. Elsie did not marry. Jane married John Crispell and
they had two sons, Peter and DuBois; both became physicians.
DuBois settled and died in Kingston, Peter died in Hurley.
A granddaughter of Joseph I., Mrs. A. M. Ronk, has in her
possession an old family Bible with the following record:

"Joseph I. Hasbrouck, born October 11, 1767, died March
24th, 1842. Married Cornelia Schoonmaker of Pa-ca-na-sink,
born February 18th, 1766, died July 14th, 1814." Their children were Sarah B., born August 28, 1788, married Daniel

Tuthill; Maria, born May 23, 1790, married Thomas Ostran-
der; Catharine, born August 17, 1792, married Samuel John-
son; Dr. Stephen, born April 24, 1794, married Elsie Schenck
of Fishkill; Levi, born December 21, 1795, married Manj
Decker; Jane, born January 27, 1798, married Cornelius De-
Witt of Marbletown; Geo., born January 26, 1800, married
Maria Johnson; Joseph Osterhoudt, born December 23, 1801,
married Eliza Ray; Abel, born December 16, 1803, married
Ruth Winfield; Augustus, born September 20, 1809, married
Jane V. W. Eltinge, daughter of Rev. Wilhelmus.

Joseph I. located and built on a portion of his father's lands
about half a mile south of the old homestead and some distance
by lane from the main road to the banks of the Wallkill. This
has sometimes been mistaken for the old homestead.

Joseph I., of Shawangunk, was Supervisor in 1797-9, 1813-4
and in 1817.

JACOB A., SON OF JOSEPH OF GUILFORD

Jacob A. Hasbrouck, son of Joseph of Guilford and grandson of Abraham the Patentee, was born in 1717. He married,
in 1746, Maria Hornbeck and located at Kyserike in the town
of Marbletown. At about the same date Isaac Hasbrouck, son
of Jacob, son of Jean the Patentee, moved from what is now
the Memorial House in this village and likewise settled in the
town of Marbletown. Both of these Hasbrouck families have
ever since had representatives in the town of Marbletown and
elsewhere, but there is a great disparity in the number of descendants bearing the Hasbrouck name for the reason that while
Isaac had six sons and a goodly number of grandsons, Jacob
had but one son, and boys have since been few in numbers in
his line of the Hasbrouck family.

Capt. Jacob L. Snyder, of High Falls, whose wife is a daugh-

ter of Calvin Hasbrouck and great-granddaughter of Jacob A.,
has in his possession a number of valuable old papers, which
have come down in this line of Hasbroucks and which make
clear the family history.   The oldest of these papers are two
deeds for land at Kyserike from Ellsje Hasbrouck, of Guilford,
widow of Joseph, to her son, Jacob A. Hasbrouck.   In one of
the deeds, dated in 1747, consideration is love and affection and
£300.   In the deed for the other tract at Kyserike the consideration mentioned is love and affection and £540.   The latter
deed is dated in 1754.

The children of Jacob A. Hasbrouck and his wife, Mary
Hornbeck, were Anitje, Elsie, Mary, Joseph and Rachel.   In
his will, also in possession of Capt. Jacob L. Snyder, Jacob A.
gives to his son Joseph all his land in the towns of Marbletown
and Rochester, but requires him to pay £400 to his sisters,
Anitje, Elsie and Mary.

Joseph Hasbrouck, son of Jacob, occupied his father's homestead, known in modern times as the Lodewyck Hasbrouck place.

In the war of the Revolution Joseph's name appears as ensign in the company of which John Hasbrouck, of Marbletown,
who had married Joseph's sister, was captain.   Subsequently
he received from Gen. Geo. Clinton a commission as lieutenant
in the Levies and his name appears as lieutenant in the Fourth
Orange County Regiment, Col. Hathorn, of which his cousin,
Joseph Hasbrouck of Guilford, was lieutenant-colonel.   His
commission is dated July 1, 1780.   At a later date, after the
close of the war, in 1787, he received a commission as captain.
The will of Joseph Hasbrouck, which was probated May 6,
1802, together with the other valuable papers mentioned are
now in the possession of Capt. Jacob L. Snyder, having come
to him from his father-in-law, Calvin Hasbrouck, who was
the son of Joseph.   Calvin resided at High Falls and was for
many years superintendent on the Delaware & Hudson canal.

BENJAMIN, SON OF JOSEPH AND GRANDSON OF ABRAHAM THE PATENTEE

Benjamin, born in 1719, son of Joseph and grandson of Abraham the Patentee, located at what is now Wallkill and built the stone house, still standing, and which forms a part of the present Mrs. John G. Borden residence. Benjamin married Elidia Schoonmaker and had three sons, Benjamin, Cornelius and Joseph, the second named of whom kept the homestead, and the son Joseph took the south part of the farm. Cornelius' farm was left to his son, Benjamin C., and Joseph's farm went to his son Thomas. The descendants of the three sons of Benjamin Hasbrouck, the first of the name at Wallkill, are thus stated by Mr. A. M. Ronk:

Benjamin married Elizabeth Dickerson, daughter of William. Their children were Eliza, who married Stephen Ronk; Lydia did not marry; Isaac married Delia Newman; Jacob married Charlotte Thorn; Elsie married Jabez Ells; Henry H. married Ruth Constable; Catharine married William Johnson; Jane, Joseph, Mary did not marry.

Cornelius married Jane Kelso. Their children were Wm. C., married Mary E. Roe; Benj. C., married Louise Lyon; Margaret, married Captain Eli Perry.

Joseph married Rebecca Kelso, a sister of Cornelius' wife. Their children were Thomas, did not marry; John, moved to Michigan, married Rachel Ann Traphagen; Maria Jane, married Nathaniel Roos; Catharine Ann married Halsey Lyon; Rebecca, married Linus Esterly; Sarah, married John Titus.

Wm. C. Hasbrouck, son of Cornelius, son of Benjamin, the first at Wallkill, was born August 23, 1800; married Mary E., daughter of William Roe, June 28, 1831; died November, 1870; had three sons, viz.: Wm. H., Henry C. and Roe, and three daughters: Maria H., Emily A. and Blandina. He graduated at Union College at the same time Wm. H. Seward was an undergraduate, and soon after removed to Franklin, Tenn., where he became principal of the academy founded by Bishop Otey. Returning to the North, he became principal of the Farmers' Hall Academy, at Goshen, in 1822, and commenced there the study of law with Mr. Wisner. He completed his legal studies with Wm. Ross, in Newburgh; was admitted to the bar in 1826, and rose rapidly to rank in his profession. He was elected to the Assembly of 1847 and was chosen Speaker of that body; he was a man of high bearing, spotless character, and a chivalric sense of honor and duty. His second son, Henry C., graduated at the West Point Military Academy, May, 1861 ·· served as lieutenant under Captain Griffin, 5th Artillery, U. S. A., in first Bull Run, also at Miner's Hill and Newport News; promoted captain 4th Artillery, and in service in the Modoc campaign.

Henry C. was for some time in command at Fortress Monroe, holding a commission as lieut.-colonel in the regular army, and in the war with Spain was appointed brigadier-general.

COL. JONATHAN, SON OF JOSEPH AND GRANDSON OF ABRAHAM THE PATENTEE

Jonathan, the youngest son of Joseph and grandson of Abraham the Patentee, was born in Guilford April 12, 1722, and died July 31, 1780. Jonathan married May, 1751, Tryntje, daughter of Cornelius DuBois of Poughwoughtenonk. Jonathan located at Newburgh, purchasing, in 1747, the property on which he built, in 1750, part of the house known as Washington's Headquarters. Subsequently he built an addition to this house and here he resided until his death. He was the first Supervisor of the precinct in 1763. He held at different times commissions as ensign, captain and colonel, his commission to the latter office being issued October 25, 1775. His regiment saw much active service in the Revolutionary war, but, owing to the ill health of its colonel, was much of the time commanded by Lieutenant-Colonel Johannes Hardenbergh. On account of continued ill health Col. Jonathan Hasbrouck resigned in 1777. The diary of his brother, Col. Abraham of Kingston, gives the following account of Col. Jonathan:

"He was a loving husband to his wife, a tender and loving father to his children, a loving brother to his brothers and sisters, an obedient and dutiful child to his parents, a kind master to his servants, a good neighbor, a hospitable man, a good, industrious, sober man, and a very good liver, and a very good commonwealth's-man (whig). He was a pious worthy man, paid a good deal of reverence in hearing and reading the word of God. He was good natured, not soon ruffled or put in a passion, but with a great deal of forbearance. He had very good sense, and strong natural parts and understanding— especially in divinity, and very knowing in common affairs of life. He was a man of stature above six feet and four inches, well shaped and proportioned of body, good features, full visage of face, but of brown complexion, dark blue eyes, black hair, with a single curl, strong of body, arms, legs; was inclined to be corpulent and fat in his younger days, but meeting so many sicknesses and disorders he was not so fat the last thirty years of his life as he was in his youth. He had a great many good qualities that I don't write down here. He died on Monday morning and was buried on Tuesday in the burying place on his own land, between his house and the North River, lying along side two of his sons (Abraham and Joseph), who lay buried in the same ground." ·

The other children of Jonathan were Cornelius, Isaac, Jonathan, Mary and Rachel. The son, Cornelius, born in 1755, espoused the cause of the king and removed to Canada where he founded a creditable family. The son Isaac, born in 1761, died in 1806, married Hannah Birdsall and continued to reside at Headquarters. The daughter Mary, born in 1763, married Capt. Israel Smith and during the Revolutionary war resided with her father's family at Headquarters, at the time that Gen. and Mrs. Washington were there. A cloak presented by Lady Washington to little Mary Smith is still treasured up as an heirloom. The son Jonathan did not marry. The daughter Rachel married her cousin Daniel, son of Col. Abraham of Kingston, and located at Montgomery, Orange county.

Col. Jonathan's son Isaac, who occupied the Headquarters after his father's death, left a family of three sons and three daughters as follows: Jonathan, Israel, Eli, Sarah, Rachel, Mary, all of whom were born at Headquarters. Sarah, who married Walter Case, was the only daughter who married. Jonathan, the oldest son of Isaac and grandson of Col. Jonathan, married Phebe Field and left a large family of sons and daughters, all of whom were born at Headquarters.

Eli, son of Isaac and grandson of Col. Jonathan, married Harriet Belknap and left a large family of children, six of whom · married and left children. Eli's second son, Charles H., deceased, was for many years cashier of the Quassaick Bank.

Rachel, daughter of Col. Jonathan, married her cousin Daniel, son of Col. Abraham Hasbrouck of Kingston, and located at Montgomery, Orange county. They left a family of two sons, Asa and Samuel, neither of whom married, and four daughters who married as follows: Margaret, married Severyn Bruyn of Bruynswick; Betsey, married Edward Wait of Montgomery; Clara, married Nicholas Evertson of Newburgh, and Elsie, married Dr. Hornbeck.

RACHEL HASBROUCK'S RIDE FROM NEWBURGH TO GUILFORD

One of the most romantic stories that we hear of the Revolutionary times is thus related to us by Mrs. Peter Miller of Montgomery, Orange county (who is a daughter of Edward Wait), and was told to her when a child by her grandmother, who is the heroine of the tale:

The British were approaching Newburgh; we presume it was Vaughn's expedition to relieve Burgoyne. Whatever else the red coats might spare if they stopped at Newburgh it was a plain case that the family plate of so noted a rebel as Col. Jonathan Hasbrouck would not be left at its owner's home. So Rachel, who was eighteen years old, mounted a mare called Firefly and with the family plate in the saddle bags the brave girl started alone for the old home of her grandfather, Joseph, at Guilford. Part of the way the route was only to be found by the marks blazed on the trees. At the foot of a mountain on the route she was stopped by tories. But the leader of the band declared with an oath that she was too pretty to be molested. While the members of the party were debating the question Rachel struck Firefly with the whip and flew on. The tories fired at her, but she was not hit by the bullets and arrived safe at the ancestral home at Guilford.

Until quite recently Mrs. Miller owned the saddle in which her grandmother made this famous ride. Other Revolutionary reminiscences related to Mrs. Miller by her grandmother are that when the British sailed past Newburgh on the way to help Burgoyne the family of her father, Col. Jonathan, took refuge in the cellar, expecting that the British ships would cannonade the house. They were not disappointed, but the cannon were aimed too low and the balls struck below the house, in the ground. When Washington had his headquarters at this house

he and Mrs. Washington boarded with Col. Jonathan's family.
Part of the time while Washington was at Newburgh the
Marquis de La Fayette and his wife were their guests. La
Fayette was a very large, heavy man—so large that his wife
was obliged to use five needles in knitting his stockings, and
when he went out his valet would take an extra horse along
for his use. When Washington said good bye to the headquarters Lady Washington presented Rachel Hasbrouck with
a chair, which is now owned by Mrs. Elizabeth Eager of Great
Bend, Pa. Another daughter of Col. Jonathan was likewise
presented with a chair by Lady Washington.

BENJAMIN, SON OF ABRAHAM, THE PATENTEE

Benjamin, the youngest son of Abraham the Patentee, born
in 1696, located in Dutchess county about 1720. His wife was
Janitje De Long, whom he married February 13, 1737. In
1755 Benjamin built a stone house, which is still standing near
Hopewell, in which he resided until his death, in 1763. Benjamin had a family of four sons and two daughters, as follows:
Daniel, Benjamin, Jacob, Mary, Heiltje and Francis. Benjamin did not marry. Daniel married ——— Van Vlecken and
had four sons, Tunis, Benjamin, John and Daniel; also two
daughters, Catharine and Rachel. Tunis lived in the town of
Fishkill, where he left two sons. John married Mary Backus
and moved to Onondaga county. Benjamin married Hannah
Green and left a large family of children, eleven in all. Daniel
did not marry.

Francis, son of Benjamin (the first in Dutchess county) married Elizabeth Swartwout and they had four children, Benjamin, Abraham, James and Gilbert. All died young, except the
oldest son, Benjamin. He was a private in Capt. Abraham

Brinkerhoff's company, in Col. John Cantine's Ulster County Regiment. During his lifetime he occupied the old stone house of his grandfather, Benjamin. He married Rachel Storm. Their children were Francis, Sarah, Catharine, Elizabeth, Caroline and Isaac.

This ends the history of the family of Abraham Hasbrouck, the New Paltz Patentee.

THE JEAN HASBROUCK HOUSE, NOW THE MEMORIAL HOUSE

CHAPTER XXXII

The Family of Jean Hasbrouck, the Patentee

Directly across the street from the site of the first stone church stands the house of Jean Hasbrouck, the Patentee, which was purchased by the New Paltz Huguenot Memorial Society in 1899, to preserve the memory of the early settlers and as a store-house of relics and ancient documents.

This is the largest and finest of all the old houses, except the DuBois house, and that has lost a great part of its attraction from having been modernized many years ago.

The house of which we speak bears the letters I. H., surmounted by a sort of crown, cut in a stone just above and to the left of the door. In the mortar, near one of the front windows, is the date 1712. The I in the olden time was the same as J, and the letters above mentioned are the initials of the builder. The date 1712 is found in two places on the building, and doubtless marks the date of its erection—thirty-five years after the date of the patent and seven years after the erection of the DuBois house, which still bears the figures 1705 in iron letters. The only other stone house in this village ever bearing a date of which we are aware is the original Bevier house, afterward the Elting store, which stands with its gable end to the street, opposite the DuBois house, and which bore on its chimney until about 1890 the date of 1735.

The first houses were doubtless all of logs. As the settlers found time they were replaced by the stone edifices still standing. Probably every one in the settlement assisted in the building. The house we are describing is the only one in the village with an exceedingly tall and steep roof, nor do we recollect any other old stone house in all the country round with such a roof.

Entering at the front door we find ourselves in the broad hall, extending through the center of the building. To the right and left are large rooms, with high ceilings, the great beams being about nine feet from the floor.

The room to the right was used in Revolutionary times, and probably for half a century before, as a store where the few goods that were not produced in the place were sold to the settlers. In one side of the chimney is a closet with a door fitting so closely as to be almost unnoticed except by careful inspection. This, it is said, was the money drawer. High up on the garret is a railing which was formerly in this room and was the bar, behind which stood the merchant of the olden time. This railing was not taken up on the garret until about 1850. Levi Hasbrouck, during his lifetime would not allow any important changes to be made in the appearance of the old homestead, and this is the reason why this bar railing was kept in this room so long after it was unused for mercantile purposes.

The large room to the left, as we enter, was without doubt the living room of the family. In the rear is the kitchen.

The kitchen chimney is about ten feet wide at the base, the mortar apparently of lime and clay—tough and firm. Stepping into the fireplace from the kitchen, the old trammels and pot hooks are still to be seen. These were in common use in the old stone houses before the day of cook stoves. These chimneys, with their wide fireplaces, were meant to consume the great logs without the trouble of cutting them up. The mantle-piece is high up so as to be out of the way of the flames. The brick, of course, must have been hauled from Kingston and doubtless brought from Holland, as there were, we presume, no brickyards in this country at that early date. But what an immense quantity of brick went into one of these old chimneys!

Everything about the house is evidently hand-made. The nails in the doors, the bolts and hinges are made by the home blacksmith, and their appearance shows that they were hammered out. The wood work was made before the day of sawmills and shows the hand planing of the home carpenter.

The work is all substantial. There was evidently no slighting of the work by mechanics in those days. The old settlers meant to stay, and they meant that their houses should be for their descendants as well as themselves.

Descending to the cellar we find a higher ceiling than in the other old houses. There is one dark room, without a window, in the cellar, but we do not find the sub-cellar which two or three of the other stone houses in the village had and which we are informed was to store liquor in or to put things in for safe keeping, to have them out of the way of the slaves. Doubtless this dark room and the sub-cellar in other old buildings were for the same purpose. Part of the cellar is paved with stone, part of it with brick, an evidence of comfort we have not seen in other old houses.

Ascending to the upper portion of the building, we find the airy loft. Here in olden times the grain was stored in hogsheads. Even in the memory of the people now living, this custom was continued in this building. The light streamed in through the windows with their little panes of glass. This was not the only one of the old houses in which the grain was stored in the loft. Doubtless that custom was universal in the early settlement.

From cellar to garret the house is full of quaint reminders of the olden time—over two centuries ago, when the country around was a wilderness and New Paltz a little hamlet in its midst, where a handful of French Huguenots, fleeing from persecution, had found a home and a refuge, where they might worship God in peace and rear their families in comfort.

Jean Hasbrouck, the Patentee, left three daughters, Mary, who married Isaac DuBois; Hester, who married Peter Gumaer, and Elizabeth, who married Louis Bevier of Marbletown. He also had three sons, Abraham, Isaac and Jacob. The first went to England and never returned. Isaac died before his father. His name appears in the list of members of Capt. Wessell Tenbrouck's company that marched to the invasion of Canada in 1711. He probably lost his life in this campaign. Jacob married Hester Bevier and kept the old homestead. Jacob left three sons, Jacob, Isaac and Benjamin. Jacob, who wrote his name Jacob, Jr., married Jane DuBois, daughter of Cornelius DuBois, Sr., and sister of Cornelius DuBois, Jr., of Poughwoughtenonk. He continued to reside in the homestead. Isaac married Maria Bruyn. Benjamin was killed by a falling tree in 1747. Isaac is the ancestor of the Stone Ridge Hasbroucks.

Jacob, Jr., of New Paltz, who lived in the old homestead, was Supervisor of the town in 1762-5 and again in 1771-6. From a tax list of the town, dated 1765, we find that Jacob Hasbrouck, Jr., Josiah Elting and Cornelius DuBois of Poughwoughtenonk, were the three wealthiest men in the town and each possessed of about an equal amount of property.

Jacob, Jr., was captain of the Second New Paltz Company, Third Regiment of Ulster County Militia, in Revolutionary times, his commission being issued October 25, 1775. He was promoted subsequently to the position of major in the same regiment, February 21, 1778. We have no account of any battles in which he was engaged, but there is good evidence that he was with the army when Kingston was burned.

Jacob, Jr., left two sons, Josiah and Jacob J., Jr.; also one daughter, Hester, who married Dr. George Wirtz, the ancestor of the Wurts family at New Paltz. On the tombstone in the old graveyard marking the spot of her interment is the inscription, "daughter of Major Jacob Hasbrouck."

In his old age, Jacob, Jr., built and perhaps moved to the old stone house in the north bounds of the present corporation, where his great-grandson, Abm. M. Hasbrouck, now lives. The son Josiah kept the old homestead. He carried on the mercantile business in this ancient house after the Revolution and accumulated a very large amount of property. He was a Member of Congress in the 8th session in 1803-5, was Member of Assembly in 1796, 1802 and 1806, and Supervisor of the town in 1784-6, 1793-4 and from 1799 to 1805. Josiah was commissioned as second lieutenant in the Second Company, Third Regiment of Ulster County Militia in 1780. He was usually called Colonel. Perhaps that rank may have been bestowed during the war of 1812. We know nothing of his military record.

In his old age Josiah moved from the old family residence in this village to the Plattekill. His wife was Sarah Decker. They had three daughters, Elizabeth, Jane and Maria, and one son, Levi, who occupied the Plattekill residence during his lifetime, as did his only son, Josiah, who died about 1885.

Col. Josiah's daughters married as follows: Elizabeth was Josiah DuBois' first wife, Jane married Joseph Hasbrouck of Guilford and Maria married Christopher Reese of Newburgh.

We have said that Col. Josiah had one brother, Jacob J., Jr. After his father's death he continued to occupy the house where Abm. M. now resides until in middle age when he gave up this house to his son, Maurice, and moved to Bontecoe and built the brick house which his grandson, Luther, now owns. He was twice married. His first wife, Margaret Hardenbergh, died young, leaving one son, Louis, who went to Sullivan county when a young man and was never seen again. The second wife, Anna DuBois, left a large family of sons and daughters, as follows: Maurice, Jacob J., DuBois, Huram, Asenath, Albina.

Coming back now to the village and to the ancient house which is now the Memorial House, we note that after Col. Josiah's removal to the Plattekill, near Jenkintown, the old homestead was occupied for a time by his son-in-law, Josiah DuBois, who had previously carried on the mercantile business in partnership with him, but discontinued it after a time, and about 1820 built the brick house now owned by Wm. H. D. Blake. After that date the old stone house, until its purchase by the Huguenot Memorial Society in 1899, was occupied by tenants.

Col. Josiah Hasbrouck was quite certainly the richest man in New Paltz, perhaps the richest man in the county. His father before him was a rich man for those days. Yet it must be noticed that although this old house was for successive generations the residence of wealthy people it was a very plain edifice.

The people of those old days did not put all their money into houses. They lived, we dare say, in comfort, but had not as yet learned to be discontented with the plain, old stone houses of their ancestors.

The Stone Ridge Hasbroucks

Isaac Hasbrouck, son of Jacob, son of Jean the Patentee, was born in 1722. He married, in 1745, Mary, daughter of Jacobus Bruyn of Shawangunk. They moved to the town of Marbletown and lived in the house in which their son, Severyn, afterwards resided, which is still standing, about a mile east of Stone Ridge and now owned by James Pine.

Isaac Hasbrouck and his wife, Mary Bruyn, left a large family of children, as follows: Jacob I., John, Jacobus Bruyn, Severyn, Maria, Esther, Catharine, Benjamin and Louis.

The names of four of these sons appear as soldiers in the Revolutionary war: John, as captain, Jacobus Bruyn as lieutenant, Severyn and Louis as privates. The name of Jacob I. appears among the signers of the Articles of Association.

Jacob I., the oldest son, who was born in 1746, married Sarah, daughter of Cornelius DuBois of Poughwoughtenonk, in the town of New Paltz. They located at the place, still known as the Colabargh, about a mile north of Stone Ridge. The property remained in the family for several generations, passing from Jacob I. to his son Josiah, and then to Josiah's son DuBois, and then to his son Dr. Josiah Hasbrouck, who was an only son, as was his father DuBois. On removing to Port Ewen he sold the farm to Lucas E. Schoonmaker.

Jacob I. had another son, Cornelius D., who married Hannah Van Wagenen, studied medicine and became a doctor. In the division of the estate of his maternal grandfather, Cornelius DuBois, Senior, of Poughwoughtenonk, he received the old stone house and about 120 acres of land. Dr. Hasbrouck moved to this tract about 1820, tore down the stone house, which had been built about 100 years before by Solomon Du-Bois, and built the frame house still standing and now occupied as a residence by the present owner of the farm, LeFevre Du-Bois. Dr. Hasbrouck resided on this place and practiced medicine about twenty-five years. He left one son, Hiram, who went to Michigan, and one daughter, Eliza, who married Peter Barnhart and lived on the place until in old age.

Other children of Jacob I. Hasbrouck and Sarah DuBois

were: Isaac, born in 1769; Margaret, born in 1773 (married Dr. Wm. Peters); Wilhelmus, born in 1775 (was the owner of Kingston Point); Jacobus, born in 1777; Cornelius, born in 1778; Jacob I., Jr., born June 7, 1780; Louis I., born 1785; Abraham, born in 1787; Maria, born in 1789.

Of this numerous family we have additional account of the following: Louis I. married Margaret Van Vleck. Maria married Dr. Matthew Dewitt of Stone Ridge and left no children. Jacob I., Jr., married, November 18, 1809, Catharine Knickerbocker. They had a large family of children, as follows: Cyrus (killed in the civil war), Rufus, Sarah DuBois, Wm. Peters, Matthew Dewitt, Annie Ingraham, Maria Dewitt, Margaret Peters, Josiah Lewis, Anna Chittenden. The daughter, Margaret Peters, married James C. Cornish. Rev. Marion Cornish of Kingston is their son.

Benjamin, son of Isaac, wrote his name Benjamin I. He was born in 1764 and located at Kyserike, his old stone house, which is still standing, being on what is now the Matthew Steen place. Benjamin was twice married. His first wife was Catrina Smedes. After her death he married Rachel, daughter of David Hasbrouck, whose home was what is now the Louis H. Deyo place, near Butterville. By the second wife there were four daughters, one of whom married Stephen Stilwell. Benjamin I. Hasbrouck died in 1843, aged eighty years. The farm passed into the possession of his son, Alexander, usually called Bony, who was a child by the first wife.

John, son of Isaac, the first Hasbrouck at Stone Ridge, married Mary, daughter of Jacob A. Hasbrouck of Kyserike, who was the son of Joseph Hasbrouck of Guilford. John located about one mile south of Stone Ridge at what was called Rest place and here he built a stone house. In the Revolutionary war he served as captain in the Third Ulster County Militia, of which John Cantine was colonel. The name of John Hasbrouck, Jr., perhaps the same person, appears as a private in the Third Regiment of the Line, commanded by Col. Jas. Clinton. From one of the family, Mrs. James Oliver Hasbrouck, residing in extreme old age at Washington, D. C., comes the following account of the services of Capt. John Hasbrouck and his family in the Revolutionary war:

Capt. John inherited a homestead from his father, which was located in the county of Ulster, town of Marbletown. On it he built a stone house. When the war broke out he went himself and gave everything except his homestead for freedom's cause. On this homestead or farm he left his wife and four small children; and she, taking up the burden of both man and wife, worked the land, which was in a splendid state of cultivation. Finally the Indians and Tories, who were all around them, became so troublesome and dangerous that it was necessary to have a fort for the safety of the families. So Capt. John's wife offered her house, which was turned into a fort. It had to be guarded day and night by the soldiers—even men who worked in the fields had to have a guard with them or they would be shot while at work. At this fort the people were cared for and given a place where they could sleep in safety, and besides the table was always on the floor for those that were hungry. The homestead was handed down from generation to generation until it came to Gross Hasbrouck, grandson of Capt. John. Capt. John Hasbrouck's descendants likewise have an account of his presence at the capture of Burgoyne's army, also in Sullivan's expedition against the Indians.

Severyn, son of Isaac Hasbrouck, the first of the name at Stone Ridge, was born in 1756. He lived about a mile east of Stone Ridge on what is now the James Pine place. He was twice married. By his first wife, Maria Depuy, he had one son, Isaac S., born in 1786. By his second wife, Maria Conklin, he had one son, Henry C., and one daughter, Maria. Isaac S. studied for a doctor and practiced medicine for a time, and afterwards carried on the mercantile business at Stone Ridge. His wife was Matilda Barnes. Their children were Severyn, Edgar, Charlotte and Matthew. The two first named sons continued their father's business as merchants at Stone Ridge. Henry C. Hasbrouck lived on a farm about a mile east of Stone Ridge. His wife was Nancy Barnes. Their children were Lorenzo, who died when a young man, and Elmira, who married Abm. V. N. Elting of New Paltz.

Jacobus Bruyn, son of Isaac Hasbrouck, the first of the name at Stone Ridge, was born in 1753, married Ann Abeel. They resided at High Falls.

We have no further information concerning the family of Jacobus and none concerning that of Louis, the youngest son of Isaac, except that he was born in 1767, married Catharine Decker and lived at Stone Ridge.

CHAPTER XXXIII.

THE LeFEVRE FAMILY IN AMERICA

Among the Huguenots who settled in America at an early date we have accounts of six different families of LeFevres, namely at New York, in New Paltz, in New Jersey, in Penn-sylvania and at New Rochelle. We have no certain evidence that these families were related, although it is quite probable that Isaac LeFevre, the ancestor of the Pennsylvania tribe, was the nephew of Andre and Simon LeFevre, of New Paltz, and quite possibly all these Huguenot families bearing the name of LeFevre were nearly related.

For our account of the LeFevre family outside of Ulster county we are mainly indebted to the researches of Mrs. C. A. Weber Lindsay, of Pittsburg, Penn.

The first LeFevre in America of whom we have any record was Peter LeFevre, who was in New Amsterdam in 1653. His name appears on the records at subsequent dates during the next few years in New York and Brooklyn as an owner of real estate. It is thought that he or his widow moved to New Jersey. Hippolytus LeFevre settled at Salem in western New Jersey and was one of John Fenwick's council in 1676. He became a large landholder and his descendants are believed to have been engaged in navigation, as nearly half a century afterward vessels bearing the name of members of the LeFevre family were running from this part of New Jersey to the New England coast. In 1683 another LeFevre, Isaac by name, crossed the ocean and settled in New Jersey. His son, Myn-dert, in 1731, advertised his father's farm for sale, between

Perth Amboy and New Brunswick. These New Jersey Le-
Fevres have moved to other states or become extinct in the
male line, as the name has been lost a long time in that country.

Isaac, the ancestor of the Pennsylvania LeFevres, has a
numerous line of descendants and the family history has been
carefully traced. A brief statement is as follows: Isaac was
born in France in 1669. When he was a youth of fourteen
his parents, brothers and sisters were massacred on account of
their religion. He escaped and fled to the Palatinate, carrying
with him the family Bible, which is still in existence and is now
the property of Samuel T. LeFevre of Iowa City, Iowa. It
is about 300 years old, was printed at Geneva and contains the
name of Isaac's brothers and sisters, but not of his parents.
Isaac fled from France to the Palatinate in company with the
family of Madam Ferree and married the daughter, Catharine
Ferree. One son, Abraham, was born to them in the Palatinate. In 1708 they emigrated to America and in 1711 were
in Kingston, when their second son, Philip, was baptised April
1, 1711, Isaac DuBois and Rachel DuBois, both of New Paltz,
being sponsors. In 1712 Isaac went with his wife and two
sons to Lancaster county (then Chester county), Pa., nine
miles from the present town of Lancaster, where he made purchases of land amounting to 2,200 acres, and here in 1713 their
son Daniel was born, being the first white child born in the
Pequea Valley. At about the same date Abm. DuBois, one of
the New Paltz Patentees, bought a large tract of land in this
.part of Pennsylvania and in this section three of his daughters
and their husbands located. Isaac LeFevre, of Pennsylvania,
has a numerous and highly respectable line of descendants. In
December, 1896, an ·organization of the LeFevre and Ferree
families was formed for historical purposes.

The New Rochelle LeFevres came to this country at a much

later date than the others of the name. They are descended from John LeFevre, a native of Havre de Grace in France, who went from his native country to St. Domingo. His son John, born in 1752, died in 1837, emigrated to New Rochelle, N. Y. John left a family of seven children, of whom the eldest was the late Peter E. LeFevre, captain of one of the Atlantic steamers sailing from New York. Hon. Ben. LeFevre, of Ohio, is a grandson of John.

With this brief notice of other families of Huguenot descent bearing the name of LeFevre we take up the history of the two brothers, Andre and Simon, who settled at New Paltz.

THE LeFEVRE FAMILY AT NEW PALTZ

The old people, in noting the family characteristics of the LeFevres, said they lacked the energy of the Hasbroucks and DuBoises; they would not work hard themselves, nor make their slaves work hard; they were not so noted for book learning as the Beviers; they could not talk well; but on the other hand they knew when to keep the mouth shut. This is a most important quality, meaning prudence and oftentimes good sense and judgment. The LeFevres certainly held their own very well among the other settlers; when the church sought release from Holland rule and when the country sought release from British rule they were on the right side; in building each of the old stone churches they contributed a full share, and in the war of the Revolution did not waver; no feuds or family quarrels are reported among the LeFevres in the olden days.

Simon and Andre LeFevre, after leaving France, resided in the Palatinate. They arrived at Kingston at an earlier date than most of the New Paltz Patentees and united with the church at that place in April, 1665. The LeFevre family has a large share of well-preserved traditional lore and ample documentary evidence concerning its later members, but of these two brothers we have little knowledge. Probably they were mere boys when they came to Kingston, and that is the reason their names do not appear on the records for the next twelve years, and that would also explain why there have been found no certificates of their church membership in the Palatinate, as have turned up in the case of others of the Patentees. We have been told that Grandfather Peter LeFevre had a French testament and, according to the best recollection of our informant, the word "Lyons" was on the flyleaf. This testament can not now be found. We think it probable that the LeFevre brothers were of the kindred of Jas. LeFevre, the great French Reformer and Bible translator, who was born at Calais, from whence came the Hasbrouck brothers. Lille, the home of Louis DuBois, was not far off. Louis Bevier was a cousin of the Hasbroucks. It is probable that all the Patentees were from the same portion of France. In 1635 Adam LeFevre, who may have been a relative, went from Calais to Leyden. Thirty years afterwards Andre and Simon are in Kingston, but probably we shall never know the place of their birth or who were their parents, as the baptismal records of Huguenot families were destroyed by order of Louis XIV.

At the granting of the New Paltz Patent in 1677 the names of the LeFevre brothers appear with the other Patentees. Simon married Elizabeth Deyo, daughter of Christian, the Patentee. Their first born child, Abram, who died young, was baptised at Kingston in 1679; their son Isaac, the ancestor of the Bontecoe tribe, was baptised at New Paltz, October 28, 1683, and their son Jean (Jan in Dutch, John in English) was baptised October 28, 1685. We find no record of the baptism of the son Andre (in English Andrew, in Dutch Andries). He is first mentioned as joining the church here in 1700.

Of Simon and Andre, the Patentee, we find but little account in the early records of New Paltz. Neither of them lived very long after the settlement here. In 1680 Andre sold to Hyman Albertson Rosa a house at Hurley, which he had bought of the executors of Cornelius Wynkoop. In 1681 his name appears as godfather at the baptism of Andre, son of Louis Bevier, and in 1694 as godfather at the baptism of Daniel, son of Abraham Hasbrouck. Andre was the only one of the Patentees who did not marry. He doubtless made his home with his brother, whose children at his death inherited his property. He certainly outlived his brother, but we can not give the date of his death. An ancient tombstone in the old graveyard, bearing simply the initials A. L. F., marks the grave either of the Patentee or of his nephew who bore his name.

Simon, the Patentee, built his house in the northern part of the present churchyard, where it stood until the present church was built, in 1839. In 1678 Simon, acting for his father-in-law, Christian Deyo, transferred a house at Hurley to Cornelius Wolverson. In 1689 the names of the LeFevre brothers and the other Patentees, except Christian Deyo (who was dead), appear in the list of persons taking the oath of allegiance.

The only family paper in existence, so far as we know, relating to Simon is an agreement between the son and four sons-in-law of Christian Deyo in 1687 for an equitable division of his property. Simon must have died about 1690. His widow married Moyse (Moses) Cantain, a French Protestant, whose wife had died on the passage to America. In 1693, May 21, they had a son, Peter, baptised and he is the ancestor of the Cantine family.

Cantain occupied the house until the LeFevre boys were grown and then moved to Ponckhockie. In 1700 we find his name as lieutenant in a military company, the rest of whose officers were New Paltz men. He probably left our village shortly after that date. In the tax list of 1712 the property is assessed to "Andre LeFevre & Co.," meaning, of course, the three brothers and their sister Mary, who married Daniel Du-Bois, son of Isaac, the Patentee.

The LeFevre property in this assessment roll is valued at £270 and is the largest assessment on the roll, except those of Louis Bevier and Abm. DuBois.

In 1713 a division was made among the children, who had until that date jointly owned the one-sixth of all the lands in the patent, which they had heired from their father Simon and their uncle Andre, and likewise the one-fifth of the share of Christian Deyo, which had come to them from their mother. The paper containing the apportionment to the sister Mary, who had married Daniel DuBois, has come down among the papers of that family and is as follows, certain portions being illegible and marked with stars:

To all Christian people to whom this present writing shall or may come Andre Lefevre of the town of new palls in the County of Ulster and province of New York in America Isaac Lefevre of the same place Jean Lefevre of the same place the heires of Andre Lefevre and Symon Lefevre both late of the new palls Deceased Send Greeting Whereas the said Andre Lefevre and Symon Lefevre in theire lifetime were possessed & seized of two-twelfths and of the one-fifth part of a twelfth part of all the land and appurtenances * * * within the bounds and limmitts of the Pattent of the Town * * aforesaid and whereas the Partners of the said lands of the * * by theire certain deed or instrument in writing under their hand * * the twenty-fifth day of Jany anno Domini * * Did convey unto the said Andre LeFevre Isaac Lefevre Jean Lefevre and Mary Lefevre * * now wife of Daniel Du-

Bois of the new palls aforesaid all their lotts and parts of the
Lands within the bounds and Limmitts of the new palls aforesaid as in and by the said deed or instrument in writing thereunto being had doth and   *   appear and whereas by the
division of the said parts and lotts of the said new palls aforesaid The Lotts and parts hereafter in these presents more particularly mentioned and expressed are fallen unto the said Daniel
DuBois and Mary his wife Now for a confirmation of the same
unto them the said Daniel Dubois & Mary his wife their heirs
and assigns forever Know Yee that the said Andre Lefevre
Isaac Lefevre and Jean Lefevre Have given granted conveyed
assured Ratified Released and confirmed and by these presents
for themselves and their heirs Do freely and Clearly give grant
convey assure Release Ratifie and confirme unto the said Daniel
Dubois and Mary his wife & to their heirs and assigns forever
all that certain lott lying and being on the north side of the
palls creek on a certain piece of land call avienjer or piece of
oates Between the lotts of Jean Hasbrouck and the said Daniel
Dubois and also a certaine lott lying on the north side of the
palls creek on a piece of land called pasture between the lotts
of Jean Hasbrouck and Abram DuBois allso a certaine lott of
land on the northeast of the high bridge so called between the
lotts of Daniel Dubois & Lewies Bevier and also a certaine lott
of land lying on the north of the palls creek on a piece of land
called the Little bontekow between the lotts of the said Daniel
DuBois and Pieter Doyo and also a home lott and pasture land
thereunto adjoining lying in the Town of the new palls on the
east side of the   *   *   Lewies Beviere being in length from
the street to the pas—   *   *   Lefevre equal with the said
lotts & pastures in length   *   *   Beviere and also to a certain
parcell of land lying to the north   *   *   of the new palls and
to the east of the waggon path between the   *   *   Dubois

and Jean Hasbrouck and also to a just fourth part of * *
two twelfth parts & one fifth part of a twelfth part of said
* * new palls aforesaid which is nott yett devided and layd
out to have and to hold the said lotts parts and parcels of lands
with all and singular the * appurtenances thereunto belonging or in anywise appertaining unto them the said Daniel
DuBois and Mary his wife their heirs and assigns forever to
the sole and only proper use benefit and behof of them the said
Daniel Dubois and Mary his said wife their heirs and assigns
forever they paying rendering and yielding yearly and year
forever the just fourth part of the quit Rent due to her majestie
for the above mentioned two twelfth parts & one fifth part of
a twelfth part of the said land in the new palls in witness
whereof the said Andre Lefevre Isaac Lefevre and Jean Lefevre have hereunto put their hands and seals this twenty-
second day of October annoy domini 1713.

> Andre le Fevre.
> isaac le Fevre.
> jean le Fevre.

Sealed and delivered in the presence of us

> Joseph Hasbrouck.
> solomon hasbroucq.
> Jacob hasbroucq.

In the presence of me Joseph Hasbrouck justice of the peace

> W. Nottingham Clerk.

Recorded in libra * *

> W. Nottingham Clerk.

It is interesting to note that the names of "little (in Dutch klein) bontekow" and "avienjer," which have come down to the present day, were at that early date applied to certain tracts of land along the Wallkill, "little bontekow" being the Beaver place, near Springtown, and "avienjer" a piece of land on the west side of the Wallkill a short distance from our village. It is also worthy of note that the name Bontekow, applied to lowland along the Wallkill, is at a date when the French language is still the common speech of the people. This would seem to indicate that the name was of French origin, and in that case it means "neck of good land," if written "Bon-ter-cou."

Jean LeFevre, son of the Patentee, was one of the volunteers who marched to the invasion of Canada in 1711. The next year, November 20th, he was married by Dominie Peter Vas at Kingston, to Catharine Blanshan of Hurley. They located on the Paltz Plains.

Isaac was married at Kingston, May 16, 1718, by Dominie Peter Vas, to Marytjen Freer, daughter of Hugo Freer, Sen. They located at Bontecoe, about four miles north of this village.

Andre married Cornelia Blanshan. We do not find the marriage recorded in the church records either at New Paltz or Kingston. Their eldest child, Simon, was baptised in 1709. Andre kept his father's homestead in this village.

The names of the three sons of Simon, the Patentee, are found in the list of those who built the first stone church in 1718 and in the list of those who were assigned seats in the church in 1720. At the later date it is noticed that their sister Mary, wife of Daniel DuBois, was dead.

Andre, son of Simon, the Patentee, who married Cornelia Blanshan and kept the homestead in this village, had a family

TOMBSTONE IN THE OLD BURRYING GROUND IN THIS VILLAGE

of two sons, Matthew and Simon, and seven daughters, who were known as the "seven sisters."

In the list of militia officers in Ulster county, in 1717, we find Andre's name as sole lieutenant in Capt. Hoffman's company, which embraced New Paltz and Shawangunk. In the same list the names of his brothers, Isaac and Jean, appear as privates.

Isaac's name appears in 1738 as corporal in Capt. Zacharias Hoffman's company, and at the same date appear as privates the names of his eldest son, Isaac, Jr. (who died unmarried when a young man), and of his nephews, Abraham and Nathaniel, sons of Jean, and of his nephew Simon, son of Andre. The name of Matthew, the other son of Andre, does not appear and he had probably moved from New Paltz the previous year when he married.

Matthew moved to Bloomingdale in the northern part of the town of Rosendale and the history of his family is given under that head.

Simon married Petronella Hasbrouck and kept the old homestead in this village. They had but one son, who was named Andries, Junior, born in 1740. Simon died young and his widow, who long outlived him, in 1771 sold to the Reformed church the southern part of the present churchyard, where the second stone church was shortly after erected. The "seven sisters" married as follows: Elizabeth married Jonathan DuBois of Nescotack, Mary married Conrad Vernoy of Wawarsing, Sarah married Samuel Bevier of Wawarsing, Maritje married her cousin Nathaniel LeFevre on the Plains, Cathirintje married Simon DuBois, Magdalen married Johannes Bevier and Rachel married Johannes Bevier of Wawarsing.

Andries, Jr., who was the only son of Simon and Petronella LeFevre, kept the old homestead in this village and married

27

Magdalena LeFevre. They had no children. Andries is re
membered by the old people under the name of "Flaggus" or
"Uncle Flaggus." He died in 1811, at the age of 71 years, as
is shown by the tombstone still standing in the old graveyard.
After his death the old homestead became the property of
Andries DuBois of Wallkill and his wife, Elizabeth LeFevre,
who was a sister of "Flaggus." The DuBoises occupied the
house until the present brick church was erected, in 1839, when
it was torn down and the stone went into the church foundation.

This ends our account of the family of Andre, the eldest son
of Simon, the Patentee, the male line of the son Simon having
become extinct and the line of his son Matthew being given
under the head "Bloomingdale LeFevres."

The Homestead on the Plains

Jean (in Dutch Jan), the third and youngest son of Simon,
the Patentee, married Catharine Blanshan and built his house
on the Paltz Plains, between the present cemetery and the railroad track. The old stone house was torn down about 1885. A
clump of old lucust trees marks the site and the cellar remains.
In this house we may suppose that Jean lived from the time of
his marriage, in 1712, until his death, in 1744. Jean left one
daughter, Margaret, who married Jacob Hoffman of Shawangunk, and three sons, Nathaniel, Abraham and Andries. The
history of the two last named is given under the head "Kettleborough LeFevres." Nathaniel, who was born November 2,
1718, married his cousin, Maritje LeFevre, and kept the homestead on the Plains. In the list of slaveholders, in 1755, he is
set down as the owner of two slaves. In the tax list of 1765
he is assessed for £23 and his mother at £3. Nathaniel and
his brother Abraham of Kettleborough were both members of
the building committee when the second stone church was

erected, in 1772, and the initials of his name, with those of
other members of the building committee, are still to be seen
in a large stone, which was doubtless the corner stone of that
church, under the horse block at the south end of the present
portico. Nathaniel's subscription to the building of the church
was £18.

In 1748 Nathaniel obtained, in partnership with his neighbor,
Noah Eltinge, a grant for a tract of 3,000 acres adjoining the
Paltz patent on the south. This grant led to a long dispute,
it being claimed that part of the tract belonged to the Paltz
patent. After a few years the matter was settled and Noah
and Nathaniel retained the land. Nathaniel kept a store at
his home on the Plains, as did his brother Andries at Kettleboro.

Nathaniel left a family of three sons, Matthew, John and
Jonathan; also two daughters, Margaret and Catharine. John
was baptised at Shawangunk in 1746, Margaret at Kingston in
1743, Matthew at Kingston in 1749 and Jonathan at Shawangunk in 1753. Margaret married Daniel Deyo, the first of the
name at Ireland Corners. Catharine married Daniel Jansen of
New Paltz, John married Eglie Swart, widow of Capt. Simon
LeFevre of Bloomingdale and moved to Owasco, where he was
probably one of the first settlers and where he had descendants
living at a recent date, but none we believe in the male line.

Matthew retained the family homestead on the Plains. He
married Elizabeth, daughter of Daniel LeFevre of Bontecoe.
The name of Matthew LeFevre appears as a lieutenant in the
First Company, Third Ulster County Regiment, Col. John
Cantine. The other officers of the company are New Paltz men.
The name Matthew LeFevre also appears as a lieutenant in the
Fourth Ulster County Regiment, in the Revolution, Col. Johan-
nes Hardenbergh commanding. The only other Matthew Le-

Fevre was the one who moved many years before the Revolution to Bloomingdale. Probably one was a lieutenant in the Third and the other in the Fourth Regiment. The name Matthew LeFevre also appears as a private in the 2nd New Paltz company. There was no other person at New Paltz of that name. He was probably a private at first and afterwards promoted.

The names of Matthew's brothers, John and Jonathan, appear as privates in the Second New Paltz Company, Capt. Abm. Deyo, Third Ulster County Regiment, Col. John Cantine.

The names of the three brothers, Matthew, John and Jonathan, appear in the list of those who, in 1775, signed the famous "Articles of Association," in which so many citizens of Ulster county and other parts of the State expressed their hatred of British oppression and their determination never to be slaves.

We have stated that Matthew kept the homestead on the Plains and John moved to Owasco. The youngest brother, Jonathan, who married Catharine Freer, located on a portion of the patent which his father had obtained and his house was built some distance east of the old homestead and some distance west of the present residence of his grandson, Hon. Jacob LeFevre. Matthew, the oldest son, who married Elizabeth LeFevre and kept the homestead, had a family of six children, Moses, Simon, Catharine, Nathaniel, Gitty and Magdalen. Nathaniel married Margaret Jansen and kept the old homestead for a time, but afterwards sold it to —— Ackerman and located on the New Paltz turnpike, about one-fourth of a mile east of Ohioville, where Dr. Maurice Wurts long afterwards resided. Nathaniel left no children. Matthew's son Moses married Margaret Vernooy and located on the turnpike, in the town of Lloyd, where his grandson Moses lately lived. His children were Elizabeth, Cornelia, Matthew and Cornelius, the last named of whom kept his father's house on the turnpike, and the other three spent a great portion of their days on the Paltz Plains not far from the old stone house of their ancestors.

Matthew's daughter Catharine married Roelif S. Elting and her sister Gitty made her home there until in old age, when she removed to the residence of her neice, Mrs. F. S. McKinstry, where she died about 1885, aged nearly 100 years, and retaining until extreme old age the vivacity and kindly interest in the welfare of others, which we love to think formed a delightful trait in the character of our Huguenot great-grandmothers. The family Bible of Daniel LeFevre of Bontecoe passed to his daughter Elizabeth, wife of Matthew Le-Fevre, and then to their daughter Gitty, who retained it during her long liftime. Since her death it has been placed in the Memorial House in this village. It is in Dutch, was printed in 1741, and contains the family record of Daniel LeFevre in English, commencing with his marriage to Catharine Cantine in 1751.

Simon, the remaining son of Matthew, married Elizabeth Deyo. They had their home at what is now the LeFevre Deyo place, on South street. Simon was a captain in the army in the war of 1812, but his company was stationed on Long Island and did not do any fighting. Simon left a large family of children, as follows: Gitty, Eliza, Matthew, Philip, Nathaniel, Magdalen, Maria, Moses and Andrew. Nearly all of these children located at New Paltz or at New Paltz Landing. Gitty was Jacob Elting's first wife. Eliza married Clinton Hasbrouck. Magdalen married Nathaniel J. LeFevre. Maria married C. Wynkoop. Nathaniel lived at New Paltz. Matthew located at Wurtsboro. The other brothers, Moses, Philip and Andrew, engaged in navigation on the Hudson, Philip and Andrew long running a barge from Highland to New York in partnership, and Moses passing a great portion of his life on the river as mate or captain of a vessel.

Going back now once more to the old homestead on the Plains, we will take up the line of Jonathan, son of Nathaniel. His wife was Catharine Freer. The house in which he resided, some distance east of the old homestead, was torn down about 1845. Jonathan left two sons, Garret and Jonathan J., and one daughter, Mary, who became the wife of Smith Ransom. Garret continued to till the ancestral acres and Jonathan located at Middletown.

THE KETTLEBOROUGH LEFEVRES

The Kettleborough LeFevres are descended from Andries and Abraham, sons of Jan, who was one of the three sons of Simon LeFevre, the Patentee. Jan settled on the Paltz Plains, in a house between the cemetery and the railroad, torn down about 1885.

Jan LeFevre's name appears in the papers, at the State library at Albany, as one of the volunteers in the Ulster county company that marched to the invasion of Canada in 1711. This Ulster county company was commanded by Capt. Wessel Tenbroeck, and with the exception of Jan LeFevre and Isaac Hasbrouck almost every name in the company is Dutch. In 1728 Jan LeFevre's name appears in a list of freeholders of New Paltz. Jan died May 27, 1744, as stated in the family record of his son Andries. Jan's son Nathaniel retained his homestead on the Paltz Plains and his other sons, Andries, born in 1722, and Abram, born in 1716, located in Kettleborough on a tract of 1,000 acres, being a part of the Thomas Garland tract.

The Thomas Garland patent was granted January 26, 1721. This patent included, likewise, a tract of 500 acres at Ireland

Corners, on which Daniel Deyo, son of Abram Deyo, settled.

This patent, sometime after it was granted to Thomas Garland, became the property of Garret Kettletas, whose name appears as a freeholder in the precinct of New Paltz in 1728.

Subsequently this tract became the property of John, Abram and Peter, sons of Garret Kettletas, and of Cornelius and Henry Clopper. There is no reason to suppose that any of these parties moved to Ulster county. The Kettletases resided in New York and were merchants or mariners. The Cloppers were merchants. Though they did not move to Ulster county themselves, they sent a man who located where the farm of Asa LeFevre now is. This man, whose name we have not learned, did not make a success at farming, and in 1742 1,000 acres of the tract were sold to Jan (in English John) LeFevre, whose brother-in-law, Daniel DuBois, went on the bond with him, as is shown in the following paper :

Know all men by these presents that I John Lefever of the Newpaltz In the County of Ulster and Colony of New York am Held and firmly bound unto Daniel Duboys of the Newpals In County and Colony as aforesaid in the sum of sixteen hundred pounds current money of the Colony of New York as aforesaid to be paid to the said Daniel Duboys his certain attorneys Executors Administrators or assigns for the which payment Well and truly to be made and Done I do bind my Self and heirs Executors and administrators and Every of them firmly by these presence Sealed with my Seal Dated this Twenty first Day of March In the Sixteenth Year of His Majestes Reign annoq Domini 1742-3.

The condition of this obligation is that whereas the above named Daniel Duboys at the Special Instance and Request of the above named bounden John Lefever and for his only debt,

Duty, matter and Cause, together with the said John Lefever is jointly held and firmly bound Unto Gerret Keteltas of the City of New York In and by three obligations In the pennell sum of Eleven Hundred and Eighty pound Conditioned for the true payment of five hundred and ninty pound Current money of the Colony of New York unto the Said Gerret Keteltas his Executors administrators or assigns on or before the first day of June one thousand seven hundred and forty three the sum of four hundred and ninty pounds and the sum of fifty pounds on the first day of June one thousand seven hundred and forty four and the Sum of fifty pounds the first Day of June then next following as by the said obligation and Condition thereof (relation being there unto Had) doth and may more fully appear If therefor the Said John Lefever his heirs Executors administrators Shall do well and truly pay or Cause to be paid to the above named Gerret Keteltas his Heirs Executors administrators or assigns the just and full sum five hundred and Ninty pounds Current money and the Collony as aforesaid In Discharge of the above mention obligation, and also save harmless and keep Indempnified the Said Daniel Deboys heirs Executors administrators as above writing from all Cost, charges, Suits or troubles that may happen for or by reason of his being bound, as first above mentioned then this obligation to be void and of none effect as else to stand and remain In full force and virtue.   Jean lefevre.

Sealed and delivered In the presence of
          Benjamin Dubois.
          Simon Dubois.

Andries' wife was Rachel, daughter of Nathaniel Dubois of Blooming Grove, Orange county, and granddaughter of Louis DuBois, Jr., of New Paltz. They were married October 20,

1745. Andries' house stood near Andries A. DuBois' late residence and was torn down about 1850.

The traditions all agree that when the first settlers located in Kettleborough the gravelly soil of that region was considered very poor. There was not sufficient stone for building purposes and an arrangement was made by which stone could be procured elsewhere. There was little timber on the eastern portion of this tract, as the Indians used to burn over the land and it was now just growing up in bushes, over which the deer leaped. In those old days wheat was the staple crop and a gravelly soil is not good wheat land. There was, however, a certain proportion of clay land, and when a farm was divided the son who took clay land was obliged to accept fewer acres than the other. One of the stories told illustrating the hard lot of the Kettleborough farmer, on his gravelly acres in those old days, is that at a certain wedding the Kettleborough people were not invited and when the question was asked why they had been omitted the answer was made that they had enough hard times without being put to the trouble of attending weddings.

We think the stories about the early settlers in Kettleborough being poverty stricken are much exaggerated. At any rate Andries LeFevre was a member of the Provincial Congress, which met in New York in 1775 and 1776, adjourning in May of the latter year. Andries likewise kept a store, as did his brother Nathaniel, on the Paltz Plains, and the Hasbroucks at Guilford at the same date. Andries' account book, as well as his family Bible with the family record in Dutch, are now in the possession of the family of his great-granddaughter, Mrs. Josiah P. LeFevre. The account book is also in Dutch and the items are quite interesting. After a while he discontinued the mercantile business, assigning as a reason that his money was "all in the bushes," that is scattered around and could not be collected of the neighbors who had bought his goods.

Andries LeFevre lived to the extreme age of 90 years. He is buried in the family burying-ground now on the John H. Wurts farm. His grave is marked by a tombstone erected long afterwards by his son Johannes.

Andries left a family of two sons and six daughters. These all married as follows: Nathaniel married Mary Deyo, Johannes married Elizabeth DuBois, Gertrude married Philip Deyo, Mary married Isaac LeFevre of Bontecoe, Catharine married Wessel DuBois, Elizabeth married Zachariah Bruyn, Cornelia married Solomon Elting, Sarah married Josiah R. Elting.

It is quite a prevalent idea with the present generation that the New Paltz people in Colonial times did not work very much. This may have been true sometimes, but it was not always the case.   Mother tells us the following story as related by her grandmother, Elizabeth DuBois, daughter of Andries DuBois: When she married her husband, Johannes LeFevre, and moved from Wallkill, then called New Hurley, to Kettleborough, she "moved in" with the family of her husband's father, Andries LeFevre, who with his brother Abraham were the first settlers in Kettleborough. Her husband had six sisters, all of whom married sooner or later, but these young women before they married and left the Kettleborough home had learned to work, and to work hard—they would hurry up to get the washing out of the way in the forenoon in order that they might sort or pare apples in the afternoon, and then in the evening they would spin. The eldest of these sisters married Philip Deyo and the youngest married Josiah R. Elting, and these alone have a large number of descendants in New Paltz, while the other four have a smaller number of great-grandchildren in this vicinity.

Andries' son Johannes (usually called Squire Hons) was baptized January 18, 1761. He lived at his father's homestead for a number of years, but built for his son Andries J. and finally lived himself in the house, now owned by his great-grandson, J. Elting LeFevre. Johannes was a young man in the time of the Revolutionary war and performed some service for the patriot cause by taking a load of arms from New Paltz to the army.

Johannes left a family of two sons, Andries J. and Nathaniel, born November 5, 1786, and four daughters, all of whom married as follows: Andries J. married Hannah DuBois, Nathaniel married Magdalene Hornbeck, Sarah married Matthew J. LeFevre, Rachel married James Jenkins, Petronella married Daniel A. Deyo and Cornelia married George Wurts.

Andries J., son of Johannes, married Hannah DuBois, daughter of Cornelius DuBois, Jr., of Poughwaughtenonk. Andries J. occupied the house and farm now owned by his grandson, J. Elting LeFevre. The house was a very fine building for those old days and the farm is still considered the best in the neighborhood. Andries died at the early age of thirty-five and his wife about ten years afterwards. Their children were Cornelius D., who kept his father's homestead; Johannes A., who moved to Michigan; Andries A., who located near Modena; Gertrude, who married Roelif DuBois, and Elizabeth, who married Josiah P. LeFevre.

Nathaniel, the son of Johannes, married Magdalen Hornbeck. They lived for a while in the old stone house of Andries, the pioneer, and afterwards built a new house a short distance south. They had a large family of sons and one daughter, as follows: Johannes, C. Hornbeck, Luther, Andries, DuBois, Sarah M., James, Egbert, Matthew. Sarah M. married Joseph Hasbrouck, Andries and Johannes emigrated to Kalamazoo county,

Mich., in their youth and Matthew in middle age. DuBois tills a portion of the ancestral acres, James was for many years a preacher of the gospel at Middlebush, N. J., Hornbeck and Luther are dead. Egbert died when a young man.

Nathaniel, the son of Andries, the pioneer, located about a mile south of the residence of his brother Johannes. His wife was Mary Deyo. He kept a store, as his father had done before him, and raised a large and robust family of sons, as follows: Andries, Jonas, Lewis, Abram N., Jacobus.

Nathaniel is spoken of as an energetic man, who made money and saved it. As an evidence of the healthfulness of his family, it is said that the door of his house usually stood open in all sorts of weather. His house burned down about 1825. Nathaniel's sons located as follows:

Jonas located at New Hurley. He had one son, John, who married Nancy Ransom.

Nathaniel's son, Abraham N., lived near Modena, where his son-in-law, Andries A. LeFevre, afterward resided. His wife was Sarah LeFevre, daughter of Isaac LeFevre of Bontecoe. They had three sons: Josiah, Nathaniel and Abm. A., and three daughters: Maria, who married Andries A. LeFevre; Rachel, who married Andrew Brodhead, and Gertrude.

Nathaniel's son Andries lived on what is known as the Jacob Westbrook place of late years. He had a large family of daughters, all of whom married.

Nathaniel's youngest son, Jacobus, married Elizabeth Jansen. They lived on what is now known as the John H. Wurts farm. Their children were as follows: Maria, who married Josiah LeFevre; Blandina, who married Rœlif Elting; Eliza, who married Deyo DuBois; Margaret, who married Cornelius Wurts; Lewis, who married Christina Hornbeck; Daniel, who married Ellen LeFevre; Rachel, who married Wm. Deyo.

THE HOUSE OF ABRAHAM LE FEVRE, ONE OF THE FIRST SETTLERS AT
KETTLEBOROUGH

Nathaniel's son Lewis kept his father's homestead, an old stone house, which was burned down and rebuilt as a frame house many years ago. Lewis married Rachel Bell. They left but one child, Nathaniel, usually called "Sing" because he was often singing to himself.

Going back now to Abraham, brother of Andries, the other pioneer settler at Kettleborough, we find that he was born in 1716, married Maria Bevier and located at Kettleborough about 1742. His stone house is still standing and is now the tenant house on the Solomon Van Orden farm. Abraham left a family of six sons, John Solomon, Noah, Nathan, Samuel, Philip, and four daughters, Catharine, Magdalene, Margaret and Rachel. Catharine married Daniel DuBois, Rachel married Johannes DuBois, Margaret married ———— Vernoy and after his death Abm. Bevier. Magdalene married Andries Le-Fevre, usually called "Flagus," and lived with him in the old LeFevre homestead at New Paltz village. They had no children.

We find that the names of four of Abraham's sons, John, Solomon, Noah and Philip, are recorded as soldiers in the Revolution. Of the army record of Noah we have this brief account: He was a sergeant in Brodhead's Company, Hathorn's Regiment, Orange County Militia. He was at the battle of Stillwater—not under fire, but stationed in the reserve, within hearing of the battle, expecting every moment to get the order to advance. However, night came on before they were needed, and the battle was not renewed the next day. He was, we believe, a three months man and returned home shortly after this battle and was never again engaged. Solomon was a private in the same company with his brother Noah. The two other brothers, John and Philip, were privates in Col. John Cantine's regiment. Philip was stationed at one time in the fort at Wawarsing.

John, the eldest son of Abraham the pioneer, married Mary LeFevre. He lived in the stone house in which Johnston Hasbrouck now resides. This house passed from John to his son Matthew, who married Sarah LeFevre, and from him to his son John M., who resides in his old age at Peekskill. Matthew had one brother, Abraham, who lived at Ireland Corners.

Noah married Cornelia Bevier of New Hurley. He lived in a house built by his father Abraham, the pioneer, where Nathaniel Deyo now lives. Noah left two sons, John N. (Capt. Hans) and Jonas N., and four daughters, one of whom married Cornelius DuBois of Marlborough. The first named son married Sarah DuBois, daughter of Cornelius DuBois, Jr., of Poughwoughtenonk. He remained with his father-in-law for several years, until the death of the latter, when in 1817 his father purchased land of Charles Brodhead, to which he moved and there he resided on the place where his son Josiah lived until he removed to this village. Jonas N. married Catharine Budd and after her death Jane Westbrook, widow of Luther Hasbrouck. He occupied the homestead until his death.

Philip, the youngest son of Abram the pioneer, occupied his father's homestead, and had twice as much land as his brothers each had, as he heired the entire portion of his brother Solomon, who did not marry. Philip's farm comprised the present farms of his grandsons, Abram and Asa LeFevre, and the Solomon Van Orden farm.

Philip's wife was Elsie DuBois of Wallkill, sister of the wife of his neighbor, Johannes LeFevre (Squire Hans). Their children were Abraham P., Andries P., Solomon P., Magdalene, who married Mathusalem Elting; Maria, who married Abraham Van Orden, and Sarah.

Abraham P. married Margaret, daughter of Daniel Jansen, and occupied his father-in-law's farm after his death. His second wife was Maria Elting, widow of Dr. Bogardus.   Andries P. married Magdalene, daughter of Philip Elting.   He lived in the house built for him by his father, where his son Asa now lives.   Solomon P. married Sarah, daughter of Philip Deyo, and after her death Jane, daughter of Ezekiel Elting.

There are two LeFevre burying-grounds at Kettleborough, in one of which Andries and his descendants are interred.   In the other the descendants of Abraham are buried.   Andries' grave is marked by a stone erected some time after his death by his son Johannes.   The burying-ground has been kept in good order.

In 1820 there were eleven families of LeFevres living in Kettleborough.   The heads of the families were as follows:

Johannes (Squire Hans), Nathaniel, Lewis, Jacobus, John N., Philip, Solomon P., Andries P., Noah, Jonas N., Matthew J.

The LeFevre Family at Bontecoe

On the banks of the Wallkill, four miles north of this village, on the farm of Simon LeFevre, stand two old stone houses. A little farther up the Wallkill is the cellar of another, which was torn down about 1825.   The locality is dear to the writer as the home of his childhood.   The first half dozen years of his life were spent in the northernmost of these houses.   Here father and grandfather and great-grandfather and great-great-grandfather tilled the soil.

The surroundings have changed considerably since the days of childhood.   But the house is there and the Wallkill is there, and a portion at least of the old grove of pear trees on the bank of the stream.   The well is unchanged, and the low cellar with its immense beams, and the old loft, and the curious little closets and carved chimney front, where the Franklin used to stand in old days.   The Franklin is gone and most of the orchard is gone and the kitchen has been torn down, but most interesting of all, there still remains the *"Slawbonk"*—the square bunk, let down from the chimney side in the living room of the house, open in the evening and closed up in the day-time. Here, when the writer was a little fellow, three brothers lay side by side. Here, father tells us, when he was a boy also three little children lay side by side.

The "rift" in the Wallkill is not the same as of old, for the hateful "rebel" weeds have found a foothold there, but the swimming place is unchanged.

But from a description of the place we must pass to our account of the houses and the people that lived in them.

The old houses have been occupied by tenants for half a century. For the same period there has been but one family of LeFevres in the neighborhood.

But, next to New Paltz, Bontecoe is perhaps the oldest settled place in this vicinity, and many years before the Revolution there were three families of brothers—sons of Isaac LeFevre, living at this locality. Scattered over Ulster county and elsewhere there is now quite a numerous tribe that can trace their ancestry to one or another of these three brothers.

Simon LeFevre, the Patentee, left three sons, named Andre, Jean and Isaac. The first named kept the homestead in this village; Jean lived in the house on the Plains, torn down about 1885, and Isaac, who was born in 1683—half a dozen years after the first settlement of the place—moved to Bontecoe, four miles north of the village. The date of his settlement at Bontecoe was about 1718, when he was married and was 35 years old. His wife was Maria, daughter of Hugo Freer, Senior.

The original house in which Isaac LeFevre first lived at Bontecoe was on the bank of the Wallkill a few rods north of

28

the southernmost of the two old stone houses of Simon Le-Fevre, now standing.

This pioneer house was destroyed by fire when Isaac's children were quite small—the oldest about ten years old. The parents had gone to the Paltz on a winter's evening visit to friends, leaving the little children, four sons and a daughter, at home and with the doors locked.

The house caught fire in some manner not related. The oldest son, Isaac, was sometimes able to unbolt the cellar door, but at other times his strength was not sufficient. In this case he was able to move the bolt and the little ones escaped and found shelter at an outbuilding—a bee house. Here their parents found them on their return from their visit, safe and unhurt.

The house which had been burned was replaced by a new one at about the same site. Here we may suppose that Isaac LeFevre lived and died in peace. No Indians troubled the settlers. Bontecoe land in those early days was noted for the production of wheat. Although four miles from the old settlement at the Paltz, we may suppose that the family of Isaac LeFevre was not lonesome, for the whole community of settlers had a joint ownership and cultivated in common the "Bontecoes"—necks of good land, of which there were at least four lying in the bends of the Wallkill between New Paltz and Isaac's house.

There is still in existence an ancient paper, written in Dutch, which is the quit claim from his brothers and sisters to Isaac for their interest in the property at Bontecoe.

It must be noted that these first settlers cared nothing for the upland, and it was not until the last century that much of the upland was cleared off. So late as 1810 there were but two clearings east of the old homestead in all the Gerhow neighborhood.

There are no tales of encounters with Indians, and no very exciting ones of wild animals. In one case the story goes that two of the sons of Isaac LeFevre found the tracks of a "panther" around the house in the morning, after a heavy fall of snow. They followed the tracks and, after a weary tramp, found the animal in a tree.

One of the brothers laid his gun over the shoulder of the other to get a good aim, then fired and killed the savage beast.

It is related of Isaac LeFevre, that being in Albany once on some business, he ran a foot race and that while the race was in progress his friends to cheer his drooping spirits cried to him in the French language, "Courage Isaac." He won the race. One son of Isaac, who bore his father's name, went to the Potomac, lived there a while, then returned home and died. He was never married. Four other children, three sons and one daughter, married and left families. The oldest son, Petrus, was born in 1720, December 25th. He died in 1806, aged 85 years. He married Elizabeth Vernooy and occupied his father's homestead. The next son, Johannes, was born in 1722, October 10th. He married Sarah Vernooy and for him a stone house was built about 150 yards farther up the Wallkill. Daniel, the youngest son, was born in 1725, November 8th. He married, in 1750, Catharine Cantine, who was the granddaughter of Moses Cantine, who married the widow of Simon LeFevre, the Patentee. The house in which Daniel lived was about 150 yards down the Wallkill from the one in which his father had spent his days and which the oldest son, Petrus, continued to occupy.

Besides these three sons mentioned, Isaac LeFevre had one daughter, Mary, who married Col. Johannes Hardenburgh, Jr.,

HOUSE BUILT BY MAJ. ISAAC LE FEVRE ON THE SITE OF THAT OF HIS
GRANDFATHER ISAAC

of Esopus, who owned a large tract of country at Swartekill and saw much active service in the Revolutionary war. Isaac LeFevre died October 31, 1752, aged 69 years. He was buried in the Freer burying-ground about two miles north of his house.

PETRUS, THE OLDEST SON AND HIS DESCENDANTS

The oldest son, Petrus, occupied his father's house during a long life. Tradition says that Petrus LeFevre could have claimed the entire estate, under the old English law, but that he shared it equally with his brothers.

Petrus died in 1806, at the age of 85, and is buried in the old family burying-ground on the farm of Simon LeFevre. Petrus left a large family of sons and daughters, as follows: Jacob, Isaac, Cornelius, John P., Sarah, Jane and Ann. Jacob, the oldest son, married Lydia Deyo, and lived near this village, on the other side of the Wallkill, where Jacob Wurts now lives. He was the father of Christopher LeFevre and Tjerck.

Christopher's family lived after his death in this village, in the house now owned and occupied by Josiah J. Hasbrouck.

Petrus' next son was Isaac, Major Isaac, as he was called. He married Catharine Burhans. He built a new house where his father had lived. This was the third house on that site and is still standing. It was a fine house in its day. He was a noted man and a famous surveyor.

Major Isaac afterwards moved to Rifton and built a large frame house, which is still standing. The Major was one of the best remembered men of that period. He was a member of the Legislature in 1803, and Supervisor of New Paltz in 1807 and 1808.

After moving to Swartekill he was Supervisor of the town of Esopus from 1820 to 1825. He was at one time a State surveyor, going on this business a great distance from home.

About all the surveys in this vicinity for a long period were made by him.

He was for a time the owner of a famous race horse called the Grand Bey, which, we believe, was never beaten in Ulster county.

Petrus' next son was Cornelius, who married Maritje Van Wagenen and moved to Creek Locks or LeFevre Falls. He was the father of Peter C., Isaac C. and Washington.

Cornelius was Supervisor of the town of Hurley from 1839 to 1841. Hurley at that time included a considerable portion of the town of Rosendale, which was not created as a town until 1844.

The other son of Petrus, John P., settled at first at Swartekill and afterwards exchanged property with his brother Isaac and moved to the old Bontecoe homestead. His widow, whose maiden name was Mary Hardenburgh, long survived him and occupied the old homestead with her family until it was sold, about 1840.

Besides these sons, Petrus left three daughters, one of whom married Samuel DuBois of New Paltz, another Charles Hardenburgh of Esopus, and another married Elias Bevier and moved to Broome county.

This ends the history of the most central and oldest of the three stone houses, as far as it was owned by the family who built it. It passed into the hands of strangers about 1840, and from that time to the present has frequently changed hands. It is now owned by Simon LeFevre.

We will now take up the history of the northernmost of the three houses, which was built for Daniel LeFevre, the great-grandfather of the writer.

Daniel LeFevre was born November 8, 1725, and died February 10, 1800, aged 74 years. He is buried in the old family

TREE NEAR CELLAR OF JOHANNES LE FEVRE'S HOUSE

burying-ground, and the spot is marked by a stone of the species of brown sandstone used in those days. Daniel always lived in the house which is still standing—the northernmost of the three. Slavery existed in New York in those days, and in his will Daniel disposed of four slaves. We have no record of any notable events in his life, and believe that he lived as a quiet citizen. Not long ago we looked over his will and, from the expressions contained therein, we doubt not that he was a pious, God-fearing man. The north room, now standing, was added to the house in Daniel's day.

Daniel had two brothers-in-law, Johannes Hardenburgh, Jr., and John Cantine, who were colonels in the patriot army, and another brother-in-law, Matthew Cantine, who was a member of the Council of Safety, but he did not serve himself in the army and was too old in fact. Daniel's Bible in Dutch, containing the family record in English, is in the Memorial House in New Paltz, likewise his old arm chair.

Daniel left but one son, Peter, born in 1759, February 10, and two daughters, Mary and Elizabeth. Mary married Jonathan Deyo and lived with him near the place where his great-grandson, Perry Deyo, lately lived, near the village. Elizabeth married Matthew LeFevre and lived with him in the old homestead of Jan LeFevre, on the Paltz Plains.

Peter LeFevre continued to occupy the old homestead of his father Daniel. By his father's will he received that portion of his estate lying west of the Black Creek swamp.

JOHANNES LEFEVRE'S HOUSE

We will leave for the present the history of the descendants of Daniel LeFevre, who continued to occupy his homestead, and pass to the other brother, Johannes, who lived all his life in the stone house farthest up the Wallkill, of which the cellar is still seen but the house has been long torn down.

We have stated that Johannes was born in 1722, and that he married Sarah Vernooy. Johannes died June 27, 1771, at the comparatively early age of 49 years, and was buried in the old family burying-ground, on the farm of Simon LeFevre. Johannes left but one child, a son named Isaac, who married Mary LeFevre, daughter of Andries, the first settler in Kettleborough. Isaac occupied his father's homestead all his life. He died in middle age, leaving a large family of children. His widow married again, her second husband being Capt. Abm. Deyo, who was a widower at this time, living in the old Deyo homestead in this village. She did not move to her second husband's home, but continued to reside at Bontecoe. She bore one son as the fruit of this second marriage. This child was named Abram. His mother died when he was an infant, only a few days old, and he was taken on a pillow to his mother's brother, Johannes LeFevre, at Kettleborough. Afterwards this infant became Judge Abram A. Deyo of Modena.

The family of Isaac LeFevre, after the death of their mother, scattered. Both parents were dead. The farm was sold to Benj. Deyo, who afterwards traded it with Jacob J. Hasbrouck, who thus became owner of the old homestead, and shortly afterwards moved to Bontecoe and built the brick house which his grandson Luther now owns. Soon afterwards, about 1830, this old stone house was torn down.

This Isaac, son of Johannes, was an only child, but his family was large enough to make ample amends. His children were John I., Andries, Rachel, Peter, Daniel, Sarah and Gitty. These children scattered far and wide. Daniel settled in Delaware county, and two of his sons afterwards carried on business in Johnstown, Fulton county, and one of them, Gilbert, resided in Albany. John I. settled at Elmore's Corner, and afterwards at Highland. Andries, Peter and Rachel located in the town of Wawarsing—the two boys at Greenfield, on land coming from their grandmother Vernooy—Rachel married John Brodhead at Lurenkill, father of Henry, Andrew and others. Sarah married Abram N. LeFevre and lived near Modena in the house now occupied by H. B. LeFevre. Gitty married Dr. John Bogardus, who was a leading citizen of New Paltz in 1830. John I., the eldest son, who settled at Elmore's Corners and afterwards moved to Highland, carried on business on the dock. He ran for State Senator once, but was beaten by Wells Lake. He was Supervisor of New Paltz in 1816 and 1817. He left but one son, Alexander, who for many years was on the barge running from Highland.

This completes the history of the third house and the family who built it.

The northernmost of the three old stone houses still remained in the family and Grandfather Peter LeFevre remained the sole representative of the old settlers' stock. He was of pure French blood, and was a tall, spare, dark-complexioned man. Being an only son, he was well educated for those days. He was a lad of seventeen at the time of the Declaration of American Independence. He did some service in the patriot cause as a teamster, going with a load of arms to the American army. Part of the time during the war he had charge of the ferry of his uncle, Moses Cantine, at Ponckhockie.

He married, in 1789, Magdalen, daughter of Roelif J. Elting. Grandfather had something of a taste for politics. He was Supervisor of the town in 1797-8, and a member of the Legislature in 1799. We have seen the curious-looking old knee breeches worn by him when in the Legislature. For a long time he was one of the associate judges of Ulster county, and in that capacity transacted a great amount of business. The book in which he recorded a summary statement of the cases which were tried before him is still in the possession of the family. He also performed a great amount of business in the way of drawing up wills, deeds and legal papers generally. We believe that most of the papers of that nature in New Paltz were written by him. The desk on which this work was done about 1800, is now in possession of the writer.

But One Family Remaining

As the northernmost house was the only one of the three now left in the family, we will continue its history a generation farther. Peter LeFevre left four sons, Daniel, Ralph, Moses P. and Josiah P. Daniel, the eldest son, married Mary Blanshan, widow of Abm. Hasbrouck, and settled on a portion of his father's estate, where his son Peter D. afterwards lived, in the present town of Rosendale. Daniel was a general of militia in the old times, and a Member of Assembly in 1834. He was a short, stout-built, black-eyed man, a surveyor as well as a farmer. Although a strong, robust man, he died at the early age of forty-five. Ralph, the second son, married Rachel Elting. He lived on the portion of his father's estate in the present town of Rosendale, where his son Josiah R. afterwards lived, near his brother Daniel. Afterwards he moved to the farm in Lloyd, where his sons, Peter R. and Josiah R., afterwards lived. Though like his brother Daniel, a robust man, he died at the age of forty-nine.

Family Characteristics

We have alluded to the practice of the old people of bestowing names upon the clearings which they opened in the forest. The name *"Vantyntje"* (spring field) still is borne by one of

IN THIS HOUSE THE WRITER SPENT HIS EARLY YEARS. IT WAS OCCUPIED
BY HIS FATHER, JOSIAH P., HIS GRANDFATHER PETER AND
HIS GREAT GRAND-FATHER, DANIEL LE FEVRE

the best fields on the old farm. The name *"Maugerstuck"* (poor field) has been dropped for the more pretentious one of flat meadow. A sandy knoll on the land of Abram Ean, a short distance south of the LeFevre burying-ground, is still called by the Eans *Daun Favre's bowery.* At some distance ₴ast of the public highway a clearing of perhaps twenty acres was made about 1815, but the rest of Daniel LeFevre's land east of the highway remained a forest until a comparatively recent period.

Farming in Bontecoe and at New Paltz in those days was very much as it had been for the hundred of years preceding.

Some of the old people, instead of having a farm in one body, had a piece of land here and another there. This came from dividing the land among the children.

The highways were not fenced until perhaps 1825. There was but little travel in those days, and when people journeyed they had to stop and open the gates.

We spoke of Major Isaac LeFevre building the southern-most of the stone houses still standing. He also built a barn on the same premises, which was torn down about 1850. Part of the timber of this old barn was of yellow pine and was hauled all the way from Greenfield, in the town of Wawarsing, where his mother, who was a Vernooy, owned land. This barn was torn down by Josiah P. LeFevre, and some of this yellow pine lumber put into his barn which he was then building where he afterwards resided. We can not imagine why it was considered necessary to draw the lumber so far.

We must confess that as a general rule, the old people at Bontecoe or elsewhere were not apparently inclined to over-work themselves. Had they been bent in that direction, the cellars might have been dug deeper, so that one would not be obliged to stoop so much in entering them. Slavery, as it

existed here and in the South, doubtless prevented the whites
from exerting themselves as they do at the present day. What
work great-grandfather Daniel LeFevre found for four slaves
to do on no greater quantity of cleared land than he had we
cannot guess. As an instance, perhaps exaggerated, of management in the olden times, it is related that the well on the
Petrus LeFevre place near by, not being in good order, instead
of deepening it, or digging another, it was filled up, and thence-
forth, when drinking water was needed, some one of the family
paddled out on the Wallkill and sank a jug down where the
springs bubbled up in the stream. There was less necessity
for hard labor in those old days than at present. There was
little market for produce. The horses and cattle ran in the
woods and stock was branded. Grandfather's branding iron
is still preserved and is now in the Memorial House. We may
imagine that snow fell to a greater depth then than of late
years, for a pair of snow shoes of the olden times made of
thongs of deer hide, intersecting each other and stretching from
side to side of a wooden frame, is among the other old articles
that we have seen.

One of the undertakings, 100 years ago or more, was to
build a wall a part of the way across the Wallkill and put in
timbers for the purpose of constructing a fish weir, just below
Daniel LeFevre's house. But the wall raised the water in the
stream so much that the project was abandoned.

The building of the mill at Dashville about 1810 was another
enterprise of considerable moment for those old days. The
deed for this property was procured by grandfather of ———
Hardenburgh, and the mill was erected by him, in partnership
with his brothers-in-law, Philip and Ezekiel Elting. Before
that time handmills had been in use although not in New Paltz,

and Levi Schryver informs us that he has seen a handmill used at Swartekill to supply the neighborhood.

As a general rule it must be confessed, perhaps, that the Bontecoe people in the Colonial period did not show any very remarkable degree of enterprise. But on the other hand, if they did not work themselves to death, at least they lived together in harmony, none of them sold whiskey, they treated their slaves well, no family quarrels are recorded, they lived on good terms with their neighbors. None of them in those old days were as rich as certain members of the Elting or Hasbrouck family at New Paltz; but on the other hand, they were generally quite well to do—not poverty stricken by any means.

Altogether they held their own among the old settlers very creditably, and it may do their descendants good to study their characters and revisit their old homes.

The following are the names of old people of the LeFevre family interred in the graveyard on the farm at Bontecoe, now owned by Simon LeFevre:

Johannes LeFevre, d. 1771, a. 49 years.

Sarah Vernooy, wife of Johannes LeFevre.

Daniel LeFevre, d. 1800, a. 74 years.

Catharine Cantine, wife of Daniel LeFevre, d. 1799, a. 72 years.

Petrus LeFevre, d. 1806, a. 85 years.

Elizabeth Vernooy, wife of Petrus LeFevre, d. 1807, a. 74 years.

Isaac LeFevre, son of Johannes LeFevre, born 1753.

Peter LeFevre, son of Daniel, d. 1830, a. 71 years.

Magdalen Eltinge, wife of Peter LeFevre, d. 1823, a. 57 years.

John P. LeFevre, son of Petrus, d. 1810, a. 34 years.

Mary Hardenburgh, wife of John P. LeFevre, d. 1841, a. 59 years.

Jane LeFevre, d. 1852, a. 52 years.

Catharine LeFevre, d. 1834, a. 42 years.

Zebedee LeFevre, d. 1836, a. 33 years.

THE BLOOMINGDALE LEFEVRES

The first settler at Bloomingdale, in the northern part of the present town of Rosendale, was undoubtedly Matthew Le-Fevre, who moved from the LeFevre homestead in this village.

Matthew LeFevre was one of the two sons of Andre Le-Fevre, who was one of the three sons of Simon, the Paltz patentee. Matthew's location at Bloomingdale was on a tract of 700 acres, which was purchased for $700. We can not fix the date exactly, but it was about 1740, at about which same time his cousins, Andries and Abram LeFevre, located at Kettleboro and about twenty years after his uncle, Isaac Le-Fevre, located at Bontecoe.

Matthew's wife was a Bevier. His house is still standing at what is now called Rock Lock. It is of stone and was lately owned by Benj. Hardenburgh and occupied by tenants. Matthew had four sons, Conrad, Jonathan, Samuel and Simon. Each of these brothers married a Swart from Kingston and, we believe, they were all sisters.

Matthew was a lieutenant in the 3d Regiment of Ulster County Militia, John Cantine, colonel, commissions being issued October 25, 1775. He subsequently became a captain. He was familiarly called the "Old Captain," and took his four sons with him to the army, preferring to do so though the youngest was not more than fifteen or sixteen years of age.

One of the sons died from a wound received in the Revolutionary war. In the records at Albany appears the name of Matthew's son Jonathan as a private in Col. Cantine's regiment. The name of Simon LeFevre appears as a lieutenant and subsequently a captain, commissioned in 1779, in the 1st Ulster County Regiment. This was Matthew's son Simon. Moses P. LeFevre recalls one or two incidents in regard to Matthew's record as captain, as related by his grand-mother's brother, Col. Cantine.

Matthew's four sons settled as follows: Conrad in a stone house, part of which is still standing in the forks of the creek (that is between the Wallkill and Rondout) not far from the powder mill. The house passed from Conrad to his sons, Moses, Adam and Jonathan (the last named of whom did not marry), and all three brothers continued to occupy the house of their father. They had one sister, Affie, who married Daniel Blanshan and moved to Western New York. Lorenzo Le-Fevre, of Rosendale, was a son of Adam.

Matthew's son Jonathan occupied the original homestead after his father's death. He left but one son, Levi, who married a Newkirk. Levi is the father of our informant, Garret, and of Jonathan J. LeFevre of Creek Locks, formerly justice of the peace, deceased.

Matthew's son Samuel lived in a stone house built for him by his father on the top of the Bloomingdale hill. He died when a young man, it is said, from a wound received in the Revolutionary army. His widow married John LeFevre of the Paltz Plains and moved with him to Owasco, in western New York, being doubtless among the first settlers there. Samuel left one son, Simon, who married a Hendricks and left a family of three sons, one of whom, George, resided some years ago near Cold Spring Corner.

29

Matthew (the first settler's) son, Capt. Simon, lived in a stone house built for him by his father on part of his tract, about a mile north-east of the Quaker meeting house on the Rosendale Plains. Simon was one of the organizers and first elders of the Bloomingdale church, which was organized in 1796 and was built on part of the LeFevre tract. Simon's children were Anna, who married Abm. DuBois (father of Simon L. and Daniel A.) ; Magdalen, who married Solomon Hasbrouck (father of Alexander) ; Samuel and Matthew, the last named of whom long kept the lower toll-gate on the Paltz turnpike.

All of the LeFevres of the first and second generations who settled at Bloomingdale are buried in the old burying-ground, on the Conrad LeFevre place, in the forks of the creek, now owned by Mr. Hardenbergh. Most of the original tract of 700 acres has passed out of the family. Jonathan's place was sold to Judge Jonathan Hasbrouck, of Kingston.

CHAPTER XXXIV

The Auchmoody Family

The ancestor of the Auchmoody family in Ulster county is Gemes Acmoidec, as the name is entered in the marriage record on the church book at New Paltz. The record is in French, translated thus: 1731 Oct. 8, Gemes Acmoidec married Mari Doyo, daughter of Christianne Doyo and Mary Le Conte. The bans for this marriage appear in the Kingston church record as published Sept. 19, and the record is: Jeames Auchmoide, young man, born in Scotland, and Maria de Joo, young woman, born in New Paltz and both residing there. A few months earlier, in March of the same year, Mr. Auchmoody's name appears for the first time on the New Paltz church records as godfather at the baptism of a child. There was no other person of Scottish nationality who settled in New Paltz in the early days.

Mr. Auchmoody's house was built somewhere in the Bontecoe neighborhood; at least he owned land there. James Auchmoody and wife had three sons, David, Christian and Jacobus; also three daughters, Maria, Elizabeth and Rachel. David married Maria DeGraff in 1764. At that time he lived in Dutchess county, but afterwards moved to Elmore's Corners in Esopus and finally located near Plutarch, where his grandson Jeremiah lived in modern times. The name of David Auchmoody appears as one of the enlisted men in the First Regiment of Ulster County Militia in the Revolution. Christian Auchmoody located in the present town of Rosendale, on a farm which passed to his son Abraham and then to Abraham's son

Jonathan, who spent a long life there and was a highly respected man. Jacobus, the remaining son of Jeames Auchmoody, located on the farm now owned by Alonzo Neil, in the Middletown neighborhood, about three miles north of our village. He married Elizabeth Smith and afterwards Margaret Irwin. They had but one son, William, who did not remain at New Paltz.

CHAPTER XXXV

THE BUDD FAMILY AT NEW PALTZ

Samuel Budd was a very prominent citizen of New Paltz for a long term of years about 1810. He had a wheelwright shop, procured the establishment of a stage line through our village and had an inn at the corner of Chestnut and North Front streets, where Luther Schoonmaker's hotel is now located and the fame of this inn extended far and wide. Samuel Budd's father, Thomas Budd, was a sea captain and obtained a grant for a large tract of land where the city of Monmouth, N. J., was afterwards located. From some technicality he failed to get or retain possession of this land, though even of late years efforts have been made to secure the property. Thomas Budd lost his life, and the privateer vessel which he commanded was sunk during an engagement with a British cruiser in the Revolutionary war. During the battle of Monmouth, the house and other buildings on the Budd property were burned by the British and Hessians and the family scattered to the winds. Samuel Budd, then a boy of ten, fled to the residence of an uncle in Philadelphia and did not see his mother until a considerable time afterwards.

Samuel Budd's wife was Mary LaRue. They were married in 1796. Five children of the Budd family grew up and married. They were Hiram, Wade Hampton, Catharine, Gertrude and Laura. Hiram married Maria Deyo, and as his second wife Catharine Ann Smedes. Catharine Budd married Jonas LeFevre of Kettleborough. Gertrude Budd married Robert

Lawson of Newburgh.   Laura Budd married Joseph Harris.
Wade Hampton married Martha J. Brundage.

A pamphlet containing a history of the Budd family has been
published.   Two brothers, named John and Joseph, came to
America from England about 1632.   Another brother, Thomas,
came to this country at a later date and settled in New Jersey.
Samuel Budd, who lived in New Paltz, was descended from
Thomas Budd.

CHAPTER XXXVI

THE HARDENBERGH FAMILY

The Hardenbergh family has been one of the most respected and influential in Ulster county, its members occupying positions of trust and responsibility in church and state, in peace and war. Of late years there have been comparatively few of the name in Ulster county.

Dr. Corwin in his last edition of "The Manuel of the Reformed Church" says:

Sir Johannes (Hardenbergh) was knighted by Queen Anne at the recommendation of the Duke of Marlborough for gallantry at the decisive battle of Blenheim. With the order of Knighthood he also received the patent which bears his name and which comprised a considerable portion of what now constitutes the counties of Ulster, Delaware and Sullivan in the state of New York.

In signing his name, Johannes Hardenbergh sometimes simply signed "Hardenberg" as was the custom with those in England who held titles.

The Hardenbergh family is of German origin and the ruins of the Hardenbergh castle are still pointed out near Nordheim, in Germany. Gerrit Jans Hardenbergh, the progenitor of the family in Ulster county, came to America with his father from Maarden, near Utrecht, in the Netherlands. He first appears on record at Albany in 1667. His wife was Jeapie Schepmoes. Their son Johannes became an owner of real estate in the village of Kingston in 1689, was commissioned high sheriff of

Ulster county by Gov. Leisler in 1690, and again by Gov. Lovelace in 1709. He was commissioned as major in the Ulster county regiment in 1728, and was afterwards a colonel in the same regiment. He was one of the patentees in the great or Hardenbergh Patent, by which an immense tract, estimated at 2,000,000 acres in the present counties of Ulster, Orange, Greene, Delaware and Sullivan was granted by Queen Ann in 1708. There was considerable dissatisfaction among the Indians for a long term of years at the granting of so large a tract, but they became satisfied on the payment of an additional sum.

By his wife, Catharine Rutzen, he had a large family of sons and daughters. Two of the sons married New Paltz women and settled within the bounds of the New Paltz congregation, although but one of them, Abraham, lived in the New Paltz precinct, his home being at Guilford. The brother Johannes lived at what is now Rosendale village. Other members of the family located elsewhere.

Abraham, who was born in 1706, married Marytje Roosa, daughter of Nicholas Roosa, who had moved from Hurley to New Paltz. After her death he married, in 1752, Mary, daughter of Joseph Hasbrouck of Guilford and widow of James Gasherie. Abraham Hardenbergh's house was built on the Wallkill, a short distance below Tuthill and commanded a fine view of the stream. A very large tract of land in this vicinity had been granted to Jacob Rutzen, the father of Abraham's mother. The portion of the tract on which the house stood descended in the Hardenbergh family for several generations to Mrs. Crines Jenkins. The old stone house has now tumbled into ruins. The land is owned by Josiah LeFevre.

Abraham Hardenbergh was a man of wealth and influence. He was Supervisor of the town of New Paltz from 1751 to

1761 and again in 1770. He was one of the Justices of the Peace of the county in 1766. In the list of slave-holders in 1755 he is set down as the owner of seven slaves, a number only equalled by one other resident of the town, Solomon Du-Bois, who likewise owned seven slaves. In the tax list of 1765 Abraham's name appears as Supervisor, and the amount of his assessment is exceeded only by that of Col. Abraham Has-brouck, of Kingston, for his Guilford farm, and by Josiah Elting of the village. In 1759 he was an elder in the church.

The children of Abraham Hardenbergh by his first wife were Johannes, baptized at Kingston in 1743, and Sarah, also baptized at Kingston. The children by the second wife were Nicholas, Elias, Maritje and Rachel, all baptized at New Paltz from 1753 to 1758. Abraham died 1771. His name does not appear on the subscription for the erection of the second stone church in 1771, but the names of his widow and son John A. appear.

From Abraham Hardenbergh the farm at Guilford passed to his eldest son, Johannes, who wrote his name John A. Elias married and had his residence somewhere within the congregation, as we find his name on the church book. Where the other children lived we do not know. John A. was a captain in the patriot army in the Revolutionary war, serving in the Third Ulster County Regiment, John Cantine, colonel. His name also appears as lieutenant in the Fourth Ulster County Regiment, of which his cousin, Johannes Hardenberg of Swartekill, was colonel a part of the time. His wife was Rachel, daughter of his neighbor, Hendricus DuBois.

The children of John A. Hardenbergh and his wife, Rachel DuBois, were Marichie, born in 1771; Jacob, born in 1780; Charles, born in 1782; Alexander, born in 1784, and Abraham, born in 1777. The last named built on the ancestral estate the fine old brick house, near the Guilford church, long unoccupied and now commencing to tumble into ruins. Abraham, who wrote his name Abraham J., married Margaret DuBois and his brother Jacob married Jane DuBois, both of whom were daughters of Cornelius DuBois, Jr., of Poughwoughtenonk.

It is related that the parents wanted the last named young woman to marry another young man and that she jumped out of a window and then ran away from home in her every-day dress to marry the man of her choice. Her husband died young. Alexander became a doctor. He died from an accident, his neck being broken by a fall from his horse, which stumbled over a log. Jacob left one son, Jacob, and one daughter, who married Crines Jenkins.

The brother Charles became a minister, was settled at Warwick, N. Y., Bedminster, N. J., and was a colleague of Rev. Dr. Thomas Dewitt in the collegiate churches in New York. He was one of the trustees of Rutgers College.

Abraham. J. Hardenbergh, who built the brick house, was a member of the Legislature in 1813. In the war of 1812 he was a colonel of militia and was able to get part of his men across the Niagara river, which was more than some others did, when the invasion of Canada was made.

It is a striking illustration of the lack of all interest in an honorable military career that was felt in the days of our grandfathers, that Abm. J. Hardenbergh subsequently had two butcher knives made out of the sword that he carried in the war of 1812. What a contrast with the feeling of pride, with which the people of to-day look upon the military record of their ancestors!

The sons of Abm. J. Hardenbergh and his wife, Margaret DuBois, were Charles, David, Josiah and Ditmas. There was only one daughter, Gertrude, who married Aldert Schoonmaker

HOUSE OF COL. ABRAHAM HARDENBERGH AT GUILFORD

and lived in this village. The son Charles became a doctor and settled at Port Jervis; David went to Michigan; Ditmas located at Ellenville; Josiah settled on the farm of his father at Pecanisink in Shawangunk and there his father likewise lived in his latter days.

COL. JOHANNES HARDENBERGH OF ROSENDALE

Going back now to Col. Johannes Hardenbergh we shall make but brief mention of his family, because he did not live within the precinct of New Paltz, although included in the congregation of the New Paltz church.

Johannes Hardenbergh, of Rosendale, was Colonel of the First Regiment of Ulster County Militia for twenty years, was a member of the Colonial Assembly from 1743 to 1750, and of the State Legislature in 1781 and 1782, and he was a member of the First Provincial Congress. He repeatedly served as an elder in the New Paltz church, acting in that capacity as a delegate to the Conference in New York, when the differences between the Cœtus and Conferentie parties were harmonized.

A few years before his death, when General Washington, in June, 1783, visited the county of Ulster, Colonel Hardenbergh entertained the General and Mrs. Washington, with Governor and Mrs. Clinton, at his residence in Rosendale.

The wife of Col. Johannes Hardenbergh, of Rosendale, was Maria DuBois, who was born in 1706 and was the daughter of Louis DuBois, Jr., of Nescatack, in the town of New Paltz. Their children were: Johannes, born in 1729; Lewis, born in 1731, married Catharine Waldron; Charles, born in 1733, married Catharine Smedes; Jacob Rutze, born in 1736, married Dina VanBergh, widow of Rev. John Frelinghuysen;

Rachel, born in 1739, married Rev. Hermans Myer, D. D.; Catharine, born in 1741; Gerardus, born in 1744, married Nancy Ryerson.

Jacob Rutze Hardenbergh became a minister of the gospel, settled first in New Jersey and afterwards over the churches at Marbletown, Rochester and Wawarsing. He was the first president of Queens, now Rutgers College.

Johannes Hardenbergh, Jr., eldest son of Col. Johannes Hardenbergh of Rosendale, located at Swartekill, a short distance north of Rifton. His house we believe is still standing a short distance east of the highway. His wife was Mary LeFevre, daughter of Isaac LeFevre of Bontecoe.

In the Revolutionary war he served a great portion of the time as lieutenant-colonel of the 4th Ulster County Regiment, of which Jonathan Hasbrouck of Newburgh was colonel. On account of the ill health of the colonel the regiment was a considerable portion of the time under the command of the lieutenant-colonel. In 1779 he received his commission as colonel.

Sojourner Truth, the famous negro woman, who acquired a great reputation as a public speaker and died in Chicago about 1870, after having long passed the century mark, was in her early days a slave in the family of Colonel Hardenbergh at Swartekill and related that she and a number of sheep were once sold for $100.

There was a standing dispute between New Paltz people and the Hardenberghs as to the boundary line of the respective patents. The Hardenberghs at Swartekill claimed the land up to about where Perrine's Bridge is located. The Paltz people claimed that the surveyor had been bribed by the present of a cow to run a false line and that the Paltz Patent really included the valuable water privilege at Dashville Falls. But the Hardenberghs retained Dashville Falls till about 1810, when the

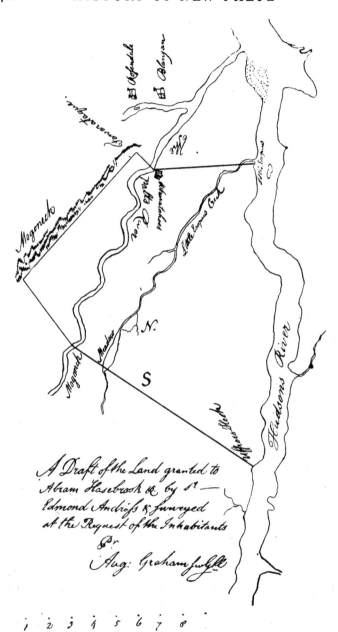

*A Draft of the Land granted to
Abram Hasebrook &c by Sr ——
Edmond Andriss & Surveyed
at the Request of the Inhabitants
Pr
Aug: Graham Surv*

The original of this map is in the town clerk's office at New Paltz. It was made in 1709, one year after the grant of the Hardenbergh Patent.

The bends in the Wallkill are not laid down accurately on the map and probably the angle in the north line of the Patent is what the New Paltz people denounced as the running of a false line to give the Hardenberghs' the water privilege at Dashville Falls, the surveyor having been bribed, as the New Paltz people claimed, by the present of a cow.

privilege was purchased by Peter LeFevre of Bontecoe of his uncle, Johannes Hardenbergh, Jr. Peter LeFevre proceeded with his brother-in-law, Ezekiel Eltinge, to build the mill torn down a short time ago. Some time previous the Hardenberghs had built a mill at Swartekill, which was one of the first in this county. The sons of Johannes Hardenbergh, Jr., of Swartekill, and Mary LeFevre, his wife, were Issac, Peter, Charles and Louis. Peter moved to Pennsylvania, Isaac went to Catskill, where he became a merchant and was a prominent man. Charles resided in the neighborhood. He is the ancestor of the late Benj. F. Hardenbergh of Rock Lock. Louis was a blacksmith by trade. He lived part of the time on the paternal estate at Swartekill. Afterwards he had a shop at Bontecoe north of the lane leading to the old house of Simon LeFevre. Louis had three sons, Richard, Simon and John. Richard is well remembered by the old men of the present generation. He resided for a time at New Paltz and was the father of Hon. Jacob Hardenbergh and of Louis Hardenbergh of Gardiner, who until his death, two or three years ago, occupied the farm purchased by his father about 1830.

CHAPTER XXXVII

The Wurts Family

The Wurts family is of Swiss origin. The ancestor of the family at New Paltz was George Wirtz, M. D., who was the first physician in the place. He was a near relative of the Goetschius family, which was likewise of Swiss blood, three of whose members served the New Paltz church, acceptably in the early days, the first as a supply and the others as regularly ordained pastors. Maurities Goetschius, the second of the name to occupy the pulpit at New Paltz, served the people here as a physician, as well as pastor, and was known as the "doctor dominie." Dr. George Wirtz's name first appears on the New Paltz records in 1773, when he married Esther, daughter of Major Jacob Hasbrouck. Rev. Stephen Goetschius succeeded his uncle, Rev. Maurities Goetschius, as pastor of the church in 1775. Dr. Wirtz was on the ground at the time of the arrival of the new pastor, who was his cousin, and may have come before the death of his uncle, the "doctor-dominie," which occurred in 1771. He united with the church at the village of New Paltz in 1776 by certificate from the church at Shawangunk. It seems certain, therefore, that he must have lived at Shawangunk at least a short time before coming to New Paltz. His uncle had his home at Shawangunk and preached there, as well as at New Paltz.

Dr. Wirtz was doubtless a busy man, with a large territory to travel over in visiting patients. So when he thought of selecting a partner for life he could not spend much time in courtship. The story, as we have heard it related, is that he made his proposal of marriage without preliminary and completed it with the statement that if it was accepted he would take tea with the family. The proposal met with an affirmative response and the young doctor took tea with the family in the old steep-roofed house, now the "New Paltz Memorial House," in which they resided.

Dr. Wirtz built as his residence the house at the foot of Main street, torn down about 1880, the site of which is now occupied by the Riverside Cottage. His name appears as one of the signers of the Articles of Association at the outbreak of the Revolutionary war. He was a deacon in the church in 1776 and an elder in 1797.

The children of Dr. George Wirtz and his wife, Esther Hasbrouck, were Jacob (born in 1776), Janetje, Catharine, Mauritius (born in 1784).

Dr. Wirtz died in 1802. The tombstones in the old graveyard marking the last resting place of himself and wife bear these inscriptions:

In memory of George Wirtz, M. D., who departed this life April 20, 1802, aged 55 years, 5 months and 6 days:

In memory of Esther Hasbrouck, daughter of Maj. Jacob Hasbrouck and relict of doctor George Wirtz, who died June 4th, 1826, aged 68 years, 4 months and 26 days.

The sons, Jacob and Maurities, both became doctors. The first named married Catharine DuBois. During his long life he attended to the duties of his profession as a physician, riding about the country on horseback, according to the custom of those days, to visit his patients. He lived in the house which his father built until in middle age, when he built and moved into the house in the southern part of our village where his son Cornelius afterward lived.

The children of Dr. Jacob Wurtz and his wife, Catharine

30

DuBois, were George, born in 1798; Gertrude, born in 1803; Mathusalem, born in 1806; Gitty Jane, born in 1809; David, born in 1812; Maurice, born in 1815. By his second wife, Mary Hornbeck, Dr. Jacob Wurts had one son, Cornelius.

Maurities (in English Maurice), the younger son of Dr. George Wirtz, engaged in the practice of medicine, living for a while in Esopus and likewise for a time at Springtown, on the farm where his son-in-law, Gilbert Elting, afterwards lived. His wife was Maria Jansen. He died in middle age, leaving two sons, John H. and Jansen, and two daughters, one of whom married Gilbert Elting and the other Nathaniel Elting.

CHAPTER XXXVIII

Old Dutch Families at New Paltz and Vicinity

The Dutch families residing at New Paltz and vicinity previous to the Revolution for a greater or less length of time include the Eltings, the Lows, the Roses, the Clearwaters, the Van Wagenens, the Ostranders of Plattekill and the Eans.

The Dutch element was always quite small at New Paltz.

None of the Dutch families who located in New Paltz became permanent settlers here except the Eltings, the Van Wagenens and the Eans, though the Lows remained through several generations.

There is this difficulty in tracing the ancestry of Dutch families: that is while the Huguenots all had surnames when they came to Ulster county nearly all the Dutch are first recorded on the church book by their Christian names alone, although some of them had surnames used in legal documents. The Jansens are descended from Jan Mattys, the Lows from Peter Cornelis, the Clearwaters from Tunis Jacobse, the Roses from Albert Hymans, the Van Wagenens from Aaert Jacobson, who was the son of Jacob Geritson. The Ostranders took the name from "east strand," where the ancestor of the family lived. The name Ean simply means "one." Where it is recorded in the church book by a French minister it is written "un" and when by a Dutch minister Ein or Een.

CHAPTER XXXIX

THE LOW FAMILY AT NEW PALTZ

The ancestor of the Low family in Ulster county is Peter Cornelius, who sailed from Holstein in 1659. He married Elizabeth Blanshan, daughter of Matthew Blanshan and sister of the wife of Louis DuBois, the New Paltz Patentee, at Kingston in 1668. His name was entered on the church record simply as Peter Cornelis, the surname of Low not yet having been adopted. His sons were Matthew, Peter, Cornelius, Jacob, born in 1683; Johannis and Abraham, born in 1688. Peter and Cornelius received land grants in Shawangunk and Wawarsing.

Matthew married Jannetje Van Harring. His two sons, Peter, born in 1700, and Johannes, born in 1706, located in New Paltz. Peter married Catharine, daughter of Solomon DuBois of Paughwaughtanonk, in New Paltz, in 1722, and his name on the marriage register is set down as residing at New Paltz. He quite certainly lived on the southern part of the land of his father-in-law at Paughwaughtanonk and his descendants afterwards lived there for many years.

The name of Peter Low appears as a freeholder in New Paltz in 1728 and again on the tax list of 1765 as still living in the Paughwaugtanonk neighborhood. His sons were Jonathan, born in 1724; Solomon, born in 1725 (located at Springtown), and Isaac, born in 1730, who lived where his father had lived. When the Conferentia church was organized, in 1767, Peter Low and his two sons, Solomon and Isaac, united with it. The Low family long had a blacksmith shop at Paughwaughtanonk and the name is found on one or more tombstones in the burying-ground near where the blacksmith shop stood on the farm now occupied by LeFevre DuBois on the County House Plains.

Johannes, the brother of Peter, sometimes wrote his name Johannes M. and sometimes Johannes, Jr. He located in New Paltz village, married, about 1735, Rebecca, daughter of Hugo Freer, Senior, and after his father-in-law's death occupied his house, the northernmost of the old stone houses, still standing on Huguenot street in this village, and here his descendants lived for many years.

The children of Johannes M. Low and Rebecca Freer were Johannes, born in 1736; Maria, born in 1738 (married Roelif J. Elting) ; Jacob, born in 1743; Lena, born in 1745; Simeon, born in 1747. Johannes M. Low still occupied the homestead in 1765. After his death it passed into the possession of his son Simeon, who married Christina McMullen. The children were Ezekiel, born in 1777, David, Janitje, Maria, Jacob and Samuel. All of the Low family at New Paltz finally died out or moved away.

CHAPTER XL

The Klaarwater (Clearwater) Family

The Klaarwaters were one of the most ancient families in Holland. For centuries they owned and to this day own estates at Baarn, near Rotterdam. Its members were among the founders of the Dutch Republic, and achieved distinction in the wars of Holland.

Theunis Jacobsen Klaarwater, the founder of the Clearwater family in America, was born at Baarn in 1624. He was a soldier of Holland and a graduate of the University of Leyden. He came from Holland to Niew Amsterdam, went to Esopus (Kingston) and subsequently to Bontecoe.

In the year 1709 Queen Anne granted to him, to his son, Jacob Klaarwater, his brother-in-law, Hendrick Vernooy, his son's father-in-law, Abraham Doiau (Deyo), Rip Van Dam, Adolph Phillipse, Dr. Gerardus Beekman and Colonel William Peartree a patent of 4,000 acres of land in this county.

The patent is recorded in the office of the Secretary of State, in Book 7 of patents, at page 54, and embraces that tract in the present town of Shawangunk bounded by the Wallkill on the east, the Dwaarskill on the south and the Shawangunkkill on the west.

Theunis Jacobsen was one of the founders of the Reformed Protestant Dutch church at Kingston, commonly known as the First Dutch. He was chosen by the citizens of Kingston commissioner to present to the British Crown their protest against the arrogant and illegal conduct of the commandant of the English garrison stationed at Kingston under the English rule, a duty discharged with ability and dignity.

After his removal to Bontecoe he joined the Huguenot church at New Paltz. His son Jacob, who was born in Holland, married Marie, daughter of Abraham Doiau (Deyo), one of the patentees. He was the first Dutchman to marry a daughter of one of the New Paltz Patentees.

Theunis Jacobsen and Jacob were among the freeholders of the New Paltz Patent whose names appear upon the oldest tax list of the Patent now extant, that of 1712, which is preserved among the archives of the Memorial House.

Theunis Jacobson died in 1715 and was buried in the orchard of his farm at Bontecoe, which is still owned by one of his descendants.

A tablet, designed by Charles R. Lamb, the architect of the Dewey Arch, was erected on the anniversary of the Battle of Lexington, 1899, in the Dutch church at Kingston to his memory, and that of some of his lineal descendants by Judge Clearwater of Kingston, his descendant six degrees removed.

The tablet is of white marble, framed by Corinthian pilasters, with capitals and frieze supported by heavy corbels. Upon the frieze is a scroll, on which is carved a pair of crossed swords on the model of those used by the officers of the continental army, intertwined with oak leaves, the symbol of strength and heroism, surmounted by the words "In Memoriam." At the base of the tablet is the inscription, "Fide Et Fortitudine," intertwined with ivy leaves, the symbol of remembrance and longevity. Each capital is crowned with a scallop shell, the emblem of the Pilgrim. The inscription is of bronze letters executed in high relief, and is as follows:

1624   THEUNIS JACOBSEN KLAARWATER   1715
Whose ancestors were among the founders of the

DUTCH REPUBLIC.
A soldier of Holland.
An early settler of Ulster County.

1663   JACOB KLAARWATER.   1747
A native of Holland who fought in the wars of the
American frontier.

1699   ABRAHAM KLAARWATER   1782
Sergeant in the provincial army during the
Colonial Wars.
Signer of the Articles of Association 1775.
Dragoon in the Marbletown Troop of Horse during the
war of the Revolution.

1757   THOMAS KLAARWATER   1830
Signer of the Articles of Association 1775.
Trooper in the Marbletown Horse.
Soldier in the Continental Army.

1787   THOMAS TEUNIS CLEARWATER   1860
Soldier of the War of 1812.

The bronze is made of old cannon captured in battle during
the American wars. The marble is from American quarries.
The tablet is placed in the west wall of the church and is a
fine addition to the beautiful interior of that stately edifice.
Among the descendants of Theunis Jacobsen who will be
recalled by the readers of this volume are the Honorable Hiram

Clearwater, who for many years was the president of the Board of Education and the president of the Board of Water Commissioners of the city of Cincinnati; the Reverend Charles Knapp Clearwater, now pastor of the old Reformed Protestant Dutch church of Newton, L. I.; Charles Hiram Clearwater, one of the pioneer manufacturers of Rosendale cement in this county; Colonel Alfred Clearwater, one of the leading citizens of Northern Pennsylvania, and the Honorable Alphonso Trumpbour Clearwater, LL. D., who three times has been District Attorney and twice County Judge of Ulster county, and afterwards Justice of the Supreme Court of the State of New York. During the two hundred and forty years the family has been settled here its members have intermarried with many of the old Dutch and Huguenot county families, and those interested in tracing their descent from its founder should consult among other family genealogies, those of Beekman, Burger, Davis, DePew, DeWitt, Deyo, DuBois, Elmendorf, Freer, Helm, Houghtaling, Hoffman, Kortright, Schoonmaker, Terwilliger, Trumpbour, Van Leuven, Van Wagenen, Vernooy, Wood.

CHAPTER XLI

THE EAN FAMILY AT NEW PALTZ

The Ean family was the first of Dutch extraction to settle at New Paltz and remain here permanently. The Ean family is unique in another respect: from generation to generation there have been few boys in the family. Consequently the Ean name has increased but slowly. The first at New Paltz was Elias Eign (spelled by the French Un or Yn), who married Elizabeth, daughter of Anthoine Crespel, the Patentee. Another daughter of Anthoine Crespel, the Patentee, named Maria (or Maria Maddaleen), also settled at New Paltz and also married a Dutchman, Mattys C. Sleght. We have very little knowledge of Sleght or his children, although as late as 1724 we find the name of Mattys Sleght, Jun., signed to the agreement of the 24 proprietors of the Patent at that time, authorizing the Duzine to give title to land. The Sleght family certainly did not long remain at New Paltz. Ean and his descendants always remained here. In the tax list of 1712 he is assessed £35. In 1718 his name appears as the only person, not of the Patentees' families, who assisted in building the first stone church. In the agreement of the 24 proprietors in 1724, authorizing the Duzine to give title to land, appear the names of Jan Een, Elizabeth Een, Sarah Een and Maria Maddaleen Een. These were undoubtedly the widow and children of Elias. We have no means of determining whether he lived always in the village or moved in his later years to the homestead at Bontecoe, where his descendants have lived ever since. In the tax list of 1728 the property is assessed to "Elias Ean's

RUINS OF THE EAN HOUSE AT BONTECOE

widow" at £20. Her father, Anthony Crespel, always remained at Hurley, and in 1693 he sold a plot of land in this
village, probably the lot assigned to him for a home to Hugo
Freer, Sen., as is shown by the original deed, in the possession
of the writer.

Jan Ean, son of Elias, married, in 1735, Geesje Roosa. In
the marriage record, recorded in the church book at Kingston,
the bride is set down as being from Marbletown and the groom
as born at Hurley and residing "at Mond-Albany, in the juris-
diction of Paltz." The clerk who made the record undoubtedly
misunderstood the name of the locality and should have written
Bontecoe, where, on the farm about 3½ miles north of the
village, Jan Ean lived and died and his grave is pointed out
till the present day, and on this farm his descendants still live.

The children of Jan Ean were Elizabeth, Margaret, Elias,
Abraham (born in 1741) and Isaac. We have no account of
these sons except Abraham. The others probably died in infancy or boyhood. In the old stone house, which has lately
tumbled into ruins, on a stone beside the front door appear the
initials A. E. and J. E., showing that Jan Ean and his son
Abraham together built the house. About two miles down the
Wallkill a lot of about ten acres of fertile lowland in one of the
great bends of the stream belonged to the Eans as early as
1730, as shown by a paper in possession of the writer. It is
called the Half Moon in this paper and retains that name until
the present day. It was owned by the Eans until about 1880.
Jan Ean died before 1755 and in that year Geesje Ean, widow
of Jan, is set down in the list of slave-owners in the town. In
a map of the Patent, made in 1760 by Louis Bevier, the house
of Geesje Ean is the only one set down. She was a woman of
note in the community and is still remembered by the Le-
Fevres, who owned the adjoining farm, for her help to the sick.

Abraham Ean came next in possession of the farm. In 1765 Abraham was married, at Kingston, to Catharine Van Wagenen, who was born at Hurley and resided at Wagondahl (Creek Locks) at the time of the marriage, as stated in the record on the church book. In the division in the church between the Cœtus and Conferentia parties Abraham seems to have sided with the latter party and his mother with the Cœtus, as Abraham's name appears as one of the subscribers to the Conferentia church then built, and in 1772 his mother's name appears as a contributor to the building of the second church in our village.

In the Revolutionary War Abraham Ean served on the frontier as a member of Capt. Abraham Deyo's company, Third Ulster County Regiment.

The children of Abraham Ean and Catharine Van Wagenen, his wife, were Elias (born in 1768), Annetje, Rachel, Catharine and Peter (born in 1781). The three daughters all married and located directly across the Wallkill in the Springtown neighborhood. Rachel married David Deyo (grandfather of Rev. Paul T.). Catharine married Jonathan Deyo (grandfather of James E.). Annetje married Benjamin Hasbrouck. Peter, who was the younger son, occupied the farm during his long life. He married Maria Freer. From Peter the farm descended to Abraham Ean, who was an only son, and occupied the farm during his lifetime.

Going back now to Elias, son of Abraham, we find that he married Elizabeth Hasbrouck of Springtown. He built the stone house at Middletown, which passed to his son, Elias, Jun., and in the next generation to James Ean. This house, still standing with its gable end to the road, bears, deeply cut in a stone in the southwest corner of the building, the date of erection, 1789, and the initials of the builders, E. E. (Elias Ean) and R. H. B. (Roelif Hasbrouck). A peculiarity of this old house was that the stone oven, instead of being incorporated in the building as in other stone houses was built on a rock across the street, where it stood until modern times. Elias Ean was for a number of years an officer in the church and was a much respected man. His sons were Elias, who occupied the farm after his father's death, and Jacobus, who spent his days in the Middletown neighborhood. A daughter, Elizabeth, born in 1807, married ———— Snyder. She lived to the extraordinary age of 95 years.

CHAPTER XLII

THE VAN WAGENEN FAMILY AT NEW PALTZ

The first Van Wagenen at New Paltz was Petrus Van Wagenen, whose father Archa resided at Creek Locks (called by the old people Wagondahl) in a house near the residence of the late Washington LeFevre.

Petrus married, at Kingston, June 15, 1760, Sarah Low, daughter of Simeon Low of New Paltz village. In the marriage record on the church book Petrus is set down as residing at Wagondale and his wife as residing at New Paltz. They probably took up their residence at New Paltz immediately after the marriage. Petrus' house, one mile northeast of the village, is still standing, but has not been occupied for many years. Part of the eastern wall has tumbled down. It is the most picturesque ruin anywhere in the vicinity of New Paltz, and the artist's brush of Mr. A. Scott Cox has placed it on canvass in a very attractive manner. It stands in a field about half a mile northwest of Put Corners.

In the tax list of 1765 Petrus is assessed £8 10s. In 1767 he, with other New Paltz people of Dutch descent transferred his membership from the church at Kingston to the newly-organized Conferentia church at New Paltz, which had just erected a house of worship about two miles from the village on the west side of the Wallkill. Petrus lived to the extraordinary age of 92 years. He was by trade a stone mason. His name appears as one of the enlisted men in the Third Ulster County Regiment in the Revolutionary war.

Petrus and his wife had a large family of children. The following are recorded on the church book at Kingston as being baptized from 1761 to 1766: Jonathan, Daniel, Ezekiel, Levi. The following are recorded on the church book at New Paltz as being baptized from 1766 to 1778: Catharine, Lucas, Maria, Aert (in English Archa) and Sarah.

In the Revolutionary war Daniel and Levi served in the stockade at Wawarsing and Daniel was in the stockade when it was attacked by Tories and Indians. Daniel left three sons, all of whom went west. Archa wrote his name Archa P. He married, in 1800, Maria Freer. They lived for a time in the old homestead and for a time on what is now the Abner DuBois farm at Middletown. Archa P. served in the war of 1812 in the 92d Regiment, Heavy Artillery. He was on Lake Ontario and in the fight at Lake Mills in Canada. He received 160 acres of land for his services in war, but it was afterwards sold for taxes. Archa P. left two sons, Jonas, who resided at Plutarch, and Alexander; also one daughter, Magdalen, who married Jacob Bedford.

Lucas Van Wagenen, son of Petrus, married Cornelia Markle. They lived in the house still standing just south of the present church-yard ; at least Mrs. Van Wagenen lived there after her husband's death, which occurred in 1811, at the age of 41. The children of Lucas and Cornelia Van Wagenen were Benjamin, born in 1796; Jonathan, born in 1798; Janetje, born in 1800; Maria, born in 1803. We have no account of any of these children except Benjamin and one daughter, who married James Mitchell of Shawangunk. Benjamin married Catharine, daughter of Judge Jonathan DuBois of Springtown. They lived in the building now the Huguenot bank. Benjamin Van Wagenen was a very prominent citizen of our village in his day. There was no lawyer in New Paltz until long after that time and the legal business required in the place was done by Benj. Van. Wagenen.

CHAPTER XLIII

THE ELTINGE FAMILY IN NEW PALTZ

The following account of the Eltinge family so far as it relates to Jan, the original Eltinge in Ulster county, was derived mainly from the researches of Jonathan W. Hasbrouck and is given in his words:

Jan Elten, the ancestor of all the Eltinges in Ulster county, was born in Holland, at Beyle, a dependency of Switchsaelen, in the province of Drenthe, on the 29th day of July (old style) 1632. He was the son of Roelif and Aeltje Elten and known to be of a numerous and respectable family. The first mention I find on record concerning him I find in one of the volumes of the Transactions of the Dutch, at Albany, in a commission, issued Sept. 6, 1665, by authority of E. Andross, Governor, constituting and appointing Capt. Thomas Chambers to be a justice of the peace for Kingston, Hurley and Marbletown and dependencies in Esopus and also for him and George Hall, the sheriff, Cornelius Slecht, W. Nottingham, John Elten (or Jan Eltinge) and John Briggs, or any four or more of them to hold a court of sessions twice a year at Kingston, to hear and determine all appeals and causes, as a court of sessions, according to law. He must therefore have emigrated from Holland a considerable time prior to that date. In 1680 a certificate, signed by the church officers at Beyle was executed for his benefit, in which he is commended by them to the favorable regard of all to whose knowledge its contents should be made known. This must have been sent to him years after his residence here.

31

Being associated, as above, with Cornelius Slecht, one of the first settlers of Esopus, he doubtless became intimate with him and his family, thus forming an acquaintance with Cornelius' daughter Jacomyntje, whom he married about the year 1677. The mother of Jacomyntje was Tryntje Tynebrouck. Jacomyntje had had a previous husband, by whom she had four children, one of whom named Tryntje married Solomon DuBois of New Paltz. Jan Elten took out a patent for land in Hurley in ————. Jan Eltinge and his wife Jacomyntje had five children, as follows: Roelif, baptized in 1678, who settled in New Paltz and married Sarah DuBois; Cornelius, baptized in 1681, who settled in Marbletown and married Rebecca Van Metten; William, who settled in Kingston and married Jane LeSaeur; Greitje, married Thos. Wall of Somerset county, N. J., and Aaltje, who married Garret Aertson of Kingston, son of Aert Jacobson, son of Jacob Gerritsen. Notice peculiar changes of names from one generation to another. Gerrit had a brother Jacob. The children of both are called Van Waggennegar or Van Wegener.

Jan Eltinge signed the treaty made by the Paltz Huguenots and the Indians, in the spring of 1677, as one of the witnesses. On the 8th of June, 1686, Jan Eltinge and Gerrit Aertson, his son-in-law, and Arien Post bought a lot of land at Rhinebeck; "Right over against the Rondout Creek" by a small creek called Quaawanoss. This is now the home of Hon. Levi P. Morton. The price paid for the land was 6 suits of stremuater (a kind of coarse cloth), 6 duffels, 4 blankets, 5 kettles, 4 guns, 5 hoes, 5 axes, 10 cases powder, 10 bars of lead, 8 sheets, 8 pairs stockings, 40 fathoms wampum, 2 drawing knives, two adzes, ten knives, half an anker of rum (anker is ten gallons) and one frying pan.

ROELIF THE FIRST ELTINGE AT NEW PALTZ

Roelif, the eldest son of Jan Eltinge, was baptized October 27, 1678, and married, in 1703, Sarah, daughter of Abm. DuBois, the Patentee, who was the son of Louis DuBois, the Patentee. He settled at New Paltz about 1720. We have reason to believe that Roelif lived for several years on Huguenot street in this village, in a house which stood a short distance south of the old stone house of Isaiah Hasbrouck and was torn down in 1800. In his later days he located a short distance outside the south bounds of the Paltz patent, where Edmund Eltinge resided, on a portion of a patent of land, lying on both sides of the Wallkill, granted to the Patentee, Louis DuBois, and by him conveyed to his sons, Solomon and Louis, Jr., both of whom settled on a part of this tract lying on the west side of the Wallkill. The deed from Solomon and Louis DuBois to Roelif Eltinge was in the possession of Edmund Eltinge and is dated February 4, 1726-7. (The last two figures are written in a fractional form, customary in those days, to indicate the difference of old and new style.) Geo. Van Wagoner is one of the witnesses of this deed. On this tract, a short distance south of Edmund Eltinge's residence, Roelif built a stone house and here ended his days. This house was burned about 1820. Some of the stones of the old house are in the kitchen walls of the present residence. One of these bears the inscription "Anno 1742." This old stone house was erected at different periods and a part of it may have been erected by Roelif Eltinge at a still earlier date. Roelif had four sons, Noah, Josias, Abraham and Johannes, and three daughters, Jacomyntje, Margaretta and Cattrina. We have little further knowledge of any of these children except Noah, Josias and Margaretta.

Tradition says that when Roelif came from Kingston to

New Paltz he had a belt of gold around his waist.   He was one
of the justices of the county before moving to New Paltz.   He
became a man of much influence in the little settlement, and
in 1728 was still one of the justices of the county.   Roelif was
an executor of the will of his father-in-law, Abm. DuBois, who
died in 1731 and was the last survivor of the twelve patentees,
as stated on his tombstone, still standing in the old burying-
ground in this village.   We can not state the exact date of
the death of Roelif Eltinge or the place of his burial.   His will,
a copy of which is in the possession of Jacob Eltinge, is dated
in 1745 and probated in 1747.   It is in English.   In this will,
after provision is made for the support of the widow, the son,
Noah, is given the homestead on which he afterwards resided
and certain lands in the New Paltz Patent.   The grandson,
Roelif Elting, son of the testator's son Abraham, late of the
Potomac, is given certain sums of money and land which is
to be sold.   His uncles, Josiah and Noah, are made his guar-
dians until he arrives at the age of 21 years.   The testator's
eldest son, John of Mormel (Marbletown), is given certain
property and tan pits in the corporation of Kingston; to John
and his sons, Peter and Roelif, are given a share in certain
lands in the Paltz Patent.   The will gives to the testator's son
Josiah the property which he had purchased of his brother-in-
law, Abraham DuBois, and a share in certain undivided lots
in the Patent.   The daughter, Jacomyntje, wife of Wm. Code-
bec, and the daughter Margaret, wife of Abraham Bevier, are
given certain sums of money to be paid by their brothers.   The
sons, John, Josiah and Noah, are appointed executors.

ROELIF ELTINGE'S CHILDREN

Roelif's sons, Noah and Josias, settled at New Paltz.   Noah,
who was born in 1721, lived in the homestead of his father on

the Plains, where his descendants have lived ever since. He married his cousin, Jacomyntje Elting, October 16, 1742. They had but one child, Sarah, who married Dirck Wynkoop. Though his descendants are not numerous, we have more extended information concerning Noah than any man of that day. In 1748 he obtained, in conjunction with Nathaniel LeFevre, who lived in the old stone house some distance further north, torn down about 1885, a grant for 3,000 acres of land. This land has remained in the possession of the descendants of each, to a considerable extent, to the present day. This grant was comprised in three tracts, lying on both sides of the Wallkill. The whole, or at least a part of it, had been previously granted to Capt. John Evans, but had been vacated for some cause and the title reassumed by the government. The patent for the 3,000 acres, written on parchment, with the colonial seal, several inches in diameter, attached, was in the possession of Edmund Eltinge. This grant of the 3,000 acres brought a great deal of trouble. It was claimed that the original Paltz patent covered a part of the tract. Louis Bevier of Marbletown, Col. Abm. Hasbrouck of Kingston and Jacob Hasbrouck, Jr., in behalf of the descendants of the patentees, began proceedings, alleging, furthermore, that Noah had no good title to the homestead, where he resided and which had come to him from his father. Finally the matter was settled without being tried in court. Noah Eltinge and Nathaniel LeFevre retained their 3,000 acres, and for a very moderate sum (perhaps enough to pay the expenses of litigation) a release was signed, in 1754, by Jacob Hasbrouck, Jr., Louis Bevier and Col. Abm. Hasbrouck, confirming to Noah Eltinge his title to one lot of 179 acres and another of 22 acres, comprising, undoubtedly, the homestead. A full and lengthy account of these matters, drawn up by Noah, was in the possession of Edmund Eltinge.

The old barn, still standing on this place, is thought to have
been built by Roelif Eltinge.   It was rebuilt in 1811.   The timbers are of pitch pine, which formerly grew to some extent
along the Plattekill.   Noah was the first elder in the Conferentia church at New Paltz, which was organized in 1767.   In
1773 he owned one-seventeenth of all the undivided land
in the Paltz patent.   The road from Plattekill to New
Paltz was laid out in Noah Eltinge's day, and among his
documents is one throwing some light on this matter.   Noah
Eltinge died in 1778, aged 57 years, and is interred in the
old graveyard in this village.   By his side is the grave of
his wife, who died in 1790, aged 75 years.   We have said
that Noah Eltinge left but one child, a daughter named Sarah,
who married Dirck Wynkoop and continued to occupy her
father's homestead.   Dirck Wynkoop was a prominent man.
He was one of the delegates from this county to the convention in Poughkeepsie which decided to adopt the Federal constitution.   Mr. Wynkoop voted against the measure.   During
his lifetime he held various important public positions.   Dirck
and wife left but two children, both daughters, Gertrude, who
married Alexander Colden and afterwards David Colden, and
Cornelia, who married Peter Eltinge.   Peter was the son of
William, who was the grandson of William, who was the second son of the original Jan Eltinge of Kingston.   Peter continued to occupy the old homestead up to the time of his death,
and it was afterwards occupied by his son Edmund.

JOSIAS ELTING AND HIS DESCENDANTS

The history of the family of Noah Eltinge being brought
down to modern times, we will take up that of his brother,
Josias (or Josiah), baptized October 12, 1712, and this should
take more space, as his descendants are more numerous.   There

is no reasonable doubt that Josiah lived in the old Eltinge house, still standing, on Huguenot street, nearly opposite the late residence of Mrs. Berry. This house bore on one of its chimneys till recently the date 1735. It was originally a Bevier house, but passed into the possession of the Eltings about 1740. Josiah married Helena, daughter of Solomon DuBois, July 15, 1734. In a tax list dated 1765 Josiah's name appears as the wealthiest man in the town. To a list of owners of slaves, dated in 1755, Josiah's name is signed as captain. In the building of the Conferentia church his name and that of Hendricus DuBois appear as the most liberal subscribers. We do not know when Josiah Eltinge died. Doubtless he was interred in the old burying-ground in this village, and it is singular that no stone marks his grave. Josiah left one daughter, Catharine, who married Jacobus Hardenbergh of Hurley, and four sons as follows: Roelif J., Abram, Cornelius and Solomon. The last named left no children. Cornelius married Blandina Elmendorf and settled in Hurley, where he left a line of descendants. Abram married Dinah DuBois and located where his son Philip, his grandson, Mathusalem and his great-grandson, Sol. L. F., have since resided. Roelif J. married Maria Low, daughter of Johannes M. Low. He occupied his father's homestead in this village and carried on the mercantile business.

THE ELTINGE HOMESTEAD

We have a feeling of pity for any one who does not love old houses, something akin to the pity we would feel for any one who says he does not love flowers or the song of birds. In the whole village there is no more interesting house than the one we are about to describe. There are none about which cluster more associations and traditions, and there is probably no old house in the county that has sheltered beneath its roof

THE ELTINGE HOMESTEAD, ORIGINALLY THE BEVIER HOUSE

the ancestors of so numerous a line of descendants, now living. What makes this old structure much more interesting is the fact that there has been no attempt to spoil it by modern improvements. This house is now the property of Jesse M. Eltinge. It is about 50 feet in length and 25 feet wide. It has evidently been built at two different periods—the rear or eastern end last. On this eastern end the chimney bore until a few years ago the figures 1735. The western end, which fronts on the street, is evidently the oldest portion of the building, but there is no date to determine its age exactly. Before entering we must notice the well, which is about 20 feet deep, the water of excellent quality and the stones covered with moss and ferns all the way from top to bottom. Every Eltinge who visits the home of his ancestors must take a drink from this well. The house is shaded by locust trees, such as the old folks used to plant. On the north side of the building the roof projects a dozen feet and the earth is paved with flat stones. Here we are told the people used to sit in the olden times on Sunday and chat until the bell summoned them to attend Divine service at church. Looking at the house we notice the gutters sustained in part on stones projecting from the wall; also the old shutters, held open by long, twisted hooks. No regulation style of architecture seems to have existed in the early days of the settlement. In this house the window above the door with its ten small panes was doubtless considered quite an attempt at style in its day. The main window by the side of the door is very grand with its 30 panes of 7x9 glass. Entering at the front door we find a room which in the old times has been about 16x24 and this is undoubtedly the room in which the merchant's wares were kept. From floor to beams above is a distance about eight feet and the great beams are about 10x15. In the chimney still hangs the crane.

Descending to the cellar we find the most interesting portion of the building.   Here is a sub-cellar, which now exists in none of the other old houses.   This sub-cellar is under the other cellar and is about four feet deep and walled all round, the mortar being made of loam and the floor of the cellar proper resting on these walls.   Although there is no drain the ground is dry as dust owing to its porous, gravelly nature. The chimney is about ten feet wide in the cellar and on the east side there has been evidently an oven.   In the cellar is a fireplace and an outside door.   The sub-cellars, where they existed in the old houses, were, we understand, for wine cellars, to be used in the storing of liquors.   Ascending now to the first floor we notice the huge door frames, of pitch pine timber, 12x6 inches and fastened together by wooden pins.   The nails used in the building are hand-made and the work of the home carpenter is to be seen in the planing of the timbers.   Ascending the back stairs by the original staircase we notice that it has no banister, and doubtless many children and probably some grown people have got a tumble in descending it.   One room on the stairs has been finished off, but in the rest of the house there is nothing overhead but the roof and rafters.   The rafters are very heavy—about 6x4 inches.   The floor boards are of pitch pine, about 15 inches wide.   The bricks in the chimneys are of the same length as modern brick, but only about $1\frac{1}{2}$ inches thick.   Probably they were brought across the ocean as ballast and hauled from Kingston.   The mortar used in the building is of loam, lime and chopped straw.   The stone in the walls are only such as a farmer would use in building an ordinary stone fence, but the excellence of the mortar has held the stones together until the present day.

So ends our description of the house of the richest man in the town in 1765, for as such do we find Josiah Eltinge's name in a tax list of that date. From Josiah Eltinge the old homestead passed to his son, Roelif J., who owned it during the Revolutionary period. In the contest between the Coetus and Conferentia parties in the church a few years before the Revolutionary war, which doubtless shook the little community to its center, Roelif sided with the latter party, attended their church when erected, near Mr. Wm. H. D. Blake's, and when after a few years the quarrel was settled and the church had stood, unused for awhile, he removed it to this village.

Roelif J. Eltinge is buried in the old graveyard in this village and his tombstone, of dark sandstone, states that he died on the 21st of July, 1796, aged 58 years, 6 months and 4 days. By his side is another tombstone, stating that "Mary Louw, wife of R. Elting, departed this life Aug. 24th, 1800, aged 62 years and 7 days." This couple left five sons: Josiah, Ezekiel, Solomon, John, Roelif; also four daughters: Magdalen, Sarah, Catharine and Maria. Each of these nine children of Roelif J. married and settled in this vicinity and each one raised a large family of children.

Josiah, the eldest son, married Sarah LeFevre and settled on the Turnpike where his grandson, Philip L. F., now lives. Josiah had eight children, who grew up and married, of whom the last survivor was Gitty, wife of Cornelius D. LeFevre. Josiah's sons were Andries, Roelif and Abm. D. B. The daughters of Josiah were Maria, wife of Dr. John Bogardus and afterward of Abm. P. LeFevre; Rachel, wife of Ralph LeFevre; Cornelia, wife of Peter Deyo, and Magdalen, wife of Derick W. Elting.

Ezekiel, Roelif J.'s second son, kept the old homestead and long carried on the mercantile business in partnership with his cousin, Philip Elting, who was also his brother-in-law. Later in life, in 1800, Ezekiel built the large stone house where Jesse

M. Elting lived many years in our day. Here the mercantile
business continued to be carried on. Ezekiel married Magdalen Elting and they left a family of eight children, of whom
Jacob Elting of Clintondale was the last survivor. The other
children of Ezekiel were Solomon, Alexander, Dinah, Maria,
Sarah, Catharine and Jane. All of these lived in New Paltz or
adjoining towns except Alexander, who located at Owasco in
western New York. Dinah married C. Brodhead and long
carried on the milling business at Dashville Falls, Maria
married Andries DuBois, Catharine married Andries Deyo.
Ezekiel's son Solomon lived two or three years in the "Old
Homestead" and afterwards lived and carried on the mercantile
business in the store across the street from the Huguenot Bank.
Solomon was elected sheriff of the county in 1837. He was
the father of Abm. V. N. of this village and Ezekiel of
Highland.

Going back now to the next son of Roelif J., who was named
Solomon, we find that he was first married to Cornelia LeFevre
and afterwards to Rachel Eckert and left a family of eleven
children, of whom Tobias was the last survivor. Several of
this family located at a distance. Roelif, the eldest son, lived
on South street in Lloyd. There were only two other sons,
David and Solomon, the rest of the eleven children being
daughters.

The next of Roelif J.'s sons, John, married Jane Wurts and
lived in Esopus opposite Hyde Park. He left four daughters
and only one son, George, who has a son, John, who is now
and has been for many years engaged in business in this village.
Roelif J.'s son Roelif lived in the north part of the village,
where Philip D. Elting now lives. He married Dinah Elting.
They left a family of four sons and five daughters, not any of
whom located in this vicinity. Roelif built the dyke along the

Wallkill about 1795. Three of the sons were Daniel of Ellenville and Brodhead and Ezekiel of Port Ewen.

We have said that Roelif J. left four daughters, Magdalen, Sarah, Catharine and Maria. All of these married in this town and all left large families of children. The eldest daughter, Magdalen, married Peter LeFevre and they left a family of nine children, of whom Moses P., Magdalen and Josiah P. were the last survivors, the two first named each living until upwards of 90 years of age. Magdalen, who died in 1900, aged nearly 93 years, was the last survivor of the 77 grandchildren of Roelif J. Elting.

The next of Roelif J.'s daughters, Sarah, married Wm. Deyo and lived with him on what is now Oscar Tschirkey's farm, about four miles north of this village. This couple raised a family of five sons and six daughters, all of these eleven marrying and nearly all settling in this immediate vicinity. The sons of this family were William W., Roelif, Ezekiel, Cornelius and Abram W.

Roelif J.'s next daughter, Catharine, married Philip Elting and they lived about a mile north of this village, where their grandson, Sol. L. F., now lives. This couple left seven children who reached maturity and five married.

Roelif J.'s youngest daughter, Maria, married Garret DuBois. They lived on what is now the southern bound of the town, where their son Jacob G. and their grandsons, Philip and Solomon, resided. This couple left four sons, Henry, Jacob, Roelif and Solomon, all of whom married, and three daughters, Catharine, Rebecca and Maria. Of this family Solomon, who lived at Vigo, Ross county, Ohio, was the last survivor.

In all Roelif J. Elting and his wife had 77 grandchildren who grew up. Most of these married and settled in this vicinity. There is such a host of the second cousins that the old homestead would not begin to hold them.

Abram, son of Josiah and brother of Roelif J., located where his great-grandson, Sol. L. Eltinge, now lives, about a mile north of this village, which place has been in possession of his descendants ever since. Abram married Dinah, daughter of Hendricus DuBois of Nescatack. They left four sons, Josiah, Henry, Noah and Philip, and two daughters, Jane and Margaret; also one son, Jacobus, by the second wife, Dorothy Bessimer. Of these sons Philip kept his father's homestead. He carried on the mercantile business in this village, many years in partnership with his cousin, Ezekiel Eltinge, who was also his double brother-in-law (each marrying the other's sister) in the stone house with a brick front, now owned by his grandson, Jesse M. Elting.

Abram's son Josiah married Hester Brodhead and, together with his brother Henry, who did not marry, built, about 1786, the brick house now owned and occupied by Mr. Terpenning, about 2½ miles north of this village and which is by far the oldest brick house in this town. Josiah died in 1813, May 15th, aged 52 years, and his wife, Hester, in 1848, at the ripe age of 86 years. Both lie buried in the northwest corner of the old graveyard in this village. Josiah left four sons, Cornelius, Abm. J., Charles and Richard. The last named studied medicine and located in Rondout, where he became a very noted physician. Charles lived on part of the old homestead and built his house where his grandson, Watson, lived. Abm. J. lived for a time in the brick house of his father. One of Abm. J.'s sons, Edgar, became a doctor and settled in Kingston. Another, Norman, was educated at West Point Military Academy and was in the service of the government a considerable time.

HOUSE BUILT BY JOSIAH ELTING—THE OLDEST BRICK HOUSE IN THE TOWN

We will now take up the history of Abram Elting's son Noah, who was born in 1763. He married Hannah Deyo and located at New Paltz Landing on a tract of 500 acres. His house was built near the ferry landing. He established the ferry to Poughkeepsie, which at first was propelled by oars and sails, giving place afterwards to horse power, and finally to steam as the propelling force. Noah died in 1813 and is buried in the old cemetery at Highland. His brother Henry, of whom we have previously spoken, died three years earlier and is buried in the same cemetery. Noah left a family of five sons, viz.: Abram, Henry D., Joseph, Philip and David. Abram commenced the freighting business by running a sloop to New York about the time of the close of the second war with England and he continued in the business for perhaps 40 years, his son Luther being latterly associated with him and the sloop giving place to a barge. Noah's son Philip erected the first buildings, in the present village of Highland, about 1825.

Going back now to the family of Abram's son Philip at New Paltz, who we have said lived about a mile north of this village and long carried on the mercantile business here, we find that he married Catharine Eltinge. They left a family of three sons, Moses, Mathusalem and Jesse, and five daughters, Maria, Rebecca, Dinah, Magdalen and Gertrude. Mathusalem occupied the homestead of his father up to the time of his death, since which time it has been occupied by the son, Solomon L. F.

Right here we will note a curious instance of heredity from a female ancestor. The Eltings are not generally noted for their large size, but, as we have stated, Abram Elting married Dinah, daughter of Hendricus DuBois. The family of Hendricus were noted for their goodly stature, a saying of an old negro being still remembered that more large people had probably come out of his house than any other in the country. Now, among the descendants of Abram Elting and his wife, Dinah DuBois, are found to this day men of large size. The Eltings, not descended from this line, are not above the average in physical proportions.

THE HURLEY ELTINGES

The Hurley Eltinges are descended from Cornelius, the son of Josiah and brother of Roelif J., and Abram, who moved from New Paltz about the time of the Revolutionary war and located on a farm about a mile south of Kingston, which is still owned by the family. Cornelius Eltinge married Blandina Elmendorf and left a family of three sons, Solomon, Cornelius and Wilhelmus, and four daughters, Jane, who married Matthew Oliver; Polly, who married David Bevier; Blandina, who did not marry, and Katie, who married Dr. Peter Crispell. Two of Cornelius' sons, Wilhelmus and Cornelius, became ministers of the gospel. The first named located at Paramus, New Jersey. Cornelius located at Port Jervis. The son, Solomon, kept his father's homestead at Hurley and he has descendants still living at the place.

Rev. Wilhelmus Elting married Jane Houseman and they had three children, Maria, who married Cornelius Van Winkle, Jane V. W., who married Augustus Hasbrouck of Shawangunk, and Cornelius, who married Catharine Hardenburgh, daughter of Jacobus Hardenburgh of Marbletown.

We have now completed the history of the Eltings at New Paltz—the only family not of original Huguenot stock that settled here at an early date and increased and flourished at New Paltz.

32

Before closing this chapter we will allude to the personal characteristics of the Eltings, as noted by the old people. They are an active, thrifty, energetic race, given to sociability and hospitality. They have been, almost without exception, upright, moral and church-going people. Bluntness of speech and positiveness in dislikes and likes may be considered to some extent as family traits. A tendency to turn gray at a comparatively early age has been considered by the old people as a physical characteristic.

CHAPTER XLIV

FAMILIES LIVING IN THE CONGREGATION BUT NOT IN THE
PRECINCT OF NEW PALTZ

THE SCHOONMAKER FAMILY IN GARDINER

Hendrick Jochensen Schoonmaker, founder of the Schoonmaker family in America, was a native of Hamburg, Germany. He came to this country from Holland as lieutenant in the military service of the Dutch East India Company, in 1654. He was sent with his company to Fort Orange (Albany), where he later became an innkeeper. In 1659 he was sent with his company on order of Governor Stuyvesant to the Esopus (Kingston) to assist the settlers there in defending themselves against the Indians. He was so attracted by the beautiful lands in the Esopus country that on his return to Fort Orange he sold his property there and located among the people he had been sent to defend. He married, at Fort Orange, Elsie, daughter of Jan Janse Van Breestede. He died in 1681. He left five children, of whom the eldest, Jochem Hendrick, married Petronella Sleght in 1679. After her death he married Ann Hussey. He was one of the pioneer settlers of the town of Rochester and was one of the three trustees to whom a patent was granted in 1703. He died in 1713.

By his first wife he had four children. The eldest of these, Cornelius B., married, in 1711, Engeltje Roosa. They had three daughters and only one son, Cornelius, who married, in 1744, Arriantje Hornbeck of Rochester.

Cornelius settled on a large tract of land on the north side of Shawangunk, which he purchased from the James Henderson patent, which adjoined on the south the Zachariah Hoffman patent. He died in Shawangunk January 21, 1778.

He had three sons: Cornelius C., Abraham and Isaac, all of
whom located in what is still called Schoonmakertown, in the
present town of Gardiner. The son Cornelius C. did not remain in that locality. Abram and Isaac staid. Abram had a
family of seven sons: John A., George, David, Moses, Selah,
Cornelius and Abram. All of the sons, with probably one exception, settled along the Marakill and all married and left
children.

Isaac married Sarah DuBois. Their eldest child, Mathusa-
lem, was baptized at New Paltz in 1783. Mathusalem lived at
Tuthill. Isaac had four other children: Harriet, who married
———— Goetcheous; Polley, who married Tjerick DeWitt;
Abraham, who married Rachel Deyo, and Jacob I. The last
named married Arriantje Schoonmaker, and after her death
Ann Baird. Jacob I. carried on the blacksmith business at
Libertyville, and afterwards put up a store building and long
carried on the mercantile business at that place. He was a
member of Assembly in 1828 and again in 1831. It was during
his term of office that measures were taken to erect the first
county poorhouse and he was one of the committee.

From the late Elihu Schoonmaker, who was a son of Jacob
I., the information was obtained concerning the location of the
Schoonmaker family in Gardiner.

THE RONK FAMILY

The ancestor of the Ronk family in Ulster county was John
George de Ranke. He lived in Belgium near the French line
and was educated for the ministry. About the year 1740, Belgium being under the dominion of Holland, having incurred
the hostility of the government, de Ranke left the country and
fled to America. He married his wife, Clara Battie, on board
the ship.

In 1750 he purchased of Frances Barbarie, daughter of Peter Barbarie, the patentee of that tract, 245 acres, at $2.50 an acre, on the Shawangunk Plains road. He built a log house on this tract by a big spring about the centre of the portion of this tract lying on the west side of the road, and afterwards a stone house on the extreme north part of the tract. This house was lately owned and occupied by Mr. Jacob Tears. In the same year (1750) he joined the church at New Paltz by letter and he was elected a deacon.

Some time afterwards de Ranke made a second purchase of Frances Barbarie amounting to 277 acres. Afterwards de Ranke made a purchase of land from James Erwin joining his previous purchases on the south and joining Dr. Phinney's farm.

Ronk's name and that of his wife appear at different times on the New Paltz church records as sponsors at the baptism of children, and in 1760 Ronk's name appears as sponsor at the baptism of his grandchild, Johannes Ostrander.

John George de Rank or Ronk (as it was afterwards written) left four sons, Laurents, John, Philip and Cornelius; also four daughters: Christina, who married Peter Ostrander; Margaret, who married Peter Pich; Janet, who married Ezekiel Masten, and Anna, who married Dr. Plum of Plattekill.

The two brothers, John and Philip Ronk, were at Fort Montgomery, when it was taken by the British in the Revolutionary war, but they escaped to the mountains and returned home.

The name of Cornelius Ronk appears as a private in the 4th Regiment, Ulster County Militia.

Laurents Ronk left but one child, a son named John George. He sold his father's farm and bought the place south of the Flint, where J. J. Van Steenbergh lived before emigrating to California.

John Ronk, one of the four brothers, married a Sinsabagh.

He left several sons, one of whom, whose name was Joseph, kept the farm.

Laurents Ronk, the eldest son of John George, was one of the organizers of the church at New Hurley in 1770.

The name of his father, John George, does not appear in the church records until three or four years after the organization of the church, when he served several years as an elder. He was probably connected with the church at New Paltz and did not unite with the church at New Hurley at its first organization. The name in this church record is spelled in various ways—de Rank, Ranke, Rank, Rancke.

John George divided his land among his four sons, Laurents, John, Philip and Cornelius. The first named received five shillings as his birthright. He had only 100 acres of land from his father, but was given £800 in money. The daughters received £250 in money.

Laurents (who is the grandfather of the late A. M. Ronk of Brooklyn), lived in a stone house which he built, south of the New Hurley church on the road to Wallkill. John, the second son, built and lived in a stone house on the road to the Wallkill. This house was of late occupied by Mr. Sutton. Philip built and occupied a stone house, still standing, adjoining the Dr. Phinney place. Cornelius, the youngest son, kept his father's homestead. The houses of the four brothers are all still standing except that built by Laurents.

THE RELYEA FAMILY

The first mention we find of any Relyea is when the name of Dennis Relje appears as godfather at the baptism of a child of Hugo Freer and his wife, Mary LeRoy, in 1693. Dennis' wife's name was Joanna LeRoy. Probably she and Hugo Freer's wife were sisters. Dennis Reljea long occupied the house on the Hudson, just south of Juffrow's Hook, as the point was called, where the south bounds of the patent struck the river. He and his wife, Joanna LeRoy, had several children baptized in the Kingston church—David in 1703, Claudina in 1706, Hester in 1708.

Although the first Dennis Relje had children, it is learned from the manner in which the location is mentioned in the contract of 1744, that they did not occupy the house on the Hudson after his death, nor do we find any further mention of the family until in 1759, when David Relyea, doubtless the same whose christening is recorded in 1703, appears as godfather at the baptism of David, child of Dennis Relje and Marytje Van Vleit at Kingston. In 1771 Dennis and his wife, Marytje Van Vleit, joined the church at New Paltz. It was probably at about this time that Dennis located at New Hurley. In the list of soldiers of the Revolution we find the names of Dennis, Peter, John and Simeon Relje. About this time the name of Simeon also appears in the New Paltz church book. In 1793 David Relyea and his wife, Lana Ostrander, joined the New Paltz church by letter from New Hurley. In 1795 Dennis Relyea was an elder in the New Paltz church.

THE SMITH FAMILY AT SWARTEKILL

The territory lying north of the Paltz patent in the present town of Esopus, on the east side of the Wallkill, was called Swartekill by the old people, and the name is still applied to the locality a little north of Rifton. We are indebted to Mr. William Smith, the Sunday school missionary, for information concerning the early history of the Swartekill neighborhood, derived mainly from his grandfather, William Smith, as follows: Probably the first settler in this neighborhood was his ancestor, Hendrick Smit, the first of the name in this country.

He came from Holland in the same ship with Jacob Rutsen, who was the first settler at Rosendale and father-in-law of Johannes Hardenbergh, the first of the name in Ulster county. Rutsen paid Smit's passage across the ocean and the latter worked for some time to repay the money advanced. He then got a life lease for eighty acres of land on the east side of the Wallkill and included in the Hardenbergh patent. There were no definite bounds assigned to the eighty acres, except that it bounded on the south on the Paltz patent. It lay east of the Dashville falls. The house was built about 1715, at about the same date that Hugo Freer, Jr., Hendricus Deyo and Isaac LeFevre located on the Wallkill in the northern part of the Paltz patent. The annual rent paid by Smit was "a hen and a rooster." In his old days he obtained a deed for the eighty acres, which has never been put on record. But the property has descended in the family from father to son for 175 years, and the name of the owner has alternated from William to Henry for the whole time. During the entire period there never has been a mortgage on the property. Our informant has a son, Henry, who has a son named William, so the custom of naming the infant son for its grandfather has been continued to the present day.

The house, partly of stone and partly of frame, is situated a snort distance east of Rifton. The very first house on the place was of logs. Some time ago an examination of the walls disclosed a small loose stone, which on being pulled out proved to be a whetstone, bearing the date 1704.

Our informant's grandfather, William Smith, was a soldier in the army of the Revolution. At the age of seventy-two he attended the gathering of Revolutionary soldiers at Kingston, in 1831, half a century after the surrender of Yorktown. He drew a pension of three dollars a month in his old age and was assigned bounty lands at Hurley.

CHAPTER XLV

GENEALOGY OF THE FRENCH SETTLERS OF NEW PALTZ
TO THE THIRD GENERATION

BY LOUIS BEVIER

The reformation in France in the sixteenth century included among its adherents many of the nobility as well as the common people who, as a whole, constituted a large and influential part of the population of most of the provinces of France.

Whenever the persecutions of the government and Romish hierarchy became particularly oppressive and violent the Huguenots, as they were called in derision by their enemies, living in Catholic communities and under Catholic rulers, were often obliged to seek refuge from the storm in those communities, where their co-religionists were in greater number so as to be able to afford them some protection, more particularly to those provinces where the Huguenot princes were in authority. These movements of the Huguenot population continued at intervals down to 1628, when Rochelle, the last of their strongholds, was taken by Cardinal Richelieu, the minister of Louis XIII, and the power of the Huguenots as a political party was broken, and from this time all prudent persons foresaw that there remained no adequate security that the peace and toleration now freely promised by the king would be maintained. They had too often proved by sad experience that Catholic princes acted on the maxim that "no faith should be kept with heretics," to trust the sincerity of the king and his advisers; hence large numbers sought asylums in the neighboring Calvinistic States where they might enjoy those rights and privi-

MR. LOUIS BEVIER, OF MARBLETOWN

leges which were denied them at home. So a more general emigration was inaugurated throughout the kingdom, and France lost thousands of her most quiet and industrious citizens to the manifest and acknowledged advantage of the Netherlands, England, Switzerland and the Palatine provinces. The French government from time to time increased the difficulties in the way of these fugitives until after the revocation of the Edict of Nantes, in 1685, their flight was absolutely forbidden. Yet still members, by one device or another, managed to escape to their brethren who had preceded them.

About the year 1650 the band of Huguenots who afterward associated as patentees of New Paltz, began to gather from their several homes in France in the vicinity of Manheim in the Palatinate where they sojourned about ten years, during which time some of those friendships and connections were formed which survived the transplanting to the new world.

Whilst they were in the Palatinate they affiliated with the churches there and enjoyed the confidence and respect of the church officials. This is evidenced by the certificates given by the pastors to many of the emigrants on leaving for their new homes.

One of these given by Jacob Amyot, the noted pastor of the church at Mutterstadt near Manheim, to Pierre Deio, is still in possession of one of his descendants at New Paltz, by whom it is valued as a precious relic of the past. This is dated January 31, 1675, the year preceding his arrival at Wiltwyck. It is said that the heirs of Jean Hasbrouck, one of the patentees, held a similar certificate dated March 16, 1672, and Peter Gumaer's heirs hold a similar paper dated Moise, April 20, 1686. Doubtless others of a like character were brought by each of these emigrant families.

Matthew Blanshan and his wife, Maddeleen Jorisse, and

their son-in-law, Anthony Chrispel, with his wife, Maria Blanshan, and three younger children of Blanshan, were the first
of these refugees to set sail for the new world in the Gilded
Otter, April 27, 1660. They arrived at Wiltwyck before December 7, 1660, for at that date we find Dominie Blom's
record of their presence at his first celebration of the Lord's
Supper.

The next arrival from this band was another son-in-law of
Blanshan, Louis DuBois, who, with his wife, Catharine Blanshan, and their two young children, Abraham and Isaac, aged
respectively four and two years, arrived at Wiltwyck in 1661.
Matthew Blanshan and his two sons-in-law settled at the new
village (now Hurley) as early as 1662. At the time of its
burning by the Indians, June 7, 1663, Matthys Blanshan's two
children, Louis DuBois' wife and three children and Anthony
Chrispel's wife and child were taken prisoners and remained
among their captors about three months, when they were at
length restored to their friends. It was during the efforts to
recover the prisoners, held by the Indians, that attention was
first drawn to the lands along the Wallkill where New Paltz
was subsequently located.

The LeFevre brothers, Simon and Andre, were in Wiltwyck
and united with the church there April 23, 1665. The exact
date of their emigration is unknown. They were young, unmarried men at this time and brought to their new home the
energy and enthusiasm for the reformed faith, which charac-
terized the eminent scholar of their name, Jacobus Stapulensis
Faber or LeFevre.

Advised of the unsettled condition of the New Netherlands,
no more emigrants left the colony in the Palatinate until May
17, 1672, when Jean Hasbrouck and wife, Anna, daughter of
Christian Deyo, and their two daughters, Mary and Hester,

set out from Manheim and arrived at Wiltwyck in the spring
of 1673. Jean Hasbrouck and his brother Abraham (of whom
we shall speak later) were originally from the vicinity of Calais
before their emigration to the Palatinate.

Louis Beviere and his wife Maria LaBlan followed shortly
after to New York, in 1673, but made no permanent settlement until 1677 when the settlement at New Paltz took place.
His two children, born before that time, were baptized elsewhere.

Hugh Frere and his wife, Mary Haye, and three children,
Hugh, Abraham and Isaac, arrived about 1676, but there is no
record of his appearance at Wiltwyck until the purchase of
the land from the Indians and patent from Andros, September
29, 1677.

About this time Christian Deyo, with Pierre Deyo and his
wife, Agatha Nickol, and their child Christian, came over and
accompanied by the three unmarried daughters of Christian,
viz.: Maria, Elizabeth and Margaret. Maria married Abraham Hasbrouck, the brother of Jean, mentioned before, November 17, 1676; Elizabeth married Simon LeFevre, 1676; Margaret married Abraham DuBois, 1681. Thus Christian Deyo,
the oldest of the twelve patentees, gathered all of his family
around him again in the *New* Paltz, as they had been before
in the German Palatinate.

Abraham Hasbrouck sailed from Amsterdam in 1675 and
landed at Boston, and in July rejoined his brother Jean and his
other friends.

In May, 1677, Louis DuBois and his associates obtained, by
purchase, the title from the Indians to all the lands from the
Shawangunk mountains to the Hudson river, which were more
particularly described in the patent subsequently given by
Governor Andros September 29th of the same year. The Pat-

entees as named in said Patent were Louis DuBois, Christian Doyau, Abraham Hasbrouck, Andre LeFebvre, Jean Hasbrouck, Pierre Doyau, Louis Beviere, Anthoine Crespel, Abraham DuBois, Hugue Frere, Isaac DuBois and Simon LeFebvre. These men and their families removed to their patent lands and there founded the village of New Paltz in the spring of the subsequent year. Here in 1683 they organized the French Reformed church, electing Louis DuBois as elder and Hugo Frere deacon. They adopted the confession of faith framed by the first Synod of the Reformed church of France in the year 1559 and the other formularies of the French Reformed church. These continued in use in the church and its school until the change from the French to the Dutch language was made, when the Heidelberg catechism took their place and the French church was merged into the Reformed Dutch church.

Below is a short account of the twelve patentee families to the third generation.

THE CHILDREN OF LOUIS DuBOIS, THE PATENTEE

The children of Louis DuBois and Catharine Blanshan were:

Abraham, b. 1657, at Manheim; m. Margaret Deyo (daughter of Christian), March 6, 1681; settled at New Paltz, 1678; d. October 7, 1731.

Isaac, b. cir. 1659, at Manheim; m. Marie Hasbrouck (b. Mutterstadt cir. 1662), June, 1683; settled at New Paltz, 1678; d. June 28, 1690.

Jacob, b. October 9, 1661, at New Village (Hurley); m. Gitty Garretson (b. February 15, 1665), March 25, 1689; settled at Hurley; d. 1745.

Sarah, b. September 14, 1664, at Hurley; m. Joost Jansen of Marbletown, December 12, 1682.

David, b. March 13, 1667, at Hurley; m. Cornelia Vernooy (b. April 3, 1667), March 8, 1689; settled at Rochester.

Solomon, b. 1670, at Hurley; m. Tryntje Garretson (b. cir. 1671), cir. 1692; settled at New Paltz (Poughwaughtenonk); d. 1759.

Rebecca, b. June 18, 1671; d. young.

Rachel, b. April 18, 1675; d. young.

Louis, b. 1677; m. Rachel Hasbrouck (daughter of Abm., b. cir. 1679), January 19, 1701; settled at New Paltz (Nescatack); d. after 1729.

Matthew, b. January 3, 1679, at New Paltz; m. Sarah Matthysen (daughter of Matthys Matthysen and Tjatje Dewitt, b. April 17, 1678); settled at Kingston.

CHILDREN OF ABRAHAM DUBOIS

The children of Abraham and Margaret Deyo were:

Sarah, b. New Paltz, May 18, 1682; m. Rœlif Eltinge, June 13, 1703, New Paltz.

Abraham, b. April 17, 1685; m. ———; settled Somerset county, N. J.

Leah, b. New Paltz, October 16, 1687; m. Philip Ferre; settled Lancaster county, Penn.

Twins—Mary, d. young; Rachel, b. New Paltz, October 13, 1689; m. Isaac DuBois (son of Solomon), April 6, 1713; settled at PesKoine Creek, Penn.

Catharine, b. New Paltz, May 21, 1693; m. Wm. Donnelson, October 24, 1728; settled at Lancaster county, Penn.

Noah, b. February 18, 1700; d. young.

Joel, b. New Paltz, 1703; d. 1734.

CHILDREN OF ISAAC DUBOIS

The children of Isaac and Maria Hasbrouck were:

Daniel, b. April 28, 1684; m. Mary LeFevre (daughter of Simon), June 8, 1713, New Paltz.

Benjamin, b. April 16, 1689; d. young.

Philip, b. May 14, 1690; m. Esther Gumær (daughter of Peter), Rochester.

CHILDREN OF JACOB DUBOIS

The children of Jacob and Gitty Gerretson were:

Magdalena, b. May 25, 1690; m. 1st, Garret Roosa, December 30, 1710; m. 2d, Peter VanEst, October 20, 1718. Hurley.

Barent, b. May 3, 1693; m. Jacomyntje DuBois (daughter of Sol.), Pittsgrove, N. J.

Louis, b. January 6, 1695; m. 1st, Jane VanVliet, April 16, 1718; m. 2d, Margaret Jansen, May 22, 1720, Pittsgrove, N. J.

Geiltje, b. May 13, 1697; m. Cornelius NieuKirk, September 3, 1737.

Gerrit, b. March 29, 1700; d. in infancy.

Isaac, b. February 1, 1702; m. 1st, Næltje Roosa, August 5, 1732; m. 2d, Jannetje Roosa, October 15, 1760, Kingston.

Gerrit, b. February 13, 1704; m. Margaret Elmondorf, July 18, 1730.

Catrina, b. March 17, 1706; m. Petrus Smedes, January 24, 1725, Hurley.

Rebecca, b. October 31, 1708; m. Petrus Bogardus, September 15, 1726.

Johannes, b. October 10, 1710; m. Judith Wynkoop (daughter of Corn.), December 14, 1736, Hurley.

Sarah, b. December 20, 1713; m. Conrad Elmondorf (son of Conrad), May 27, 1734, Kingston.

Children of David DuBois

The children of David and Cornelia Vernooy were:

Catrina, b. May 25, 1690; d. in infancy.

Catryn, b. April 7, 1692; m. Wm. Kool (son of Leonard).

Hanna, b. October 11, 1696.

Anna, b. March 28, 1703; m. Jacob Vernooy.

Josaphat, b. March 17, 1706; m. Tjatje VanKeuren, April 21, 1730.

Elizabeth, b. October 31, 1708.

Children of Solomon DuBois

The children of Solomon and Trintje Garretson were:

Isaac, b. September 27, 1691; m. Rachel DuBois (daughter of Abm.), Perkiomen, Pa.

Jacomyntje, b. 1693; m. Barrent DuBois (son of Jacob), April 23, 1715, Pennsylvania.

Benjamin, b. May 16, 1697; m. Catrina Zuyland, Catskill.

Sarah, b. January 1, 1700; m. Simon Jacobse Van Wagenen, November 17, 1720, Marbletown.

Catryn, b. October 18, 1702; d. in infancy.

Cornelius, b. ———; m. Anna Margaret Hotaling, April 7, 1729, Poughwoughtenonk.

Magdalena, b. April 15, 1705; d. young.

Catharine, b. ———; m. Petrus Mathens Louw, December 9, 1722, Poughwoughtenonk.

Deborah, b. ———; probably died young.

Hendricus, b. December 31, 1710; m. Jannetje Hotaling, April 15, 1733, Nescatack.

Magdalena, b. December 20, 1713; m. Josiah Elting (son of Roelif), May 6, 1734. New Paltz.

Children of Louis DuBois

The children of Louis and Rachel Hasbrouck were:

Maria, b. December 1, 1701; d. in infancy.

Nathaniel, b. June 6, 1703; m. 1st, Gertrude Bruyn, May 17, 1726; m. 2d, Gertrude Hoffman, Salisbury Mills, Orange county.

Mary, b. March 24, 1706.

Jonas, b. June 20, 1708.

Jonathan, b. December 31, 1710; m. Eliz. LeFevre (daughter of Andries), December 25, 1732, Nescatack.

Catrina, b. October 31, 1715; m. Wessel Brodhead, January 25, 1734.

Louis, b. 1717; m. Charity Andrevelt, Staten Island.

Children of Matthew DuBois

The children of Matthew and Sarah Matthysen were:

Louis, b. July 18, 1697.

Matthens, b. October 9, 1698.

Hiskiah, b. January 26, 1701; m. Anna Pierson, June 17, 1722.

Ephraim, b. May 30, 1703; m. Anna Catrien Delamater.

Johannes, b. March 17, 1706; m. Rebecca Tappen, November 16, 1728.

Tjatje, b. November 2, 1707.

Jesse, b. February, 1709.

Eliza, b. October 4, 1713.

Catrina, b. December 4, 1715.

Gideon, b. January 11, 1719.

Jeremiah, b. May 18, 1721.

THE CHILDREN OF CHRISTIAN DEYO, THE PATENTEE

Christian Deyo had five children who were all probably born before he went to Germany.

Anna, b. 1644; m. Jean Hasbrouck.

Pierre (Peter), b. between 1646-1650; m. Agatha Nickol, about 1672; settled at New Paltz, and was one of the Patentees.

Maria, b. 1653; m. Abraham Hasbrouck, November 17, 1676.

Elizabeth, ———; m. Simon LeFevre, about 1678.

Margaret, ———; m. Abm. DuBois, about 1680 or 1681.

CHILDREN OF PIERRE DEYO

The children of Pierre Deyo and Agatha Nickol were:

Christian, b. 1674, in Palatinate; m. Mary Le Conte (or as translated into Dutch DeGroff, in church records it appears in both forms), February 20, 1702.

Abraham, b. October 16, 1676; m. Elsie Clearwater, October, 1725. New Paltz (Village).

Mary, b. April 20, 1679.

Pierre, baptized October 14, 1683.

Margaret, baptized October 14, 1683.

Maddeline, b. April 16, 1689.

Henricus, b. October 12, 1690; m. December 31, 1715, Margaret Wanboom (or VanBummel). New Paltz (Bontecoe).

CHILDREN OF CHRISTIAN DEYO

The children of Christian and Mary Le Conte were:

Peter, b. 1702; probably d. young.

Jacobus, b. January 16, 1704; m. Janetje Freer, October 28, 1724; removed to Kingston before 1738.

Moses, b. January 26, 1706; m. Clarissa Stohraad, of Hoog-drytslandt, April 17, 1728.

Maria, b. September 11, 1709; m. Jeems Achmootie, September 19, 1731, Bontecoe.

Angenieter, b. March 30, 1712; probably d. young.

Esther, b. February 27, 1715; m. Hugo Hugosen Freer, August 18, 1738.

Margaret, b. January 27, 1717; m. Marinus Van Acken, August 30, 1740 (2d wife).

CHILDREN OF ABRAHAM DEYO

The children of Abraham and Elsie Clearwater were:

Marytje, b. November 7, 1708; m. Isaac Freer, August 24, 1723. New Paltz.

Wyntje, b. January 24, 1708; m. Daniel Hasbrouck.

Abraham, b. October 16, 1710; m. Elizabeth DuBois. New Paltz (Village).

CHILDREN OF HENRY DEYO

The children of Henry and Margaret Wamboom were:

Debora, b. January 27, 1717; m. Petrus Ostrander, February 19, 1749. New Hurley.

Peter, Jr., b. November 9, 1718; m. Eliz. Helm, January 14, 1765. Tuthill.

Isaac, b. March 11, 1723; m. Agatha Freer.

Benjamin, b. May 30, 1725; m. Jennek Van Vliet, November 10, 1751. Bontecoe.

Johannis, b. November 6, 1726; m. Sara Van Wagenen, November 20, 1756. Springtown.

Christoffel, b. February 4, 1728; m. Debora Van Vliet. Springtown.

Haggetta, b. October 19, 1729; m. John Freer, May 5, 1769. Buntecoe.

Henricus, b. 1731; m. Eliz. Beem, October 13, 1753; buried at Highland, 1805.

Sarah, b. September 16, 1733; m. Isaac Van Wagenen.

David, b. January 9, 1739.

The Children of Abraham Hasbrouck, the Patentee

Abraham Hasbrouck with his wife, Maria Deyo, emigrated in 1675 and settled at Kingston, 1676. Their children were:

Anna, b. October 9, 1682; d. young.

Joseph, b. January 28, 1684; m. Elsie Schoonmaker (daughter of Joachim), October 27, 1706. Guilford.

Solomon, b. October 6, 1686; m. Sara Van Wagenen, April 7, 1721. New Paltz (Middletown).

Jonas, b. October 14, 1691; probably d. young.

Daniel, b. June 23, 1692; m. Wyntje Deyo (daughter of Abm.), April 2, 1734; d. June, 1759. New Paltz (Village).

Benjamin, b. May 31, 1696; m. Jannetje DeLange, February 13, 1737. Dutchess county.

Rachel (probably the oldest child); m. Louis DuBois, January 19, 1701.

Children of Joseph Hasbrouck

The children of Joseph and Elsie Schoonmaker were:

Abraham, b. October 19, 1707; m. Catharine Bruyn, January 5, 1739. Kingston.

Sarah, b. February 18, 1709; m. William Osterhoudt.

Isaac, b. March 17, 1712; m. Antje Low (widow of John Van Gasbeck). Shawangunk, south of Tuthill.

Mary, b. January 10, 1714; m. 1st, John Gasherie; m. 2d, Abm. Hardenberg.

Petronella, b. December 25, 1710; m. Simon LeFevre, June 24, 1735. New Paltz (Village).

Rachel, b. November 11, 1715; m. Jan Eltinge.

Jacob, b. May 5, 1717; m. Mary Hornbeck, October 17, 1746. Kyserike.

Benjamin, b. June 28, 1719; m. Ellidia Schoonmaker. Shawangunk (Borden Home Farm).

Cornelius, b. September 5, 1720.

Jonathan, b. April 12, 1722; m. Cath. DuBois (daughter of Cor's), May, 1751. Newburgh.

CHILDREN OF SOLOMON HASBROUCK

The children of Solomon and Sarah Van Wagenen were:

Abraham, Jr., b. March 11, 1722; m. Rachel Sleight, June 28, 1749.

Jacobus, b. January 3, 1725; d. in infancy.

Jacobus, b. January 1, 1727; m. Divertje Van Wagenen, March 19, 1755.

John, b. February 1, 1730; m. Rachel Van Wagenen, December 24, 1763.

Daniel, b. October 18, 1732 (no records).

Simon, b. December 25, 1735.

Petrus, b. August 20, 1738; m. Sarah Bevier (daughter of Abraham), October 25, 1765. New Paltz.

Elias, b. June 21, 1741; m. Elizabeth Sleight. Kingston.

CHILDREN OF DANIEL HASBROUCK

The children of Daniel and Wyntje Deyo were:

Maria, b. January 9, 1735.

Jonas, b. May 16, 1736; m. Catharine DuBois, August 1, 1765.

Josaphat, b. April 29, 1739; m. Cornelia DuBois. Plattekill.

David, b. June 8, 1740; m. Maritje Haughland. New Paltz, Butterville.

Elsie, b. July 4, 1742; m. Petrus Smedes. Hurley.

Rachel, b. October 30, 1743.

Isaiah, b. April 13, 1746; m. Mary Bevier (daughter of Abm.). New Paltz.

Benjamin, b. January 31, 1748; m. 1st, Antje Bevier; m. 2d, Maria Bevier. New Paltz.

Zachariah, b. June 24, 1749; m. Rebecca Waring.

CHILDREN OF BENJAMIN HASBROUCK

The children of Benjamin and Jannetje DeLange were:

Daniel.
Benjamin.
John.
Jacob.
Mary, m. John Halstead.
Heiltje, m. Dr. Nathaniel House.
Francis, m. Elizabeth Brinkerhoff.

THE CHILDREN OF JEAN HASBROUCK, THE PATENTEE

The children of Jean Hasbrouck and Anna Deyo were:

Mary, b. ———; m. Isaac DuBois (son of Louis), 1683. New Paltz (Village).

Hester, b. ———; m. Peter Gumær, April 1, 1692. Minisink.

Abraham, b. March 31, 1678 (went abroad and never returned. See will.)

Isaac, b. April 17, 1680; d. before 1712. (See will.)

Elizabeth, b. February 25, 1685; m. Louis Bevier, June 2, 1713. Marbletown.

Jacob, b. April 15, 1688; m. Hester Bevier (daughter of Louis 1st), December 14, 1717. New Paltz (Village).

CHILDREN OF JACOB HASBROUCK

The children of Jacob and Hester Bevier were:

Jan, b. December 16, 1716; d. young.

Benjamin, b. April 17, 1719; d. October 14, 1747. (Killed by a falling tree.)

Isaac, b. March 11, 1722; m. Maria Bruyn, August 30, 1745. Marbletown.

Lowies, b. February 21, 1725; d. in infancy.

Jacob, b. May 7, 1727; m. Jannetje DuBois, April 12, 1756. New Paltz.

CHILDREN OF ISAAC HASBROUCK

The children of Isaac and Maria Bruyn were:

Jacob I., b. September 28, 1746; m. Sarah DuBois (daughter of Cor's). Calbergh, Marbletown.

John, b. ———; m. Mary Hasbrouck (daughter of Jacob A.). Rest Place, Marbletown.

Jacobus, b. February 19, 1749; d. in infancy.

Jacobus Bruyn, b. December 1, 1753; m. Ann Abeel. High Falls.

Severyn, b. January 1, 1756; m. 1st, Maria Depew; m. 2d, Nancy Concklin. Stone Ridge.

Maria, b. February 5, 1758; m. Cor's Stilwell. Stone Ridge.

Esther, b. January 8, 1760; m. Abm. Sahler. High Falls.

Catharine, b. August 12, 1762; m. 1st, Patterson; m. 2d, Wigton. Stone Ridge.

Benjamin, b. January 8, 1764; m. 1st, Catrina Smedes; m. 2d, Rachel Hasbrouck. Kyserike.

Louis, b. February 1, 1767; m. Catharine Decker. Stone Ridge.

Anna, b. June 23, 1769; d. in infancy.

CHILDREN OF JACOB HASBROUCK

The children of Jacob and Jannetje DuBois were:

Hester, b. May 18, 1752; m. Dr. Geo. Wurts. New Paltz.

Josiah, b. March 5, 1755; m. Sarah Decker. New Paltz.

Lowies, b. July 26, 1758; d. in infancy.

Jacob J., b. October 25, 1767; m. 1st, Margaret Hardenberg; m. 2d, Ann DuBois. New Paltz.

THE CHILDREN OF LOUIS BEVIER, THE PATENTEE

The children of Louis Bevier and Maria LaBlan were:

Maria, b. July 19, 1674; d. in infancy.

Jean, b. January 2, 1676; m. Cath. Montanye, April 14, 1712. Wawarsing.

Abraham, b. January 20, 1678; m. Rachel Vernooy, February 18, 1707. Wawarsing.

Samuel, b. January 21, 1680; m. Magdalena Blanjean. New Paltz.

Andries, b. July 12, 1682. Unmarried.

Louis, b. November 16, 1684; m. Elizabeth Hasbrouck (daughter of Jean), May 5, 1713.

Esther, b. November, 1686; m. Jacob Hasbrouck (son of Jean).

Solomon, b. July 12, 1689; d. in infancy.

CHILDREN OF JEAN BEVIER

The children of Jean and Catharine Montanye were:

Maria, b. March 1, 1713; d. in infancy.

Elenora, b. March 23, 1714; m. Benj. Rolscher. Wawarsing.

Elizabeth, b. February 10, 1717; m. Isaac Bevier (son of Samuel), 1715. Wawarsing.

Johanna, b. May 15, 1720; m. Michæl Sax, April 23, 1753. Wawarsing.

Ester, b. September 23, 1722; m. Solomon Westbrook, May 4, 1748. Minisink.

Louis J., b. October 18, 1724. Unmarried. (See will.) Wawarsing.

Jesse, b. May 11, 1729; m. Elizabeth Hoffman. Wawarsing.

CHILDREN OF ABRAHAM BEVIER

The children of Abraham and Rachel Vernooy were:

Louis, b. 1708; d. before 1750. No heirs. (See will.)

Anna, b. May 17, 1710; d. in infancy.

Cornelius, b. July 20, 1712; d. after 1770. Apparently unmarried.

Samuel, b. August 28, 1715; m. Sarah LeFevre (daughter of Andries), June 10, 1739. Wawarsing.

Jacobus, b. September 28, 1717; m. Anna Vernooy, February 23, 1757. Wawarsing.

Abraham, b. January 10, 1720; d. aged 18.

Maria, b. January 28, 1722; m. Benj. DuBois, June 20, 1755. New Paltz.

Johannes, b. April 26, 1724; m. 1st, Rachel LeFevre, August 10, 1747; m. 2d, Elizabeth Van Vliet, September 18, 1764. Wawarsing.

Benjamin, b. May 7, 1727; m. Eliz. VanKeuren (daughter of Tjerck), December 13, 1760. Wawarsing.

Daniel.

CHILDREN OF SAMUEL BEVIER

The children of Samuel Bevier and Magdalena Blanjean were:

Solomon, b. May 13, 1711; d. young.

Abraham S., b. June 14, 1713; m. Margaret Elting (daughter of Roelof), January 22, 1742. New Paltz (Butterville).

Isaac, b. December 25, 1714; m. Eliz. Bevier (daughter of Jean). Wawarsing.

Jacobus, b. April 29, 1716; m. Antje Freer. New Paltz.

Margaret, b. June 30, 1717; m. Matthew LeFevre, June 7, 1737. Bloomingdale.

Maria, b. October 5, 1718; m. Abm. LeFevre. Wawarsing.

Louis S. Unmarried.

Esther, b. January 18, 1721; m. Cornelius Brink. Shawangunk.

Johannes, b. September 9, 1722; m. Magdalena LeFevre, September 2, 1748. Shawangunk.

Philip, b. February 9, 1723; m. Tryntje Low, July 10, 1748. Shawangunk.

Matthew, b. June 28, 1712; d. young.

The only child of Louis Bevier and Elizabeth Hasbrouck was:

Louis, b. April 10, 1717; m. Esther DuBois (daughter of Philip, d. October 7, 1790), October 24, 1745; d. April 29, 1772. Marbletown. They left five children.

The Children of Anthoine Crispel, the Patentee

The children of Anthoine Crispel and Maria Blanshan were:

Maria Maddaleen, b. February 15, 1662; m. Matthys Cor's Sleight. New Paltz.

Pieter, b. December 21, 1664; m. Neeltje Gerretsen (m. 2d husband, Joannes Schepmoes), February 18, 1697.

Lysbet, b. October 3, 1666; d. in infancy.

Lysbet, b. October 15, 1668; m. Elias Eijn. New Paltz.

Sara, b. June 18, 1671; m. Huybert Suyland.

Jan, b. July 24, 1674; d. young.

Children of Second Wife

Jannetje, b. January 4, 1682; d. in infancy.

Jan, b. October 12, 1684; m. Geetje Jans Roosa.

Jannetje, b. February 7, 1686; m. Nic's Hoffman.

Children of Pieter Crispel

The children of Pieter Crispel and Neeltje Gerretsen were:

Antony, b. April 17, 1692; m. Lea Roosa, September 11, Arriantje, b. June 31, 1694; m. Andries, March 20, 1712. 1719.

Joannes, b. October 27, 1695; m. Anna Margaret Roosa, December 15, 1725. Hurley.

Children of Jan Chrispel

The children of Jan Chrispel and Geertje Jans Roosa were:

Marytje, b. March 15, 1702; m. Jacob Heermance, April 28, 1725.

Rebecca, b. March 17, 1706; d.

Antoine, b. October 12, 1707; m. Catrina Van Benthuysen.

Helena, b. May 7, 1710; m. Teunis Van Steenberg, April 24, 1731. Kingston.

Jan, b. September 21, 1712; m. Sara Janse, December 10, 1736; m. 2d, Maria Dorothea Kraft, December 29, 1753.

Petrus, b. January 24, 1727; m. Lea Roosa, January 14, 1743.

Rebecca, b. April 7, 1717.

Zara, b. November 26, 1721.

CHILDREN OF ANTHONY CHRISPEL

The children of Anthony Chrispel (son of Peter) and Leah Roosa were:

Petrus, b. May 1, 1720; d. in infancy.

Neeltje, b. February 4, 1722; m. Dirk Roosa.

Petrus, b. August 11, 1723; m. Leah Roosa, January 14, 1743.

Johannes, b. November 8, 1724.

Cornelius, b. September 4, 1726.

Anna Margriet, b. December 22, 1728.

Arriantje, b. October 8, 1732.

Wilhelmus, b. August 17, 1740.

CHILDREN OF JOHANNES CHRISPEL

The children of Johannes (son of Peter) and Anna Margaret Roosa were:

Petrus, b. November 26, 1727; d. young.

Aldert, b. November 10, 1728; d. young.

Rachel, b. October 1, 1732.

Arriantje, b. August 25, 1734.

Petrus, b. September 19, 1736.

Elizabeth, b. September 24, 1738.

Lea, b. December 14, 1740.

Allert, b. February 13, 1743.

Johannes, b. April 21, 1745.

CHILDREN OF ANTOINE CHRISPEL

The children of Antoine (son of Jan) and **Catharine Van** Benthuysen were:

Lidia, b. April 28, 1734.

Geertje, b. October 3, 1736.

Jan, b. May 28, 1738.

Rebekka, b. October 12, 1740.

Maria, b. October 10, 1742.

CHILDREN OF JAN CHRISPEL

Jan married 1st, Sarah Janse; 2d, **Maria Dorothea Kraft.** The children were:

FIRST WIFE

Mayke, b. August 27, 1738.

Jan, b. August 16, 1741.

Thomas, b. January 22, 1744.

Hendricus, b. June 21, 1745.

Thomas, b. May 8, 1748.

SECOND WIFE

Matthens, b. December 1, 1754.

Sara, b. July 15, 1759.

Matthens, Elisa [twins], b. November 17, 1761.

David, b. November 26, 1763.

Solomon, b. November 24, 1764.

CHILDREN OF PETRUS CHRISPEL

The children of Petrus and Lea Roosa were:

Petrus, b. October 9, 1743.

Benjamin, b. January 13, 1745.

Anthony, b. July 20, 1746.

Abraham, b. March 5, 1749.

Maria, b. February 24, 1751.

Rachel, b. April 1, 1753.

Rachel, b. October 13, 1754.

Jacob, b. June 6, 1762.

THE CHILDREN OF HUGO FRERE, THE PATENTEE

Hugo Frere married 1st, Mary Haye; 2d, Jannetje Wibau. The children were:

Hugo, ———; m. Mary Ann Leroy, June 7, 1690. New Paltz.

Abraham, ———; m. Aagien Tietsorte, April 28, 1694.

Isaac, b. 1672; d. August 9, 1690.

Jacob, b. June 9, 1679; m. Antje Van Weyen, September, 1705. Bontecoe.

Jean, b. April 16, 1682; m. Rebecca Wagener. Kingston.

Mary, ———; m. Lewis Veille. Schenectady.

Sarah, ———; m. Teunis Clausen Van Volgen. Schenectady.

CHILDREN OF HUGO FRERE

The children of Hugo Frere and Mary Ann Leroy were:

Hugo, Jr., b. October 14, 1691. Bontecoe.

Isaac, b. May 21, 1693. New Paltz.

Mary, b. May 31, 1696.

Sarah, b. May 15, 1698.

Esther, b. October 15, 1699.

Benjamin, b. October 20, 1706.

Rachel, b. November 10, 1710.

Jannette, b. January 25, 1713.

Elizabeth, b. May 25, 1718.

CHILDREN OF ABRAHAM FREER

The children of Abraham Freer and Aagien Tietsorte were:

Hugo b. *1695*

Neeltje Maeltje, b. May 5, 1696. New Paltz.

Abraham, b. October 31, 1697. Kingston.

Solomon, b. October 23, 1698; m. Klaartje Westvall, September 22, 1721. Minnesink.

Willem, b. January 14, 1700.

Helena Jelena, b. January 16, 1704.

* Phillipus, b. August 16, 1706. *b. 1705 Bap. 11 Aug 1706*

Sara, b. October 12, 1707.

Naritje, b. September 11, 1709.

Jacomyntje, b. November 4, 1711.

Aagien, b. April 11, 1714.

Johanna, b. November 13, 1715.

Catryntjen, b. January 11, 1719.

CHILDREN OF JACOB FRERE

The children of Jacob Frere and Antje Van Weyen were:

Jannetje, b. October 20, 1706.

Sarajte, b. September 11, 1709.

Abraham, Isaac [twins], b. February 27, 1715.

Jacob, b. January 27, 1717.

Maritje, Annatje [twins], b. January 3, 1720.

Antjen, b. April 2, 1721.

Jacob, b. September 1, 1723.

Daniel, b. January 2, 1726.

Cornelis, b. June 29, 1720.

THE CHILDREN OF SIMON LEFEVRE, THE PATENTEE

Simon LeFevre married Elizabeth Deyo (whose second husband was Moses Cantain). He died about 1690. The children were:

Andries, ——; m. Cornelia Blanjean. New Paltz (Village.).

Abraham, b. May 11, 1679; died before his father.

Isaac, b. August 5, 1683; m. Maritje Freer, May 16, 1718. New Paltz (Bontecoe).

Jan, b. October 28, 1685; m. Catharine Blanjean, November 20, 1712. New Paltz (Plains).

Maritje, b. October 15, 1689; m. Daniel DuBois, June 18, 1713. New Paltz (Village).

CHILDREN OF ANDRIES LEFEVRE

The children of Andries and Cornelia Blanjean were:

Simon, b. September 11, 1709; m. Pieternella Hasbrouck, June 24, 1725. New Paltz (Village).

Matthens, b. April 10, 1710; m. Margaret Bevier, June 17, 1737. Rosendale (Bloomingdale).

Elizabeth, b. September 8, 1712; m. Jonathan DuBois (son of Louis), December 23, 1732. Nescatack.

Margaret, b. March 13, 1715; m. Conraed Vernooy, June 10, 1739. Wawarsing.

Zara, b. February 3, 1717; m. Samuel Bevier, June 10, 1739.

Maritje, b. March 1, 1719; m. Nathaniel LeFevre. New Paltz (Plains).

Catarina, b. April 2, 1721; m. Simon DuBois. New Paltz (Village).

34

Magdalena, b. October 11, 1724; m. Johannis Bevier, September 2, 1749.   Shawangunk.

Benjamin.

Rachel, b. June 23, 1728; m. Johs Bevier, September 2, 1749. Wawarsing.

CHILDREN OF ISAAC LEFEVRE

Isaac LeFevre married Maritje Frere.   The children were:

Isaac, b. December 14, 1718; died unmarried.

Peter, b. February 19, 1721; m. Elizabeth Vernooy, January 2, 1760.   New Paltz (Bontecoe).

Johannes, b. November 18, 1722; m. Sarah Vernooy, May 29, 1752.   New Paltz (Bontecoe).

Daniel, b. November 8, 1725; m. Catharine Cantine.   New Paltz (Bontecoe).

Simon, b. November 10, 1728; died young.

Mary, b. March 20, 1732; m. Johannes Hardenberg, Jr. Swartekill.

Simon, b. December 17, 1738; died young.

CHILDREN OF JAN LEFEVRE

The children of Jan LeFevre and Catharine Blanshan were:

Margaret, b. December 20, 1713; d. young.

Abraham, b. March 25, 1716; m. Maria Bevier.   New Paltz (Kettleborough).

Elizabeth, b. October 2, 1717.

Nathaniel, b. November 2, 1718; m. Maritje LeFevre.   New Paltz (Plains).

Andries J., b. March 18, 1722; m. Rachel DuBois (daughter of Nathaniel), October 20, 1745.   New Paltz (Kettleborough).

Margaret, b. February 9, 1724; m. 1st, Jacob Hoffman; m. 2d, Abm. Richards.   Shawangunk.

INDEX

INDEX

535

INDEX 569

INDEX

587